GOSPEL WOMEN

GOSPEL WOMEN

Studies of the Named Women in the Gospels

Richard Bauckham

WILLIAM B. EERDMANS PUBLISHING COMPANY
GRAND RAPIDS, MICHIGAN / CAMBRIDGE, U.K.

Wm. B. Eerdmans Publishing Co.
255 Jefferson Ave. S.E., Grand Rapids, Michigan 49503 /
P.O. Box 163, Cambridge CB3 9PU U.K.

Printed in the United States of America

07 06 05 04 03 02   7 6 5 4 3 2 1

Library of Congress Cataloging-in-Publication Data

Bauckham, Richard
Gospel women: studies of the named women in the gospels /
Richard Bauckham.
p.   cm.
ISBN 0-8028-4999-7 (pbk.: alk. paper)
1. Women in the Bible.
2. Bible. N.T. Gospels — Biography.   I. Title.

BS2445.B38   2002
226.09221082 — dc21

2001059216

www.eerdmans.com

This book is dedicated to my mother
Stephania Lilian Bauckham (née Wells)
1911-1998

who used to say she was a Martha

Contents

CONTENTS

Acknowledgments

Chapter 1 is a revised version of "The Book of Ruth and the Possibility of a Feminist Canonical Hermeneutic," *Biblical Interpretation* 5 (1997) 29-45.

Part of chapter 2 was published as "Tamar's Ancestry and Rahab's Marriage: Two Problems in the Matthean Genealogy," *Novum Testamentum* 37 (1995) 313-29.

Chapter 4 is an expanded version of "Anna of the Tribe of Asher (Luke 2:36-38)," *Revue biblique* 104 (1997) 161-91.

Chapter 6 is a slightly revised version of "Mary of Clopas (John 19:25)," in G. J. Brooke, ed., *Women in the Biblical Tradition* (Lewiston, N.Y.: Edwin Mellen, 1992) 231-55.

Chapter 7 is a revised version of "Salome the Sister of Jesus, Salome the Disciple of Jesus, and the Secret Gospel of Mark," *Novum Testamentum* 33 (1991) 245-75.

Chapters 3, 5, and 8 have not been previously published. (A short version of chapter 8 was given as the Laing Lecture for 2001 at the London Bible College.)

Introduction

Imaginatively adopting the perspective of biblical wo/men rather than just looking at them as fixed objects in texts in a fixed context yields a different world and set of possibilities.[1]

This is not just another book on women in the Gospels. Of course, it *is* a book that reflects the huge wave of interest in this subject over the last two decades, especially since Elisabeth Schüssler Fiorenza's pioneering and immensely influential *In Memory of Her: A Feminist Theological Reconstruction of Christian Origins* (1983).[2] A succession of books have studied women in the ministry of the historical Jesus or in the Gospels in general,[3] while others have taken one or

---

1. E. Schüssler Fiorenza, *Jesus and the Politics of Interpretation* (New York: Continuum, 2000) 36.

2. E. Schüssler Fiorenza, *In Memory of Her: A Feminist Theological Reconstruction of Christian Origins* (New York: Crossroad; London: SCM, 1983).

3. E. Moltmann-Wendel, *The Women Around Jesus* (tr. J. Bowden; New York: Crossroad; London: SCM, 1982); B. Witherington III, *Women in the Ministry of Jesus* (SNTSMS 51; Cambridge: Cambridge University Press, 1984); S. Heine, *Women and Early Christianity: Are the Feminist Scholars Right?* (tr. J. Bowden; Minneapolis: Augsburg; London: SCM, 1987); J. A. Grassi, *The Hidden Heroes of the Gospels* (Collegeville, Minn.: Liturgical, 1989); L. Schottroff, *Let the Oppressed Go Free: Feminist Perspectives on the New Testament* (Louisville: Westminster/John Knox, 1991); K. E. Corley, *Private Women, Public Meals: Social Conflict in the Synoptic Tradition* (Peabody, Mass.: Hendrickson, 1993); C. Ricci, *Mary Magdalene and Many Others* (tr. P. Burns; Minneapolis: Fortress, 1994); E. Schüssler Fiorenza, *Jesus: Miriam's Child, Sophia's Prophet* (New York: Continuum; London: SCM, 1994); L. Schottroff, *Lydia's Impatient Sisters: A Feminist So-*

other of the four canonical Gospels for its subject.[4] Other books that are significant in marking out an area of scholarship in which I would place my work in
this volume are recent studies of women in the life and literature of Jewish Palestine in the late Second Temple period,[5] especially the studies by the Israeli
scholar Tal Ilan.[6] Of course, in addition to the books listed in the notes to this
paragraph, there have been a host of journal articles and articles in multi-
authored volumes on the theme, some of which appear in footnotes throughout this book. There has also been much work on women in the Pauline
churches and in the early church generally, including the period immediately
after that of the New Testament writings: it would be artificial and unhelpful to
isolate studies of women in the Gospels from such work. Less often acknowledged as important for its relevance to the Gospels is the large literature of fem-

---

cial History of Early Christianity (tr. B. and M. Rumscheidt; Louisville: Westminster John Knox;
London: SCM, 1995); H. M. Keller, *Jesus und die Frauen: Eine Verhältnisverstimmung nach dem
synoptischen Evangelien* (Freiburg: Herder, 1997); I. R. Kitzberger, ed., *Transformative Encounters: Jesus and Women Re-viewed* (BibIntSer 43; Leiden: Brill, 2000). Note also volumes of essays
that include a significant number on women in the Gospels: G. J. Brooke, ed., *Women in the Biblical Tradition* (Studies in Women and Religion 31; Lewiston, N.Y.: Mellen, 1992); R. S. Kraemer
and M. R. D'Angelo, eds., *Women and Christian Origins* (New York: Oxford University Press,
1999).

4. Matthew: E. M. Wainwright, *Towards a Feminist Critical Reading of the Gospel of Matthew* (BZNW 60; Berlin/New York: de Gruyter, 1991); E. M. Wainwright, *Shall We Look for Another? A Feminist Rereading of the Matthean Jesus* (Maryknoll, N.Y.: Orbis, 1998).

Mark: H. Kinukawa, *Women and Jesus in Mark: A Japanese Feminist Perspective* (Maryknoll, N.Y.: Orbis, 1994).

Luke or Luke-Acts: T. K. Seim, *The Double Message: Patterns of Gender in Luke-Acts*
(Nashville: Abingdon; Edinburgh: T. & T. Clark, 1994); B. E. Reid, *Choosing the Better Part?
Women in the Gospel of Luke* (Collegeville, Minn.: Liturgical, 1996); J. M. Arlandson, *Women,
Class, and Society in Early Christianity: Models from Luke-Acts* (Peabody, Mass.: Hendrickson,
1997).

John: M. Scott, *Sophia and the Johannine Jesus* (JSNTSup 71; Sheffield: Sheffield Academic Press, 1992); R. G. Maccini, *Her Testimony Is True: Women as Witnesses according to John*
(JSNTSup 125; Sheffield: Sheffield Academic Press, 1996); A. Fehribach, *The Women in the Life of
the Bridegroom: A Feminist Historical-Literary Analysis of the Female Characters in the Fourth
Gospel* (Collegeville, Minn.: Liturgical, 1998).

5. L. J. Archer, *Her Price Is Beyond Rubies: The Jewish Woman in Graeco-Roman Palestine*
(JSOTSup 60; Sheffield: Sheffield Academic Press, 1990); A.-J. Levine, ed., *"Women Like This":
New Perspectives on Jewish Women in the Greco-Roman World* (SBLEJIL 01; Atlanta: Scholars
Press, 1991); C. A. Brown, *No Longer Be Silent: First Century Jewish Portraits of Biblical Women*
(Louisville: Westminster/John Knox, 1992).

6. T. Ilan, *Jewish Women in Greco-Roman Palestine* (TSAJ 44; Tübingen: Mohr [Siebeck],
1995; Peabody, Mass.: Hendrickson, 1996); idem, *Mine and Yours Are Hers: Retrieving Women's
History from Rabbinic Literature* (AGAJU 41; Leiden: Brill, 1997).

inist scholarship in the field of Hebrew Bible/Old Testament;[7] from some of the best of this work I have learned things I could not have learned from New Testament feminist scholarship.

This literature is quite varied in its methodological approaches, and, while almost all of its authors would identify themselves and their approach to the subject as feminist, they would understand that in somewhat different ways. But, taken as a whole, this body of work has considerable achievements to its credit, achievements to which I am much indebted and which, to a large extent, I take here as achievements on which subsequent scholarship can build. (Of course, I take issue with many of these scholars on specific points, sometimes on quite wide-ranging arguments, just as they do with one another.) Most fundamentally, these scholars have made the women in the Gospels visible simply by attending to the evidence of the texts that generations of male scholars had (to put it charitably) not found very interesting or had not thought significant enough to deserve their labors. It is remarkable, for example, how cavalierly major scholars once dismissed the key role of the women disciples in the resurrection narratives as the stuff of apologetic legend and therefore, in effect, best ignored in any properly scholarly account of Christian origins.[8] In this sense modern historical-critical study achieved what centuries of androcentric but (to use the pejorative cliché) precritical interpretation could not: it denied the Gospel women their prominent place in the saving events of the Gospel story of Jesus: his incarnation, cross, and resurrection. After feminist criticism, such a move can no longer be regarded as a purely objective historical judgment, though many feminist critics (this is a distinction among them) are no less skeptical about the general historical reliability of the Gospels. Historical or not, the women are prominent in the birth, passion, and resurrection narratives, and the least that feminist scholarship has done for us all is to make us realize that this is significant and interesting.

If feminist scholarship has drawn our attention to what is really there in the texts about women and exposed the androcentric prejudice that prevented this evidence from claiming our attention, feminist scholarship has also drawn our attention to what is not there in the texts. Once we pay attention to the Gospel women, we begin to wonder whether they were more important than

7. Among many other books, the ten volumes of the *Feminist Companion to the Bible* (first series; Sheffield: Sheffield Academic Press, 1993-96; all are on Hebrew Bible/OT, but the last volume is on the Hebrew Bible in the NT), edited by Athalya Brenner, are notable. A second series has recently begun to appear.

8. This is still done, in different ways, by J. D. Crossan, *The Historical Jesus: The Life of a Mediterranean Jewish Peasant* (San Francisco: HarperSanFrancisco; Edinburgh: T. & T. Clark, 1991).

appears in the texts: have they been marginalized and others like them pushed altogether out of the story by the androcentric perspective of the male evangelists or, before them, male transmitters of the oral traditions? Has even Luke, traditionally thought especially favorable to women, given them greater representation in his Gospel only at the cost of putting them firmly in their place? These are important questions, but they can be answered only by attending as seriously as possible to what *is* in the texts, and it is therefore primarily to that task that I have devoted the essays in this book. Before we get to wondering what might have been left out, it is essential to read the texts themselves for all they are worth and with self-critical alertness to our assumptions and prejudices. Behind many a judgment of what is historically plausible or probable lie assumptions derived from patriarchal traditions of historiography or (more recently) from androcentric traditions of social anthropology, and sometimes the most "radical" feminist criticism is captive to just such assumptions, failing to attend to what the texts might mean if considered afresh, all too precipitately eager to expose every Gospel text as irredeemably oppressive to women. There is much to be said for Schüssler Fiorenza's contention that the criteria of historical plausibility or probability are too vulnerable to prejudice, and that we should look instead for what is *possible*.[9] History in the biblical-Christian tradition is the sphere of ever-new possibility, and hermeneutics is about discovering the possibilities of the text as possibilities for new living today.

When we consider the roles of women in the Jesus movement and in society there are two sorts of possibility, and it is useful to be aware of both: one is that women should step outside their accepted social roles or (as I would prefer to say of the Jesus movement) that women and men together should step outside their accepted social roles; the other is that women (or, again, women and men together) should discover new possibilities within the socially accepted framework of their lives. My own judgment is that we can see both possibilities actualized in the Gospels, but we should be careful to distinguish them and not to take evidence for one as evidence for the other, and we should not insist on assimilating all the evidence to one or the other possibility. Some confusion here seems to me to account in part for the difference between more radical and more conservative readings of the Gospels' portrayals of the roles of women. There is also an aspect of the kind of perception of the Gospels that a feminist concern for the visibility of women should have promoted among us that is not, in itself, concerned with either of the forms of new possibility but is nonetheless significant. In contrast to the androcentric perspective of much ancient narrative, which focuses on the aspects of life in which men were most impor-

9. Schüssler Fiorenza, *Jesus and the Politics*, 52-53.

tant and interested, this is about the way that gynocentric narratives open up for us the world of women simply as it was for them. While some feminist critics, more with respect to the Hebrew Bible than to the New Testament, have been alert to this, others have been slow to recognize that narratives can be gynocentric without being overtly critical of patriarchal structures. We need to learn more discrimination in deciding whether a passage presents a male view of women or an authentically (i.e., authentically with due regard to its time and place) women's perspective.

A point at which I find myself dissenting from a strong tendency in some feminist critical work on early Christian literature is what seems to me excessive and dogmatic use of a feminist hermeneutic of suspicion. A proper use of a hermeneutic of suspicion should make us conscious that men and women were in different positions in a society where those who exercised authority in the public world were almost all men. We should be alert to whose interests texts or ideas may serve, and we should be aware that the world that texts present from the perspective of men might look very different from the perspective of women. Texts are not ideologically neutral. (Of course, such considerations should not be confined to the difference made by gender, as socially constructed, but must also extend to social and economic place in the hierarchy of power.) But a problem arises when a feminist hermeneutic of suspicion becomes the only controlling principle of a reading of the texts. Then the result of interpretation is already determined by the methodological starting point and approach. The texts are bound to be read as supporting patriarchal oppression of women. They are, so to speak, not assumed innocent until proved guilty, but assumed guilty without a chance of a fair hearing. Clichés about patriarchy or ancient patriarchal society take the place of patient interpretation that attends carefully to the text. If our interpretation is not to be subject to immovable prejudice, we must attend to the particularity of the texts and the persons and situations they portray and be open to the perhaps surprising possibilities they disclose. Although I might easily be misunderstood here, I suspect that part of the problem lies in "one-issue exegesis": the issue of patriarchal oppression of women is the only interest the exegete brings to the text and therefore the feminist hermeneutic of suspicion the only exegetical tool that is employed. It is hard to attend fairly and openly to a text unless one is genuinely interested in all that the text is about, and unless one takes the trouble to approach it with the rich resources of interpretation available in the form of historical and literary methods that are designed to open up the text for its own sake and not just for ideological illustration. Blinkered use of a feminist hermeneutic of suspicion is much like an old-fashioned form of dogmatic theological interpretation, which knew in advance what was to be found in all the texts and whose exegesis of them was just one illustration after another of predetermined dogmas. The word "blinkered" in that sentence should make clear that I am not saying we should (or can) come to the texts without perspectives and interests and frameworks of interpretation, only that these should be adequate to what the texts are about and should promote rather than impede patient attention to the texts in their own particular integrity.

Resuming my account of the major achievements of two decades of work on women in the Gospels, I must mention the issue of anti-Judaism, especially since the essays in this volume all, in one way or another, place the Gospels and their women characters in a thoroughly Jewish context. Essential to the particularity of these texts, in my view, is their Jewishness, and, much though Jewish Palestine participated in the general culture of the Mediterranean world and whether we read that in terms of hellenization or Mediterranean anthropology or both, the Jewish religious and cultural tradition had strong distinctives with which any interpretation of the Gospels or study of Christian origins must come to terms. As is now well recognized, some of the early scholarly work on women in the Gospels, while well aware of the importance of their Jewish context, succumbed to what was still a not uncommon model in New Testament scholarship: portraying Jesus and his movement only by contrast with contemporary Judaism, such that whatever the scholars found admirable about Jesus and his movement was set against a dark background of its opposite in Judaism. One could sometimes get the impression that women followers of Jesus were perhaps not in an enviable position by modern standards, but when compared with how truly awful it was to be a Jewish woman at that time the position of those women who joined Jesus' movement looks wonderful. In my judgment the danger of Christian or feminist anti-Judaism has been well recognized and largely avoided in most recent work on women in the Gospels. Jewish women scholars have played an important role in counteracting it. Of course, we cannot substitute as an a priori principle that the roles or status of women in the Jesus movement could not have been any different from those which prevailed in Palestinian Jewish society in general. What seems to me the most effective safeguard against the ideological abuse of Jewish history is a different principle: that scholars should give as much attention to the Jewish texts and evidence that indicate different possibilities for women as we do to the Christian texts and evidence of this kind. The literature of Second Temple Judaism includes both texts that one can only call misogynist (such as Sirach) and texts (such as Pseudo-Philo's *Biblical Antiquities*, a retelling of the biblical history from creation to Saul, a Palestinian work of the second half of the first century CE) that one is tempted to call "feminist" and probably could do without too much anachronism. Again this requires attention to the particularity of the texts without the prejudgment that they are all bound to be patriarchal (even if some are more subtly so than others), whether one's interests in making such a prejudgment are feminist or androcentric.

I have not yet justified the claim that this is not just another book about women in the Gospels, but I have said enough about the achievements of recent work on women in the Gospels to make clear that I am far from depreciating it. But I have a sense that there may not be much further to go with the approaches hitherto taken, and I have not wished to go over ground already well trodden. Therefore this is not a generalized study of the women around Jesus nor a redactional or literary study of women in one of the Gospels. I have written only on particular persons or passages in the Gospels about which I have genuinely fresh things to say. In place of an overview or synthesis, I have conducted a series of deep probes. Of course, others have made studies of individual women in the Gospels. Most of the studies in this volume are of women who have not been so studied or have only been studied much more briefly. I hope readers will be surprised to discover how much can be known about some of these women. I have attended to these individuals not primarily as representative of anything (of the roles of women in early Christian communities or of the Gospel writer's view of women in general), but primarily as individuals (whether historical or as characters in the Gospels: often both, sometimes only the latter). Therefore I have asked not only "feminist" questions about them, but whatever questions seemed capable of interesting answers. For me these have been a series of exciting journeys of discovery. I have realized afresh what I formulated for myself on an earlier occasion: that although the Gospels are primarily the story of Jesus (biographies of Jesus in the sense of the ancient genre of biography), they are also, precisely because of the nature of Jesus' story, also the stories of many individuals who encountered him and followed him. His story is not well served by allowing it to crowd out the other stories, as happens in most of the current "historical Jesus" research and writing (in which his women disciples still have very little place). Though it was not a matter of conscious intention, I realize now that there is hardly anything in this book about "Jesus' attitude to women," not because I find that unimportant or uninteresting, but because I have focused rather on the women's side of their relationship to Jesus and the events of his story. I also realize that this is also how the Gospels themselves largely enable us to see things.

Methodologically, these essays are doubtless quite eclectic. I think the character of the Gospels and the range of questions that can properly be brought to them make a range of methods of interpretation appropriate. Historical and literary approaches are certainly not mutually exclusive, and indeed should not normally proceed without some reference to each other. Especially in chapters 4, 5, and 8 I deploy them in close conjunction with each other to illuminate both the world of the text and the world to which the text makes historical reference. What happened, how the text constructs its literary version of what happened, and how the text invites us to read its narrative are all important, and the first is certainly not accessible at all without attention to the others. Some readers may be surprised that one currently dominant model for the interpretation of the Gospels is conspicuous by its absence from these essays: the Gospels as products of, addressed and tailored to the specific needs and circumstances of each evangelist's own Christian community. I have argued elsewhere that the Gospels were not addressed to specific Christian communities, about which we can know very little, but to a wide audience in all the Christian churches to which they would naturally be expected to circulate.[10]

I would like to think that my methods in these essays are historically rigorous (which is not at all the same as historically skeptical) and imaginatively literary — or I could just as appropriately say: literarily rigorous and imaginatively historical, since it is important to remember that good historiography entails the use of the imagination in an appropriate degree and in a properly disciplined way. As far as the historical goes, I find inexhaustibly fruitful the pursuit of a kind of detailed, even meticulous, historical investigation that not many New Testament scholars now trouble to undertake. I have long been a determined enemy of the secondhand references that take the place of real immersion in the ancient sources and evidence, and of the uninformed historical dogmatizing that stands in for the fresh discoveries any New Testament research claiming to be *historical* (and I do not mean that New Testament study *has* to be of this kind) ought to be making. It is not the case, as some seem to imagine, that everything relevant to understanding the New Testament historically has been discovered and can be found in the reference books or older commentaries. For example, the passages of Pseudo-Philo that will prove illuminating in relation to the stories of the empty tomb (chapter 8, §3 below) have never been considered in that connection, while none of the commentators on Luke seems to have had any idea of the historical evidence relevant to her membership of the tribe of Asher (chapter 4 below). Moreover, there are continually fresh resources from the ancient world becoming available. A good example is the new evidence that has for some time now been available about Jewish women's ownership of property (chapter 5, §2), but not an inkling of which has hitherto appeared in any discussion of Luke 8:2-3. The study of women in the Gospels has not often benefited from the kind of painstaking historical work

---

10. In R. Bauckham, ed., *The Gospels for All Christians: Rethinking the Gospel Audiences* (Grand Rapids: Eerdmans; Edinburgh: T. & T. Clark, 1998).

that has seemed to me genuinely to advance our understanding of Gospel women in several of the essays in this book. Moreover, it is worth making the point about range of interest again in this context: the historical work in these essays is far from limited to questions about the lives of women as such in the ancient world and Second Temple Judaism (on which there are now fine historical studies in close touch with all the evidence), indispensable though that is, but extends also in whatever direction study of these women as particular individuals required (e.g., about the Median diaspora of the northern tribes in chapter 4 or about the court of Herod Antipas in chapter 5). It respects the fact that these women and their stories are remarkable for their particularity, rather than for their typicality or representativeness.

One historical resource that comes into its own quite frequently in these essays, but has generally been neglected in New Testament studies, is onomastics. The nature of our ancient evidence is such that names are something for which we have considerable and continually increasing evidence. We know the names of very large numbers of ancient people about whom we know not much else. Carefully used, the evidence of names can be very informative.

As far as literary methods go, two have proved especially valuable in some of these essays: intertextuality (chapter 3 explains how I understand this quite flexible concept) and the distinction between androcentric and gynocentric perspectives in narrative, which I owe especially to feminist scholars who have applied it in study of the Hebrew Bible/Old Testament. It is explained in chapter 1. It also, in a sense, explains chapter 1, which, as an essay on the book of Ruth, might seem anomalous in a book of studies of women in the Gospels (even though Ruth herself does make an appearance in the Gospels: Matt 1:5). Though some chapters of this book were written before chapter 1, it was working on that chapter that opened up for me the possibilities of applying the distinction between androcentric and gynocentric perspectives to Gospel narratives, along with the recognition that, in literary terms at least, by no means all parts of the Gospels are androcentric. The Gospels are written so that to a significant extent readers are invited to share the perspective of their female characters. Combining the androcentric/gynocentric distinction with the narratological notion of perspective in reading (often called focalization) has many implications that I have only begun to explore in this volume. But the essay on Ruth also merits its lead position for another, though connected reason. Unlike many feminist biblical critics I do not regard the canon of Scripture as a hopelessly patriarchal construction. The effects of the dominantly androcentric perspectives of the biblical texts can be counterbalanced by recognition that there are also genuinely gynocentric texts that, although they are fewer, can function canonically as a critical counterbalance to the androcentricity of others. Indeed, they can authorize gynocentric reading of otherwise androcentric texts. At the end of chapter 5, I suggest also how this notion of a text that itself authorizes the gynocentric reading of passages written from an androcentric perspective can also be applied within the Gospel of Luke. Many feminists will react against the notion that gynocentric reading should need to be authorized, especially by a male author, but the function of this notion is to propose that there can be gynocentric reading that goes with the grain of the text as a whole, even though it may run against the grain of androcentric parts of the text. Once gynocentric reading comes into its own, not subordinated to androcentric perspectives, then, of course, the two become complementary (despite that term's disrepute also for feminists). There should come a time when it will be not oppressive for women to read androcentric texts sympathetically. For the time being, it is liberating not only for women but also for men to discover the new possibilities of reading that the gynocentric narratives of Scripture open for all readers.

Finally, a comment on the fact that all the essays are about *named* women. In the four canonical Gospels fifteen women are named. Three are women from the Hebrew Bible/Old Testament included in Matthew's genealogy of Jesus: Tamar, Rahab, and Ruth (Matt 1:3, 5). One is the Herodian princess Herodias (Matt 14:3, 6; Mark 6:17, 19, 22;[11] Luke 3:19). Elizabeth the mother of John the Baptist and Anna the prophet appear in the first two chapters of Luke, along with Mary the mother of Jesus, who is also named elsewhere in the Synoptic Gospels, though not in John. The remaining eight named women are disciples of Jesus: Joanna, the sisters Martha and Mary of Bethany, Mary Magdalene, Mary the mother of James and Joses, Mary the wife of Clopas, Salome, and Susanna. The studies in this volume do not give all these women the attention they deserve, though all are at least mentioned. Among the disciples of Jesus, most attention is given to Joanna, Mary the wife of Clopas, Salome, and the women who discovered the empty tomb of Jesus (including Mary Magdalene, Mary the mother of James and Joses, Salome, and Joanna) considered as a group. Martha and Mary of Bethany are almost entirely omitted, while Mary the mother of Jesus is discussed only as she appears in Luke 1. The reasons for these omissions are that I have written essays only on the passages and persons about which I have substantially new contributions to make. In fact, the limitation of the volume to *named* women is partly accidental: I had originally intended to include essays on the Syro-Phoenician (or Canaanite) woman (who does make a significant appearance in chapter 2) and the woman healed of a hemorrhage. But it became clear that what I had written and wished to write

---

11. According to some manuscripts of Mark 6:22, a second Herodias, the daughter of Herodias and Herod Antipas, is mentioned here.

about named women was sufficient to fill a volume, and the limitation to named women gives a certain coherence to the volume. (Of course, the unnamed women of the Gospels deserve studies of the same kind, as do the Gospel men, many of whom have been as comparatively neglected as some of the women I have studied here.)

That so few of the women in the Gospels are named is not simply a result of androcentric attitudes in the traditions or the evangelists, though these cannot be discounted. Surprisingly few women are identified not by a name but by reference to a male relative (Jairus's daughter, Peter's mother-in-law, the mother of the sons of Zebedee, Pilate's wife): from the general practice of the time we would expect more. It is also the case that many men in the Gospel narratives are anonymous. No women are named in healing stories (though the names of three women who were healed are given in Luke 8:2-3), but only two men in such stories are named (Bartimaeus, Lazarus), even though there are far more healing stories involving men. It seems likely that names (apart from those of public figures such as Herod) were usually retained in the Gospel traditions only when the named persons were well-known figures in the early Christian communities. In that case, this will have been true of nine women (the eight named women disciples and Mary the mother of Jesus) and about twenty-four men. One could compare the fact that the named individuals Paul greets among the Christians of Rome in Romans 16:3-15 comprise nine women and sixteen men. These figures may give us some rough idea of the relative numbers of men and women in the leadership of the early Christian communities.

The Book of Ruth as a Key to Gynocentric Reading of Scripture

Ruth lay down with a man on the threshing floor
for Your sake. Her love was bold
for Your sake.[1]

1. The Female Voice in Ruth

André Brink's novel *The Wall of the Plague* is written in the first person. The novelist is a male Afrikaner, the "I" of the narrative is a "coloured" (mixed race) South African woman. The thoroughgoing adoption of a female character's perspective is intensified by vivid accounts even of distinctively female physical experience. But in the concluding short section of the novel the voice changes. The woman's South African white male lover speaks, and in the last two pages of the work reveals that he, not she, has written the story, as an attempt to "imagine what it is like to be you." As he approaches the task of writing the narrative the reader has just completed, he fears failure: "how can I, how dare I presume to form you from my rib? . . . To do justice to you an essential injustice is required. That is the heart of my dilemma. I can never be you: yet in order to be myself I must imagine what it is to be you."[2] By this ingenious device of two levels of fictional authorship, the real author distances himself from the attempt

---

1. Ephrem, "Hymns on the Nativity: Hymn 9," in *Ephrem the Syrian: Hymns* (tr. K. E. McVey; Classics of Western Spirituality; New York: Paulist, 1989) 127.
2. A. Brink, *The Wall of the Plague* (New York: Summit, 1984; London: Fontana, 1985) 445.

he has made to imagine what it is like to be this woman. It is, after all, *only* a white male's attempt to imagine what it is like to be a mixed-race woman. But readers have known this all along. How does the final revelation function for them? Is it the author's bid to preempt their charge that he has not been fully successful? More seriously what it does is to acknowledge, within the imaginative world the novel has created, the readers' consciousness that behind the female voice lurks a male author. Until the penultimate page of the novel this consciousness has had only extra-textual status. The more successfully the novel creates its own world that readers inhabit, the more independent it is of anything they know about the author. But for most readers, in this case, especially given the South African nationality of both author and characters, the contrast between the white male author and the mixed-race female narrator is so powerful that it inevitably impinges on their reading. Were the contrast between author and narrator less evocatively stark, the final revelation might subvert an illusion hitherto little affected by the readers' extra-textual knowledge. But as it is, the revelation draws this knowledge into the world of the novel itself and makes into an inner-textual reality the tension between extra-textual knowledge and inner-textual world that they have never entirely been able to escape.

The book of Ruth is not a first-person narrative, but it does adopt predominantly the female perspective of its two main characters, Naomi and Ruth, one an Israelite, one a Moabite. It has no author's name on its title page and so does not oblige us to think its author female or male, Moabite or Israelite. I suppose that all readers have taken for granted that the author was an Israelite, but the contrast between Moabite character and Israelite *audience* has loomed larger in their consciousness than that between Moabite character and Israelite author. (This may be in part because Ruth's Moabite origin plays no role in the story once she has committed herself to Naomi and left Moab, though it is also the case that we lack the cultural equipment to make much sense of the question whether, when the narrative adopts Ruth's perspective, it adopts a convincingly Moabite perspective.) On the other hand, the assumption of male authorship, made largely without question by traditional historical scholarship,[3] has been challenged by recent work that finds strong evidence that Ruth is "a female text"[4] or "a collective creation of women's

---

3. However, the possibility of female authorship was seriously entertained by E. F. Campbell, *Ruth* (AB; Garden City, N.Y.: Doubleday, 1975) 22-23, in a commentary that shows no awareness of feminist concerns.

4. A. Brenner, "Introduction," in A. Brenner, ed., *A Feminist Companion to Ruth* (FCB 1/3; Sheffield: Sheffield Academic Press, 1993) 14; C. Meyers, "Returning Home: Ruth 1.8 and the Gendering of the Book of Ruth," in Brenner, ed., *Ruth,* 114.

culture"[5] or "an expression of women's culture and women's concerns."[6] However, this challenge is not mainly directed at demonstrating that the author was a woman. This is a real possibility, but evidence that the text genuinely reflects women's experience and convincingly adopts a woman's perspective and so should, in that sense, be identified as a "female text" or "women's literature," cannot actually demonstrate female authorship. Just as there is no reason, other than androcentric prejudice, to accept the traditional, usually unexpressed, assumption that ancient Israelite women did not compose literature, so there is no reason to deny to a male author in ancient Israel the imaginative capacity to adopt a woman's perspective that modern male novelists such as Brink display.[7] Whether the real author was male or female we cannot know.[8] The assumption of female authorship that some recent feminist critics[9] have adopted is designed to dispel the kind of tension between extra-textual knowledge and inner-textual world that readers of Brink's novel experience and that readers of Ruth could experience if they both accepted the traditional assumption of male authorship and were alert to gender issues and perspectives in the text. Since we have no extra-textual information about the author, however, this kind of tension need not arise. We can safely leave the real author in the uncertainties of historical possibility in this case. What recent feminist discussions of Ruth seem to me to have shown is that the *voice* with which the text speaks to its readers is female.[10] Readers are offered and drawn into an ancient

5. F. van Dijk-Hemmes, "Ruth: A Product of Women's Culture?" in Brenner, ed., *Ruth,* 139.

6. A. Brenner, "Naomi and Ruth: Further Reflections," in Brenner, ed., *Ruth,* 143.

7. A nice illustration of this is that Thomas Hardy's first two novels, published anonymously, were generally thought to have a female author. I owe this point to my former colleague Peter Coxon.

8. For discussion of criteria for determining female authorship of ancient literature, see M. R. Lefkowitz, "Did Ancient Women Write Novels?" and R. S. Kraemer, "Women's Authorship of Jewish and Christian Literature in the Greco-Roman Period," both in A.-J. Levine, ed., *"Women Like This": New Perspectives on Jewish Women in the Greco-Roman World* (SBLEJL 01; Atlanta: Scholars Press, 1991) 199-219, 221-42; M. T. DesCamp, "Why Are These Women Here? An Examination of the Sociological Setting of Pseudo-Philo Through Comparative Reading," *JSP* 16 (1997) 53-80.

9. Notably A. J. Bledstein, "Female Companionships: If the Book of Ruth were Written by a Woman . . . ," in Brenner, ed., *Ruth,* 116-33.

10. Van Dijk-Hemmes, "Ruth," 136, prefers to speak of "recognizing the voice speaking in a text as an F [female/feminine] voice." For this concept see further A. Brenner and F. van Dijk-Hemmes, *On Gendering Texts: Female and Male Voices in the Hebrew Bible* (BibIntSer 1; Leiden: Brill, 1993). Meyers, "Returning Home," 89, comments that "it is perhaps better to focus on the gender perspective of a given passage rather than on the gender identity of its author."

Israelite woman's perspective[11] on ancient Israelite society. Everything in the text is coherent with such a perspective.[12]

Until, that is, the last few verses. In the genealogy (4:18-22) a male voice speaks, reciting the patrilineal descent of King David from Perez and attributing to Boaz a place of honor, as seventh name in the genealogy whose tenth generation is David. In the usual manner of Israelite genealogy, women are excluded as irrelevant to the genealogy's purpose of demonstrating the male line of descent. The male voice is unmistakable, but might be understood as the collective voice of the compilers of traditional genealogies, from which an extract is here made, or as the voice of a redactor who, for whatever reason, has appended these verses to a work that originally ended at verse 17, or, finally, as the voice of the author. Most (though not all)[13] feminist readings of Ruth, implicitly relying on the traditional critical judgment that the genealogy is a later appendix, stop short of it.[14] They allow the last word to the women of Bethlehem (4:14-17), who conclude the story with emphatically a women's perspective on the birth of Ruth's child. The male perspective of Boaz and the people at the gate, which concerns itself with maintaining the name and inheritance of Elimelech and Mahlon and securing descent for Boaz himself (4:9-12), is relativized by the quite different perspective on the same events that the women express. What for a few verses had threatened to become, after all, a men's story is thus reclaimed by the women as Ruth's and especially Naomi's story. But since it is this final ascendancy of the women's perspective in the story that establishes the meaning of the whole and its character as women's literature, it becomes important to interpret the male voice that, at least in the final form of the text as we have it, appears to have the last word.

The importance of this issue can be illustrated by suggesting, for example, that here we have a parallel to the ending of Brink's novel. The author finally reveals himself as male and — one might have to say — undermines the authority of the female voice he has adopted as narrator of the story. His concern is patrilineal descent, and he has adopted a female perspective in order to persuade his readers that the patriarchal laws and conventions that function to secure it in cases where it might otherwise be lost work in the interests of women as well as men. In this way the genealogical conclusion could support that mi-

11. It is, of course, important to recognize that gender is culturally variable.

12. See especially Meyers, "Returning Home"; van Dijk-Hemmes, "Ruth"; Brenner, "Naomi and Ruth."

13. An exception is Bledstein, "Female Companionships," 130.

14. Phyllis Trible's pioneering feminist literary analysis of Ruth ends at 4:17: *God and the Rhetoric of Sexuality* (OBT; Philadelphia: Fortress, 1978) 195; cf. also Brenner, "Naomi and Ruth," 140-41. In her more recent article, "Ruth, Book of," *ABD* 5:845, Trible comments on the genealogy.

nority of feminist critics who pass a negative verdict on Ruth, arguing that the actions of Ruth and Naomi, though seemingly courageous and independent, function to secure male interests. A male author has adopted a female voice in order to hold up for admiration and imitation women who are "paradigmatic upholders of patriarchal ideology."[15] However, this interpretation of the function of the genealogy is not very plausible, if only because the genealogy merely traces David's descent through Boaz and his father Salmon from Perez. If, as is generally supposed, Boaz's marriage to Ruth is a kind of levirate marriage designed to secure a son for her dead husband Mahlon and a grandson for Naomi's husband Elimelech, this is entirely ignored by the genealogy. As a means simply of securing a son for Boaz, which is the only fact in the story that the genealogy acknowledges, the story is ludicrously redundant.

A more conventional suggestion would explain the function of the genealogy as an editorial addition that extends the point made already by 4:17b (itself regarded by some as an addition to the original text, added before the genealogy).[16] Verse 17b serves to connect the story with the broader biblical story of God's dealings with Israel by pointing out that Naomi's grandson Obed became the grandfather of David. The addition of the genealogy "serves to formalize" this point.[17] In this case, the final verses of the book open up a canonical-critical perspective. The genealogy gives the book of Ruth a canonical setting in the larger corpus of the Hebrew Bible. However, a feminist canonical criticism could not ignore that in this addition a male voice succeeds the female voice that told the story. While the connection with David in verse 17b is made by tracing David's descent from Naomi, in the genealogy the women's perspective of the story is entirely supplanted. In this case the genealogy seems to function to subsume the gynocentric story of Ruth into the predominantly androcentric perspective of the rest of Scripture. Reading Ruth as women's literature would have to be an exercise in resisting its canonical "shaping."

In due course, I will offer an alternative to both of these suggestions for interpreting the male voice in 4:18-22. But these suggestions may serve to show both that the traditional question about the originality or otherwise of these verses needs to be reconsidered in the light of textual gendering, and also that reading Ruth as women's literature can profitably raise questions about the canon. What will it mean to read Ruth as women's literature[18] not only in itself,

---

15. E. Fuchs, quoted by Meyers, "Returning Home," 88.

16. E.g., B. Childs, *Introduction to the Old Testament as Scripture* (Philadelphia: Fortress; London: SCM, 1979) 566.

17. Childs, *Introduction*, 566.

18. I use this term in the way defined in the second paragraph of this essay: literature that "genuinely reflects women's experience and convincingly adopts a woman's perspective."

but as women's literature within a predominantly androcentric canon? Against the understandably dominant feminist tendency to evaluate the canon negatively, I shall suggest that the book of Ruth can play an essential role in a feminist canonical hermeneutic that both accepts the normative function of the canon and also resists the androcentricity of much of the canonical literature.

2. Women's and Men's Perspectives

I begin with two aspects of the relationship between social structures and the characters. First, how far are the characters at odds with patriarchal structures? The story certainly presupposes social and economic structures that make it very difficult for a woman to survive without a male provider. Naomi's plight is to have neither husband nor son, and Ruth's remarkable and courageous commitment to Naomi consists in sacrificing the chance of a husband in Moab in order to share Naomi's plight, without hope of gaining a husband thereby. It is true, as many feminist critics point out, that the two women exercise independence and initiative within the rather restricted options the structures of their society permit them, and through their solidarity and resourcefulness secure their future against the odds. It is also true that there are, in this society, some institutional structures designed to provide for their situation. One function of the narrative is surely to show the legal structures of Israelite society operating, as they should, to the advantage of the most vulnerable groups in society: childless widows and resident aliens (Naomi is one, Ruth is both). The law of gleaning provides one means of support for those who could not grow their own crops,[19] while the laws of redemption and levirate marriage enable a widow without a son to acquire economic security by marrying and bearing a son who can inherit her first husband's property.[20] But the narrative shows these legal provisions operating for the benefit of Naomi and Ruth only because Ruth, Naomi, and Boaz make them so operate — only because Ruth acts with חסד (loyalty or caring responsibility), only because both women act with initiative and mutual support, and only because Boaz responds with חסד. He allows Ruth to glean beyond her legal right (2:15-16), and, as the example of the nearer kinsman (4:6) shows, he had the

---

19. Although Naomi had inherited her husband's land (see S. J. Osgood, "Women and the Inheritance of Land in Early Israel," in G. J. Brooke, ed., *Women in the Biblical Tradition* [Lewiston, N.Y.: Mellen, 1992] 51), women in early Israel did not normally do the agricultural work involved in growing field crops; see C. Meyers, *Discovering Eve: Ancient Israelite Women in Context* (New York/Oxford: Oxford University Press, 1988) 146.

20. Cf. T. and D. Thompson, "Some Legal Problems in the Book of Ruth," *VT* 18 (1968) 79-99.

legal option not to marry her. In both cases he meets Ruth's initiative with חסד. Thus the legal structures over which the elders in the gate preside operate for the good of the women when both the women and the man make them do so. Though the women are certainly self-determinative to a significant extent, it is hardly the case, as sometimes claimed, that they subvert or circumvent the structures of society. It is more that they make those legal provisions that were designed for their advantage actually work for their advantage.

Second, it is with regard to the operation of these legal provisions that the story most effectively contrasts male and female perspectives. From the death of Elimelech (1:3) onward, the story adopts the perspective of Naomi and subsequently also of Ruth. It concerns their struggle to achieve "security" (1:9; 3:1), which is finally accomplished by Ruth's marriage and the birth of her son. But there is one major interruption of this women's perspective. Necessarily, in this society, the legal transaction takes place among the men (4:1-12). In Boaz's legal declaration and in the people's congratulation of him we are given the male perspective on his marriage to Ruth.[21] It concerns the provision of a male heir for Elimelech and Mahlon (4:9-10) and the provision of children for Boaz himself (4:11-12). The hopes expressed are fulfilled in the birth of a son to Ruth and Boaz, but this is the occasion for the women of Bethlehem to express, in their congratulation of Naomi and at their naming of Obed (4:14-15, 17), the corresponding and very different female perspective. For the women the child is Naomi's son, not in a legal sense but because he will be the security for her old age that she thought she had lost when her own sons died. And she owes him to her "daughter-in-law who loves you, who is more to you than seven sons." From the women's perspective what has happened is not that Boaz has acquired an heir for Elimelech, but that Ruth's devotion to Naomi has secured a son to be Naomi's support in her old age. From both perspectives the continuity of life into a third generation is secured and from both perspectives the biological links also serve nonbiological connections; but the concern for patrilineal descent, biological or legal, that dominates one perspective is wholly absent from the other. One should also note that the change of perspective accompanies a change of scene, from the gate where the men transact legal affairs and seem to themselves to play the dominant role in society, securing patrilineality across the generations, to the household, where the women manage the continuity of the generations, not in legal but in practical and affective terms, and seem to themselves to be the real actors in events of significance.

The women's perspective clearly completes the overall perspective of the

---

21. The people (העם) may include women, but if so they are co-opted to the male perspective in this dominantly male context.

narrative, in which there was never any concern with acquiring an heir for Elimelech until Boaz sat with the elders in the gate. The men's perspective corresponds to the form of the legal process, but the female perspective is no less true to the substance of what happens. The narrative gives the men's perspective voice in order to replace it by the women's perspective. Not that it invalidates the men's perspective as such. What Boaz says the legal transaction does for the relation of property to family structures it really does, and what the people wish for Boaz he really gains. The men's perspective is not illusory in what it claims, merely in what it leaves out. It does not touch the significance of the events for the women. Taken by itself, as though it were a universal perspective, it gives a misleading impression of the dominance of masculine concerns, which merely the juxtaposition of the women's perspective is sufficient to dispel.

Among other things the contrast of perspectives says that the legal conventions of patrilineal descent and inheritance, despite their patriarchal form, can operate in practice as structures for women just as much as for men. Seen only from the men's perspective they seem more patriarchal than they are.[22]

3. Female Power and Male Authority

This conclusion about the relation of women's and men's perspectives in Ruth can be correlated with the approach to Ruth argued by Carol Meyers, in a study exploring the significance of the term "mother's house" in Ruth 1:8 (also in Gen 24:28; Cant 3:4; 8:2). This term defines from a female perspective the ancient Israelite household, which is usually, in our literature, defined from the male perspective as the "father's house." Meyers puts it in the context of an understanding of the household — established in her earlier work[23] — as "characterized by internal gender balance rather than gender hierarchy":

> The word "internal" is critical here. Whereas outward forms of status and recognition may indicate male privilege, the dynamics within domestic units may be quite different, with women even dominating the multifarious facets of economic life, and also the social and parenting activities, that take place within the family household. Because the public record of ancient Israel, like that of most traditional societies, is so androcentric, as-

22. Cf. Meyers, *Discovering Eve,* 41: "the patrilineality of early Israel cannot simply be equated with patriarchy, if the latter implies the absolute control of males over females, or of the male head of the family over his wife and other family members, or of [*sic*] the subservience of women to men."

23. Meyers, *Discovering Eve.*

pects of female power within the Israelite household can rarely be seen. Yet the relative invisibility of female power does not mean it did not exist; and occasionally it can be glimpsed even in the male-oriented canon.[24]

Her study of the texts that use the term "mother's house" affords one glimpse of the internal world of the household from the women's perspective, revealing that "within that setting, women's voices were heard, their presence was valuable and valued, and their deeds had a profound influence on others."[25] Meyers is also careful to insist that one should not interpret this female power within the household in terms of a modern distinction between private and public, which is not appropriate to ancient societies in which the household and the workplace were virtually identical. Family life was not "distinct from the general social relations involved in economic, political and religious life."[26]

Meyers's study of Ruth serves to relate the book to the reconstruction of female roles and gender relationships in early Israel that she established in detail in her earlier work. There she applied to early Israel the model proposed by feminist anthropologist S. C. Rogers for a peasant society in which the idea of male dominance functions as a cultural myth embodied in public displays of male authority, while social reality at the all-important level of the household is characterized by a functional absence of hierarchical gender relationships and a functional balance of male and female power. "Male authority [is] offset by female power."[27] Therefore, focusing on legal rights, formal positions in society, and high-profile activities in the community makes such a society appear more patriarchal than it really is.[28] Meyers shows that the evidence for early Israel,[29] both archaeological and documentary, fits such a model.[30]

24. Meyers, "Returning Home," 99.

25. Meyers, "Returning Home," 111.

26. Meyers, "Returning Home," 111-12.

27. Meyers, *Discovering Eve*, 43. The distinction between authority and power is critical here: authority is "the culturally legitimated right to make decisions and command obedience," whereas power is "the ability to effect control despite or independent of official authority. . . . Authority is basically a hierarchical arrangement that may be expressed in formal legal or juridical traditions. Power has no such cultural sanctions but nonetheless can play a decisive role in social interaction" (Meyers, *Discovering Eve*, 41, following M. Z. Rosaldo). For this distinction applied to male authority and female power in an ancient Jewish text, see 1 (3) Esdr 4:13-32 (I owe this observation to John Geyer).

28. Meyers, *Discovering Eve*, 42-45.

29. Her reconstruction is of Israelite society in the premonarchical period. With the establishment of the monarchy, the household gradually ceased to be the dominant social unit, but the erosion of its values and gender balance in rural Israelite life would have been a very lengthy process; see Meyers, *Discovering Eve*, 189-96.

30. Meyers, *Discovering Eve*, especially chaps. 6–8.

The implication of Meyers's approach is that the predominantly androcentric texts of the Hebrew Bible, which foreground precisely the public life in which male authority is displayed, make Israelite society appear more patriarchal than in social reality it was. It renders invisible the real independence, initiative, and power that women exercised within the household and the aspects of relationship in which women and men interacted in more egalitarian than hierarchical terms. The value of Ruth as women's literature is precisely that it renders visible what is usually invisible. Naomi and Ruth, as women of independence and initiative, respected as such by their men, are not exceptions to the Israelite rule, but examples of the rule that only the women's perspective of the book allows us to recognize.

4. The Problem of the Genealogy

The book of Ruth is not polemical.[31] Its stance toward men is not adversarial or even satirical. Boaz, the only male character portrayed at length, is presented entirely favorably. While the male and female perspectives are deliberately juxtaposed and contrasted, the purpose is evidently not to reject the former so much as to complement it. The women's perspective exposes the men's as one-sided, relatively true for the men but missing completely what matters for the women. While such a strategy of complementing androcentricity with gynocentricity is a long way from a radical feminist protest against patriarchy, it would be anachronistic to deny its authenticity as an ancient Israelite women's perspective appropriate to the kind of society I have suggested as the social context for Ruth.

With this insight we may return to the problem of the genealogical conclusion. Adrien Bledstein is almost the only critic[32] who tries to integrate it into a feminist reading of the book: "With a litany of male genealogy, the story ends traditionally just as it began. As if gently mocking a too masculine cultural bias, the account of these women survivors and their man of choice is bracketed by the expected opening and closing of a tale recorded in ancient Is-

---

31. Cf. Trible, "Ruth, Book of," *ABD* 5:846: "Neither in tone nor [in] content is it polemical."

32. Another is I. Fischer, "The Book of Ruth: A 'Feminist' Commentary on the Torah?" in A. Brenner, ed., *Ruth and Esther* (FCB 2/3; Sheffield: Sheffield Academic Press, 1999) 48: "The author of Ruth uses the androcentric literary genre of the *tôlᵉdôt* in order to anchor her 'feminist' exegesis in tradition. She had already done so in presenting the scene at the city gate from a male viewpoint. So, now she chooses to change her viewpoint in order to increase the credibility of her story in an evidently patriarchal society."

rael."[33] The parallel between the opening (1:1-2) and the closing of the book, neither of which reflects the gynocentric perspective of the narrative between them, is valid so far as it goes, but "mocking" is not true to the tone of Ruth. Nor is the genealogy in fact how one would expect an Israelite tale to end: there are no comparable examples.

The striking feature of the genealogy, as observed already, is its relative lack of connection with the story the book tells. Only by starting with Perez and thereby giving Boaz the honored seventh position does it achieve a connection. The reason it lacks any greater connection is, of course, because it is no more than an extract from a traditional genealogy of David, such as appears also in 1 Chronicles, and was no doubt well known already when the book of Ruth was written. But precisely as this it serves well the book's purpose of providing a women's perspective that exposes the androcentricity of most Israelite literature. The male voice of the genealogy is that of the traditional compilers of such patrilineal texts, which served to summarize long periods of history by tracing a line of male descent. This male voice is quoted not, as I initially suggested, in order to undermine the female voice of the narrative, but, on the contrary, in order to be exposed by the female voice of the narrative as pitifully inadequate in its androcentric selectivity. The narrative and the genealogy purport to recount the same history, but the women's world of the narrative is left wholly invisible by the male line of succession that the genealogy records.[34] Thus the book of Ruth, its conclusion tells us, is the kind of story that official, masculine history leaves out.

Ilana Pardes provides a nice analogy: "If the women in the Bible usually serve as a foil against which the deeds of the fathers are presented, in this narrative the subplot becomes the main plot in, as it were, a biblical parallel to [Tom] Stoppard's *Rosencrantz and Guildenstern Are Dead*."[35] Stoppard's play includes short sections of *Hamlet* within a plot that otherwise portrays what *Hamlet* does not: the role of the minor characters Rosencrantz and Guildenstern from their own perspective. The genealogy at the end of Ruth corresponds, one may suggest, to the quotations from Hamlet in *Rosencrantz and Guildenstern Are Dead*.

Moreover, the genealogy could be regarded as representing all the androcentric narratives of the Hebrew canon. Readers of Ruth who know such texts will be constantly aware of the contrast between its female perspective and

---

33. Bledstein, "Female Companionships," 130.

34. It is also true, of course, that the genealogy omits David's Moabite ancestry, which only a female line of descent can reveal.

35. I. Pardes, *Countertraditions in the Bible: A Feminist Approach* (Cambridge: Harvard University Press, 1992) 99.

the male perspective of these other texts. They will experience the book's effect of exposing by contrast the androcentricity of these other texts. They will be aware of this as an intertextual function of the book's relation to other texts. But the genealogical conclusion finally makes the contrast an inner-textual reality of the book of Ruth itself. Thus the conclusion that functions canonically to give the book a setting in the larger corpus of the Hebrew Bible also gives it the specific canonical function of exposing the androcentricity of other biblical narratives. The book's revelation of what is elsewhere invisible can then function canonically not merely as an exception to the prevalent androcentricity of other narratives, but also representatively, authorizing the reader to supply what is elsewhere omitted and to reconstruct what is elsewhere suppressed.[36]

5. The Canonical Role of Gynocentric Texts

Those who give either the Jewish or the Christian canon of the Scriptures the role of a body of literature normative for faith and practice are familiar with a wide variety of ways in which different parts of Scripture relate and interact with one another. In the light of the whole canon, there are undoubtedly parts of Scripture that, were they to stand alone, would be seriously misleading, but which, complemented, relativized, or corrected by other parts of Scripture, play a part in the total witness of Scripture. That Ruth is a Moabite has often been seen to give the book a relativizing or corrective function in relation to elements of nationalistic particularism elsewhere in the Hebrew canon (Deuteronomy or Ezra-Nehemiah). There is therefore nothing novel in principle in suggesting for Ruth a similar function in relation to the prevalent androcentrism of other canonical texts.

One might object that this is a disproportionately large role for one short

---

36. A whole variety of appropriate reading strategies are available here. One may reconstruct from all available historical evidence, along with comparative material and social-scientific models, the circumstances and roles of women in a period of biblical history, as Meyers, *Discovering Eve*, does, thereby supplying context and depth to texts that refer to these only briefly or indirectly. One may read from the point of view of a female character a biblical narrative that is told from an androcentric perspective, supplying the women's perspective that the text omits (e.g., F. van Dijk-Hemmes, "Sarai's Exile: A Gender Motivated Reading of Genesis 12.10–13.2," in A. Brenner, ed., *A Feminist Companion to Genesis* [FCB 1/2; Sheffield: Sheffield Academic Press, 1993] 223-34); see chap. 5, §9 below. One may use historical resources to exploit to the full what little the text says about a particular woman: see chaps. 4, 5, and 7 below. One may use informed imagination to penetrate within and around the text's account of a particular woman (e.g., to some extent, E. Moltmann-Wendel, *The Women around Jesus* [tr. J. Bowden; New York: Crossroad; London: SCM, 1982]); see chap. 5, §8 below.

text in the canon to perform. But, first, a quantitative judgment here is less than appropriate. More to the point are the widely acknowledged literary qualities of Ruth, which enable readers to share its gynocentric perspective and empower it to expose the androcentrism of other texts. Readers who attend to this text can neither miss nor be content with the androcentrism of other texts.

Second, Ruth is by no means the only gynocentric interruption of the dominant androcentricity of Scripture. The kind of feminist canonical hermeneutic that is being proposed will need to explore the distinctive canonical functions of other canonical texts in which a women's perspective is dominant. For example, the Song of Songs, in which the female voice predominates and, it has been convincingly argued, expresses an authentically female perspective,[37] differs from Ruth in that male and female perspectives are not contrasted. Because the world in which the forms of male dominance are expressed scarcely impinges at all on the world in which the Song moves, it can be simply ignored. Here the mutuality of the lovers is all that counts ("My lover is mine and I am his," 2:16; 6:3; cf. 7:10 [MT 11]).[38] Equality and mutuality can only be presented here as the female perspective because the text also presents them as the male perspective. Thus, while deuteronomic laws may treat female sexuality as male property,[39] the Song of Songs' celebration of sexual mutuality is sufficiently powerful in itself that it can counteract the conventional framework of male dominance simply by ignoring it.

Female voice and women's perspectives occur not only in those few biblical books in which they predominate (Esther may be a third example), but also in books whose dominant perspective is more or less androcentric. Those parts of Genesis where the perspective of the matriarchs interrupts the more dominant perspective of the patriarchs are a good example. A feminist critique that finds in such texts androcentric marginalizations of women can also be turned around, so that such gynocentric interruptions can be allowed to throw light on their androcentric contexts. This will occur in different ways, depending on whether the women are, like Deborah, historically exceptional, in the sense that probably few women played such roles historically, or, like Hannah, textually exceptional, in the sense that they make visible what is normally invisible in the texts.

37. A. Brenner, "Women Poets and Authors," in Brenner, ed., *A Feminist Companion to the Song of Songs* (FCB 1/1; Sheffield: Sheffield Academic Press, 1993) 88-90.

38. P. Trible, "Love's Lyrics Redeemed," in Brenner, ed., *Song of Songs*, pp. 117, 119; Meyers, *Discovering Eve*, 178.

39. Cf., e.g., C. Pressler, "Sexual Violence and Deuteronomic Law," in A. Brenner, ed., *A Feminist Companion to Exodus to Deuteronomy* (FCB 1/6; Sheffield: Sheffield Academic Press, 1994) 102-12.

The New Testament Gospels are another example of biblical books that may adopt a female perspective from time to time. They share a literary characteristic that makes the project of identifying authentically women's perspectives in them worth attempting, even though the considerable literature on women in the Gospels has as yet scarcely attempted it. For the most part the Gospel narratives do not invite their readers/hearers to identify with Jesus' perspective on events. Rather the readers/hearers are invited to adopt successively the many different perspectives of those who hear, observe, encounter, and follow Jesus.[40] The perspective may be the collective perspective of crowds or disciples, but it is frequently the perspective of one of the many individuals who interact with Jesus in narratives of healing or discipleship or other forms of encounter. Many of these individuals are women. This does not guarantee that the stories about them offer authentically female perspectives, but on the other hand we should not allow the assumption of a male author to prejudice us against this possibility. As already observed with reference to André Brink, male authors can adopt a more or less authentically female voice. In the ancient world this was partly because skilled and sensitive oral storytellers, as the evangelists surely were, when relating to a mixed audience, often in situations allowing a degree of audience participation, learn to portray characters with whom their female auditors can identify, as well as characters with whom their male auditors can identify. It is also the case that relatively spare narratives like those in the Gospels, which outline and suggest rather than exhaustively portray, can authorize a reader to supply a fuller female perspective than they explicitly express. But in addition, however justified the assumption that the evangelists were male may be, it is certainly not justified to assume that all the tradents of the Gospel traditions were male.

The potential of the Gospel stories of women to suggest or to draw their readers into an authentically women's perspective has been bypassed in the tendency to redaction-critical studies that use the stories to reconstruct, for example, "Luke's view of women." But it is vital for the kind of feminist canonical hermeneutic I am proposing. One recent methodological approach to women in the Gospels that could be related to mine is that of Carla Ricci, who describes her work as an "exegesis of the silence" of the Gospels.[41] She knows, of course, that there could be no exegesis of this silence were it total silence, and her work finds its starting point in Luke 8:1-3, understood as a "revealing trace" that

---

40. This is at least one reason for the contrast between Luke's Gospel, in which women are prominent, and Acts, in which they are not.

41. C. Ricci, *Mary Magdalene and Many Others*, tr. P. Burns (Minneapolis: Fortress, 1994) 13, and subsequently.

makes it possible to exegete the silence elsewhere. Her subject is specifically the women disciples who accompanied Jesus during his ministry in Galilee. For those women in that period of the ministry, the exercise is one of recovering a perspective the Gospels themselves do not give us. But this is not the case for other women or for some of those same women later in the Gospel narratives. Exegesis of the women's narratives in the Gospels both authorizes and assists Ricci's exegesis of the silences of the Gospels. These "indicative and revealing pieces of a far wider reality that lies hidden"[42] are all the more indicative and revealing if they can be seen as in some sense women's literature, offering significant female perspectives alongside the more predominant male perspectives in the texts.

The canonical role that my proposal suggests for the scriptural exceptions to androcentrism amounts to privileging these texts for a certain purpose. It does not make them a "canon within the canon" — even for women. The mistake made by hermeneutical approaches that rely, in some form, on a canon within the canon is that they grant hermeneutical privilege to certain parts of Scripture *in every respect*. The functional diversity of Scripture is better respected by allowing various different parts of the canon hermeneutical privilege for specific purposes and in particular respects. Thus, in my proposal, the gynocentric texts have the role not of relativizing the androcentric texts in every respect, but of relativizing or correcting precisely their androcentrism. In this way androcentrism in general in Jewish or Christian thinking and practice can be corrected by the canon, instead of being endorsed and promoted by the canon.[43]

Readers familiar with feminist theology may well react to this possibility with skepticism, since it is common among feminist theologians to view the canon as a patriarchal construction.[44] This is based in part on somewhat too sweeping judgments about its contents, which are held to be without exception androcentric and supportive of patriarchal structures. But it is also based on a misleadingly authoritarian model of canonization, as though the canon was created by councils of male rabbis and bishops. The real process of canonization took place over a long period as the actual use of books in the respective religious communities tested and established their value. Rabbinic and episcopal authorities took part only in the final stages of the process, approving the

42. Ricci, *Mary Magdalene*, 23.
43. Cf. the remarks about the role of "voices of marginality" within the canon, in W. Brueggemann, "Canonization and Contextualization," in Brueggemann, *Interpretation and Obedience* (Minneapolis: Fortress, 1991) 119-42.
44. A representative example, from an ecofeminist perspective, is A. Primavesi, *From Apocalypse to Genesis* (Minneapolis: Fortress; Tunbridge Wells: Burns & Oates, 1991) chap. 9.

canons that were already in general use and adjudicating a few remaining uncertainties. The real process of canonization must therefore have been a process
in which the audience of religious literature played the decisive role through its
critical reception of the texts. Women as well as men would certainly have had a
voice in the process, and so the inclusion of some examples of women's literature in the canon need not be regarded as accidental. Rather than viewing these
texts as surprising survivors of the attempt to suppress such literature, we may
reasonably suppose that the importance of women in the grassroots processes
of canonical selection led to their inclusion precisely as women's literature, in
order to counterbalance the androcentrism of the rest of Scripture.

CHAPTER 2

The Gentile Foremothers of the Messiah

Because of You, women pursued
men: Tamar desired
a man who was widowed, and Ruth loved
a man who was old. Even Rahab,
who captivated men, by You was taken captive.[1]

1. Why Are These Women Here?

The appearance of four women from the Hebrew Bible/Old Testament
(Tamar, Rahab, Ruth, and the wife of Uriah) in the Matthean genealogy of Jesus (Matt 1:1-17) has occasioned much discussion.[2] In a patrilineal genealogy
of this kind, women have no necessary place. The most usual circumstance in
which they appear in genealogies in the Hebrew Bible/Old Testament is when
several children of one man are distinguished as born to different mothers, but
this is usual only when more than one son is listed. It is true that Judah had
sons other than by Tamar and that David had sons other than by the wife of
Uriah, but it is also true that Abraham and Jacob (who is said to have begotten

1. Ephrem, "Hymns on the Nativity: Hymn 9," in *Ephrem the Syrian: Hymns* (tr. K. E.
McVey; Classics of Western Spirituality; New York: Paulist, 1989) 126.
2. For recent summaries of the discussion, see W. D. Davies and D. C. Allison, *A Critical
and Exegetical Commentary on the Gospel according to Saint Matthew*, vol. 1 (ICC; Edinburgh:
T. & T. Clark, 1988) 170-72; R. E. Brown, *The Birth of the Messiah* (2d ed.; Garden City, N.Y.:
Doubleday, 1993) 71-74, 590-96.

"Judah and his brothers" in Matt 1:2) had sons by more than one wife. More-over, the naming of Rahab and Ruth cannot be explained in this way. After my observations on the genealogy at the end of the book of Ruth in chapter 1 of this volume, it would be tempting to see the occurrence of the four women as some kind of protest against or qualification of the androcentricity of the oth-erwise exclusively patrilineal genealogy. It is interesting to note that in at least some Jewish literature of the Second Temple period (Jubilees, Pseudo-Philo's *Biblical Antiquities*) there is a tendency to supply the lack of women in biblical genealogies: Jubilees names the wives (along with their fathers' names) of all the patriarchs from Adam to Abraham and of all the sons of Jacob, while Pseudo-Philo names the wives and daughters of all the patriarchs from Adam to Noah,[3] and generally tends to add more female names to the genealogical information he takes from Scripture or creates. However, such an approach cannot explain why specifically these four women should be mentioned in Matthew's genealogy. If Matthew simply wanted to put some women into his genealogy, why did he not name the matriarchs Sarah, Rebekah, and Leah, all better known to his readers than the four he does mention? Why include Rahab, whose union with Salma and motherhood of Boaz are nowhere men-tioned in the Hebrew Bible/Old Testament, rather than other women who are placed in this line of descent in the genealogies or narratives in the Hebrew Bi-ble/Old Testament? It seems there must be some reason other than the mere fact that they are women for including these particular women.

A first step, not often taken in discussions of the women in Matthew's gene-alogy, is to notice that this is an "annotated genealogy" like those in Genesis and 1 Chronicles 1–9.[4] Such genealogies include a variety of additional notes besides the simple succession of male names. In Matthew's genealogy the four mothers are one sort of note but there are also others. Since there is no obvious reason why this genealogy required collateral references to brothers of any men in direct suc-cession, one can also include these in the notes, indicated in italics thus:

(2) Judah *and his brothers*
(3) Perez *and Zerah by Tamar*
(5) Boaz *by Rahab*
(5) Obed *by Ruth*
(6) David *the king*

3. For the names see T. Ilan, "Biblical Women's Names in the Apocryphal Traditions," *JSP* 11 (1993): 3-67.

4. See J. Nolland, "Genealogical Annotation in Genesis as Background for the Matthean Genealogy of Jesus," *TynB* 47 (1996) 115-22.

(6) Solomon *by the wife of Uriah*

(11) Jechoniah *and his brothers at the time of the deportation to Babylon*

(12) *After he deportation to Babylon* Jechoniah

(16) Joseph *the husband of Mary of whom* was born Jesus, *who is called the Messiah.*

In part such additional notes relate to the function of genealogies in Genesis and 1 Chronicles, which is not only to trace descendants or ancestry, but to resume and to summarize history. In 1 Chronicles 1–9 the genealogies are actually a way of telling the whole course of history, as narrated in other biblical books, from Adam to the point at which Chronicles begins its narrative: the death of Saul. Similarly, Matthew's genealogy functions to summarize the story told in the whole Hebrew Bible/Old Testament from Abraham onward. For competent Jewish readers, the names would evoke the narratives. There is also a sort of parallel with Chronicles, in that the latter's narrative is the story of the Davidic monarchy and 1 Chronicles 1–9 uses genealogies to summarize all history prior to the point at which David becomes king and Chronicles' own true narrative begins. Similarly, Matthew's genealogy takes him to the point at which his narrative of the Davidic Messiah Jesus begins.

We do not need to wait until the end of the genealogy to realize this. It is clear in the introductory title Matthew gives it: "the genealogy of Jesus the Messiah, the son of David, the son of Abraham" (1:1). The genealogy is not just a resumption of the story told in the Hebrew Bible/Old Testament; it is also designed to show Jesus as the one prophesied and expected throughout that history, the descendant of Abraham and David, the Messiah who comes to initiate the climactic phase of the story. The Davidic messianic nature of the genealogy is apparent from the fact that "David the king" and "Jesus the Messiah" are the only two persons with titles. It is also apparent in the numerical structure that Matthew carefully highlights (1:17): three sets of fourteen generations, with David at the transition from the first to the second period, and the deportation to Babylon at the transition from the second to the third.[5] The first period precedes the Davidic monarchy, the second is the period when David and his descendants ruled, the third follows the demise of the monarchy, ending with its restoration and culmination in the Messiah Jesus. It has also often been noticed that the 3 × 14 structure corresponds to the numerical value (14) of the three consonants in the Hebrew name דוד (David), an instance of the practice of gematria (converting words into their numerical value) that was widespread in Jewish and early Christian scriptural exegesis

5. On this see especially Davies and Allison, *Matthew*, 1:161-65.

and speculation.[6] As in other biblical genealogies, the generations have been adjusted to produce a numerical scheme for the sake of its symbolic meaning (cf., e.g., 1 Chron 6:3-5).

Thus it is clear that several of the annotations in the genealogy serve its Davidic messianic purpose. The reference to "Judah *and his brothers*" (1:2) brings all twelve tribes of Israel into view, since the Messiah is to be the Messiah of the whole twelve-tribe people. Perhaps the reference not only to Perez but also to his twin brother Zerah (1:3) serves the same inclusive purpose, though these twins were not the only ancestors of the tribe of Judah (their half-brother Shelah also had descendants), and so it may be that Zerah has been brought in for the sake of his mother Tamar: if the mother is to be mentioned, it seemed natural to mention both twins (as in 1 Chron 2:4, but not Ruth 4:12). The reference to "Jechoniah *and his brothers at the time of the deportation to Babylon*" (1:11) entails a deliberate abbreviation of history. Since Jechoniah himself had only one brother (1 Chron 3:16), the "brothers" are doubtless those of his father Jehoiakim, whom Matthew has omitted from the genealogy. Jehoiakim's brothers were Jehoahaz and Zedekiah, two of the last four kings of Judah, of whom Jehoiakim himself and his son Jehoiachin or Jechoniah were the others (in the sequence Jehoahaz, Jehoiakim, Jechoniah, Zedekiah: 1 Kgs 23:30–25:10). Thus the reference to Jechoniah's brothers in Matthew 1:11 serves to complete the list of the kings of Judah down to the end of the dynasty. At the same time it was Jechoniah's own deportation to Babylon that was often taken as the symbolic beginning of the exile (cf. 1 Chron 3:17; Jer 22:24-30),[7] and so it is appropriate that his should be the last name of a reigning king in the genealogy. Matthew 1:11 is a masterly compressed evocation of the end of the rule of the house of David in Israel.

Thus far I have explained the structure and annotations of the genealogy as serving its purpose of portraying Jesus as the Davidic Messiah. I could also mention that the fourteenth and last name in the first section is David "the king" (the number of whose name, by gematria, is fourteen), the fourteenth and last name in the second section Jechoniah, and the fourteenth[8] and last

6. For another instance of gematria in a biblical genealogy (Gen 46:16), see Davies and Allison, *Matthew,* 1:164.

7. Note also that Matthew's term μετοικεσία is that used of the deportation of Jechoniah and others in LXX 4 Kgdms (2 Kgs) 24:16.

8. This requires counting the name Jechoniah twice, whereas David is counted only once (the second sequence of fourteen beginning with Solomon). But this difference is indicated by the fact that Jechoniah is emphatically placed on both sides of "the deportation to Babylon" (1:11-12), which in the enumeration (1:17) is made the transition from the second to the third set of fourteen generations.

name in the third section is Jesus "the Messiah." Thus the first section culminates in the establishment of the dynasty, the second reaches its end in the downfall of the dynasty, and the third concludes with the reestablishment of the dynasty in the king who will rule forever. But one should ask why the genealogy begins with Abraham, rather than with David, the founder of the dynasty and model for his greater descendant, the Messiah. The reason is that the Messiah of David is to be not only the ruler of Israel but also the promised descendant of Abraham in whom all the nations will be blessed (Gen 12:3; 22:18; 26:4; 28:14). (One expression of this conjunction is the LXX version of the royal Psalm 71[72], where v 17b, already in the Hebrew reminiscent of Gen 12:3, is made even more so: the messianic king of the psalm is also the offspring of Abraham to whom the patriarchal promises referred.) This, of course, makes the genealogy the more appropriate as a prologue to Matthew's Gospel, which goes on to embody in its birth narrative the conviction that Jesus is the Jewish Messiah for the Gentiles (2:2-12) and concludes with the exalted Messiah's commission to make disciples of all nations (28:18-19). Thus the genealogy expresses the universal direction of God's purpose as it was indicated as early as the election of Abraham and in which Israel and their Messiah find their true identity.

The remaining annotations concern the four women from the Hebrew Bible/Old Testament and Mary the mother of Jesus. Discussions of the women in the genealogy often assume that an explanation of the references to the women should relate to all five, such that the four women from the Hebrew Bible/Old Testament in some way foreshadow Mary. This assumption has strongly prejudiced many attempts to explain the references to these four women, but it is by no means a necessary assumption. The four are formally related to the genealogy in a quite different way from Mary. The whole genealogy follows a rigid formulaic pattern (A begat B, B begat C, C begat D . . .) that none of the annotations before verse 16 disturbs. They are all added to the formula without modifying it. This is true of the four biblical women, all of whom are attached to the regular pattern by means of the same simple formula (ἐκ τῆς Θαμάρ, etc.). But with Joseph the basic formula of the genealogy for the first (and last) time changes: "Joseph the husband of Mary, from whom was born Jesus . . ." (τὸν Ἰωσὴφ τὸν ἄνδρα Μαρίας, ἐξ ἧς ἐγεννήθη Ἰησοῦς). Whereas Judah did beget Perez and Zerah "by Tamar," Joseph did not beget Jesus. Mary appears in the genealogy because Matthew cannot otherwise explain Joseph's relationship to Jesus.[9] This most fundamental reason why Mary appears in the geneal-

---

9. Luke 3:23 (the beginning of Luke's genealogy of Jesus) does not refer to Mary, but this is not a true parallel because Joseph's relationship to Jesus by way of his marriage to Mary has already been explained to readers of Luke's Gospel.

ogy has no precedent in the other four women, and so it is not at all obvious why their function in the genealogy should have to be related to Mary.

(1) The suggestion that the four women are included because they were all Gentiles coheres well with all that we have so far observed about the nature and purpose of the genealogy.[10] That the Davidic Messiah is to be a blessing to all the nations, the Messiah for Gentiles as well as for Jews, is indicated symbolically in the genealogy by mentioning the Gentile women in his ancestry. By definition no descendant of Abraham through Isaac and Jacob can be a Gentile, and so the Messiah's line of descent through David from Abraham cannot include any male Gentile. But there could be Gentile wives of the men in this line, and Matthew has found four such (probably the only four he could have found, though it is not impossible that the creative exegesis that, as we shall see, made Rahab the wife of Salma might have been paralleled in other unlikely cases). This understanding of the role of the women in the genealogy has the great advantage of serving, like all the other annotations, to explicate the meaning of Jesus' messiahship. It does so in a way that highlights an aspect of Jesus' messiahship that is of prime importance for Matthew.

There seem to be three objections to this explanation. The decisive one for many commentators is, as Raymond Brown puts it, that "one would think that the four Old Testament women constitute some preparation for the role of Mary, and yet Mary was not a foreigner."[11] I have already refuted this objection. The second problem is whether all four of the women were in fact regarded as Gentiles by Jews in the late Second Temple period. There could be no doubt that Rahab was a Canaanite and Ruth a Moabite. But nothing is said in the narrative of 2 Samuel about the ethnic ancestry of Bathsheba. By connecting her father Eliam (2 Sam 11:3; Ammiel in 1 Chron 3:5) with Eliam the son of Ahitophel (2 Sam 23:34), one could regard her as of Israelite descent (so *b. Sanh.* 101a),[12] but this is not an obvious or necessary connection. Alternatively, one could assume that, like her husband Uriah, she was a Hittite (2 Sam 11:3, 6, 21; 12:9-10). This may be the reason why, unlike the other three women in Mat-

---

10. This explanation is adopted by, e.g., E. Schweizer, *The Good News according to Matthew* (tr. D. E. Green; Atlanta: John Knox; London: SPCK, 1976) 25; U. Luz, *Matthew 1–7: A Commentary* (tr. W. C. Linss; Minneapolis: Augsburg, 1989; Edinburgh: T. & T. Clark, 1990) 109-10; C. S. Keener, *A Commentary on the Gospel of Matthew* (Grand Rapids: Eerdmans, 1999) 78-80; for others who take this view, see E. M. Wainwright, *Towards a Feminist Critical Reading of the Gospel according to Matthew* (BZNW 60; Berlin/New York: de Gruyter, 1991) 65n.24.

11. Brown, *Birth*, 73.

12. See M. Bredin, "Gentiles and the Davidic Tradition in Matthew," in A. Brenner, ed., *A Feminist Companion to the Hebrew Bible in the New Testament* (FCB 1/10; Sheffield: Sheffield Academic Press, 1996) 96-97.

thew's genealogy, Bathsheba is not named but called "the wife of Uriah." Indeed, Brown thinks that "this peculiar designation constitutes the strongest argument for the proposal that the four women" are included in the genealogy as Gentiles.[13] Perhaps it is not quite so strong: the designation could be intended to draw attention to the fact that her liaison with David was adultery (cf. 2 Sam 11:26), though by the time Solomon was conceived she was widowed and married to David. But there is certainly no real problem about supposing that Bathsheba is included in the genealogy as a Gentile. The fourth woman, Tamar, is the most problematic case, both because Genesis leaves her ethnic origin indeterminate and because the evidence many scholars have adduced for supposing that Jews in the Second Temple period regarded her as a Gentile does not in fact show that. In the next section of this chapter I shall therefore discuss Tamar's ancestry in detail and show that there were divergent Jewish traditions. Some Jews, concerned for the racial purity of the tribe of Judah, connected her with the family of Abraham, but there is also evidence for another view that considered her a Canaanite.

The third objection to the suggestion that the four women are included in the genealogy as Gentiles is a feminist one. Elaine Wainwright claims that all the main proposals for explaining the presence of the women in the genealogy reflect androcentric assumptions: "The classification of the four women as foreigners reflects an androcentric perspective which sees women as outsiders to the patriarchal world and culture."[14] Of course, as she would agree, only as part of an overall interpretation of the genealogy does this constitute an objection: Matthew may indeed view the women in this androcentric way. But it is not necessary to suppose he does. As already explained, Gentiles in this genealogy have to be women. But furthermore the racial exclusivism that would treat such Gentiles as outsiders is not endorsed but strongly critiqued by Matthew's inclusion of them in the genealogy. The representation of Gentiles in the genealogy of the Messiah signifies the inclusion of Gentiles in the messianic people of God. The same could be said of them as women, though this cannot be the primary reason for their presence in the genealogy. That the patrilineal genealogy of the Messiah does not signify the exclusion of women from his people is shown by the specific mention of women in it. If it were true that first-century patriarchal thinking paralleled foreigners and women as "outsiders to the patriarchal world and culture," then the inclusion of the women as Gentiles would certainly entail their inclusion as women. But I know no evidence from Second Temple Jewish literature to support such an association of women and Gentiles. The relative

13. Brown, *Birth*, 72.
14. Wainwright, *Towards*, 65.

absence of women from biblical genealogies is due to their irrelevance to patrilineal inheritance. It is a quite different phenomenon from the desire for purity of racial descent that would exclude Gentiles from an Israelite genealogy.

I shall consider briefly the other explanations of the presence of the women in the genealogy that have been proposed and discussed. (2) An explanation that goes back to Jerome, though it is now out of favor, is that the four women were all sinners.[15] This does have the advantage that it would serve the purpose of the genealogy in contributing to an account of the nature of Jesus' messiahship. The women would be indications that the Messiah comes to "save his people from their sins" (Matt 1:21). But it is implausible to understand all four as sinners, or to suppose that their sin would be what mention of them in the genealogy would call to mind for competent first-century readers. At the end of the story in which Tamar disguises herself as a prostitute and her father-in-law Judah employs her, Judah's own verdict is: "She is more in the right than I, since I did not give her my son Shelah" (Gen 38:26). Tamar's action was for the sake of bearing an heir for her first husband, Er, when Judah had failed in his duty to give Tamar as levirate wife to his surviving son Shelah. Jewish tradition regarded her highly for her bold initiative in thus ensuring the continuance of Judah's family line. Precisely in genealogical terms she was to be commended! Rahab was a prostitute (Judg 2:1) but, however this might have been regarded (Josephus suppressed it, calling her an innkeeper [*Ant.* 5.8-10], but other Jewish writers mentioned it), it was certainly eclipsed by her bold action, said to be one of kindness (חסד, Judg 2:12) to the spies and thus to the whole people of Israel. For Jewish tradition she was a model proselyte in her faith in the God of Israel (2:10-11) and her subsequent membership of Israel (6:25). Despite the somewhat compromising circumstances in which Ruth took the initiative in placing herself under Boaz's protection, in effect proposing he exercise his right as next of kin to marry her, she too acted with חסד (Ruth 3:10), and Jewish tradition saw her in an entirely good light. As for Bathsheba, she could hardly have been expected to do other than obey the orders of the king (1 Sam 11:4), and the narrative in 1 Samuel reserves all its condemnation for David. If Matthew's phrase, "the wife of Uriah," draws attention to the adultery, it is surely at David's expense rather than Bathsheba's. As Beare comments, "Strange as it may seem to modern commentators, no moral stigma was attached to these women in Jewish tradition."[16] But that it should seem strange may say

15. For modern representatives of this view, see Wainwright, *Towards,* 64n.17; K. E. Corley, *Private Women, Public Meals* (Peabody, Mass.: Hendrickson, 1993) 149n.9.

16. F. W. Beare, *The Gospel according to Matthew* (San Francisco: Harper & Row; Oxford: Blackwell, 1981) 64.

something about the patriarchal connection of women and sexual sin not in Jewish tradition but in more modern times. One might wonder if the argument should be turned around, such that the mention of these women calls attention not to their own sin but to that of their male sexual partners. While this would work well for Judah and David, it would not for Boaz and Salma. It is remarkable, however, that no commentators seem to notice that, if sin is to be found in the genealogy, there are much more notorious biblical sinners among the men than the women. Most of the later kings of Judah are roundly condemned both in 2 Kings and in the prophets (e.g., Jer 22–23) for rampant abuse of their office, idolatry, oppression, and violence, self-indulgent failure to fulfill their God-given role of ensuring justice for the vulnerable. The genealogy itself strongly evokes God's judgment on them and the consequent cessation of the monarchy in its repeated reference to the deportation to Babylon, as well as by concluding its names of the kings with Jechoniah, on whom Jeremiah pronounced the most final verdict of judgment on the whole royal line (Jer 23:24-30). It is by contrast with this line of kings — as well as with the usurping King Herod (note the contrast between Jesus as king of the Jews and Herod, who was also so called, throughout Matt 2) — that the messianic king is to fulfill the prophetic expectations and, by implementing the justice and compassion of God, save his people from their sins. It is once again important to remember that the women are "annotations" among others in the rather sophisticated construction of this genealogy. It is not they alone who need explanation.

(3) Another feature of the four women (often combined with the next in explanations of their place in the genealogy) does not accuse them of sin, but draws on the same evidence to suggest that there were "irregular circumstances" in their union with their male partners, through which God nevertheless acted to further his purpose. Brown, who favors this as at least part of the explanation, thinks it "obvious: These five women [including Mary, an important matter for most who have adopted this approach] do have in common that their union with their partners before or at conception was scandalous or irregular."[17] One rather weak element in this view is Rahab, since we know nothing of Rahab's union with Salma except what Matthew here tells us (and, as we shall see in §3, it is unlikely that Matthew and his readers knew more about this than that Rahab married Salma and was mother to Boaz). One has to rely on the fact that she had been a prostitute to make the union "scandalous or irregular." But it should also be noted that, if the purpose were to indicate points in the genealogy where God acted through irregular circumstances that might have impeded the continuation of the line, then one might have expected mention also of Sa-

17. Brown, *Birth*, 593.

rah, Rebekah, and Leah, the barren women whom God enabled to bear the sons named in the genealogy. But this problem is met by a variation of this view that sees the references to the women as a form of apologetic against Jewish accusations that Jesus was the illegitimate child of Mary.[18] In this case, it is the scandalous nature of the circumstances in the case of each of the women from the Hebrew Bible/Old Testament that has to be emphasized. The point is that even in Solomon's ancestry there were apparently irregular unions, but in each case the reality was that the woman was in fact righteous and God was active in spite of outward appearances of irregularity. Again, one wonders whether the circumstances of the four women do not have to be squeezed rather too much to fit this common mold. The more strained the case the weaker the apologetic.

(4) Often combined with proposal (3) is the view that these women acted with initiative and resolution that God used to further his purpose. Again Brown states this with considerable assurance: "Matthew most certainly intends to call attention to the fact that in order to bring about the birth of the Messiah, God made use of these women who were more active than their partners in very difficult situations where circumstances were stacked against them."[19] Wainwright gives a feminist alternative within broadly this same approach:

> The anomalous or dangerous situation of each of the women, at a certain point, places her outside of a patriarchal marriage or family structure. Each one's actions threaten the structure further.... While the patriarchal narrative quickly domesticates these actions, they can also be seen to encode aspects of women's power. God's messianic plan unfolds in and through such power. The women's presence functions, therefore, as a critique of patriarchy and introduces a point of tension into the narrative that must guide the reader as the story unfolds.[20]

It is certainly true that Tamar, Rahab, and Ruth all show remarkable independence, initiative, and resolution in their actions in the biblical stories, which are, at least in part, told in a gynocentric way. But the problem for the view that this characteristic is the primary reason for the inclusion of the four women in the genealogy is that it does not apply to Bathsheba. As Wainwright admits[21]

---

18. E. D. Freed, "The Women in Matthew's Genealogy," *JSNT* 29 (1987) 3-19.

19. Brown, *Birth*, 595.

20. Wainwright, *Towards*, 68. For a similar but not identical proposal, see J. Schaberg, *The Illegitimacy of Jesus: A Feminist Theological Interpretation of the Infancy Narratives* (2d ed.; New York: Crossroad, 1990) 32-34.

21. Wainwright, *Towards*, 168-171.

(shifting the emphasis in Bathsheba's case from women's power to her anomalous position vis-à-vis the patriarchal family structure) and Jane Schaberg expounds in detail,[22] Bathsheba is portrayed in 2 Samuel 11 in an entirely passive way. Kathleen Corley's hint that her bathing was a sexually provocative act ("conveniently bathing in a location where David could see her")[23] is a surprisingly androcentric slur for which the narrative gives no encouragement, while Wainwright's comment that "the wife of Uriah comes to David, one of the few actions attributed to her,"[24] is misleading in that even this act was hardly chosen. Faced with the command of the king (2 Sam 11:4), Bathsheba could choose only obedience or certain disaster. The wife of Uriah turns out to be an immovable obstacle for any approach to the women in the genealogy that treats initiative and resolute action as the common factors. It is notable that Ephrem the Syrian in his ninth hymn on the nativity (quoted at the head of this chapter) takes this approach but refers only to Tamar, Rahab, and Ruth.

Another version of this fourth proposal comes from the school of social-scientific interpretation that finds in Mediterranean anthropology the key to understanding the New Testament in its context. K. C. Hanson and D. E. Oakman assert that the whole Matthean genealogy has the single purpose of expressing the ascribed honor Jesus had by virtue of his line of ancestry.[25] The five women (including Mary), by acting with honor-acquiring initiative, enhance Jesus' honor: "Jesus' ascribed honor, consequently, stems from the ascribed honor of his paternal lineage *and* the acquired honor of pivotal, exogamously related women in the lineage."[26] But this extraordinarily reductionist interpretation of the genealogy, as merely a statement about Jesus' honor, ignores the rich messianic significance with which Matthew has certainly invested it.

I conclude that the identification of the four women from the Hebrew Bible/Old Testament as Gentiles offers an interpretation of their place in the genealogy that both finds a convincing element common to all four and also accords well with the overall messianic purpose of the genealogy. The other suggestions are not so plausible in these key respects. This does not mean that some aspects of them may not be appropriate as additional overtones of meaning, but they do not seem to qualify as the primary reason for the genealogy's inclusion of precisely these four women. I have noted, however, that two

22. Schaberg, *Illegitimacy,* 29-32.

23. Corley, *Private Women,* 149.

24. Wainwright, *Towards,* 68.

25. K. C. Hanson and D. E. Oakman, *Palestine in the Time of Jesus: Social Structures and Social Conflicts* (Minneapolis: Fortress, 1998) 51-57.

26. Hanson and Oakman, *Palestine,* 57.

problems arise from the fact that the genealogy appears to presuppose information about these women that is not available in the Hebrew Bible/Old Testament itself. These are the issue of Tamar's ethnic origin, for which there is evidence in Second Temple Jewish literature, and Rahab's marriage to Salma, for which there is not. These two specific problems require a more careful examination of relevant Jewish genealogical speculation than has been undertaken up till now.

2. The Ancestry of Tamar

Genesis 38 says nothing about Tamar's race or ancestry. A natural assumption would be that, like Judah's first wife, she belonged to one of the indigenous peoples of Canaan (Gen 38:2). On the other hand, one might infer that, since Tamar is not said to be of Canaanite origin, she was not. As we shall see, both inferences were drawn by Jewish exegetes.

The earliest known Jewish tradition about Tamar's ancestry occurs in Jubilees 41:1 and in Testament of Judah 10:1, which here, as frequently in the Testaments of the Twelve Patriarchs, embodies the same tradition about the patriarchs as the book of Jubilees. (The debated issue of the provenance and date of the Testament of Judah need not concern us here, since in this instance the correspondence with Jubilees guarantees that we are dealing with an old tradition, whenever it was incorporated in the Testament.) In both texts Tamar, who was not a Canaanite, is in this respect strongly contrasted with Judah's Canaanite wife (Jub 41:1-2; TJud 10:1-2, 6). According to Jubilees 41:1, "Judah took a wife for Er, his firstborn, from the daughters of Aram, and her name was Tamar," while Testament of Judah 10:1 says that "Er brought from Mesopotamia Tamar, daughter of Aram." In the literature about the Matthean genealogy, these statements seem to have been universally understood, without any discussion, to mean that Tamar was an "Aramean."[27] This is one of those assertions that passes from scholar to scholar without further investigation. But a little study of the context of this tradition in Jubilees easily shows that the meaning of Jubilees 41:1 is not that Tamar was an Aramean.

Two persons called Aram (אֲרָם) were among the descendants of Shem, according to both Genesis and Jubilees (see table 1, p. 29). The first, a son of

27. E.g., Brown, *Birth,* 72n.28: Jub 41:1 "calls Tamar an Aramean"; Luz, *Matthew 1–7,* 110: "Tamar is considered an Aramaean"; Davies and Allison, *Matthew,* 1:170: "a 'daughter of Aram,' that is, an Aramean"; M. D. Johnson, *The Purpose of the Biblical Genealogies* (2d ed.; SNTSMS 8; Cambridge: Cambridge University Press, 1988) 159, 270 (he takes this Aram to be the Aram of Gen 10:22); cf. J. P. Heil, "The Narrative Roles of Women in Matthew's Gospel," *Bib* 72 (1991) 539.

Table 1: Aram in Genesis and Jubilees

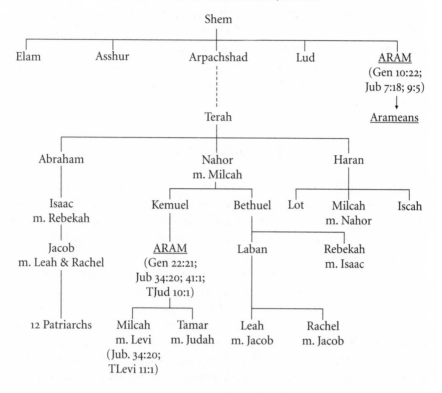

Shem (Gen 10:22; Jub 7:18; 9:5), was the eponymous progenitor of the Arameans, just as his brothers Elam, Asshur, Arpachshad, and Lud were of the Elamites, Assyrians, Chaldeans, and Lydians (according to Jub 9:2-6; Josephus, *Ant.* 1.143-44). The second Aram occurs among the descendants of Abraham's brother Nahor in Genesis 22:21, where Nahor's sons include Kemuel the father of Aram. This may originally have been intended as an indication of the origin of the Arameans (an alternative to Gen 10:22), especially since Nahor's family are located in Aram by Genesis.[28] The LXX took it in this sense (τὸν Καμουηλ πατέρα Σύρων), but Jubilees, as we shall see, did not.

The key to a correct understanding of Jubilees 41:1 lies in Jubilees' account of the wives of the twelve sons of Jacob in 34:20. In seven cases only the wife's name is given. But Naphtali's wife is said to be from Mesopotamia; I shall consider the significance of this information shortly. Levi's wife is said to be "Melka

---

28. Cf. C. Westermann, *Genesis 12–36: A Commentary* (tr. J. J. Scullion; Minneapolis: Augsburg, 1985) 368; W. T. Pitard, "Aram (Person)," *ABD* 1:338.

[Milcah],[29] from the daughters of Aram, from the seed of the sons of Terah" (cf. TLevi 11:1). Joseph's wife, following Genesis 41:45, is called "Aseneth, an Egyptian" (cf. Jub 40:10). Simeon and Judah are said to have taken Canaanite wives, as Genesis states (Gen 38:2; 46:10 [cf. Exod 6:15]).

Jubilees attaches to its interpretation of the Shechem story (30:1-7) an extremely severe prohibition of marriages between Israelites and Gentiles (30:8-17).[30] It also highlights the strict commands of Abraham, Isaac, and Rebekah, forbidding Jacob to take a Canaanite wife, as his brother Esau did (22:20; 25:1-5; 27:10). When it lists the wives of the sons of Jacob, it does not suppress the scriptural record that one did marry an Egyptian and two did take Canaanite wives.[31] But it does not approve. Following the list, it adds the nonscriptural information: "And Simeon repented and took another wife from Mesopotamia as his brothers had" (34:21). This indicates that not only Naphtali's wife but also the other wives, apart from those of Judah and Joseph, came from Mesopotamia. Mesopotamia is the name Jubilees uses for the home of Nahor's family (biblical Aram-naharaim and Paddan-aram), whence came Jacob's wives Leah and Rachel (27:10, 12, 13; 29:12, 18; also TJud 9:1). The meaning is therefore that all the sons of Jacob, except Simeon, Judah, and Joseph, followed their father's example and took wives from the family of Abraham's brother Nahor, and that Simeon later repented and followed suit. This conclusion is confirmed by the fact that Benjamin's wife bears a family name ('Iyasaka, i.e., Iscah, Gen 11:29),[32] as does Levi's (Melka, i.e., Milcah, Gen 12:29; 22:20). Moreover, Levi's wife's ancestry is more precisely stated: "from the daughters of Aram, from the seed of the sons of Terah." This must mean that she was one of the daughters of Aram, the grandson of Nahor, the son of Terah. (Terah's name is given as the ancestor common to her and Levi.) It certainly does not mean that she was an Aramean by race.[33]

---

29. The name is the same as that of Nahor's wife (Jub 19:10), the biblical Milcah (Gen 12:29; 22:20). The latter is Μελχα in LXX Gen 12:29; 22:20; Josephus, *Ant.* 1.151, 153; and Levi's wife is Μελχα in TLevi 11:1.

30. See J. C. Endres, *Biblical Interpretation in the Book of Jubilees* (CBQMS 18; Washington, D.C.: Catholic Biblical Association of America, 1987) chap. 5.

31. Contrast later Jewish attempts to deny that Simeon's and Judah's wives were Canaanites: R. H. Charles, *The Book of Jubilees* (London: A. & C. Black, 1902) 206nn.

32. "Esca" is also the name of a daughter of Nahor in *Bib. Ant.* 4:14. The Syriac fragment that parallels Jub 34:20 specifies that Gad's wife was a descendant of Nahor; see Charles, *Jubilees*, 206n.

33. Jub 27:12, following Gen 28:5, calls Bethuel son of Nahor, "Bethuel the Syrian," but this cannot be meant in a racial sense. In 37:9 (cf. 38:3) Arameans are among Esau's allies against Jacob, in a list that surely represents the author's perception of Israel's bitterest Gentile enemies (37:9-10). The biblical use of the term "Aramean" for Abraham himself (Deut 26:5), as well as his

Aram's other daughter, Milcah's sister, was Tamar. She is not mentioned in Jubilees 34:20 because the list there represents the situation at the time of Judah's first marriage to Betasu'el (41:7: Bedsuel) the Canaanite. The note about Simeon's second marriage in 34:21 is not paralleled by one about Judah, because Judah's marital situation is taken up in chapter 41, the story of Judah and Tamar. The parallel tradition in the Testament of Judah actually makes the connection with Jubilees 34 clearer: there it is Judah's son Er who follows the example of his grandfather and goes to Mesopotamia to find his wife Tamar, the daughter of Aram (TJud 10:1).[34]

The marriage of Levi and Judah to the two sisters Milcah and Tamar secures the racial purity of the two tribes most important to the author of Jubilees and the tradents of his traditions. On both male and female sides, both tribes descended entirely from Abraham's father, Terah.[35]

On this account of her ancestry, was Tamar a Gentile? Strictly speaking, the covenant with Abraham (Gen 17) was with Abraham and his descendants, not those of his brother Nahor (whose male descendants were presumably not circumcised), and Jubilees 16:30 makes explicit (what is implicit in Genesis) that even Abraham's descendants by Hagar and Keturah and through Esau are Gentiles, not members of the covenant people. Nevertheless Jubilees probably overlooks the strict implication that the wives of the patriarchs were Gentiles. They were, after all, as closely related to Abraham as it was possible to be, outside the line of Abraham's own descendants. At any rate, on this account Tamar was at least no more a Gentile than Sarah, Rebekah, Leah, and Rachel were. Of course, it would have been possible for another Jewish exegete, such

---

relatives (Gen 25:20; 28:5; 31:20, 24), became offensive to later Jews, for whom "Arameans" were Gentiles. LXX Deut 26:5 reads the text not as "An Aramean was my father," but as "My father left Syria"; cf. D. I. Brewer, *Techniques and Assumptions in Jewish Exegesis before 70 CE* (TSAJ 30; Tübingen: Mohr [Siebeck], 1992) 178.

34. Jub 41, following Gen 38:11, brings Tamar's father into the story (Jub 41:6, 13, 17), ignoring the problem that the story apparently takes place in Canaan. The Testament of Judah avoids this difficulty by omitting Tamar's father from the story.

35. Jub 41:7 implies that Shelah, the surviving son of Judah's Canaanite wife, had no descendants (cf. TJud 11:5), despite Num 26:20; 1 Chron 4:21. A parallel to Jubilees' concern for pure racial ancestry for the tribes of Judah and Levi is the way Demetrius the Chronographer, frg. 3 (*apud* Eusebius, *Praep. Evang.* 9.29.1-3), gives Moses' wife Zipporah a genealogy that traces her descent from Abraham and Keturah (by identifying Raguel [Reuel], supposed to be Jethro's father, Zipporah's grandfather [cf. Num 10:29], with the Raguel of Gen 25:3 LXX). On this text see P. W. van der Horst, "The Interpretation of the Bible by the Minor Hellenistic Jewish Authors," in J. Mulder, ed., *Mikra: Text, Translation, Reading and Interpretation of the Hebrew Bible in Ancient Judaism and Early Christianity* (CRINT 2/1; Assen/Maastricht: Van Gorcum; Philadelphia: Fortress, 1988) 531.

as the author of the Matthean genealogy, to draw the conclusion that, on this account of her ancestry, Tamar was actually a Gentile. But in that case the same argument would apply to Sarah, Rebekah, and Leah, who are not included in the genealogy. Therefore, if the Matthean genealogy presupposes this account of Tamar's ancestry, and since it does not include Sarah, Rebekah, or Leah, the reason for Tamar's appearance in the genealogy cannot be that she was regarded as a Gentile.

However, this view of Tamar's ancestry was not the only Jewish view. A view that must be considered because it has been thought relevant to the Matthean genealogy is that found in Targum Pseudo-Jonathan (Gen 38:6)[36] and later rabbinic tradition (*Gen. Rab.* 85:10; *Num. Rab.* 13:4), according to which Tamar was the daughter of Shem, whom the rabbis identified with Melchizedek (*Lev. Rab.* 25:6; *Num. Rab.* 4:8). This view does not, as Marshall Johnson oddly alleges, make "more specific" the view of Jubilees that she was a "daughter of Aram."[37] Nor can it be, as Johnson also supposes, "a way of alluding to the non-Abrahamite, hence Gentile, descent of Tamar, since Shem was but a distant ancestor of Abraham."[38] There were surely much more obvious ways of giving Tamar a Gentile origin! Whatever the precise meaning of the late and obscure passage *Ruth Rabbah* 8:1,[39] the idea that Tamar was the daughter of Shem must have originated as an attempt to give her a highly distinguished ancestry and to ensure the genealogical purity of the tribe of Judah. Since Genesis 38 gives no indication that Tamar came from outside Canaan, and implies that her "father's house" (38:11) was in Canaan, this tradition makes her the daughter of the only worshiper of the true God, apart from the family of Abraham, who could then have been found in Canaan: Shem-Melchizedek. Moreover, since Shem-Melchizedek was a priest, this could explain why the punishment of Tamar that Judah demands in Genesis 38:24 was the punishment for a priest's daughter guilty of prostitution (Lev 21:9) (so Tg. Ps.-Jon. Gen 38:24; *Gen. Rab.* 85:10). Whether this account of Tamar's ancestry was already current in the

---

36. It is extraordinary that neither Johnson's discussion of the righteousness of Tamar in Jewish tradition (*Genealogies*, 159-62) nor his appendix on the ancestry of Tamar (270-72) makes any reference to the Targums.

37. Johnson, *Genealogies*, 159; he considers this Aram the son of Shem (270).

38. Johnson, *Genealogies*, 271.

39. Against Johnson, *Genealogies*, 271-72, this passage is certainly not genuinely polemical. Johnson's whole construction of a situation of polemic about the ancestry of the Messiah is based on a failure to recognize that rabbinic literature frequently raises and answers problems (such as, in *Ruth Rab.* 2:1, David's descent from a Moabitess) not in order to answer opponents, but simply because the text of Scripture raised such problems. What Johnson takes to be polemic is often exegetical technique.

New Testament period it is impossible to tell;[40] but even if it was, it offers no plausible reason for Tamar's inclusion in the Matthean genealogy.

A reference to Tamar in Pseudo-Philo (*Bib. Ant.* 9:5) is unfortunately ambiguous with regard to Tamar's ancestry. Like all Jewish traditions, it justifies her action, but does so in a unique way: "being unwilling to separate from the sons of Israel she reflected and said, 'It is better for me to die for having intercourse with my father-in-law than to have intercourse with Gentiles.'" This reflects Pseudo-Philo's distaste for marriage with Gentiles (*Bib. Ant.* 18:13-14; 21:1; 30:1; 44:7; 45:3), but it need not mean that Tamar herself was not of Gentile origin. She could be a proselyte, though the fact that this goes unnoticed would be consistent with Pseudo-Philo's lack of interest in those righteous Gentiles of the Hebrew Bible/Old Testament whom Jewish tradition regarded as proselytes. Despite his strong interest in biblical women, Aseneth, Rahab (cf. 20:7), and Ruth all go unmentioned in his work. Thus it is possible that Pseudo-Philo assumes, without wishing to emphasize, a tradition that thought of Tamar as a Canaanite who became a proselyte when she married Er. That Pseudo-Philo assumes the Jubilees tradition of her descent from Nahor is less likely, because *Biblical Antiquities*, despite its wealth of nonbiblical genealogical information, shares none of the nonbiblical genealogical traditions found in Jubilees.

One rabbinic tradition attributes to two late-third-century rabbis the view that Tamar was a proselyte (*b. Soṭ.* 10), a view that it is not necessary to harmonize with the tradition that she was a daughter of Shem, as Johnson does.[41] But more relevant for study of the Matthean genealogy is Philo's view that Tamar was a proselyte. He describes her as a woman "from Palestinian Syria" (ἀπὸ τῆς Παλαιστίνης Συρίας), which is simply a contemporary way of saying that she was a Canaanite. From a polytheistic and idolatrous background, she converted to the worship and service of the one true God (*Virt.* 220-22). It is not clear why Johnson says that Philo does not portray her as "a proselyte in the full sense."[42] She seems to be precisely that.

Thus Philo provides clear evidence that a Jewish exegete of the time of Matthew could consider Tamar to be of unequivocally Gentile origin. Such a view may well explain her inclusion in the Matthean genealogy. But Jubilees 41:1 and Testament of Judah 10:1 should no longer be used to support this view.

---

40. Josephus makes no reference to Tamar. In *Antiquities* he omits the story in Gen 38, no doubt because of the dubious behavior of Tamar and Judah, rather than because of the issue of Tamar's ancestry.

41. Johnson, *Genealogies*, 272.

42. Johnson, *Genealogies*, 160.

3. The Marriage of Rahab

Several aspects of the reference to Rahab ('Ραχαβ) in the Matthean genealogy have puzzled readers and scholars. First, the spelling of the name is unusual. In the LXX the name of the harlot of Jericho, רחב, is transliterated 'Ρααβ (Josh 2:1, 3; 6:23, 25), and, apart from Matthew 1:5, this spelling is used consistently in early Christian literature.[43] However, some manuscripts of Josephus, *Ant.* 5.8-30, have the spelling 'Ραχαβη, though others have 'Ρααβ. Since Josephus's transliterations of biblical names are often independent of and differ from the LXX, the former is more likely to be original, the latter an assimilation to the LXX and Christian usage. There is nothing unusual about the transliteration of the Hebrew ה by the Greek χ, though the latter can also transliterate the Hebrew כ. So the spelling gives no serious reason for doubting that the mother of Boaz in the Matthean genealogy is intended to be the famous Rahab. Reference to an otherwise completely unknown Rahab or Rachab would be much more difficult to explain than an unusual spelling of the famous Rahab's name.[44] However, the unusual spelling seems to require an explanation, since most of the names in the genealogy occur in their LXX forms. All of the names down to Σαλμων (1:5) are the LXX forms, even though other Greek forms of several of these names are attested. Indeed, it seems clear that, down to Σαλμων, the genealogy follows the LXX of 1 Chronicles 1:34 and 2:1-11.[45] After Σαλμων, however, two consecutive names diverge from the LXX: Βοεσ is an otherwise unattested Greek form of בעז (LXX Βοος or Βοοζ) as 'Ραχαβ is of רחב. The only other significant departure from the LXX form of a name in the rest of the genealogy[46] is Ἀσαφ (Matt 1:7) for אסא

---

43. Heb 11:31; Jas 2:25; 1 *Clem* 12:1, 3; Justin, *Dial.* 111.4; Hippolytus, *In Dan.* 2.19.5; Origen, *In Jos.* 3.3-5; 7.5; *In Matt.* 16.5-12.

44. This consideration is surely decisive against J. D. Quinn, "Is 'PAXAB in Mt 1,5 Rahab of Jericho?" *Bib* 62 (1981) 225-28, who argues for reference to an otherwise unknown woman, but fails to explain why this woman should be named in the Matthean genealogy, in which the other three women of the period of the Hebrew Bible/OT are famous biblical characters. Women are not named in Jewish genealogies without specific reasons.

45. The spelling Ἑσρωμ is found in the A text of 1 Chron 2:5, 9 (also Ruth 4:18), Ἀραμ in most manuscripts of 1 Chron 2:9-10 (also some manuscripts of Ruth 4:19), and Σαλμων in most manuscripts of 1 Chron 2:11 (also the A text of Ruth 4:20-21).

46. Ἰωαθαμ (Matt 1:9) differs from the form in LXX 1 Chron 3:12 (Ἰωαθαν), but is the form generally used elsewhere in the LXX for this king of Judah. Ἀμως (Matt 1:10) for אמון is found in some manuscripts of LXX 1 Chron 3:14, and is the usual form of the name of this king elsewhere in the LXX in most manuscripts (cf. Josephus: Ἀμωσος). R. E. Brown, "*Rachab* in Mt 1,5 Probably Is Rahab of Jericho," *Bib* 63 (1982) 79, incorrectly treats this form as peculiar to Matthew.

(LXX Ἀσα; Josephus: Ἀσανος).[47] The striking occurrence together of the two otherwise unattested forms Βοες and Ῥαχαβ strongly suggests that at this point the genealogy has recourse to a tradition independent of the LXX, unlike the rest of the genealogy.[48]

A second feature of the reference to Rahab in Matthew 1:5 to which scholars have drawn attention is its alleged chronological incongruity: the idea that Rahab was the mother of Boaz is "curious since the famous Rahab . . . lived at the time of the conquest, nearly two centuries before Boaz' time."[49] But this is a misunderstanding. Like many genealogies in the Hebrew Bible/Old Testament, the genealogy of David's descent from Judah (Ruth 4:18-22; 1 Chron 2:1-15) has too few generations to fill the period it covers. If one reckons backward from David, as Raymond Brown has done, then Boaz's father Salma (Matt 1:4-5: Σαλμων) would have lived much later than Rahab.[50] But it would be more natural for a Jewish exegete to place Salma in the biblical history by reference to his father, Nahshon (Matt 1:4, Ναασσων), who is singled out in the genealogy in 1 Chronicles 2:10 as "the prince of the sons of Judah," referring to his position as tribal leader in the wilderness (Num 1:7; 2:3; 7:12-17; 10:14). He was also the brother of Aaron's wife Elisheba (Exod 6:23). It was therefore well known that he belonged to the generation of the exodus that died in the wilderness. His son Salma would then belong to the generation that entered Canaan with Joshua and would be a contemporary of Rahab.

The final problem about the reference to Rahab in the Matthean genealogy is the most obvious one: neither the Hebrew Bible/Old Testament nor any extant Jewish text from any period knows of Rahab's marriage to Salma or parentage of Boaz. This need not mean that Matthew was original in making Rahab an ancestor of David. For the inclusion of Rahab in the genealogy of the

---

47. Johnson, *Genealogies*, 182, strangely misstates the evidence here. The use of Ἀσαφ (Matt 1:7) for אסא may be no more than an assimilation to the more familiar name אָסָף, as in the case of Ἀμως (Matt 1:10) for אמון (see previous note), but it is possible that it represents a midrashic identification of King Asa with the author of Psalms 50 and 73–83. This should not be called a "confusion" of two biblical characters (Davies and Allison, *Matthew*, 1:175); it is an example of a frequent practice in Jewish exegesis of identifying two biblical persons with similar names. (I note other examples below.)

48. Quinn, "'PAXAB,'" 226-27.

49. Brown, *Birth*, 60, followed by Davies and Allison, *Matthew*, 1:173 ("OT chronology separates Rahab and Salmon by almost two hundred years"); Schaberg, *Illegitimacy*, 25 (unacknowledged quotation from Brown). Brown, *"Rachab,"* 79-80, takes the correct view without acknowledging his previous mistake.

50. Josephus, *Ant.* 5.318-23, places Boaz in the time of Eli, at the end of the period of the judges, no doubt by reckoning the generations backward from David. But Ruth 1:1 would permit a much earlier date in the period of the judges.

Messiah to have carried any weight as making a theological point (such as the Messiah's relevance to Gentiles), her marriage to Salma must have been an already accepted exegetical tradition. But extant Jewish literature such as Jubilees and the *Biblical Antiquities* of Pseudo-Philo shows that postbiblical Jewish writers were much interested in filling gaps in the genealogical information of the Bible, while the tantalizingly fragmentary Qumran text 4Q544, which evidently concerned the genealogies of members of the tribes of Judah and Levi in the exodus period and after, shows that there were certainly genealogical speculations that have now been lost. One is therefore justified in asking whether the general principles that Jewish genealogical speculation used to extend the genealogical information in the scriptural text can suggest, by analogy, what the exegetical basis may have been for the notion that Rahab married Salma.

One specific form that the common midrashic desire to make connections between biblical characters took was that of finding husbands for female figures to whose husbands the Bible does not refer. Women as significant as Jacob's daughter Dinah or Moses' sister Miriam must, it was no doubt reasoned, have married illustrious men who themselves appear in the biblical history. So, according to a widespread tradition, Dinah became the wife of Job (*Bib. Ant.* 8:7-8; Tg. Job 2:9; *y. B. Bat.* 15b; *Gen. Rab.* 57:4).[51] This choice was no doubt obvious, because Scripture provided few famous God-fearing men of the patriarchal period, outside Dinah's own family, whom she could suitably marry. Job could be dated to the lifetime of Dinah especially if he were identified, as he often was, with Jobab, Esau's great-grandson (Gen 36:33; 1 Chron 1:44; cf. LXX Job 42:17c-d; TJob 1:1; Aristeas the Exegete, *apud* Eusebius, *Praep. Evang.* 9.25.1-3).[52] Miriam, according to Josephus, *Ant.* 3.54, and perhaps 4Q544, married Hur, Moses' trusted assistant, who seems to rank with Aaron and Joshua in importance (Exod 17:10, 12; 24:14). Since Hur was a prominent member of the tribe of Judah (Exod 31:2; 1 Chron 2:19-20, 50; 4:1, 4), this marriage would also have been thought appropriate as creating marital ties between the leaders of the two tribes of Levi and Judah, as Aaron's marriage to Nahshon's sister also did. Later rabbinic tradition achieved the same end in a different way by identifying Miriam with Caleb's wife Ephrath (Tg. 1 Chron 2:19; 4:4; *Exod. Rab.* 1:17; 48:4).

---

51. In TJob 1:6 she is Job's second wife.

52. The marriage of Dinah to Job also satisfied another strong midrashic desire: to know the names of characters, such as Job's wife, who are anonymous in Scripture. Compare the identification of Micah's mother (anonymous in Judg 17:2-4) with Delilah in *Bib. Ant.* 44:2. On the principle of "retreat from anonymity," see E. Segal, "Sarah and Iscah: Method and Message in Midrashic Tradition," *JQR* 82 (1992) 419; and cf. R. A. Freund, "Naming Names: Some Observations on 'Nameless Women' Traditions in the MT, LXX and Hellenistic Literature," *SJOT* 6 (1992) 213-32.

Rahab was similarly in need of a husband. In Jewish tradition she was highly esteemed as a proselyte (*Num. Rab.* 8:9) who put her faith in the God of Israel into courageous action on behalf of his people (Heb 11:31; Jas 2:25; *1 Clem.* 12:1-8; Josephus, *Ant.* 5.11-14). The biblical narrative implies that she was not married when Jericho was captured (Josh 6:23),[53] but could also be interpreted to mean that she had descendants in Israel (Josh 6:25). So she must have married a suitably illustrious Israelite. Rabbinic tradition therefore held that she married Joshua (*b. Meg.* 14b-15a). That she married Salma would be an alternative solution to the same problem, not quite so obvious, but not too surprising. As the son of Nahshon, he would have been supposed to be a prominent member of the tribe of Judah. The tradition that he married Rahab was possibly linked to a tradition that he was one of the spies in Jericho.

It is worth asking, however, whether there may be a more specific exegetical reason for believing that Rahab married Salma. Johnson claimed that a rabbinic tradition of exegesis of 1 Chronicles 4:21 (preserved in *Ruth Rab.* 2:1 and *Sifre Num.* 78)[54] provides evidence of a view that Rahab married into the tribe of Judah. However, this is dubious. *Ruth Rabbah* 2:1 contains the first of a series of alternative interpretations of 1 Chronicles 4:21-23. It interprets the whole passage as referring to Rahab, the spies, and Rahab's descendants. Alternative interpretations refer either the whole passage to David and his family (2:2), or 4:22-23 to Moses and the righteous (2:3), or 4:22 to Elimelech and his family (2:4). *Sifre on Numbers* 78 combines the interpretation of 1 Chronicles 4:21 as referring to Rahab (as in *Ruth Rab.* 2:1) with the interpretation of 1 Chronicles 4:22 as referring to Elimelech and his family (as in *Ruth Rab.* 2:4). Although 1 Chronicles 4:21-23 belongs to the genealogies of the tribe of Judah, it is unlikely that these highly imaginative rabbinic exegeses were interested in placing Rahab within that tribe. After all, the interpretation of 4:22 as referring to Moses (*Ruth Rab.* 2:3) is certainly not intended to make Moses a member of the tribe of Judah. In the interpretation of the whole of 1 Chronicles 4:21-23 as referring to Rahab and her descendants (*Ruth Rab.* 2:1) it would have been easy to reach the conclusion that, according to verse 23, she was the ancestor of David, but this was not done. Instead, the tradition about her descendants (both here and in *Sifre Num.* 78) is that she was the ancestor of several priests who were also prophets.[55]

---

53. Freed, "Women," 12, thinks Josephus, *Ant.* 5.8-15 implies she was married and had children. But if so, this implication has no relation to Matt 1:5, as Freed alleges, since she could have had no children by Salma before the capture of Jericho.

54. Y. Zarowitch, "Rahab als Mutter des Boas in der Jesus-Genealogie (Matth. I 5)," *NovT* 17 (1975) 3-4, refers to the same two passages.

55. This is related to an interpretation of Josh 2:8-13 as indicating that Rahab herself prophesied; see Josephus, *Ant.* 5.12; *1 Clem* 12:5-8.

This tradition is elsewhere connected with the tradition that some of her daughters married into the priesthood (*Num. Rab.* 8:9) and that her husband was Joshua (*b. Meg.* 14b-15a). The connection is probably original, because the fact that Scripture records no sons of Joshua (cf. 1 Chron 7:27) explains why Rahab's descendants are traced through her daughters (cf. *b. Meg.* 14b). Therefore *Ruth Rabbah* 2:1 and *Sifre on Numbers* 78 are probably not evidence of a tradition that Rahab married into the tribe of Judah, but presuppose the tradition that she married Joshua.[56]

The exegetical basis for Rahab's marriage to Salma should be sought rather in 1 Chronicles 2:54-55, which refers both to Salma (שלמא, as in 2:11, 51) and to Rechab (רכב, which could be transliterated Ῥαχαβ, as in Matt 1:5). The modern reader of the genealogies of 1 Chronicles 2 distinguishes two persons called Salma (see table 2, p. 39), of whom one (2:11) was the ancestor of David, appears elsewhere in the Hebrew Bible/Old Testament only in the parallel genealogy appended to the book of Ruth (Ruth 4:20-21), and is the Σαλμων of Matthew 1:5. But it is worth noting that the other Salma (1 Chron 2:51, 54) is closely connected with Bethlehem. His grandmother Ephrath gave her name to the clan that lived around Bethlehem and came to be regarded as synonymous with Bethlehem (Gen 35:19; 48:7; Ruth 1:2; 4:11; 1 Sam 17:12; Mic 5:2 [MT 1]; LXX Josh 15:59a). His father Hur is called the father of Bethlehem in 1 Chronicles 4:4, and he himself was the father of Bethlehem according to 1 Chronicles 2:51, 54. Since Boaz and his kinsfolk and descendants were Ephrathites from Bethlehem (Ruth 1:2; 4.11; 1 Sam 17:12), it is probable that originally their descent was traced from this Salma, the father of Bethlehem

---

56. Since I first published this essay, Larry Lyke has related *Ruth Rab.* 2:1 to the Matthean genealogy in a different way from Johnson (he does not mention Johnson's treatment of the passage or mine): L. L. Lyke, "What Does Ruth Have to Do with Rahab? Midrash *Ruth Rabbah* and the Matthean Genealogy of Jesus," in C. A. Evans and J. A. Sanders, eds., *The Function of Scripture in Early Jewish and Christian Tradition* (JSNTSup 154; SSEJC 6; Sheffield: Sheffield Academic Press, 1998) 262-84. He sees it as evidence that the rabbis associated the stories of Ruth, Rahab, and Tamar. But the parallels he finds between the stories are not in the text of Ruth Rabbah at all, nor are they needed to explain it. As noted above in my text, *Ruth Rab.* 2:1-4 contains a series of three different interpretations of 1 Chron 4:21-22. Two of these (2:2 relating the text to David, 2:4 relating it to Elimelech) read 1 Chron 4:22 ("who had married into Moab") as referring to Moab and therefore make a connection with Ruth. The other two interpretations reconstruct the text of 1 Chron 4:22 in order to read the phrase as: "his/her deeds went up to the father" (as Lyke recognizes: p. 273). Thus the first interpretation, which relates the passage to Rahab, allows no connection with Moab or Ruth. It is clear that the set of four interpretations of 1 Chron 4:21-22 have been incorporated into Ruth Rabbah as a set, even though only two of them have a connection with Ruth. Cf. J. Neusner, *Ruth Rabbah: An Analytical Translation* (BJS 183; Atlanta: Scholars Press, 1989) 55-56.

Table 2: Salma in 1 Chronicles 2

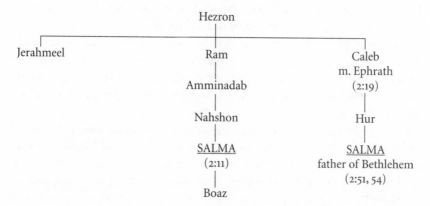

and grandson of Ephrath.[57] David's ancestor Salma would have been later made the son of Nahshon, because it was thought that David must be a descendant of the prince of Judah (1 Chron 2:10).

Jewish exegetes of the New Testament period would not have indulged in such historical-critical reconstruction, but it is likely they would have identified the Salma of 2:11 with the Salma of 2:51, 54.[58] In fact, this identification is made in the Targum to Ruth 4:20 (cf. also Tg. 1 Chron 2:54). It was virtually a principle of Jewish exegesis that persons bearing the same names should be identified if at all possible. It was not necessarily an impediment if such persons had fathers of different names.[59] But it need not have been apparent that the Salma of 2:51 was the son of Hur, since this is clear only if the MT of 2:50 is amended from בן הור (designating Caleb the son of Hur) to בני הור, in accordance with the LXX (υἱοὶ Ὤρ), so that the names that follow are designated the sons of Hur. A Jewish exegete reading 2:50-51 as in the MT could have found no indication of Salma's parentage and therefore would the more easily have identified

---

57. L. M. Luker, "Ephrathah (Person)," and "Ephrathah (Place)," *ABD* 2:557-58, emends 1 Chron 2:24 to mean that Ephrath was Hezron's wife before she was Caleb's, and so the ancestor of David. But the emendation is questionable, and in any case 1 Chron 2 does not say that Ram (David's ancestor) was the son of Hezron by Ephrath (Hezron had other wives). A rabbinic tradition (*Exod. Rab.* 1:17; 48:4), which identified Ephrath with Miriam, held that David was descended from Ephrath-Miriam (hence 1 Sam 17:12) through Hur, Uri, and Bezalel (1 Chron 2:20), but it is not clear how this genealogy of David was reconciled with that of 1 Chron 2:9-15.

58. LXX transliterates שלמא as Σαλμων in 2:11, but as Σαλωμων (usually used for שלמה, as in 1 Chron 3:5, 10) in 2:51, 54. This certainly distinguishes the two persons, but perhaps in the interests of identifying the latter with King Solomon.

59. E.g., *Num. Rab.* 10.5 identifies Joel the son of Samuel (1 Sam 8:2) with Joel the prophet, the son of Pethuel (Joel 1:1), and concludes that Pethuel is another name for Samuel.

him with the Salma of 2:11. Moreover, that the Salma of 2:54 is the ancestor of David would be confirmed by the fact that, after the obscure notes of Salma's descendants (2:54-55), the genealogy of David continues (3:1-24).

An identification of the רכב of 1 Chronicles 2:55 with Rahab (רחב) would be an example of the midrashic principle of identifying not only biblical figures with the same name, but also those with similar names. For example, Job was identified with Jobab, as already noted; Micah the prophet was identified with Micaiah the son of Imlah (LivPro 6:2); Amos the prophet was identified with Amoz the father of Isaiah (Isa 1:1; cf. AscIsa 1:2; 4:22); Eldad (Num 11:27-28) was identified with Elidad (Num 34:21; cf. *Num. Rab.* 15:19); and Hirah (Gen 38:1) was identified with Hiram of Tyre (1 Kgs 5:15; cf. *Gen. Rab.* 85:4). In the Targum to 1 Chronicles 2:55, רכב is identified with Rehabiah (רחביה) the grandson of Moses (1 Chron 23:17; 24:21; 26:25). So an exegete in search of a reference to Rahab that would establish her genealogical connection with Israel could easily have found her in the רכב of 1 Chronicles 2:55.

How could the text be taken to mean that she married Salma? There are two possible explanations. The last sentence of 1 Chronicles 2:55 is usually translated: "These are the Kenites who came from Hammath (חמת), the father of the house of Rechab." But the understanding of חמת as a place-name is problematic, and Talmon proposes that it refers to relationship by marriage, "family-in-law" (cf. חם, "father-in-law," in Gen 38:13, 25; 1 Sam 4:19, 21; חמה, "mother-in-law," in Mic 7:6), and that the sentence should therefore be translated: "These are the Kenites who came from the family-in-law of the father of the house of Rechab."[60] If our Jewish exegete understood חמת in this sense,[61] he could have read the sentence in connection with the references to Rahab's "father's house" in Joshua 2:12, 18; 6:25, and have taken it to mean that the Kenites, Salma's descendants, derived from the family-in-law of Rahab's father. They were his family-in-law because his daughter Rahab married Salma.

Another possibility is suggested by the LXX rendering of the verse. In the A text of the LXX, חמת is taken to refer to the place Hamath and translated ἐξ

---

60. S. Talmon, "המה הקינים הבאים מחמה אבי בית־רכב: 1 Chron. ii, 55," *IEJ* 10 (1960) 174-80. This interpretation is adopted in REB: "These are the Kenites who were connected by marriage with the ancestor of the Rechabites." Against Talmon's proposal, see C. H. Knights, "Kenites = Rechabites? 1 Chronicles ii 55 reconsidered," *VT* 43 (1993) 13-17. For our purposes the original meaning of the text is less important than the possibility that a Jewish exegete in the NT period could have read the text in the way Talmon does.

61. Evidence for this understanding of חמת in a later period may be found in the rabbinic exegetical tradition that read 1 Chron 2:55 in connection with Judg 1:16 (*b. Soṭ.* 11a; Mekilta de R. Ishmael to Exod 18:27; cf. Tg. Judg 1:16); cf. C. H. Knights, "Jethro Merited that his Descendants Should Sit in the Chamber of Hewn Stone," *JJS* 41 (1990) 247-49.

A½maj.[62] But most manuscripts have ἐξ Μεσημα. Here the initial מ of מחמת has been taken as the first syllable of a proper name, instead of (or rather, as well as) the prepositional prefix (= ἐκ).[63] This means that ἐξ Μεσημα cannot be a corruption of ἐξ ημαθ that occurred within the LXX manuscript tradition, as Shemaryahu Talmon argues.[64] In that case the Hebrew מ could not have been transliterated as με. We must suppose a variant Hebrew *Vorlage,* which had, instead of מחמת, probably משמע. This is the most likely *Vorlage,* because שמע, an attested Hebrew name (1 Chron 2:43-44; 5:8; 8:13), could have been regarded as the name from which שמעתים (1 Chron 2:55) comes. In this form the obscure note at the end of 1 Chronicles 2:55 would have explained that the Tirathites, the Shimeathites (שמעתים), and the Sucathites are "the Kenites who come from Shema (שמע), the father of the house of Rechab."

If our Jewish exegete read such a Hebrew text of 1 Chronicles 2:55, he had only to equate שמע with שלמא to find the statement: "These are the Kenites who came from *Salma* the father of the house of *Rahab.*" As the father of Rahab's house, Salma was her husband.

These two possible explanations of the way 1 Chronicles 2:54-55 could have yielded the information that Rahab married Salma may seem tortuous to modern readers unfamiliar with ancient Jewish exegesis, but they are well within the range of exegetical possibilities for that period. If exegesis of 1 Chronicles 2:54-55 was indeed the source of the idea, then we can see that Matthew, by retaining the unusual spelling Ῥαχαβ and not substituting the LXX form Ῥααβ, has indicated the exegetical basis for his genealogical information.

4. The Canaanite Women

In §2 we found evidence, in Jubilees and probably in Pseudo-Philo, of concern for the racial purity of the two key Israelite tribes (as they were for first-century Jews), Judah and Levi. This is an approach, doubtless not universal in Second Temple Judaism, that would not be mollified by considering such foremothers as Tamar to be proselytes, Gentiles become Jews. The Matthean genealogy stands in stark contrast to such a concern, including as it does undoubted Gentiles: Ruth and Rahab. This makes it more likely that for Matthew Tamar also belonged in the category of Gentile foremothers of the Messiah. We have also, in §3, discovered that an exegetical basis for Salma's marriage to Rahab can

---

62. Αἱμαθ or Ἐμμαθ transliterates חמת as a place-name elsewhere in LXX.
63. Talmon, "1 Chron. ii,55," 174, followed by Knights, "Kenites," 11.
64. Talmon, "1 Chron. ii,55," 175n.5.

be found, though it depends on exegetical ingenuity. Such ingenuity, though typical of Jewish exegesis, often resulted in interpretations that could be debated and would not find universal acceptance. It is therefore striking that Matthew evidently attached so much importance to including Rahab in his genealogy that he resorted to this kind of exegesis (whether his own or, more probably, a traditional Jewish exegesis he knew). Again, Rahab's importance for Matthew seems most explicable on the basis of the fact that, along with Ruth, she was one of the two best-known examples in the Hebrew Bible/Old Testament of Gentiles who professed faith in the God of Israel and became members of God's covenant people. She is a prime instance of the openness of God's people to the inclusion of Gentiles, an openness that the Messiah will confirm and extend.

The precise ethnic origins of the four women are of interest: Tamar and Rahab were Canaanites, Ruth a Moabite, and Bathsheba the wife of Uriah the Hittite. Not only Canaanites but also Hittites were among the seven peoples of the land of Canaan whom God had promised to drive out and Israel had been commanded to annihilate (Exod 23:23, 28; 33:2; 34:11; Deut 7:1; 20:17; Josh 3:10; 1 Kgs 9:20-21; Ezra 9:1). Israel should not have intermarried with them (Deut 7:3-4; Judg 3:5-6; Ezra 9:1). They were the most abhorrent of idolatrous Gentiles, polluting the holy land with their idolatry and evil. Moabites were not in the same category, but they and their descendants to the tenth generation were debarred from "the assembly of YHWH" (Deut 23:4). The contradiction given to ideas of Jewish exclusivism by the presence of these women in the Messiah's genealogy is therefore particularly sharp and unambiguous.

Tamar and Rahab are not the only Canaanite women in Matthew's Gospel.[65] The woman Mark calls, in contemporary idiom, a "Syro-Phoenician" (Mark 7:26),[66] Matthew calls by the biblical term "Canaanite" (Matt 15:22).[67] As

---

65. Bredin, "Gentiles," also connects Tamar and Rahab with the Canaanite woman, though differently, as part of a thesis about debate within the Matthean community reflected in the Gospel.

66. G. Theissen, *The Gospels in Context: Social and Political History in the Synoptic Tradition* (Minneapolis: Fortress, 1991) 245-47, argues against M. Hengel that the term "Syro-Phoenician" does not require a western (Roman) perspective but could have been used in Syria or Palestine.

67. It is not certain whether the word "Canaanite" was in use, with reference to non-Jewish inhabitants of Palestine with "Canaanite" ancestry, other than as a Jewish usage with intentional biblical allusion. But see J. E. Taylor, *Christians and the Holy Places* (Oxford: Clarendon, 1993) 71, for an inscription from the pre-Roman period: "Abdeshmun, son of Modir, Canaanite." Cf. also the reference to Canaanites in SibOr 13:56 (c. 265 CE). In Jewish usage, "Amorites" was sometimes preferred, as in Pseudo-Philo's *Biblical Antiquities,* and the later rabbinic discussion of "the ways of the Amorite" (on which see S. Stern, *Jewish Identity in*

has often been said, this is one of the most remarkable stories in the Gospels, the only one in which someone in conversation with Jesus leads him to change his mind. The woman is one of the few women in his Gospel to whom Matthew gives sustained attention, writing the story from her perspective. His account is a little longer than Mark's and significantly different, drawing (in my view) little, if at all, on Mark, mainly on a parallel tradition known to Matthew. The woman's resemblance to the women in the genealogy does not stop with the designation "Canaanite." Like Tamar, Rahab, and Ruth, she acts with initiative and resolution and, in difficult circumstances, attains her end. I cannot here deal in full detail with Matthew 15:21-28, but I shall sketch the way that making the connection with the genealogy and especially with Rahab illuminates the significance of the story.

Gerd Theissen has shown in some detail how the story reflects the local tensions between Jews and Gentiles in the borderlands between Galilee and Phoenicia, an area into which both wished to expand.[68] I may add that similar tensions were common wherever the indigenous Gentiles of Palestine lived, and that the rising tide of Jewish religious nationalism in the first century led to the attacks on the non-Jewish cities at the time of the Jewish revolt.[69] Jewish nationalism was not only directed at the Roman occupying power but also at the presence of pagans in the land of Israel, which they polluted with their idolatry and immoral lifestyle. The Messiah, son of David, was expected not only to overthrow the Roman imperial power but also to repossess the land for Israel and to cleanse it by slaughtering or driving out the idolatrous pagans. Pseudo-Philo's *Biblical Antiquities,* with its extensive focus on the period from Joshua to Saul, shows how relevant the narratives of Joshua and Judges could appear to some first-century Palestinian Jews, awaiting the leadership of a new Joshua or a new Kenaz. It follows that when Matthew calls the woman a Canaanite, this is biblicizing but certainly not archaizing. It is highly contemporary. It views her through the biblical frame that many contemporary Jews would have brought to such an encounter as hers with Jesus. It is also noteworthy that Matthew refers to "the district of Tyre and Sidon" (Matt 15:21), where Mark had spoken only of Tyre (Mark 7:24). This too is the style of the Hebrew Bible/Old Testament (as well as contemporary style). We are reminded of the reference to the

Early Rabbinic Writings [AGAJU 23; Leiden: Brill, 1994] 181-85), probably on the basis of Gen 15:16, where "Amorites" appears as a general term for the ten peoples of the land (including Amorites) listed in 15:18-21.

68. Theissen, *Gospels,* 61-80.

69. See A. Kasher, *Jews and Hellenistic Cities in Eretz-Israel* (TSAJ 21; Tübingen: Mohr [Siebeck], 1990).

Sidonians among the indigenous people who had not been driven out of the land by the time of Joshua's death (Josh 13:6).

The connection with messianic nationalism is also made by the title "son of David," with which the woman herself — remarkably, since this title should make Jesus her enemy — uses to address Jesus (15:22). But this title, of course, also evokes the genealogy that, at the opening of the Gospel, both established Jesus' right to the title and also gave a preliminary indication of what it would mean for Jesus to be the Messiah, the son of David. The presence of the Gentile women, I have argued, indicates the inclusiveness of the Messiah's role: to be a blessing to the nations as well as to save his own people from their sins. Yet when Jesus encounters one such Gentile woman, he enunciates his mission in terms restricted to Israel: "I was sent only to the lost sheep of the house of Israel" (15:24). The sentence echoes Ezekiel 34 (cf. 34:16, 30), a Davidic messianic prophecy (see 34:23-24) that is not anti-Gentile but has nothing to say about Gentiles at all. Matthew's narrative thus situates itself in intertextual relationships with Deuteronomy–Judges, with Ezekiel 34, and with Matthew's own genealogy of Jesus. Is the Davidic Messiah's role to be that of a new Joshua who, this time, will lead an obedient Israel in driving out the Canaanites who survived the original conquest, repossessing and cleansing the land? Or is his role confined to that of the shepherd of God's scattered and injured sheep, healing and gathering them, saved at last from oppressive leaders and threatening nations alike, as in Ezekiel 34? Or do the Canaanite women in his ancestry require a more positive relationship to the Gentiles? All this is at stake in Jesus' encounter with the Canaanite woman, who could have stepped out of the genealogy in order to press her claims on her descendant.[70]

It is especially instructive to see her as a new Rahab encountering a Messiah who could be a new Joshua. Her address to Jesus, "son of David," is equivalent to Rahab's confession of the true God that is inseparable from her recognition that this God has given the land to his people Israel (Josh 2:9-11). Like Rahab she takes the initiative and asks boldly for the kindness she so desperately needs (Josh 2:12-13). Like Rahab she receives the mercy for which she had asked (Josh 6:22-25). Finally, and very importantly, like Rahab, because of her faith she is a first exception to a rule about Canaanites. In the book of Joshua, Rahab, spared with her family in the first Israelite military operation against the inhabitants of the land, is a remarkable exception to the commandment Israel is engaged in obeying: that Israel should destroy the inhabitants of the land and make no covenant with them (Deut 7:2; 20:15-18). Rahab survives, her descen-

---

70. Cf. Keener, *Matthew*, 415: readers of Matthew "know that Jesus cannot ultimately reject this woman for her ethnicity without repudiating two of his ancestors in the genealogy."

dants dwell in Israel (Josh 6:25), not because Israel has been disobedient to God, but because Israel has made a covenant and has exercised mercy in a way apparently approved by God. Right at the beginning of the conquest Rahab, as it were, provides a vision of a different way that is only occasionally (cf. Josh 9) followed thereafter but remains as a precedent for a new, messianic Joshua to follow.[71]

What the Canaanite woman does, with the clever twist she gives to Jesus' own saying (Matt 15:27), is persuade Jesus that he can act compassionately to her without detracting from his mission to Israel. Like Rahab, with her exceptional faith she secures an exception that can set a precedent. Unlike Rahab's, it is a precedent that will be followed. Although Matthew, like the other evangelists, does not represent Jesus as engaged in the Gentile mission proper until after the resurrection, it is likely that in the scene of mass healing that follows the story of the Canaanite woman (15:29-31) Matthew portrays the crowds as Gentiles, since the concluding words are: "they praised the God of Israel" (15:31). The feeding of the four thousand (15:32-39) then becomes a Gentile equivalent to the feeding of the five thousand.[72] (Is it possible that, just as the number twelve in the latter story [14:20] relates to Israel, so the number seven in the former [15:36-37] relates to the seven indigenous peoples of Canaan? Alternatively, seven as the number of completeness could be read as symbolizing the Gentile nations in general.) By placing Jesus briefly in salvific relationship to many Gentiles, Matthew seems to be indicating that the Canaanite woman's precedent is not to be an isolated exception but the beginning of the messianic blessing of the nations.

It looks as though in Matthew's two stories of Gentile individuals whose faith Jesus commends and for whom he performs healings, Matthew sees represented the two hardest cases for Jewish-Gentile relationships: the centurion (7:5-13) represents the oppressive occupying power (in the form of Rome's client Herod Antipas), and the woman represents the indigenous pagans of Palestine.[73] For Jewish messianic nationalism, with plausible appeal to the Torah itself, neither should be in the land of Israel at all. That the new Joshua does not

---

71. See the insightful treatment of the story of Rahab in R. Polzin, *Moses and the Deuteronomist: A Literary Study of the Deuteronomic History, Part 1: Deuteronomy, Joshua, Judges* (New York: Seabury, 1980) 85-91, 113-14; also T. Frymer-Kensky, "Reading Rahab," in M. Cogan, B. L. Eichler, and J. H. Tigay, eds., *Tehillah le-Moshe* (M. Greenberg FS; Winona Lake, Ind.: Eisenbrauns, 1997) 57-67.

72. For scholars who take this view see Davies and Allison, *Matthew*, 2:563n.5; Allison and Davies themselves reject it.

73. Cf. J. LaGrand, *The Earliest Christian Mission to "All Nations" in the Light of Matthew's Gospel* (2d ed.; Grand Rapids: Eerdmans, 1999) 207-10.

drive them out, but on the contrary is persuaded to extend his compassionate activity to them, may seem contrary to scriptural precedent, but Matthew in his genealogy shows it to be consistent with the nature of the Davidic Messiah, since the Messiah is also the descendant of Abraham who will bless the nations, the Jewish Messiah for Gentiles as well as for Jews. Among the women in Matthew's genealogy are those who provide occasional biblical precedent for such an understanding of Israel's and their Messiah's vocation. All four Gentile women joined the Israelite people of God, becoming themselves foremothers of the Messiah, even though the laws of the Torah, enforced to the letter, would seem clearly to prohibit this. But the exceptions show that the Torah is not to be read so literally. Rahab in particular constitutes an exception, spared by God's compassion active in the compassion of his people, at the very inception of Israel's obedience to the command to slaughter and to drive out the inhabitants of the land. Such a powerful precedent, attached to the Messiah's own genealogy, is powerfully repeated by a new Rahab and the new Joshua's response to her. Taken up by Jesus the Messiah, the precedent constituted by the Canaanite women will finally be followed on a universal scale (Matt 28:18-20).

CHAPTER 3

Elizabeth and Mary in Luke 1:
Reading a Gynocentric Text Intertextually

It is right that they should delight one another
as Mary did Elizabeth, her next of kin.[1]

1. Luke 1:5-80: A Gynocentric Text

It has often been observed that "the first two chapters of Luke invite the reader
into the world of women and begin the story of Jesus from their perspective."[2]
To claim that this part of Luke's narrative is characterized by a women's perspective on the events it narrates is to distinguish it from the androcentric narratives that are much more common in the Bible. The contrast in this respect
between Luke's and Matthew's infancy narratives has often been noticed, expressed merely in the observation that Mary is prominent in one, Joseph in the
other. In Matthew's narrative Mary neither speaks nor is spoken to, whereas in
Luke's she has more words than any other character. But to demonstrate the
gynocentric character of Luke's infancy narrative and to understand its significance requires more than the observation that female characters (Elizabeth and
Anna as well as Mary) are prominent in it. After all, male characters are also
prominent (Zechariah, the shepherds, Simeon, though Joseph is relatively in-

---

1. Ephrem, "Hymns on the Nativity: Hymn 2," in *Ephrem the Syrian: Hymns* (tr. K. E.
McVey; Classics of Western Spirituality; New York: Paulist, 1989) 80.
2. B. E. Reid, *Choosing the Better Part? Women in the Gospel of Luke* (Collegeville, Minn.:
Liturgical, 1996) 55.

significant in the story). Moreover, a narrative can encourage readers to view even significant female characters from a male perspective.

Narratives like Luke's have a kind of overarching narrative perspective which is that of the narrator (not necessarily the perspective of the real author), but they may also invite readers to adopt — for longer or shorter periods — the perspective of characters within the narrative.[3] Unless the narrator is him- or herself a character in the story, which is not the case in Luke's infancy narrative, the narrator's perspective is external to the story, while those of the characters are internal. To the degree to which a narrative draws its readers into it, readers are encouraged to identify with the perspective of one or more of the characters on the events in which they participate. Texts may be "gendered" as androcentric or gynocentric, either by identifying the narrator's perspective as male or female or by the extent to which the narrator renders the perspective of the characters in the story as male or female. (These two possibilities are not neatly distinguishable or mutually exclusive.) Such gendering should not be guided by an essentialist understanding of what is distinctively male or female, but by the recognition that in the society portrayed in the text men and women had different roles and experience and therefore different perspectives on their world. Of course, this does not mean that the male and female perspectives would not also have much in common; nor should it be allowed to obscure the equally important differences of perspective resulting from social status and economic resources.[4] An aristocratic woman's perspective might have more in common with her husband's than with, say, the perspective of a blind peasant woman reduced to begging on the streets. Nevertheless it is still possible to ask whether a text or part of a text is gynocentric in the sense of conveying a perspective on the events that is recognizably different from an androcentric perspective and plausibly authentic for women of the temporal and social location portrayed.

In this study I shall confine myself to the first of the two main sections of the Lukan infancy narrative: 1:5-80. It is widely recognized that 1:5-80 (chap. 1 with the omission of the preface) and 2:1-52 (the whole of chap. 2) are distinguishable sections. Luke signals this by the opening words: "In the days of King

---

3. I use the term "perspective" in the sense in which "focalization" is also used in narrative theory; see J. L. Ska, *"Our Fathers Have Told Us": Introduction to the Analysis of Hebrew Narratives* (Subsidia Biblica 13; Rome: Pontifical Biblical Institute Press, 1990) chap. 5; M. Bal, *Narratology* (2d ed.; Toronto: University of Toronto Press, 1997) 142-61.

4. R. A. Horsley, *The Liberation of Christmas* (New York: Crossroad, 1989) 85 observes rightly that in the Song of Deborah (Judg 5) there is clear awareness of the class difference between the tent-dwelling Jael and Sisera's upper-class mother: "The Song of Deborah expresses a popular tradition of Israelite peasants struggling against domination by foreign kings whose women live in finery and whose military conquests mean sexual abuse for the Israelite women."

Herod of Judea" (1:5) and "In those days a decree went out from Caesar Augustus" (2:1). The first section is preparatory to the birth of Jesus; the second narrates the birth of Jesus and the immediately subsequent events. The first, one can argue,[5] is full of messianic promise; the second begins the fulfillment of the promise (which continues through the rest of the Gospel). Moreover, the way in which a gynocentric perspective is conveyed in chapter 2 (primarily by 2:19 and 2:51b, which gather the rest of the narrative into Mary's loving remembrance) is quite different from the way, as we shall now see, it is conveyed in 1:5-80.

Table 3: Luke 1:5-80 Structured according to Perspective

Passage	Number of words	Perspective	Theme	Correspondences	Story 1 or 2†
1:5-7	62	Narrator	John's parents	A	1
1:8-20	232	Zechariah	Annunciation of John's birth	B*	1
1:21-23	52	People (and Zechariah)	Zechariah dumb	C	1
1:24-25	30	Elizabeth	Elizabeth pregnant	D	1
1:26-38	209	Mary	Annunciation of Jesus' birth (and Mary's motherhood)	E*	2
1:39-45	112	Mary and Elizabeth	Elizabeth declares Mary blessed	F	1+2
1:46-56	119	Mary	Celebration of Mary's motherhood (and Jesus' birth)	E¹**	2
1:57-61	78	Elizabeth	Elizabeth gives birth	D¹	1
1:62-66	81	People (and Zechariah)	Zechariah no longer dumb	C¹	1
1:67-79	148	Zechariah	Celebration of John's birth	B¹**	1
1:80	19	Narrator	John's youth	A¹	1

†Story 1 = John's story; Story 2 = Jesus' story

5. See M. Coleridge, *The Birth of the Lukan Narrative: Narrative as Christology in Luke 1–2* (JSNTSup 88; Sheffield: JSOT Press, 1993).

Attending to perspective in Luke 1:5-80 enables us to perceive a more careful and coherent structure than previous attempts to discern the structure of Luke 1–2 have achieved.[6] This structure is set out in table 3. Most scholars have treated the parallelism between the two stories of the birth of John and the birth of Jesus as the key to the structure of Luke 1–2. The structure proposed here incorporates this parallelism insofar as it is visible in chapter 1: the annunciation of John's birth (B*) and the annunciation of Jesus' birth (E*) correspond within the first half of the section, as do the celebration of Jesus' (coming) birth (E[1]**: the Magnificat) and the celebration of John's birth (B[1]**: the Benedictus) in the second half. But these correspondences are subordinate to the chiastic pattern of correspondences that the analysis of perspectives reveals. There are eleven sections, of which the first five (A, B, C, D, E) correspond in inverse order to the last five (E[1], D[1], C[1], B[1], A[1]), leaving a central section without correspondence (F).[7] The correspondences can be seen not only in terms of the character whose perspective is dominant in each section, but also in terms of the theme of each section.

The structure is coherent with the way the two stories — of the forerunner John and of Jesus — are related. The story of John is told completely within this passage, and it frames the part of the story of Jesus that precedes his birth. (In chap. 2 the story of Jesus then continues with his birth.) The chiastic structure — especially since, in this case, it has a unique central section — functions to focus special attention on the center of the narrative, where the story of Jesus runs from section E through the central section F to section E[1]. But section F is not only the centerpiece of the story of Jesus; it is also the section in which the two stories intersect or meet, in the persons of the two mothers, Elizabeth and Mary. This conjunction of the two stories along with the relationship between the two stories that is indicated in section F explain its centrality. Elizabeth, pregnant with the forerunner, recognizes the mother of the Messiah — "the mother of my Lord" — and declares her blessed. Prompted by the child's leaping in her womb, she anticipates that child's relationship to Mary's child: John's role as the one who prepares for and proclaims the Messiah

---

6. For various proposals as well as his own, see R. E. Brown, *The Birth of the Messiah: A Commentary on the Infancy Narratives in the Gospels of Matthew and Luke* (rev. ed.; New York: Doubleday, 1993) 248-52, 623-25.

7. A. Troost, "Elizabeth and Mary — Naomi and Ruth: Gender-Response Criticism in Luke 1–2," in A. Brenner, ed., *A Feminist Companion to the Hebrew Bible in the New Testament* (FCB 1/10; Sheffield: Sheffield Academic Press, 1996) 167, comments that Elizabeth and Mary "play a central role, expressed by the central place occupied by their meeting in Luke 1–2." But she does not explain in what way the meeting is central, or notice that it is central specifically to Luke 1, not to Luke 1–2.

before the Messiah appears. Thus John's preparatory role, emphasized in sections B and B[1], is expressed structurally in the way his story frames that of Jesus, acknowledging the latter as the story of central importance, but also in the way John's story directly engages Jesus' story in the meeting of the two mothers. There is no sense of opposition or rivalry in the presentation of the two stories, the two mothers, the two sons[8] — only glad recognition of the Messiah by his forerunner and of the Messiah's mother by his forerunner's mother.

I have spoken of the story of John and the story of Jesus, but in the central sections of the chiasm (D-D[1]) the stories are more obviously those of Elizabeth and Mary, the two mothers. It is undoubtedly *as* the mothers of their unborn sons that they are of central importance in Luke's narrative, but it is from their female perspectives that we view the central events of the narrative. Analyzing the structure again in terms of length, we find that, counting the narrator's perspective as male, the sections told from a male perspective (A-C, C[1]-A[1]) comprise 594 words, while those told from a female perspective (D-D[1]) comprise 548 words. Thus the two perspectives are given more or less equal scope, but the chiastic structure privileges the female perspective by placing it centrally. From sections E-E[1] it is clear that the central theme of the whole narrative is Mary's motherhood of the Messiah, which is appropriately seen from Mary's and Elizabeth's perspectives.

To recognize the gynocentricity of the narrative it is important to notice that in the central scene (F) two women meet and converse without the presence of any male character (other than their unborn babies). Androcentric narratives often enough portray women, viewed from an androcentric perspective, but rarely include scenes in which women are together without men. It is a measure of the dominant androcentricity of the narratives of the Hebrew Bible or the Old Testament that few examples of women-only scenes can be found. The following list is of narratives of this kind that are sufficiently full to include speech: Genesis 19:32, 34*; 30:14-15*; Exodus 2:1-10*; Judges 5:28-30; Ruth 1:6–2:2*; 2:17–3:5*; 3:16-18*; 4:14-17*; 2 Kings 5:2-3; Tobit 3:7-9. Few even of these passages are as long as Luke 1:39-45. The asterisks indicate stories that concern mothers and the birth of children, as Luke 1:39-45 does. It is significant that a majority of the examples do have such a theme.[9]

---

8. Cf. V. K. Robbins, "Socio-Rhetorical Criticism: Mary, Elizabeth and the Magnificat as a Test Case," in E. Struthers Malbon and E. V. McKnight, eds., *The New Literary Criticism and the New Testament* (JSNTSup 109; Sheffield: Sheffield Academic Press, 1994) 197-98, though I do not share his view of the rhetorical effect of this absence of rivalry.

9. On the gynocentricity of birth narratives, see Y. Amit, "'Manoah Promptly Followed His Wife' (Judges 13.11): On the Place of the Woman in Birth Narratives," in A. Brenner, ed., *A Feminist Companion to Judges* (FCB 1/4; Sheffield: Sheffield Academic Press, 1993) 146-56.

From other Jewish literature of the Second Temple period I can add only one other example of a women-only scene, but it is a significant one. The *Biblical Antiquities* of Pseudo-Philo[10] is a work that gives exceptional prominence to several female characters in the biblical narratives it retells.[11] Among these is Hannah, whose story is already told from Hannah's own, female perspective in 1 Samuel 1–2.[12] 1 Samuel 1:6-7 refers to the fact that Peninnah, mother of all Elkanah's children, used to taunt his barren wife Hannah. Pseudo-Philo (*Bib. Ant.* 50:1-2) expands this reference into two brief scenes reporting the words of Peninnah's taunts.[13] Once again, this women-only account concerns mothers and the birth of children, as Luke 1:39-45 does. However, like Genesis 30:14-15, which reports the unhappy rivalry between Jacob's two wives Rachel and Leah, Pseudo-Philo's account of Peninnah and Hannah portrays the interaction of two women as contentious and bitter. By contrast, the two mothers in Luke 1 are certainly not rivals. From this point of view, the obviously friendly and supportive relationship between them is closer to Exodus 2:1-10, where three women collaborate in securing the survival of the infant Moses, and especially to the book of Ruth, where the mutual concern and support of the two women lead to the birth of a son who belongs noncontentiously to both.[14] These passages from Exodus and Ruth are also the only women-only narratives in the Hebrew Bible that are not shorter than Luke's account of Mary's visit to Elizabeth (excluding the Magnificat). As we shall see, Hannah is an important precedent for Luke's Mary, but the relationship of Elizabeth and Mary, a supportive relationship of old woman and young, resembles rather that of the old woman Naomi and the young Ruth.[15]

10. References to Pseudo-Philo's *Biblical Antiquities* in this chapter do not imply any relationship of literary dependence between it and Luke, only that *Biblical Antiquities* is a contemporary (first-century CE) example of one way that Jews read the Hebrew Bible/OT in Luke's time. Cf. D. J. Harrington, "Birth Narratives in Pseudo-Philo's Biblical Antiquities and the Gospels," in M. P. Hogan and P. J. Kobelski, eds., *To Touch the Text* (J. A. Fitzmyer FS; New York: Crossroad, 1989) 316-24.

11. See, most recently, M. T. DesCamp, "Why Are These Women Here? An Examination of the Sociological Setting of Pseudo-Philo Through Comparative Reading," *JSP* 16 (1997) 53-80.

12. For the gynocentricity of the story of Hannah, see C. Meyers, "Hannah and Her Sacrifice: Reclaiming Female Agency," in A. Brenner, ed., *A Feminist Companion to Samuel and Kings* (FCB 1/5; Sheffield: Sheffield Academic Press, 1994) 93-104.

13. For commentary see C. A. Brown, *No Longer Be Silent: First Century Jewish Portraits of Biblical Women* (Louisville: Westminster/John Knox, 1992) 144-51.

14. Cf. Horsley, *Liberation of Christmas*, 88: "One wonders if the sketch of Mary and Elizabeth together does not even portray, in however tentative a manner, women identified as women in solidarity with other women."

15. Cf. A. Brenner, *The Israelite Woman: Social Role and Literary Type in Biblical Narrative* (Sheffield: JSOT Press, 1985) chap. 9. Brenner is not concerned with women-only narratives, but

The nature of Luke's Gospel, as a narrative about Jesus, in which there are few scenes in which Jesus himself is not present, would not lead us to expect women-only scenes in the rest of the Gospel. In fact, there is a brief scene of this kind in the parable of the lost coin (Luke 15:9).[16] More significant is the narrative of the women who observed Jesus' burial and went to the tomb on Easter morning (Luke 23:55–24:4), though it contains no dialogue (unlike Mark 16:3) and so does not strictly meet the criteria I have used in identifying women-only narratives in the Hebrew Bible/Old Testament. It is nevertheless a clearly gynocentric passage, balancing at the end of the Gospel the gynocentric passage at its beginning.

As well as women-only stories or events, we should note two other ways in which the central part of our passage is notably gynocentric. These concern, respectively, section E and section E¹, the sections in which readers share Mary's perspective. In the former section, an angel visits Mary in order to give her a message from God. Only twice in the Hebrew Bible/Old Testament does an angel thus visit a woman, individually and alone: Genesis 16:7-14 (Hagar) and Judges 13:2-5 (the mother of Samson; cf. *Bib. Ant.* 42:3-7). In both cases, as in Luke, the scene is more specifically an angelic annunciation of the birth of a child to the woman. Two examples from extracanonical Jewish literature are available.[17] One is the case of Joseph's future wife Aseneth in Joseph and Aseneth 14-17.[18] The other occurs, again significantly, in the *Biblical Antiquities* of Pseudo-Philo: in a dream an angel tells Miriam of the birth and career of her younger brother Moses (*Bib. Ant.* 9:10).[19] Although Miriam

---

with the literary type of "mothers of great men." From this point of view she compares the competitive rivalry of pairs of mothers, in the cases of Sarah and Hagar, Rachel and Leah, Hannah and Penninah, with the cooperative relationship of Naomi and Ruth, the women in Exod 2:1-10, and Mary and Elizabeth in Luke 1. For the comparison of Elizabeth and Mary with Naomi and Ruth, see also Troost, "Elizabeth and Mary," especially 191-95. I. Pardes, *Countertraditions in the Bible: A Feminist Approach* (Cambridge: Harvard University Press, 1992) chap. 6, offers a very insightful reading of the book of Ruth as a revision of the story of Rachel and Leah: in place of the rivalry between the two sisters it places the female bonding of Ruth and Naomi.

16. For another such scene in a parable, see Matt 25:7-9.

17. Of course, there are also other forms of revelation to women or cases in which an angel is not mentioned: cf. R. D. Chesnutt, "Revelatory Experiences Attributed to Biblical Women in Early Jewish Literature," in A.-J. Levine, ed., *"Women Like This": New Perspectives on Jewish Women in the Greco-Roman World* (SBLEJL 01; Atlanta: Scholars Press, 1991) 107-25, especially his discussion of Rebekah in Jubilees.

18. But see now the case for dating this work in the fourth century CE or later, made by R. Shepard Kraemer, *When Aseneth Met Joseph* (New York: Oxford University Press, 1998), with my review, in *JTS* 51 (2000) 226-28.

19. It is interesting to note that, like the women returning from the empty tomb (Luke

is not the mother but the sister, this story, like the others, concerns the birth of a notable son.

In section E¹, Mary sings the Magnificat, celebrating the great act of salvation of which God has graciously commissioned her to be the agent. Such songs of praise and thanksgiving for a saving act of God, from which not only the singer but the whole people of God benefit, are attributed to three women in the Hebrew Bible and one in the Apocrypha: Miriam (Exod 15:21), Deborah (Judg 5), Hannah (1 Sam 2:1-10), and Judith (Jdt 16:1-17). In the last three cases, as in Mary's case, the woman singing is also an agent through whom God has brought salvation. Once again, it is Pseudo-Philo who subsequently continues this literary tradition: he substitutes new and rather longer compositions of his own for the biblical songs of Deborah and Hannah (*Bib. Ant.* 32:1-17; 51:3-6).[20] In this gynocentric form, the connection with motherhood and birth is less common, found only in the case of Hannah. As we shall see, Hannah is the most important of these precedents for Mary's role in Luke 1, but we should not ignore the relevance also of the other female singers of salvation.

In conclusion to this section, it is important to notice how structure and theme conspire to make Luke 1:5-80 a gynocentric passage in which the actions of Elizabeth and Mary are the focus of attention and supply the dominant perspectives that readers are invited to share. Although readers are certainly not encouraged to forget that their stories are also the stories of John and Jesus, the forerunner and the Messiah, and that it is as the beginning of Jesus' story that Elizabeth's and Mary's stories have their place in the Gospel, it is still the case that, as the mothers of John and Jesus, they are the responsible and acting subjects of the events related in the five central sections of the chiastic structure of this passage. In the case of Elizabeth, Zechariah's role in fathering the child is no doubt assumed, but it is never mentioned: Elizabeth is the sole agent (other than God) in the narrative of John's conception and birth (1:24-25, 36, 57-60). Zechariah is involved only when the neighbors cannot accept, without knowing his mind, such a departure from normal custom as Elizabeth proposes in not giving a family name to her son (1:59-63). In Mary's case, Joseph takes no part at all in the narrative of this chapter. It is because the narrative focuses on the two women's roles as mothers that the gynocentric perspective is adopted. In noting

---

24:11), Miriam is not believed when she reports her dream to her parents. Similarly, Pseudo-Philo portrays Manoah as disbelieving his wife when she reports the revelation given her by the angel about the birth of a son to them (*Bib. Ant.* 42:5). This detail is not in the biblical account.

20. The lamentation he attributes to Seila the daughter of Jephthah (*Bib. Ant.* 40:5-7) cannot really be put in this category, even though he makes her self-sacrifice a parallel to that of Isaac. Quite different in form but to some degree parallel in function is the psalm of Aseneth in JosAsen 21:10-21.

the few precedents that can be found for such gynocentric narrative in the Hebrew Bible/Old Testament and other early Jewish literature, we have seen that the majority of such precedents also concern mothers and the birth of children.

2. Mary as Agent of God's Salvation of Israel

The events that transpire in Luke 1 are not matters of purely personal and private significance for the two women and their families. Rather they constitute a turning point in the story of God's people Israel and the fulfillment of his purposes for them.[21] They are laden with the promises and hopes of the past and pregnant with the future in which these promises and hopes will at last be fulfilled (see especially vv 16-17, 32-33, 54-55, 68-79). Since this relationship to Israel's history and God's purposes is conveyed by the chapter's peculiarly dense intertextual relationship with the Hebrew Bible/Old Testament, in order to understand the part played by the women in it we must now supplement the notion of gynocentricity with that of intertextuality.

The term "intertextuality," now widely used in biblical studies, highlights the relationships all texts have with other texts, so that no text is self-contained or autonomous. But it is also used in a wide variety of ways.[22] It is possible to emphasize the intentionality of the text, which relates itself to other texts to which it alludes and refers: intertextuality here belongs to the intrinsic character of the text that the reader must discern. It is also possible to emphasize the activity of readers in creating intertextual relationships: meaning occurs when readers relate one text to others. Intertextuality in this second sense can in principle set up relationships between any text and any other texts. Undoubtedly this happens in the way readers understand texts, but it is not useful for discussing the sense in which a text may have a special relationship to specific other texts by virtue of features of the text itself. Here it is important to remember that texts are written and read in literary traditions.

In the case of early Christian texts, the tradition within which they situate themselves is primarily the Jewish tradition with its special relationship to the Scriptures of Israel. In this tradition, not only are writers in constant dialogue with the scriptural texts, but they also understand those texts by means of those texts' own intertextual relationships to one another. In other words, Jewish and

---

21. As signaled by the two introductions (1:5a; 2:1), the horizon of chap. 1 is limited to Israel, while that of chap. 2 broadens to envisage the world (2:32).

22. On theories of intertextuality, see G. Allen, *Intertextuality* (New Critical Idiom; London/New York: Routledge, 2000).

early Christian exegetes were constantly relating one scriptural text to others, reading the scriptural texts not merely sequentially but with continual reference to other scriptural texts to which verbal and thematic resemblances took them. This relationship to a scriptural tradition gives early Christian writings a special kind of intertextuality, characterized by the theological necessity to validate and develop meaning through constant intertextual reference and by the particularly intense forms of textual relationship created by constant interaction with a specific body of authoritative texts.

Because of the need that each of the Gospels has to establish its relationship to the Hebrew Bible/Old Testament at the outset, Luke 1 has a remarkably rich and pervasive relationship with its scriptural intertexts. Allusions create not only the Lukan text's relationship with specific texts of the Hebrew Bible/Old Testament but also bring many such texts into relationship with one another in traditional or fresh ways. In a case of this kind, readers must attend as acutely as possible to the web of clearly intentional allusions written into the text, but the kind of relationship between itself and the Hebrew Bible/Old Testament that the text itself opens up for the reader also has a degree of communicative openness. In other words, in recognizing intentional allusions the competent reader, in this case the reader who can read the Scriptures of Israel in the manner characteristic of Second Temple Judaism, is also reminded of a range of comparable and connected scriptural passages. It is not necessary to determine whether these were specifically in the mind of the author when writing (an exercise that soon reveals the limitations, though not necessarily the invalidity, of the notion of authorial intention), only that they are the kind of intertextual relationships that the text would suggest to the kind of competent readers the text envisages. I call this "communicative openness" because it is the kind of openness to interpretation that the author of a text of this kind may well intend his or her work to have. For readers to make connections the author may not have made and certainly for which the author could not have provided unambiguous directions may be entirely in line with the author's intentions if it corresponds to the kind of text the author has created. Thus, while the discipline of identifying specific allusions to specific texts is absolutely indispensable in the exegesis of a passage like Luke 1, because such allusions are integral to the passage's literary strategy, it is not adequate to confine the intertextual relationships of the passage to such allusions, because the possibility of, even the invitation to explore, wider intertextual connections is also written into the text. Reaction against the excesses of reader-response criticism, in which the text itself plays a minimal role in the reader's creation of meaning, should not obscure for us the extent to which all texts intrinsically possess a degree of openness to interpretation, some kinds of texts more than other kinds. Insofar as this openness in early Christian texts such as

Luke 1 is to interpretation within the Jewish tradition of reading Scripture, it is far from purely subjective. Interpretation of this kind is a matter of disciplined attention to the literary tradition in which the text situates itself. This will be illustrated in the rest of this chapter.

In the Hebrew Bible and Apocrypha, a series of women are portrayed as human agents in God's deliverance of his people from their enemies, taking their place alongside such male figures as Moses, Joshua, Gideon, and David. They are:

- Shiphrah and Puah, the midwives (Exod 2:15-21);
- Deborah (Judg 4–5; cf. *Bib. Ant.* 30–33);
- Jael (Judg 4:17-22; 5:24-27; cf. *Bib. Ant.* 31:3-9; 32:12);
- Hannah (1 Sam 1–2; cf. *Bib. Ant.* 50–51);
- Esther;
- Judith; the mother of the Maccabean martyrs (2 Macc 7; 4 Macc 14–18).[23]

As these references show, Pseudo-Philo, though he ignores the midwives, characteristically plays up the roles of the other three women in this list who occur within the chronological scope of his retelling of the biblical story. The book of Jubilees (25–27) could be said to add Rebekah to the list by the way it develops her role as matriarch in the patriarchal narratives.[24] It is not appropriate to call such figures female saviors,[25] since in the Israelite and Jewish tradition it is always God who is the savior, even when humans act as his agents. As Judith says, "The Lord will deliver Israel by my hand" (Jdt 8:33). But such human agents can appropriately be praised and declared blessed by God (Judg 5:24; Jdt 13:17-20; 15:9-10, 12; 2 Macc 7:20; 4 Macc 17:5; *Bib. Ant.* 32:12). Of Pseudo-Philo's portrayal of these female agents of God's salvation, Betsy Halpern-Amaru comments: "These women confidently act out their parts, fully aware of their significance in the divine plan for Israel."[26] The same could certainly be said of Elizabeth

---

23. On the last, see R. D. Young, "The 'Woman with the Soul of Abraham': Traditions about the Mother of the Maccabean Martyrs," in Levine, ed., *Women Like This*, 67-81.

24. See R. D. Chesnutt, "Revelatory Experiences Attributed to Biblical Women in Early Jewish Literature," in Levine, ed., *Women Like This*, 108-11; B. Halpern-Amaru, *The Empowerment of Women in the Book of Jubilees* (JSJSup 60; Leiden: Brill, 1999) 55-64, 80-90.

25. Cf. G. Paterson Corrington, *Her Image of Salvation: Female Saviors and Formative Christianity* (Louisville: Westminster, 1992); Kraemer, *When Joseph Met Aseneth*, 209; C. Rakel, "'I Will Sing a New Song to My God': Some Remarks on the Intertextuality of Judith 16:1-17," in A. Brenner, ed., *Judges* (FCB 2/4; Sheffield: Sheffield Academic Press, 1999) 46.

26. B. Halpern-Amaru, "Portraits of Women in Pseudo-Philo's *Biblical Antiquities*," in Levine, ed., *Women Like This*, 103.

and Mary in Luke 1, gifted as they are with angelic revelation (1:31-37) and Spirit-inspired insight (1:41-45) into their God-given roles.

Elizabeth's role in Luke 1 is best compared with that of Israelite mothers of sons important in God's purposes for his people, including those women who were enabled to bear children by the special favor of God:

- Sarah (Gen 17–18; 21:1-7; cf. *Bib. Ant.* 23:5, 7-8);
- Rebekah (Gen 25:21; cf. *Bib. Ant.* 32:5);
- Leah and Rachel (Gen 29:31–30:24; cf. *Bib. Ant.* 50:2);
- the mother of Samson (Judg 13; cf. *Bib. Ant.* 42:1–43:1);
- Hannah (1 Sam 1:1–2:10; cf. *Bib. Ant.* 49:8; 50–51).

As these references show, Pseudo-Philo takes care to refer to all these biblical instances of barren women enabled to conceive.[27] Moreover, so impressed is he by this characteristic of God's dealing with the key women in the history of his people that he has God interpret the she-goat in Abraham's sacrifice (Gen 15:9-10) to represent "the women whose wombs I will open and they will give birth" (*Bib. Ant.* 23:7). Elizabeth's barrenness and her words after conceiving her son (Luke 1:25) put her clearly in this company of unusually favored biblical mothers (cf. especially Gen 21:6-7; 30:31-33; 31:22-24).

Mary also belongs in that company, not because she was barren but because she was a virgin and so could not have borne a child without God's miraculous intervention. Thus Mary's pregnancy both belongs in the series from Sarah to Elizabeth, in that it is enabled by a miraculous act of God, but also transcends the series, in that it is virginal.[28] In Elizabeth and her son the Hebrew Bible/Old Testament culminates, while in Mary and her son the new creation begins. It is not surprising, therefore, that, while Mary does stand in the succession of biblical mothers who conceive through God's power, she is more especially and more emphatically portrayed by Luke as in the succession of female human agents in God's deliverance of his people from their enemies, a succession that includes some of the mothers just mentioned but also the other women listed above.

This is conveyed especially by the references to Mary's blessedness. When Elizabeth, speaking prophetically in the Spirit, cries, "Blessed (εὐλογημένη) [i.e., blessed by God] are you among women" (1:42), we are reminded of Jael,

27. Note Philo's association of some of these women (Sarah, Leah, Rebekah) as miraculously enabled by God to bear children: *De Cher.* 45-47. On the dubious basis of Exod 2:22, he also includes Zipporah in the list.

28. See Brown, *Birth*, 300-301; J. A. Fitzmyer, *The Gospel According to Luke I–IX* (AB 28; Garden City, N.Y.: Doubleday, 1981) 338.

whom Deborah called "most blessed (LXX εὐλογηθείη) of women" (Judg 5:24; cf. *Bib. Ant.* 32:12), and of Judith, whom Uzziah called "blessed (εὐλογητή)[29] by the Most High above all other women on earth" (Jdt 13:18). When Mary says of herself that "from now on all generations shall call me blessed (μακαριοῦσιν)" (Luke 1:48), we are reminded of Uzziah's words to Judith: "Your praise will never depart from the hearts of those who remember the power of God. May God grant this to be a perpetual honour to you" (Jdt 13:19-20).[30] This perpetuity of reputation for Judith is connected with her own sense of the memorableness of the act of salvation God accomplishes through her: "I am about to do something that will go down through all generations of our descendants" (Jdt 8:32). Similarly, that Mary will be called fortunate by all generations is due to the eternally enduring significance of her motherhood. Her child "will reign over the house of Israel forever, and of his kingdom there will be no end" (Luke 1:33). Passages of the Hebrew Bible/Old Testament with which this eternity of the Davidic Messiah's kingdom is connected speak of "all generations" (Ps 72:5; 89:4 [MT 5]).

Both Jael and Judith (whose successful attack on Israel's prime enemy is closely modeled on Jael's) served God's purpose of delivering his people by acts of gruesome violence. Mary does so by her willing acceptance of the role of mother of the Messiah. Despite this difference, these intertextual echoes serve to highlight that Mary's motherhood is celebrated not as a purely domestic and familial matter, but as her active role in a great act of God for the salvation of his people. Mary's motherhood is of national and even world-changing significance. As such it transcends the distinction between the domestic sphere, in which women had real power despite the overall formal authority of men, and the sphere of public and political affairs, which was largely reserved for men. In the above list of female agents in God's salvation of his people, only Deborah and Judith undertake roles in society that would normally have been male, and even Judith exploits her femininity to considerable effect in doing so. (Jael's act of slaughter is exceptional, but only as a woman was she in a position to do it.) Deborah's and Judith's exercise of authority in the public, political sphere is remarkable and very unusual in the biblical narratives. The other women listed do not formally step outside the roles that would have been usual for women, but they exercise them in such a way as to affect drastically and decisively the course of public life. What we glimpse in these cases is the actual power and potential of women in such societies seen from a gynocentric perspective. From

29. The word "blessed" (εὐλογητός) occurs a significant seven times in Judith.

30. See also Leah's words in Gen 29:32, which are verbally closer to Luke 1:48 than Uzziah's are, but lack the feature of perpetuity.

the androcentric perspective, which most narrative in the Hebrew Bible/Old Testament adopts, the domestic sphere in which women have power and authority is relatively invisible. It is taken for granted as the backdrop to narratives of government and war in which men are the main actors. The extent to which women, without exceeding their socially accepted roles in domestic familial and economic matters, influenced events outside the household is usually unnoticed, from this androcentric perspective. But some of the gynocentric narratives reveal it in ways that may be representative, though also in cases that are of special importance for the narrative of God's saving purpose in Israel's history.

From this point of view the most revealing predecessor of Mary is Hannah.[31] The closest verbal contact between Luke's story of Mary and 1 Samuel's story of Hannah comes in Hannah's prayer for a child (1 Sam 1:11: "if you will look on the lowliness of your servant" [LXX ἐπιβλέψῃς ἐπὶ τὴν ταπείνωσιν τῆς δούλης σου]) and Mary's words in the Magnificat (Luke 1:48: "he has looked on the lowliness of his servant" [ἐπέβλεψεν ἐπὶ τὴν ταπείνωσιν τῆς δούλης αὐτοῦ]). But beyond this the songs of Hannah and Mary are strikingly parallel in both form and function, probably more so than has usually been noticed. The Magnificat is a collage of phrases drawn more or less verbatim from many parts of the Hebrew Bible/Old Testament.[32] Their original context is not always significant. The overall parallels of theme and function between Hannah's and Mary's songs, not dependent on precise verbal parallels, are of greater importance. The case is rather like the relation of Judith's song (Jdt 16) to Deborah's (Judg 5): there are few verbal echoes but a clear parallel in the function the two songs play in their respective narrative contexts.[33]

Both begin with personal declarations of praise and thanksgiving to God in view of his action on behalf of the singer herself. Both continue with celebra-

---

31. On the three versions of 1 Sam 1:24–2:11 (LXX, 4QSamᵃ, MT), see E. Tov, "Different Editions of the Song of Hannah and of Its Narrative Framework," in M. Cogan, B. L. Eichler, and J. H. Tigay, eds., *Tehillah le-Moshe* (M. Greenberg FS; Winona Lake, Ind.: Eisenbrauns, 1997) 149-70. It is a common mistake to assume that Luke, in his biblical allusions, works from the LXX without reference to a Hebrew text, but for our purposes now it makes no difference which version of 1 Sam 1–2 was known to Luke (or to the author of the Magnificat, if Luke was not).

32. M. P. Hogan and P. J. Kobelski, "The Hodayot (1QH) and New Testament Poetry," in Hogan and Kobelski, eds., *To Touch*, 188-90, compare this feature with the Qumran *Hodayot*, and comment: "This use of traditional language in new contexts is not a sign of a lack of originality, but it is testimony to the art of the poet who can take language already laden with meaning for people familiar with the heritage of the Greek Old Testament and use it to describe a new situation" (190).

33. S. Weitzman, *Song and Story in Biblical Narrative* (Bloomington/Indianapolis: Indiana University Press, 1997) 66.

tion of God's action for the humiliated in general (including, in both cases, the oppressed and the starving) and against the powerful in general (including, in both cases, the proud, the rulers, and the rich), effecting a reversal of status. By the end of the two songs both have in view God's saving action for his people Israel. It is significant that in both cases the scholarly consensus has been that the song is only loosely appropriate to its present context in the biblical narrative and must have originated as celebrations of God's salvation of Israel unconnected with the specific circumstances of Hannah[34] and Mary.[35] But this judgment misses the point of both songs, which is to celebrate God's gracious action for the singer herself *in its significance for all* who are also in humiliated circumstances of various kinds and so for God's faithful people in general.[36]

34. F. van Dijk-Hemmes, "Traces of Women's Texts in the Hebrew Bible," in A. Brenner and F. van Dijk-Hemmes, *On Gendering Texts: Female and Male Voices in the Hebrew Bible* (BibIntSer 1; Leiden: Brill, 1993) 93-97, discusses Hannah's song in the context of other birth songs and makes an interesting case for seeing it as an authentically female song of thanksgiving after birth. She rightly reminds us that giving birth was "often experienced by women as a struggle for life and against death" (94), so that the expression of joy in the form of a victory song "has nothing to do with typical 'masculinity'" (95) but is not unexpected after the "victory" of successful labor. The same point is made by J. Bekkenkamp and F. van Dijk, "The Canon of the Old Testament and Women's Cultural Traditions," in A. Brenner, ed., *A Feminist Companion to the Song of Songs* (FCB 1/1; Sheffield: Sheffield Academic Press, 1993) 85, where they cite (from H. Granquist) the remarkable parallel to Hannah's song (cf. 1 Sam 2:6) in a birth song improvised by a contemporary Middle Eastern mother: "He brings to life and he condemns to death/ he makes rich and he makes poor/he gives and he withholds./Everything comes from God, praise and thanks be to God." This argument vindicates the appropriateness of Hannah's song to its literary context, but cannot be directly applied to Mary's song, which is not a thanksgiving after birth. That Hannah's Song is an interpolation in the earlier text of 1 Samuel can also be argued on textual grounds (Weitzman, *Song*, 113-14), but it is quite possible that the song is both a secondary addition to the text *and* entirely appropriate to its new context.

35. E.g., Fitzmyer, *Luke I–IX*, 359 (the Magnificat "fits so loosely into the present context"); S. Farris, *The Hymns of Luke's Infancy Narrative* (JSNTSup 9; Sheffield: JSOT Press, 1985) 20-21; Brown, *Birth*, 346-49, 645. Hebrew Bible/OT scholars have often supposed that several of the songs attributed to characters in the biblical narratives (Exod 15; Judg 5; 1 Sam 2; Isa 38; Jonah 2) already existed independently of these narratives before being interpolated into them. These precedents may be partly responsible for the popularity of the view that the songs in Luke 1–2 similarly preexisted Luke's inclusion of them in the narrative. But the parallel is not valid. By the time Luke wrote, it was a scriptural literary convention that an account of a saving act of God should be followed by a song of praise to God. Luke's careful imitation of scriptural style in his first two chapters could well have included the composition of songs designed for their place in the narrative, modeled on the songs Luke knew in the narratives of the Hebrew Bible/OT. His practice would then be similar to that of the authors of Judith and Tobit, who composed songs for their characters on the model of those in the narratives of the Hebrew Bible/OT.

36. L. Legrand, "The 'Visitation' in Context," in T. Fornberg and D. Hellholm, eds., *Texts and Contexts* (L. Hartman FS; Oslo: Scandinavian University Press, 1995) 135, comments on the

Hannah's motherhood and her consecration of her son to God's service would lead to the deliverance of Israel from their enemies under Samuel's leadership and, beyond that, to the elevation (through Samuel's act of anointing) of David to national leadership and the exercise of his rule, on God's behalf, in the interests of the oppressed and the lowly.[37] (It is relevant to notice that this is clearly the way the Song of Hannah is interpreted in Pseudo-Philo's rewritten version of it [*Bib. Ant.* 51:3-6]. In this version the national and international consequences of Hannah's motherhood of Samuel are even more explicit and emphatic.[38] As Joan Cook puts it: Hannah "signals to the world the transition to a new era of leadership [and] claims a significant role for herself in the transition."[39] In Targum Jonathan to the Former Prophets, Hannah's Song is transformed into a prophecy of the historical events in which God will reverse the fortunes of Israel and their oppressors, ending with the judgment of God and the arrival of the messianic kingdom.[40] Though this passage of the Targum cannot be confidently dated as early as Luke, its messianic reading of the Song of Hannah and of the Song's theme of reversal of status makes it an interesting parallel to the Magnificat, and at least it can be said that similar Jewish exegetical approaches are at work in both cases.)

As in Hannah's case, so in Mary's, her motherhood will lead to the salvation of Israel by her son, salvation that characteristically reverses the status of the

---

way, in the Magnificat, Mary's own story assumes the grander dimensions of God's plan (1) in time (forever: vv 48, 55), (2) in space (reaching "all who fear him": v 55), and (3) in society (reaching the lowly and the destitute: vv 48, 52-53).

37. Cf. W. Brueggemann, *First and Second Samuel* (Interpretation; Louisville: Westminster/John Knox, 1990) 15-21; P. E. Satterthwaite, "David in the Books of Samuel: A Messianic Expectation?" in P. E. Satterthwaite, R. S. Hess, and G. J. Wenham, eds., *The Lord's Anointed: Interpretation of Old Testament Messianic Texts* (Grand Rapids: Baker; Carlisle: Paternoster, 1995) 43-47.

38. The point is illustrated by J. E. Cook, "Pseudo-Philo's Song of Hannah: Testament of a Mother in Israel," *JSP* 9 (1991) 103-14: Hannah "signals to the world the transition to a new era of leadership" (113).

39. Cook, "Pseudo-Philo's Song," 113.

40. Translation in D. J. Harrington and A. J. Saldarini, *Targum Jonathan of the Former Prophets* (Aramaic Bible 10; Wilmington, Del.: Glazier; Edinburgh: T. & T. Clark, 1987) 105-6; discussion in D. J. Harrington, "The Apocalypse of Hannah: Targum Jonathan of 1 Samuel 2:1-10," in D. M. Golomb and S. T. Hollis, eds., *"Working with No Data": Semitic and Egyptian Studies Presented to Thomas O. Lambdin* (Winona Lake, Ind.: Eisenbrauns, 1987) 147-52; J. E. Cook, "Hannah's Later Songs: A Study in Comparative Methods of Interpretation," in C. A. Evans and J. A. Sanders, eds., *The Function of Scripture in Early Jewish and Christian Tradition* (JSNTSup 154; Sheffield: Sheffield Academic Press, 1998) 244-49. For further discussion see R. Bauckham, "The Restoration of Israel in Luke-Acts," in J. M. Scott, ed., *Restoration: Old Testament, Jewish, and Christian Perspectives* (JSJSup 72; Leiden: Brill, 2001) 459-62.

lowly and the exalted. In her humiliation as a barren wife, Hannah is representative of oppressed Israel, whose liberation her son will achieve, and so reversal of status between the barren woman and the woman with many children is an appropriate example included in the instances of reversal of status described in her song (1 Sam 2:5b; cf. the parallel in Ps 113:7-9). This instance is not appropriate in Mary's case (though it would have been in Elizabeth's) and so does not occur in Mary's song, but in an unspecified way (which will be further discussed below) Mary is herself one of the humiliated whose exaltation at the expense of the exalted she sees occurring in consequence of her motherhood of the Messiah. Thus in both cases the singer's own experience of God's favor is representative of what will follow for others in consequence. In both cases what happens in the domestic and familial sphere of the woman transcends that sphere, achieving, in God's purpose, national and even worldwide significance and effect. The combination, in each song in its context, of the individual and the general, the personal and the political, the domestic and the public, is precisely the point of the song, which is merely obscured by theories of sources that represent this combination as secondary and artificial. In Hannah's song the combination is signaled by the *inclusio* formed by Hannah's reference to "my horn" at the beginning of the song (v 1) and her reference to "the horn of [God's] anointed," that is, the king, at the end (v 10). In Mary's song, as we shall see, there are also literary links that signal the deliberate combination of the personal and the public.[41]

The parallel in function between Hannah's story and song, on the one hand, and Mary's story and song, on the other, can be further extended to their respective functions in the larger narrative of which they constitute the beginning. The story of Hannah's motherhood of Samuel is the source of the rest of the narrative of 1-2 Samuel, and Hannah's song not only anticipates but sketches in advance the theological significance of this narrative as the outworking of God's purpose for his people.[42] Not only oppressed Israel's liberation from the Philistines is anticipated, but also David's rise to power from his origins as the socially insignificant youngest son of a peasant farmer (for David's social insignificance, see 1 Sam 18:23; and cf. 2 Sam 22:28). Also implied is

---

41. In an unpublished paper A. C. Thiselton writes: "What links Luke's interest in riches, politics, history and women is his concern with the inter-subjective public world as the domain of the profession of faith." Given the traditional identification of women with the private sphere, this is striking, and depends on Luke's sympathy with a gynocentric view that recognizes the public significance of women's apparently private activity. Since the narratives of motherhood in the Hebrew Bible/OT take such a gynocentric view, it was readily available to Luke in the literary models for his narrative in Luke 1–2.

42. Cf. B. S. Childs, *Introduction to the Old Testament as Scripture* (Philadelphia: Fortress; London: SCM, 1979) 272-73.

God's purpose in giving power to David that David should exercise God's rule on behalf of the humiliated and the poor, from whose ranks he himself rose — even if this purpose was only imperfectly realized in the actual history of David's reign. Hannah's song concludes with reference to the king, who is God's anointed (1 Sam 2:10b; cf. 2 Sam 23:1), not by some editorial oversight that allowed this anachronism in the premonarchical period in which Hannah lived, but because her song is programmatic of the whole history of God's acts of salvation as far as David's rule, all of which actually stems from God's gift of a child to her and her consecration of the child to God, even though this may initially seem an insignificant occurrence as far as the great affairs of national and international history are concerned.

Mary's song is similarly programmatic for the story of her son that the rest of Luke's Gospel (and even the Acts of the Apostles) narrates. The theme of reversal of status that characterizes God's salvation as described in the Magnificat is echoed again in Simeon's words to Mary (Luke 2:34: "this child is destined for the falling and rising of many in Israel") and is characteristic of Luke's Gospel as a whole.[43]

From a contemporary feminist perspective it is no doubt disappointing that Mary's role as an agent of God's salvation, while celebrated here as of far-reaching effect and significance, is nevertheless confined to the socially expected woman's role of motherhood[44] — unlike Deborah and Judith, who assume traditionally male roles and responsibilities. But this should not lead us to overlook that the narrative offers an authentically gynocentric perspective on the role of motherhood, such as is not to be seen in Matthew's androcentric version of Jesus' origins. Some feminist critics are inclined to see motherhood in the Bible solely in patriarchal terms, as a role to which women are stereotypically confined and as serving the interests of husbands and fathers in patrilineal descent. Every biblical portrayal of a woman as mother is then understood as a patriarchal construction, defining women in ways that served the patriarchal structure of power in society. But, while this is valid as a heuristic suspicion, to impose it woodenly or dogmatically is to rule out in advance the possibility that there are texts that reflect women's own independent sense of the importance of motherhood.

43. See J. O. York, *The Last Shall be First: The Rhetoric of Reversal in Luke* (JSNTSup 46; Sheffield: Sheffield Academic Press, 1991); J. M. Arlandson, *Women, Class, and Society in Early Christianity: Models from Luke-Acts* (Peabody, Mass.: Hendrickson, 1997) chap. 5. For a brief survey of the theme in both testaments, see E. Hamel, "Le Magnificat et le Renversement des Situations: Réflexion théologico-biblique," *Greg* 60 (1979) 60-70.

44. Cf. J. Capel Anderson, "Mary's Difference: Gender and Patriarchy in the Birth Narratives," *JR* 67 (1987) 190-91, 200-201.

As we have often found already, Pseudo-Philo again provides a helpful angle of approach to the intertextuality of the Lukan narrative.[45] Not only does Pseudo-Philo's Hannah celebrate her motherhood as a role decisive in God's purpose for Israel and the nations, in effect being the nursing mother of Israel (*Bib. Ant.* 51:2-6),[46] but also Pseudo-Philo's Deborah, not literally a mother at all, is portrayed as the mother of her people. The biblical description of her as "a mother in Israel" (Judg 5:7; cf. *Bib. Ant.* 33:6) is developed as an image of her political authority. She instructs her people, "warning" them "as a woman of God" and "enlightening" them "as one from the female race," asking them to "obey me as your mother" (33:1; cf. 33:4). In Hannah's case literal motherhood is exalted as the decisive role of an agent of God in the salvation of his people. But so exalted is the notion of motherhood here, not as a role subservient to patriarchal power but as a role of privileged obedience to God alone, that motherhood can also be, in Deborah's case, the metaphor for her exceptional role, outside the normal social expectations of women. This is only possible because literal motherhood is seen from a gynocentric perspective as owned by women themselves, not by their husbands. This is motherhood in the tradition of its first scriptural example, when Eve, naming her first child, declared with astonishment at her own God-given power to produce new life: "I have produced a man by means of YHWH" (Gen 4:1).[47]

Similarly, it would be quite misleading to see either Elizabeth's or Mary's motherhood as serving the patriarchal and patrilineal interests of their husbands, which would be the expected androcentric perspective on their roles as mother. Though Elizabeth does suffer the social stigma of the barren woman (the couple's infertility seems to be blamed axiomatically on her rather than her husband, as often in ancient culture)[48] and is delivered from this disgrace (Luke 1:25), the importance of her son has nothing to do with continuing his father's line. The refusal to give him the name of any of his paternal relatives (1:59-63) symbolizes this.[49] Like Hannah's son, John is consecrated to God from before

45. For Pseudo-Philo's remarkable emphasis on motherhood, see especially DesCamp, "Why Are These Women Here?" 76-78.

46. Cf. Cook, "Pseudo-Philo's Song," 103-14.

47. LXX Ἐκτησάμην ἄνθρωπον διὰ τοῦ θεοῦ. The Hebrew phrase את־יהוה is often translated "with the help of YHWH," but this does not seem to be possible (there are no true parallels to such a use of את). The translation "by means of YHWH" is how LXX (διά) and Vulgate *(per)* understood the Hebrew.

48. That this could not necessarily be taken for granted is shown by *Bib. Ant.* 42, in which Samson's parents debate which of them is sterile, though it turns out that it is the woman.

49. That Elizabeth names her son (Luke 1:59-60), though in accordance with the angel's instruction to Zechariah (1:13), is not unusual in the biblical tradition. In the Hebrew Bible/OT there are 27 cases of naming by the mother, compared with 17 by the father: I. Pardes, "Beyond

his birth (1 Sam 1:11; Luke 1:15). Even more striking is Joseph's complete absence from the story of Mary's motherhood in Luke 1. Even though Joseph inevitably becomes the publicly putative father of Jesus in Luke 2, Mary does not bear a son for Joseph. A certain kind of feminist critique would say that in all this Elizabeth and Mary merely become instrumental in the desires and designs of the divine Patriarch, in place of an earthly husband.[50] But this is to equate subservience to another human being with obedience to God in a crassly literalistic way, neglecting one of the central insights of biblical spirituality: that the service of God is the true liberation and fulfillment of the self. Mary is most fully herself, the active and responsible subject of her own story, when she acts as the Lord's servant (Luke 1:38, 48), taking God at his word and taking responsibility for acting with trust in that word (1:38, 45).

The title "servant" of God is certainly not demeaning. In Mary's own use it is no doubt indicative of her readiness to serve God (cf. Hannah's usage, 1 Sam 1:11), but in the context it is also an honorific title that puts Mary in the company of the special "servants" of God, the great leaders of God's people, active agents of his salvific acts, such as Abraham (Ps 105:42), Moses (Neh 9:14; Mal 4:4 [MT 3:22]), Joshua (Josh 24:29; Judg 2:8), David (Ps 89:3 [MT 4]), Daniel (Dan 6:20 [MT 21]), and even the Davidic Messiah himself (Ezek 34:23; 37:24). This raises the question whether the intertextual allusions in Luke's story of Mary function to compare her only with the female agents of God's deliverance in the biblical history, or also with male figures of that kind. From this point of view it is suggestive that Pseudo-Philo, who delights in finding parallels within the biblical story and especially in paralleling a male figure and a female, depicts the great victory of Deborah and Barak over Sisera as parallel to the victory over the Egyptians at the exodus (*Bib. Ant.* 32:16-17), and implicitly compares Deborah with Moses.[51] The introduction to his version of the Song of Deborah and Barak (*Bib. Ant.* 32:1) seems to reflect the introduction to Moses' Song at the Sea (Exod 15:1).[52] Moreover, while Judith's song (Jdt 16) most

Genesis 3: The Politics of Maternal Naming," in A. Brenner, ed., *A Feminist Companion to Genesis* (FCB 1/2; Sheffield: Sheffield Academic Press, 1993) 175n.1.

50. Capel Anderson, "Mary's Difference," 195, suggests this as a possible reading, but does not adopt it. She rightly points out that "God is not portrayed as a male sexual figure" (195-96). Robbins, "Socio-Rhetorical Criticism," 196, 198, apparently thinks that God obliges Mary to perpetuate patrilineal hierarchical ideology.

51. See Brown, *No Longer Be Silent*, 41-71.

52. Bauckham, "The *Liber Antiquitatum Biblicarum* of Pseudo-Philo and the Gospels as 'Midrash,'" in R. T. France and D. Wenham, eds., *Gospel Perspectives III: Studies in Midrash and Historiography* (Sheffield: JSOT Press, 1983) 47; Brown, *No Longer Be Silent*, 56-57; Weitzman, *Song*, 71.

obviously parallels Deborah's (Judg 5) in its narrative function, its verbal allusions are more impressively with the Song of Moses (Exod 15),[53] suggesting to some scholars that Judith is portrayed not only as a new Deborah and a new Jael,[54] but also as a new Moses.[55] Most recently, Claudia Rakel, on the basis of her study of the intertextual relationship between Judith 16 and Exodus 15, concludes that the book of Judith reproduces the theological structure of the exodus and, by attributing to Judith herself a new song of exodus like that of Moses, makes her the leader of a new exodus from Egypt.[56]

The opening words of Mary's song are notable for their first-person reference to the singer's praise of God. In this respect, the Magnificat does not conform to the model of a psalm of praise, like many psalms in the Psalter and Judith's hymn of victory (Jdt 16:1), which begin rather with a summons to others to join in praising God. In this respect Mary's song is, once again, similar to Hannah's (1 Sam 2:1), but it also resembles Moses' Song at the Sea (Exod 15:1-2; note that the parallel in Miriam's song [15:21] to the opening words of Moses' song does not preserve the first-person reference, substituting a call to others to praise) and the song given to Israel to sing at the new exodus of the future (Isa 12:1).[57] Other elements in the language of the Magnificat echo references to the exodus in the Hebrew Bible/Old Testament: God "has done great things for me" (Luke 1:49; cf. Deut 10:21); "strength with his arm" (Luke 1:51; cf. Exod 15:16). These are not compelling evidence for understanding the Magnificat as a song of the new Moses at the new exodus,[58] since other Hebrew Bible/Old Testament parallels are verbally quite as close (e.g., Ps 71:19; 89:10 [MT 11]).

53. Weitzman, *Song*, 66; cf. also C. A. Moore, *Judith* (AB 40; Garden City, N.Y.: Doubleday, 1985) 256-57 (also 193 on echoes of the Song of Moses in Jdt 9:11).

54. S. A. White, "In the Steps of Jael and Deborah: Judith as Heroine," in J. C. VanderKam, ed., *"No One Spoke Ill of Her": Essays on Judith* (SBLEJL 2; Atlanta: Scholars Press, 1992) 5-16.

55. J. W. van Henten, "Judith as a Female Moses," in F. van Dijk-Hemmes and E. Brenner, eds., *Reflections on Theology and Gender* (Kampen: Pharos, 1994) 33-48; idem, "Judith as Alternative Leader: A Rereading of Judith 7–13," in A. Brenner, ed., *A Feminist Companion to Esther, Judith and Susanna* (FCB 1/7; Sheffield: Sheffield Academic Press, 1995) 232-45.

56. Rakel, "I Will Sing," 43-44, 46-47. She also sees Judith's song as, so to speak, restoring to Miriam the role of victory singer that the redaction of Exod 15 removed from her by giving the principal song to Moses and only a response to Miriam (Exod 15:20-21): "The fact that a woman, Judith, now sings in praise of a new Exodus restores to Miriam the voice she has lost in the book of Exodus" (45).

57. The two songs in Isa 12 echo Exod 15, and the formal difference between the first-person praise of the first (vv 1-2) and the invitation to praise of the second (vv 4-6) shows that they correspond, respectively, to the songs of Moses and of Miriam.

58. Cf. K. E. Bailey, "The Song of Mary: A Vision of a New Exodus (Luke 1:46-55)," *Near East School of Theology Theological Review* 2/1 (1979) 29-35 (not seen).

However, one other consideration is worth taking into account. In the Hebrew Bible/Old Testament and the Apocrypha, there is a series of songs of praise sung to God following his great acts of salvation of his people:

- Exodus 15:1-18 (Moses); 15:21 (Miriam);
- Judges 5 (Deborah and Barak);
- 1 Samuel 2 (Hannah);
- 2 Samuel 22 (David);
- Isaiah 38:9-20 (Hezekiah);
- Judith 16 (Judith);
- Additions to Daniel 3 (Shadrach, Meshach, and Abednego);
- Tobit 13 (Tobit);[59]
- Isaiah 12 (Israel at the new exodus).

For early Jewish readers of Scripture, Moses' Song at the Sea would appear "as the initiating member of a tradition of praise and thanksgiving that Israel would repeat consistently throughout its history."[60] Against this background, the Magnificat does not need to allude specifically to the words of Moses' song in order to be recognized as belonging to this series. Read intertextually, Mary's song stands in the great tradition initiated by Moses' song (as do Zechariah's and Simeon's songs), and the salvation it celebrates has its ultimate precedent in the exodus. As a human agent of salvation, Mary stands in succession to other singers of such songs: Moses and Miriam, Deborah and Barak, Hannah and David. But it should be noted that the narrative function of these songs, beginning with the literary model set by Exodus 15, is not to celebrate the singer, but to give all the glory to God, the mighty Savior of his people.[61]

59. The hymn in Tob 13 resembles the Song of Hannah not only in its theme of reversal of status (13:2), but also in that it celebrates at the same time both the acts of God for Tobit and his family and also the great deliverance of the nation in the future presaged by these seemingly just personal events. On Tobit's hymn, see S. Weitzman, "Allusion, Artifice, and Exile in the Hymn of Tobit," *JBL* 115 (1996) 49-61.

60. Weitzman, *Song,* 123.

61. Weitzman, *Song,* chap. 2, on Exod 15. This is also true of Judith's song. She is indeed honored by the women of Israel for her part in the deliverance (15:12), but in singing the song she then invites the people to give all the glory to God. This does not deny Judith's agency in the events, but it makes it inappropriate to interpret the reference to "the hand of a woman" (16:6) as Rakel does: "Thus she is an epiphany of God. Judith is an embodiment of God in the new Exodus" (Rakel, "I Will Sing," 43). This move from agency to embodiment is not characteristic of Second Temple Judaism and does not correspond to the way the book of Judith speaks of her.

3. Mary's Lowly Status

No reading of the Magnificat can fail to observe a parallel between the "lowly status" of Mary, God's "servant" (Luke 1:48), for whom God "has done great things" (v 49), and "the lowly," whom God "has exalted" (v 52), as well as "his servant Israel," whom God has helped. But discerning the structure of Mary's song assists us in recognizing this connection as its main theme. In table 4 (on p. 70) I have suggested that it divides into two stanzas of equal length, with a transitional or core verse (51) in the center.[62] I have italicized words in each stanza that echo words in the other stanza. These correspondences confirm the parallel between what God has done for Mary herself (stanza 1) and what he has done for his lowly people (stanza 2). The first stanza, though it finally (v 50) broadens the subject of God's favor from Mary alone to all who fear God, does not introduce the negative counterpart to this: God's judgment on the exalted. The second stanza begins with four lines depicting, in chiastic manner (A the powerful, B the lowly, A[1] the hungry, B[1] the rich) the reversal of status that God's salvific action involves. The transitional verse refers back to God's gracious act for Mary herself in the first stanza ("he has shown strength with his arm") and forward to the judgment on the exalted in the second stanza ("he has scattered the proud in the thoughts of their hearts"). But it states implicitly the theme of reversal of status in a way that links Mary in the first stanza with the more general statements of the second stanza: with the strength of his arm God has exalted his lowly servant Mary and brought low the arrogant.

As in Hannah's song the theme of reversal of status seems to apply, on the one hand, to the lowly and the exalted within Israel and, on the other hand, also to Israel as God's humiliated servant and their powerful pagan oppressors. In a first-century Jewish context the latter can hardly fail to be evoked by the second stanza as a whole, but (as Simeon's words in 2:34 later confirm) there must also be the thought of the distinction within Israel between those who are truly God's lowly servants and those who range themselves with the Gentile enemies of God in oppressing or exploiting their fellow Jews. ("Lowliness" [ταπείνωσις] can certainly describe either Israel as oppressed and humiliated [e.g., Deut 26:7; 1 Sam 9:16; 1 Macc 3:51; 3 Macc 2:12] or the humiliated status of the poor within Israel [1 Sam 18:23; Isa 11:4; 14:32],[63] as

---

62. This analysis of the structure is a simplified version of that given by S. Terrien, *The Magnificat: Musicians as Biblical Interpreters* (New York: Paulist, 1995) 6-9, to which I owe especially the notion of v 51 as a transitional or, in Terrien's term, "core verse." Unlike Terrien's, my structure does not rely on a putative original Hebrew version of the Magnificat.

63. Cf. K. Wengst, *Humility: Solidarity of the Humiliated* (tr. J. Bowden; Philadelphia: Fortress; London: SCM, 1988) 16-30.

Table 4: Structure of the Magnificat (Luke 1:46-55)

Stanza 1

46 My soul magnifies the Lord,

47 and my spirit rejoices in God my Savior,

48 for he has looked with favor on the *lowliness* of *his servant*.
    Surely, from now on *all generations* will call me blessed;

49 for the *Mighty One* has done great things for me,
    and holy is his name.

50 *His mercy* is for those who fear him
    for generation after generation.

Transitional verse

51 He has shown strength with his arm;
    he has scattered the proud in the thoughts of their hearts.

Stanza 2

52 He has brought down the *powerful* from their thrones,
    and lifted up the *lowly;*

53 he has filled the hungry with good things,
    and sent the rich away empty.

54 He has helped *his servant* Israel,
    in remembrance of *his mercy,*

55 according to the promise he made to our ancestors,
    to Abraham and to his descendants *forever.*

well as the barrenness of women like Hannah and Elizabeth [Gen 16:11; 1 Sam 1:11].) In any case Mary, in her "low status" (v 48), is clearly paradigmatic of those whom God exalts. But she does not only represent them. In her exaltation by God, from low status to being the mother of the Messiah, she becomes the means of the exaltation of the lowly in general through the coming of the Messiah. The whole can be described in the song, with its aorist verbs throughout,[64] as a single act of salvation for God's people by God, since his making Mary the mother of his Messiah entails also the exaltation of the lowly and the humiliation of the exalted in Israel that her son will accomplish.

64. For the various views of these aorists, see Farris, *Hymns,* 114-16; Brown, *Birth,* 362-63, 648-49; York, *Last,* 52-53; M. Coleridge, *The Birth of the Lukan Narrative* (JSNTSup 88; Sheffield: Sheffield Academic Press, 1993) 93-94n.2. These discussions fail to take proper account of the fact that Mary's exaltation is her motherhood of the Messiah, which is not therefore just *comparable* with God's exaltation of the lowly in general, but *instrumental* in God's exaltation of the lowly through his Messiah Jesus.

But in what does Mary's "low status" (ταπείνωσις) consist? Although "the poor" and "the lowly" had acquired in Jewish tradition a strong sense of religious attitude as well as social and economic status, it is a mistake to suppose that these terms can indicate attitudes of humility before God and trust in God without any implication of status. Rather there is an assumption that, in the ordinary way of things, the rich and powerful are likely to trust arrogantly in themselves and disregard God, while those without worldly security tend to recognize their need of God and to approach him in humble trust. The theme of reversal of status usually combines the attitudinal-religious and the socio-economic.[65]

The Magnificat (1:48, 52) therefore contradicts the view of those who argue that Luke's Mary is *not* of low social status, since she has the ascribed honor of Aaronide priestly descent (cf. 1:36) and/or of her husband-to-be's Davidic descent (1:27).[66] The first point is dubious in any case. Since priestly status belonged only to descent in the male line from Aaron, we cannot tell whether her (unspecified) relationship with Elizabeth, who was the daughter of an Aaronide priest (1:5), indicates that Mary herself was of priestly descent. We should also not be as confident as many scholars appear to be in supposing that priests were ipso facto of high social status. The ordinary priests who, like Zechariah, lived like peasants in the villages of Palestine and officiated in the temple only one week in the year, were certainly not of the status of the priestly aristocracy who ran the temple and profited from its wealth and the power their relationship to the temple gave them. The honor associated with pedigree was only one factor determining status and could be largely counteracted by lack of economic resources and of the power and influence in society that went with them. Joel Green's argument that Luke deliberately depicts Zechariah and Elizabeth as of high social status according to current social values and intends that to contrast with the reversal of values effected by God in his choice of the socially insignificant Mary is unconvincing, since Elizabeth also benefits from

---

65. It is probably also a mistake to think, as Brown, *Birth*, 350-55, does, that the term "the poor ones" (אנוים), used in this way, would suggest a reference to specific religious groups, such as the Qumran community or the early Jerusalem church (with the resulting hypothesis that the Magnificat derives from such circles of *Anawim*). That such groups sometimes used this term and similar ones to describe themselves does not make it as such a technical term for specific communities.

66. I. J. Mosala, *Biblical Hermeneutics and Black Theology in South Africa* (Grand Rapids: Eerdmans, 1989) 166-71; B. J. Malina and J. H. Neyrey, "Honor and Shame in Luke-Acts: Pivotal Values of the Mediterranean World," in Neyrey, ed., *The Social World of Luke-Acts* (Peabody, Mass.: Hendrickson, 1991) 47-48; J. H. Neyrey, "The Symbolic Universe of Luke-Acts: 'They Turn the World Upside Down,'" in Neyrey, ed., *Social World*, 289.

God's reversal of status.[67] The relevant social fact about Elizabeth is the social disgrace of her barrenness (1:35), which, as in Hannah's case, God reverses in enabling her to conceive a son with a high calling in God's service. This also makes questionable the reading of the meeting of Elizabeth and Mary according to which a reversal of status takes place between them, with Elizabeth the old woman of Aaronide descent submitting to the socially insignificant young girl whom God has made the mother of Elizabeth's lord (1:43).[68] This reading runs counter to the clear parallel between the two as both recipients of God's grace to the lowly, both in different ways compared with Hannah.

It is a mistake to think that pedigree is only ever mentioned for the sake of the ascribed honor it implies. Joseph's descent from David (1:27) has to be mentioned because it is the way in which Mary's son can be reckoned a descendant of David (1:32) and therefore fulfill the prophecies of the Messiah descended from David. On the other hand, this makes it unlikely that, as Green argues, Joseph's descent from David implies ascribed honor that Mary, as no more than his betrothed and lacking any reference to her own paternity or ancestry (1:27), does not share. If the angel's words in 1:32 already imply that Mary's son will count as a descendant of David by virtue of Joseph's Davidic descent, then it is hardly credible that Mary herself does not participate in whatever in the way of ascribed honor her betrothed has by virtue of his pedigree. In any case, the nature of betrothal in first-century Jewish society makes it unlikely that a betrothed girl would not already share the social status of the man legally pledged to become her husband.

One proposal about the nature of Mary's "low status" that would explain it without also implying Joseph's low social status is that it is the disgrace resulting from her pregnancy while not yet living with Joseph.[69] While such disgrace might well be so obviously entailed by her situation as not to need explicit mention for first-century readers, there is a serious difficulty in this suggestion. The social disgrace, if it exists, actually results from God's choice of Mary to be the virginal mother of the Messiah, and so cannot be the lowly status from which God raises her by choosing her as the mother of the Messiah. Arie Troost's argument that in her question to Gabriel in 1:34 Mary's "concern is for facing the social awkwardness of her position, and for the child to be born," and that what she requests is "protection for herself and assistance in bearing the consequences of the announced pregnancy," cannot be sustained.[70] Mary asks how her pregnancy can come about, not how she will face the social disgrace of it.

67. J. B. Green, "The Social Status of Mary in Luke 1,5–2,52: A Plea for Methodological Integration," *Bib* 73 (1992) 457-72.

68. Green, "Social Status," 469-70.

69. E.g., Robbins, "Socio-Rhetorical Criticism," 182-84, following J. Schaberg.

70. Troost, "Elizabeth and Mary," 174.

It is true that, unlike Matthew and Mark, Luke does not mention that Joseph was an artisan (cf. Luke 4:22 with Matt 13:55; Mark 6:3).[71] But nor does he do anything analogous to the tactics adopted by the later *Protevangelium of James*, which is clearly concerned to provide Jesus with higher social origins than the Gospels imply, probably in response to non-Christian Jewish criticisms of the Christian account of Jesus as Messiah. In this work Mary's father Joachim is a rich Jerusalem aristocrat (1:1), to whose banquets all the elite of Israel are invited (5:2). Joseph, though he does work with an axe (9:1), is evidently no ordinary artisan but a master builder (9:2; 13:1).

By contrast, Luke's account of the sacrifice offered by Mary and Joseph (2:24) implies their lack of economic resources (cf. Lev 12:6-8). The story of the shepherds (2:8-20), though not necessarily requiring that Mary and Joseph be low in the social and economic scale, surely reveals Luke's intention to situate Jesus' birth in humble circumstances among the poor. In this context Jesus' birth in Bethlehem, "the city of David" (2:11), recognized as Messiah by shepherds, suggests not his birth into the honor and status of the royal line of the kings of Judah, but rather David's own social insignificance, as a shepherd boy in Bethlehem, before his rise to power. The Messiah who is to be the ideal David, ruling righteously for the benefit of the poor (Isa 11:4), comes, like David himself, from the ranks of the poor, so that he may rule in solidarity with the poor. He is a king who meets not the expectations of the elite, but the hope of the poor for a ruler who will exalt the lowly and feed the hungry.[72]

It seems that Luke wishes descent from David to evoke not the high status of royal descent, but the low status of David's humble origins. This is confirmed by the genealogy Luke gives to Jesus, a genealogy that traces Jesus' descent through Joseph from David and back to Adam (Luke 3:23-38). As I have demonstrated in detail elsewhere,[73] Luke's genealogy is a sophisticated theological text, embodying, as biblical genealogies can, much more than biological information. According to this genealogy Jesus was descended from David not through Solomon and the kings of Judah, as in Matthew's genealogy (Matt 1:6-11), but through David's little-known ninth son Nathan (cf. 1 Chron 3:5). While making contact with the official line of heirs to the Davidic throne in Zerubbabel and his father Shealtiel (Luke 3:27; cf. Matt 1:12-13), the genealogy otherwise consists

71. Cf. Arlandson, *Women, Class*, 141-42.

72. R. A. Horsley and J. S. Hanson, *Bandits, Prophets, and Messiahs: Popular Movements at the Time of Jesus* (San Francisco: Harper & Row, 1985) chap. 3, misunderstand Davidic Messianism (as necessarily elitist or scribal) by failing to see that in this sense it could embody the hopes of the poor for precisely what Horsley and Hanson call "popular kingship."

73. R. Bauckham, *Jude and the Relatives of Jesus in the Early Church* (Edinburgh: T. & T. Clark, 1990) chap. 7.

of entirely unknown names between Nathan and Joseph. This genealogy embodies an interpretation of the prophecies of the Davidic Messiah, according to which the Messiah is to come not from the line of David's royal successors but from David's own family origins in Bethlehem. This is the significance of the key Davidic messianic text Isaiah 11:1: "A shoot shall come out from the stump of Jesse, and a branch shall grow from out of his roots." The image is of a tree cut down to a stump. A new shoot grows up from the roots. The natural meaning is that the tree of the royal house of David is to be cut down in judgment (cf. 10:33-34), and the ideal king of the future will derive not from the royal line of the kings of Judah, but from the origins of the dynasty, indicated by the reference to David's father, Jesse. The implication of the prophecy of the Messiah's birth in Bethlehem, in Micah 5:2 (MT 1), is similar. The new king is not to be born in the royal palace in Jerusalem, but in insignificant Bethlehem, where David's line began.[74] Bethlehem had no role in Israelite history once David became king. Solomon and all his successors were born not in Bethlehem but in Jerusalem. Thus Jesus' birth in Bethlehem, in both Matthew's and Luke's Gospels, but more clearly in Luke's, is a return to the authentic source of David's line among the ordinary people. Bethlehem is the city of David (Luke 2:11), but not of any of David's descendants through Solomon.

We see, then, that Mary's own low social status, expressed in the Magnificat, is consistent with the kind of Messiah she is to bear, one who comes from lowly origins in order to exalt the lowly and to abase the haughty. But finally we may ask whether there is any intrinsic connection between this important motif of Mary's low status and the fact that she is a woman. Is there only an incidental connection in the obvious fact that the mother of the Messiah must be a woman, or is there a sense in which Mary's femaleness reinforces her status as lowly?

One approach to this issue is to notice how the theme of reversal of status, which, as we have seen, dominates the Magnificat, occurs in earlier songs in this biblical tradition of songs sung by the human agents of God's salvation. It occurs, appropriately, in David's song (2 Sam 22:28 par. Ps 18:27 [MT 28]), but more emphatically in Hannah's (1 Sam 2:4-8), which offers much the best literary precedent for the development of this theme in the Magnificat. Like Mary, Hannah presents herself as a notable instance of God's characteristic practice of exalting the lowly. However, striking as this parallel between the two women, Hannah and Mary, is, one has to say that it is not because Hannah is a woman as such that she is aligned with the weak, the hungry, and the poor, but because she is a *barren* woman, whose condition is reversed by the gift of a child.

74. On this theme in the messianic prophecies, see more fully Bauckham, *Jude*, 334-39.

Judith's song also refers to the theme of the reversal of status. Judith herself is the agent through whom God's oppressed people, helpless before the vast army of the arrogant Assyrian general, are delivered and exalted, while the mighty Holofernes is struck down and his army perishes (Jdt 16:5-12). In this God proves to be, as Judith has addressed him earlier in the book, "the God of the lowly, helper of the oppressed, upholder of the weak, protector of the forsaken, savior of those without hope" (9:11). But what is especially noteworthy is the way the book relates this theme to the fact that God's agent of salvation in this case is a woman. Much is made of the fact that Holofernes is defeated not by young warriors or mighty giants, but "by the hand of a woman" (16:5-6), a phrase that recurs several times (9:10; 13:15; 16:5).[75] It is borrowed from Judges 4:9, where it refers to Sisera's downfall at the hands of the woman Jael, one of the biblical prototypes on whom the figure of Judith is modeled. Pseudo-Philo's re-telling of the story of Jael also savors this phrase (*Bib. Ant.* 31:1, 7, 9). It is a peculiar ignominy that Sisera should die not in an equal struggle with a male warrior, but by "the arm of a weak woman" (*Bib. Ant.* 31:1; and for the shame of being killed by a woman, see also Judg 9:54). This shaming of the arrogant is also implied in Judith (9:10), but probably more important is that Judith's supposed powerlessness as a woman aligns her with the helpless condition of her people (cf. 9:9-11). This does not necessarily reflect a view of women as "weak" in every respect, but simply the lack of power generally attributed to women in the male worlds of politics and war.[76] That Judith is a widow is explicitly cited to enhance the impression of her powerlessness, since, although she is rich and so not the typical Israelite widow at all, nevertheless as a childless widow she is without a man.[77] Alone, with only her maid, in Holofernes' tent, Judith is the archetypically vulnerable woman faced with superior male strength. That she is the agent of his defeat dramatizes superbly the way God destroys the powerful and the arrogant, giving victory to those they oppress and despise.[78]

Mary too, in the context of Luke 1, is a lone woman, with only her female relative Elizabeth for support. While we cannot extrapolate from Judith's case

75. See P. W. Skehan, "The Hand of Judith," *CBQ* 25 (1963) 94-109.

76. Similarly 1 *Clem* 5:2 praises the women martyrs for their steadfastness, although they were "weak in body."

77. Cf. A. LaCocque, *The Feminine Unconventional* (OBT; Minneapolis: Fortress, 1990) 35-37.

78. Cf. P. F. Esler, "'By the Hand of a Woman': Culture, Story and Theology in the Book of Judith," in J. J. Pilch, ed., *Social Scientific Models for Interpreting the Bible* (B. J. Malina FS; BibIntSer 53; Leiden: Brill, 2001) 64-101, who compares Judith with David in his victory over Goliath, stressing the social insignificance of both (in Judith's case, as a woman) and the unlikelihood they would single-handedly win a great military victory.

to hers in every respect, there may be a sense in which Mary, who as God's lowly servant is representative of his servant Israel, precisely *as a woman* instantiates the weakness of the lowly before the oppressive power of the haughty. And like Judith, Mary too is not only aligned with the lowly, but herself is empowered by God to act as his agent in his exaltation of the lowly.

CHAPTER 4

Anna of the Tribe of Asher

Blessed also is that Anna who hated
her house and loved the Temple of her Lord.
She gazed intently at hidden beauty
for eighty years but was not sated.[1]

1. Introduction

According to Luke 2:36, the prophet Anna was a member of the tribe of Asher. She is thus the only Jewish character in the New Testament who is said to belong not to the tribe of Judah, Benjamin, or Levi, but to one of the northern tribes of Israel.[2] While most commentators on Luke pass over her tribal mem-

---

1. Ephrem, "Hymns on Virginity: Hymn 24," in *Ephrem the Syrian: Hymns* (tr. K. E. McVey; Classics of Western Spirituality; New York: Paulist, 1989) 367.

2. Using the term "Jewish" of members of the northern Israelite tribes seems awkward, but can be justified. In the late Second Temple period such Israelites who were not Samaritans belonged to the same nation as descendants of the southern tribes, and would have been called "Jews" by Gentiles and by Jews (especially diaspora Jews) who adopted this Gentile terminology. (Palestinian Jews normally used the term only in the geographical sense — meaning Judeans — and called their nation "Israel.") The "Jews" in Esther surely include the exiles of the northern tribes. The use of "Jews" for exiles of the northern tribes in Nineveh in Tob 11:17 may be due to the Greek translator (this verse is not extant in the Aramaic and Hebrew fragments of Tobit from Qumran), but shows that a Greek translator thought the usage appropriate.

bership in silence,[3] some who do comment on it find it surprising. Joseph Fitzmyer comments: "What a prophetess from a tribe like Asher would be doing in the Jerusalem Temple is a bit puzzling; Luke is probably little interested in the geographical location of Asher, as his attempt to describe Anna in the following phrases would suggest."[4] Raymond Brown also uses the word "puzzling": "This genealogical indication is puzzling, for Israelites in Jerusalem were principally of the tribe of Judah ('Jews') or of Benjamin or of Levi; and genealogical memories are normally of those tribes."[5] While this sentence, with some further discussion of the point, occurs in a note on Luke 2:36, Brown evidently agrees with Fitzmyer that Anna's tribal membership is of no real significance, since his extensive exegetical comment on Anna ignores it.[6] In this chapter I shall argue that to an informed first-century reader of Luke, Anna's membership of the tribe of Asher would not have been puzzling. On the contrary, it would not only be readily intelligible, but would also form a significant and coherent part of Luke's total characterization of Anna.

In the first two sections below, I shall argue that Anna, as a member of the tribe of Asher in Jerusalem, is a historically credible character. A Jewish reader of Luke who knew or knew about pre-70 Jerusalem would not find her tribal membership puzzling, but would find her an entirely credible participant in Luke's narrative. Thus, even if she is a fictional character, she is portrayed with verisimilitude, not least in her membership of the tribe of Asher. In the third and fourth sections I shall suggest that there is also reason to suppose that she is a genuinely historical character, and that the details of her descent and tribal membership are a reliable historical memory.

---

3. This is also true of the discussion of Anna in B. Witherington III, *Women in the Earliest Churches* (SNTSMS 59; Cambridge: Cambridge University Press, 1988) 140; M. Coleridge, *The Birth of the Lukan Narrative: Narrative as Christology in Luke 1–2* (JSNTSup 88; Sheffield: JSOT Press, 1993) 178-83.

4. J. Fitzmyer, *The Gospel According to Luke I–IX* (AB 28; Garden City, N.Y.: Doubleday, 1981) 431.

5. R. E. Brown, *The Birth of the Messiah* (rev. ed.; New York: Doubleday, 1993) 441.

6. Brown, *Birth*, 466-68. In his 1993 supplementary comments, Brown refers to "an enduring suspicion that the biographical information about her in 2:36-37, lavish for a minor character, has special significance," but finds the parallel between Anna and rabbinic understanding of Serah the daughter of Asher (Gen 46:17; Num 26:46), argued by M. Wilcox, "of uncertain value," because of the late date of *Pirqe de-Rabbi Eliezer* and Targum Pseudo-Jonathan, on which Wilcox depends (Brown, *Birth*, 688). The reference is to M. Wilcox, "Luke 2,36-38: 'Anna bat Phanuel, of the tribe of Asher, a prophetess . . .': A Study in Midrash in Material Special to Luke," in F. Van Segbroeck, et al., eds., *The Four Gospels 1992*, vol. 2 (F. Neirynck FS; BETL 100; Leuven: Leuven University Press and Peeters, 1992) 1571-79.

2. Where Were the Asherites?

In this section I ask: Where could members of the tribe of Asher be found in the late Second Temple period? We must rid ourselves of the popular notion of the "lost" ten tribes. The northern tribes (reckoned by Jewish writers of this period as ten[7] or nine and a half)[8] were not then thought to be "lost."[9] But where would Jews of this period expect to find people who traced their descent from a tribe such as Asher?

a. Galilee

The original tribal territory of Asher was in the western hills of Galilee, adjoining the Phoenician coast (which belonged only nominally to Asher), with the territories of Naphtali and Zebulun to the east and southeast (Josh 19:24-31; Judg 1:31-32; 1 Kgs 4:16; cf. Judg 5:17; 1 Kgs 9:13). When Tiglath-pileser III of Assyria conquered Galilee, probably in 733 BCE, large numbers of the inhabitants were deported (2 Kgs 15:29; Assyrian inscriptions in *ANET*, 283-84). Though the Galilean towns mentioned in connection with this campaign seem all to be in the territories of Dan (cf. also Judg 18:30), Naphtali, and Zebulun (cf. also Isa 9:1 [MT 8:23]), we can assume that Asherites would also have been deported. After this we hear of Asherites in Galilee only in 2 Chronicles 30:11, in connection with Hezekiah's attempt to win the northern tribes' allegiance to the Jerusalem temple. Though the account of Hezekiah's endeavor to extend Jerusalem's in-

---

7. E.g., Josephus, *Ant.* 11.133; TMos 3:4, 6; 4:9; SibOr 2:171; *m. Sanh.* 10:3.

8. E.g., 2 Bar 62:5; 77:17; 78:1; 4 Ezra 13:40 (some witnesses); AscIsa 3:2.

9. For the legendary notion that the exiles of the northern tribes had migrated to an extremely remote and inaccessible place, first attested in 4 Ezra 13, see Additional Note A at the end of this essay. The reported discussion between rabbis Aqiba and Eliezer ben Hyrcanus on whether the ten tribes would ever return to the land (*m. Sanh.* 10:3; *b. Sanh.* 110b) is a typically exegetical discussion of the meaning of Deut 29:28 (evidently an accepted reference to the exile of the northern tribes, since 4 Ezra 13:45 also refers to it, adopting Eliezer ben Hyrcanus's view): on the basis of different interpretations of this verse Aqiba maintains that the ten tribes will never return, Eliezer that they will. But this is not a discussion about whether exiles of the ten tribes still exist, and cannot be treated as evidence that these rabbis (supposing the attribution to be reliable) thought the ten tribes were "lost," as it is by J. Mann, "Anna, 'a prophetess of the tribe of Asher' (Luke ii.30)," *ExpT* 28 (1916-17) 332. According to *Sifra* 269:1, Aqiba also applied Lev 26:38 ("you shall perish among the nations") to "the ten tribes who went into exile in Media," whereas others took "perish" to mean only going into exile. This makes Aqiba's view clearer, but still need not mean that the ten tribes had already perished when this opinion was given.

fluence in the north probably has a historical basis,[10] the specific reference to Asher may be due to no more than the writer's desire to instance representative tribes as far north as Zebulun (cf. v 18, where Asher does not appear, but Issachar, not in v 11, does).[11] One should note, however, that the Chronicler takes for granted that members of the Galilean tribes, including Asher, were still to be found in Galilee after the deportations of many Israelite inhabitants of the region to Assyria (cf. also 34:6). Presumably, he knew this to be still the case in his own time.[12] One should note that Galilee, unlike Samaria (1 Kgs 17:24), is never said to have been resettled by the Assyrians with colonists from elsewhere.

However, the extent to which an identifiably Israelite population survived in Galilee is difficult to determine.[13] 1 Maccabees 5:21-23 seems to indicate, at the time of the Maccabean revolt, an Israelite minority in a predominantly Gentile territory, and archaeological evidence now bears out the idea that Upper Galilee, at least, was predominantly Gentile until the Hasmonean conquest of Galilee at the end of the second century BCE. Pagan settlements were then replaced by new Jewish settlements all over Galilee.[14] Most settlers were new immigrants from Judea. Thus the Galilean Jewish population in the first century BCE and the first century CE would have included the remnants of the old Israelite population from the First Temple period, large numbers of Judean immigrant families from the Hasmonean settlement program, and perhaps also converted pagans. Although the evidence is lacking, it is possible that prominent families still maintained the tradition of their descent from the old Israelite tribes of the Galilean area. If such families belonging to the tribe of Asher were still living in the old tribal territories, they would be on the borders of Jewish Galilee and Phoenicia, an area subject, from the late Hasmonean period onwards, to Jewish-Gentile friction and competition for hegemony.[15] The kind of

---

10. H. G. M. Williamson, *1 and 2 Chronicles* (NCB; Grand Rapids: Eerdmans; London: Marshall, Morgan & Scott, 1982) 361.

11. The rather notable absence of Naphtali, the most prominent of the Galilean tribes, from 30:10-11 and 18 contrasts with the stereotypical phrase "from Beersheba to Dan" (30:5), and suggests that the Chronicler relies on historical information that Hezekiah's influence did not extend as far north as Naphtali. Contrast the account of Josiah's activity "as far as Naphtali" (34:6).

12. He seems to think otherwise of the Transjordanian tribes: 1 Chron 5:26.

13. R. Frankel, "Galilee (Prehellenistic)," *ABD* 2:893-94.

14. I rely especially on a paper by Mordechai Aviam, given at the annual SBL meeting, Chicago, November 1994.

15. A. Kasher, *Jews and Hellenistic Cities in Eretz-Israel* (TSAJ 21; Tübingen: Mohr [Siebeck], 1990) chaps. 3–5; G. Theissen, *The Gospels in Context* (tr. L. M. Maloney; Minneapolis: Fortress, 1991) 65-78.

Jewish eschatological nationalism with which Luke associates Anna (Luke 2:38) would surely appeal to them. Moreover, it is clear that Galilee in the Herodian period was strongly loyal to Jerusalem and the temple.[16] That a Galilean prophet, expecting the redemption of Israel from pagan rule, should move to the religious heart of the nation and the expected center of God's eschatological restoration of the nation, in order to spend her time in the temple, would not be at all "puzzling."

b. Northern Judea

For the sake of completeness, we should take account of the fact that in the biblical period there were Asherite clans not only in the tribal territory in the northwest, but also in an Asherite enclave in the southern Ephraimite hill country, adjoining Benjamin to the south. The genealogy of Asher in 1 Chronicles 7:30-40 refers, from verse 31 onward, solely to the families of this southern Asherite enclave.[17] This Asherite enclave was probably part of the kingdom of Judah by the end of the monarchical period and perhaps included in the postexilic province of Yehud.[18] It might therefore be possible to argue that Asherite families belonged to the Jewish community in Judea throughout the Second Temple period and that Anna belonged to one such family. However, that the names Beriah (1 Chron 7:30) and Heber (7:30-31), the progenitors of this branch of the tribe of Asher, also occur in genealogies of Ephraim (1 Chron 7:23) and Benjamin (1 Chron 8:13, 16, 17) suggests that these southern Asherite families eventually lost their Asherite tribal identity and came to be regarded as Ephraimites or

16. S. Freyne, *Galilee from Alexander the Great to Hadrian 323 B.C.E. to 135 C.E.* (Wilmington, Del.: Glazier; Notre Dame, Ind.: University of Notre Dame Press, 1980) 259-304; idem, *Galilee, Jesus, and the Gospels* (Philadelphia: Fortress; Dublin: Gill & Macmillan, 1988) 178-90. A case can be made for a centuries-old distinction, in this respect, between Samaria and Galilee, since close links between Jerusalem and Galilee can be seen in the period after the Assyrian conquest (2 Chron 30:10-11; 2 Kgs 21:19; 23:36); cf. Frankel, *ABD* 2:894.

17. D. Edelman, "The Asherite Genealogy in 1 Chronicles 7:30-40," *BR* 23 (1988) 13-23; S. Japhet, *I & II Chronicles* (OTL; Louisville: Westminster/John Knox; London: SCM, 1993) 185-87.

18. The northern and northwestern boundaries of the province cannot be determined with certainty. The reconstruction in Y. Aharoni, *The Land of the Bible* (tr. and ed. A. F. Rainey; 2d ed.; Philadelphia: Westminster; Burns & Oates, 1979) 417, includes the Asherite enclave, but the more restricted boundaries for which C. E. Carter, "The Province of Yehud in the Post-Biblical Period: Soundings in Site Distribution and Demography," in T. C. Eskenazi and K. H. Richards, eds., *Second Temple Studies*, vol. 2, *Temple Community in the Persian Period* (JSOTSup 175; Sheffield: JSOT Press, 1994) 106-45, argues would include little of the Asherite enclave.

Benjaminites.[19] Thus it seems unlikely that even a well-informed contemporary reader of Luke 2:36 would consider the possibility that Anna belonged to an Asherite family located in northern Judaea since preexilic times.

c. Adiabene and Media

Although the places of settlement of the later exiles from Samaria are specified with some precision in 2 Kings (17:6; 18:11), the exiles of the Galilean tribes are merely said to have been taken to Assyria (15:29). The Transjordanian tribes, deported in the same campaign of Tiglath-pileser, are said in 1 Chronicles 5:26 to have been taken to the same places as 2 Kings gives as the places of settlement of the exiles from Samaria,[20] but probably the Chronicler's information is taken from 2 Kings 17:6 and 18:11,[21] and does not constitute independent evidence for locating Tiglath-pileser's deportees. It is not improbable, however, that the same places of settlement were used for the two phases of Israelite exile, only twelve years apart. As we shall see, this would conform with later evidence as to the whereabouts of the northern Israelite exiles. Second Kings 17:6 and 18:11 refer to three areas:[22] (1) Halah (cf. also Obad 20, text as corrected in NRSV), which is the Assyrian Halahhu, a region and a town northeast of Nineveh; (2) the Habor River, which flows into the Euphrates in northern Mesopotamia, and on which the city of Gozan stood;[23] and (3) the cities of Media. On the last, Bustenay Obed comments: "The purpose of bringing deportees from the west to Madai was to strengthen the Assyrian hold in that area, mainly against the Elamites, and to resettle the evacuated lands with new inhabitants, just as they did with the land of Samaria and many other conquered regions."[24]

The descendants of the exiles in the first and second of these three areas of settlement probably formed the core of the later Jewish communities of

19. Japhet, *Chronicles*, 185.

20. By comparison with the lists in 2 Kgs 17:6 and 18:11, that in 1 Chron 5:26 lacks a reference to the cities of Media, and adds the otherwise unknown Hara. Most likely the word "Hara" (הרא) represents a corruption of a reference to the cities (ערי) of Media.

21. So Williamson, *Chronicles*, 67; Japhet, *Chronicles*, 141.

22. On these see B. Obed, "The Settlements of the Israelite and the Judean Exiles in Mesopotamia in the 8th-6th Centuries BCE," in G. Galil and M. Weinfeld, eds., *Studies in Historical Geography and Biblical Historiography* (Z. Kallai FS; VTSup 81; Leiden: Brill, 2000) 94-99, who also refers to the epigraphic evidence of Israelites in the first two areas.

23. For epigraphic evidence of Israelites in Gozan and other parts of Assyria, see R. Zadok, *The Jews in Babylonia during the Chaldean and Achaemenian Periods according to the Babylonian Sources* (Haifa: University of Haifa Press, 1979) 35-37.

24. Obed, "Settlements," 97.

Nisibis and Adiabene (Hadyav),[25] as the north Mesopotamian area west and east of the Tigris came to be called in the Hellenistic and Roman periods.[26] But although Nisibis and Adiabene became especially important to Jews because of the conversion of the Gentile royal house of Adiabene to Judaism in the early 30s of the first century CE, it seems that after the Assyrian period it was with Media, the third of the areas of settlement of the northern Israelite exiles, that they were most often associated.[27] In the book of Tobit, Tobit and his relatives, depicted as Naphtalites from Galilee, are taken captive to Nineveh (1:10), where he lives throughout the story, as do other Israelites (11:17).[28] But relatives of his live in the cities of Media, Ecbatana and Rhagae (1:14; 3:7; 4:1; 5:6), and after his death his son Tobias takes his family to Media, which is going to prove a safer place to be than Assyria and Babylonia (14:4, 12-15). The impression the book gives is that, subsequent to the fall of Nineveh, Media is where descendants of the exiles of the northern tribes live. No reference is made to the other two areas of settlement mentioned in 2 Kings 17:6 and 18:11.

Writing of the fall of Samaria, Josephus says that its inhabitants were deported to "Media and Persia" (*Ant.* 9.279).[29] Josephus's eastern geography was not good, and he evidently did not know the real identity of the other localities mentioned in 2 Kings 17:6 (just as even the Babylonian rabbis later did not: *b. Qid.* 72a; *b. Yeb.* 16b-17a). But it is notable that his guesswork produces an area even further to the east than Media.[30] In a later passage, whose further implications we shall have to consider later, Josephus makes an interesting addition to the story of the return under Ezra. When Ezra received King Xerxes' let-

---

25. Mann, "Anna," cites a good deal of the evidence for the diaspora in this area and in Media, but consistently treats it as evidence for exiles of the southern tribes, not the northern tribes. It is much more natural to suppose that Jews in these areas in subsequent centuries were descendants of the exiles of the northern tribes.

26. Adiabene was originally the area east of the Tigris, between the Greater Zab and the Lesser Zab rivers, of which Arbela was the principal city, but could also include the area between the Greater Zab and the Tigris, where Nineveh was situated. Later Adiabene increased west of the Tigris, and the city of Nisibis was put under Adiabenian rule in 36 CE (Josephus, *Ant.* 20.68). Nisibis stood on the Mygdonius River, a tributary of the Habor. For Jews in Adiabene and Nisibis, see A. Oppenheimer, *Babylonia Judaica in the Talmudic Period* (Beihefte zur Tübinger Atlas des vorderen Orients B47; Wiesbaden: Reichert, 1983) 21-24, 319-34; J. Neusner, *A History of the Jews in Babylonia*, vol. 1, *The Parthian Period* (SPB 9; rev. ed.; Leiden: Brill, 1969) 13-14.

27. Note that AscIsa 3:2, dependent on 1 Kgs 17:6 and 18:11, refers to "the rivers of Gozan," but gives priority to Media and ignores Halah and Habor.

28. See Obed, "Settlements," 93-94, for epigraphic evidence of Israelites in Nineveh.

29. Cf. also *Sifra* 269:1 (on Lev 26:38): "the ten tribes who went into exile in Media."

30. Perhaps Josephus's eastern geography is vague enough for him to be thinking of the well-known Jewish community in Hyrcania, northeast of Media. Cf. the reference to Parthia in Acts 2:9. There seems to be no evidence of Jewish communities in Persia proper in this period.

ter, permitting the Jews to return with him to Jerusalem, he not only read it to the Jews in Babylonia, but also sent a copy "to his compatriots (ὁμοεθνεῖς) who were in Media." The latter rejoiced to hear the news, and many traveled to Babylon in order to join the return to Jerusalem. "But," comments Josephus, "the nation of the Israelites as a whole remained in the country. In this way it has come about that there are two tribes in Asia and Europe subject to the Romans, and up till now ten tribes beyond the Euphrates, countless myriads whose number cannot be ascertained" (*Ant.* 11.131-33). It is curious that Josephus here gives the impression that all the exiles of the southern tribes in Babylonia returned, leaving only the ten tribes, of whom only a minority returned, to form the eastern diaspora. He certainly knew that there were still descendants of the exiles of Judah in Babylonia. He must mean merely that the majority of Israelites in the eastern diaspora are descendants of the ten tribes, whereas the majority in the western diaspora belong to the two tribes. In any case, it is notable that Media is here the only location of the northern exiles that he mentions. Josephus's exaggerated idea of their numbers results, apparently, from seeking in them the fulfillment of the promise to the patriarchs that their descendants would be innumerable (Gen 13:16; 15:5; 32:12 [MT 13]; Hos 1:10).[31] Media was remote enough from Rome, where he wrote the *Antiquities,* for such an idea to meet no contradiction. But that the descendants of the ten tribes were to be found in Media was something Josephus knew not only from Scripture, but also from the close contacts between Jerusalem and the eastern diaspora in the pre-70 period (see §3 below), of which Josephus would have had direct experience earlier in his life. Finally, among explicit references to the location of the exiles of the northern tribes in Media, mention can be made of *Lives of the Prophets* 3:17, which has Ezekiel prophesy that "the people would not return to its land but would be in Media until the consummation of their error." The passage reflects the same tradition,[32] but we cannot be confident it dates from the Second Temple period.[33] Second Baruch 77:22 locates the nine and a half tribes "over the breadth of the many waters of the Euphrates" (cf. 78:1), which could refer to Adiabene as well as Media.

31. For related interpretations of this promise, see R. Bauckham, *The Climax of Prophecy* (Edinburgh: T. & T. Clark, 1993) 223-24.

32. In view of the specific reference to the tribes of Dan and Gad in LivPro 3:16, there may also be a connection with TAsher 7:6.

33. D. Satran, *Biblical Prophets in Byzantine Palestine: Reassessing the Lives of the Prophets* (SVTP 11; Leiden: Brill, 1995), is critical of most earlier scholarship on the *Lives of the Prophets* and treats it as an early Byzantine Christian work. He allows that it certainly incorporates earlier traditions, but considers that its complex history of redaction makes it virtually impossible to recover such traditions in their earlier form.

Further evidence of the Median diaspora will be discussed in §3 below, where I also note the evidence that, despite their origins in the northern kingdom, many (if not all) of the exiles of the northern tribes in the Second Temple period adopted the same kind of Judaism as their fellow exiles from the southern tribes in Babylonia, that is, they acknowledged the Jerusalem temple and its form of the Torah. For the moment one should note that awareness of tribal membership may be more likely to have survived in the eastern diaspora than in Galilee. In Media the northern exiles formed distinctive communities, intent on preserving their identity in a Gentile context. The book of Tobit depicts the exiles as highly conscious not only of tribe but also of family. The duty to marry within the family is a major concern of the book (1:9; 3:15; 4:12-13). Though the book is fictional, it likely reflects life in the eastern diaspora.[34] Thus an informed reader of Luke could easily think of Anna as a member of an Asherite family that had returned from the diaspora to live in Jerusalem.

d. Jerusalem

Specific evidence of members of the northern tribes resident in Jerusalem in the Second Temple period is sparse, but not completely lacking. First Chronicles 9:2-34 is a version of an account of the inhabitants of Jerusalem that also occurs in a variant form in Nehemiah 11. But whereas Nehemiah 11:4 reads "And in Jerusalem lived some of the Judahites and some of the Benjaminites," the corresponding introductory formula in 1 Chronicles 9:3 adds members of northern tribes: "And some of the people of Judah, Benjamin, Ephraim, and Manasseh lived in Jerusalem." "Ephraim and Manasseh" presumably stand for the whole of the northern kingdom. The purpose is to indicate that members of the whole community of Israel, north and south, were to be found in its center, Jerusalem. The reference to Ephraim and Manasseh is clearly a redactional addition that has no support from the detail of the rest of the account, in which members only of the tribes of Judah, Benjamin, and Levi appear. Further assessment of this addition depends on whether, as most commentators suppose, the chapter is intended by the Chronicler to depict the postexilic community after the return from the Babylonian exile (certainly the original intention of

---

34. G. W. E. Nickelsburg, "Stories of Biblical and Early Post-Biblical Times," in M. E. Stone, ed., *Jewish Writings of the Second Temple Period* (CRINT 2/2; Assen: Van Gorcum; Philadelphia: Fortress, 1984) 45. On tribal and family structures in Tobit, see P. Deselaers, *Das Buch Tobit: Studien zur seiner Entstehung, Komposition und Theologie* (OBO 43; Freiburg: Universitätsverlag; Göttingen: Vandenhoeck & Ruprecht, 1982) 309-20, though he argues for an Egyptian Jewish origin.

the main source document; cf. Neh 11), or whether, as Sara Japhet argues, the Chronicler intends the account to depict Jerusalem in the time of David.[35] In the latter case, 9:2 can be translated: "Now those who dwelled of old in their possessions in their towns. . . ." In the former case, this verse ("Now the first dwellers in their possessions . . .") is to be understood in the light of the reference to the exile of Judah in verse 1b, and refers to those who first lived in Judah after the return. If the account depicts Jerusalem in David's time, then the reference to Ephraim and Manasseh, reflecting the Chronicler's view that Jerusalem had always been the center of all Israel, is of no relevance to our inquiry. If the account depicts postexilic Jerusalem, then the addition of Ephraim and Manasseh reflects the Chronicler's conviction of the continuing role of Jerusalem as a center for Israelite unity, down to his own time: "Following the Chronicler's portrayal of the restoration of Israel's unity under Hezekiah [2 Chron 30], he is anxious to emphasise that the later community was representative of all Israel, not just the former southern kingdom alone, so that it would act as a nucleus for a return of any who had a legitimate claim to participation."[36]

In the latter case, we can scarcely determine from the Chronicler's text whether the reference to members of northern tribes resident in postexilic Jerusalem is wholly ideal or corresponded in any degree to historical fact. But two later writers share the same conception. The Letter of Aristeas, in its fictional account of the origin of the Septuagint, recounts how Eleazar the high priest in Jerusalem was able to carry out King Ptolemy's request that he select six men from each of the twelve tribes and send them to Egypt to be the translators of the Torah into Greek (32, 39, 46-50). While this is interesting evidence that an Egyptian Jewish writer of the late Second Temple period could suppose that members of all twelve tribes of Israel lived in Jerusalem, no confidence can be placed in this writer's knowledge of the real situation in Jerusalem.[37] But it is otherwise with Josephus, who knew Jerusalem well.

We have already noticed how, in his account of the return under Ezra,

---

35. Japhet, *Chronicles*, 207-8.

36. Williamson, *Chronicles*, 88-89; cf. idem, *Israel in the Books of Chronicles* (Cambridge: Cambridge University Press, 1977) 140; T. Willi, "Late Persian Judaism and Its Conception of an Integral Israel according to Chronicles," in Eskenazi and Richards, eds., *Second Temple Studies*, 2:146-62.

37. N. G. Cohen, "The Names of the Translators in the Letter of Aristeas: A Study in the Dynamics of Cultural Transition," *JJS* 15 (1984) 62, defends the possible historicity of the division of the list of translators into twelve tribes, on the grounds that it could be purely formal and has Greek parallels, and she relevantly points out that the tribes are not named. But she seems to accept the erroneous assumption that "the 12 tribes of Israel had long ago disappeared."

Josephus adds to the biblical account (1 Esdr 8)[38] the information that Ezra invited the exiles of the northern tribes in Media to join the return, and that "many of them" actually did (*Ant.* 11.131-32). Why should Josephus have expanded the biblical account in this way? It is possible that he made an exegetical deduction. He may have read 1 Chronicles 9:3 as a reference to the inhabitants of postexilic Jerusalem, and wished to explain how they included returnees from the northern tribes. But the verse is too obscure to make this likely. More plausible is the possibility that Josephus noticed that the list of those who returned with Ezra consists, after reference to two Aaronide leaders and one Davidic leader (1 Esdr 8:29 = Ezra 8:2-3a), of a list of the number of returnees from each of twelve families (1 Esdr 8:30-40 = Ezra 8:3b-14). He could have supposed that these twelve families must correspond to the twelve tribes of Israel: one family from each tribe.[39] However, there is a problem with this explanation. Several of these twelve families (Parosh, Pahath-moab, Zattu, Adin) occur in a passage of the Mishnah (*m. Ta'an.* 4:5, where all are said to be families of the tribe of Judah) that lists the families entitled to supply the wood offering to the temple. Both these and other families in the list also occur in other lists in Ezra and Nehemiah, but it does not seem that the passage in the Mishnah depends directly on any such biblical source. It may well be evidence that these families continued to be prominent Jerusalem families late in the Second Temple period. In that case Josephus, himself a member of the Jerusalem priestly aristocracy, would have known these families, and known that several of the families in the list of twelve families that returned with Ezra were Judahite and Benjaminite families. So it may be that Josephus's addition of members of the northern tribes to the return under Ezra was based not on exegetical deduction, but on his own knowledge that there were, in his time, Jerusalem families who claimed descent from Israelite families of the Median diaspora. He therefore included their forebears in the return under Ezra.

This cannot be said to be strong evidence for families of northern tribal descent resident in Second Temple Jerusalem, but we do know of one historical individual in this category. Rabbi Nahum the Mede was remembered in rabbinic tradition as active in Jerusalem in the last years of the Second Temple (*m. Naz.* 5:4; *b. Ket.* 105a; other references to him are *m. Shab.* 2:1; *m. B. Bat.* 5:2; *b. 'Abod. Zar.* 7b). Whether or not the content of the traditions is otherwise his-

---

38. Josephus depends on 1 Esdras rather than Ezra.

39. No doubt the twelve families are intended to correspond symbolically to the number of the tribes of Israel, but probably "it suggests not so much that Ezra was aiming to reunite all the remnants of former Israel . . . as that he regarded his own more restricted community as the sole legitimate representative and heir of Israel" (H. G. M. Williamson, *Ezra, Nehemiah* [WBC 16; Waco: Word, 1985] 111).

torically reliable, it is reasonable to suppose that they accurately locate him in Jerusalem.[40] For him to have been known as "the Mede," either he or his parents must have moved to Jerusalem from Media. He has the distinction of being the one member of the Median diaspora in the Second Temple period whose name has been preserved,[41] unless, as I shall argue, Anna and her father Phanuel were also historical persons in this category.

3. Jerusalem and the Median Diaspora

So far I have established that a competent contemporary reader of Luke 2:36 might have supposed Anna to belong to a Galilean family and to have moved to Jerusalem, but that he or she is perhaps more likely to have supposed that Anna or her family must have moved to Jerusalem from the eastern diaspora of the northern tribes. To support the latter possibility, we must now present wider evidence for contacts between Jerusalem and the Median diaspora in the later Second Temple period.

With the exception of Hyrcania, which lay beyond Media, Media was, among major diaspora communities, the least accessible from Jerusalem, since, although the distance was not greater than that to many parts of the western diaspora, the journey had to be made entirely by land. The perceived remoteness of Media is reflected in a rabbinic tradition about a rabbi[42] in Palestine whose father died in Ginzaq (the town of Gazaca[43] in Media Atropatene, the most western part of Media). Since the news of his father's death took three years to reach him, a halakic question about how he should conduct the mourning arose (*b. Mo'ed Q.* 20a; *b. Naz.* 44a; *b. Ṣem.* 12:2).[44] Nevertheless the remoteness of Media did not prevent contact with Jerusalem. No doubt some pilgrims from Media made the journey to festivals in the temple, as Acts 2:9 claims. More

40. J. Neusner, *The Rabbinic Traditions about the Pharisees before 70*, vol. 1 (Leiden: Brill, 1971) 413-14, accepts that he was active in pre-70 Jerusalem.

41. From a later period, there is Benjamin of Ginzaq (*t. Ber.* 2:5b), the Median city of Gazaca or Ganzaca (Oppenheimer, *Babylonia*, 120-26). One should also note that the use of the name Hyrcanus among Palestinian Jews in the later Second Temple period (2 Macc 3:11; the Hasmonean rulers Hyrcanus I and II; Rabbi Eliezer ben Hyrcanus) probably derived from families returning to Palestine from the exile in Hyrcania. But most of the exiles in Hyrcania were probably members of the southern tribes, deported by Artaxerxes III Ochus in the fourth century BCE (E. Schürer, *The History of the Jewish People in the Age of Jesus Christ (175 B.C.–A.D. 135)*, rev. by G. Vermes, F. Millar, and M. Goodman, vol. 3/1 [Edinburgh: T. & T. Clark, 1986] 6).

42. His name is variously given as Zadok and Isaac.

43. The site cannot be confidently identified; see Oppenheimer, *Babylonia*, 123-24.

44. For the remoteness of Media, cf. also *m. B. Qam.* 9:5; *m. B. Meṣ.* 4:7.

would have sent their temple tax (cf. *m. Sheq.* 3:4; Philo, *Leg. ad Gai.* 216), which by helping to finance the daily burnt offerings ensured their participation in the temple cult despite their physical distance from it. Josephus recounts (*Ant.* 18.311-13; cf. 379) how the two cities of Nehardea and Nisibis served as the collecting points for the temple tax contributions from the eastern diaspora, where the resulting huge sums of money could be kept safe until they were conveyed to Jerusalem along with the caravans of pilgrims, whom Josephus numbers at tens of thousands. Nehardea was the most important center of the Jewish exiles in Babylonia, located on the Euphrates to the west of Seleucia and Ctesiphon. Because Josephus appears to locate Nisibis on the Euphrates near Nehardea (*Ant.* 18.311), many scholars have saved his geographical accuracy by supposing it to be not the famous Nisibis in northern Mesopotamia, but another, otherwise unknown Nisibis near Nehardea.[45] It is more likely, however, that Josephus makes a geographical mistake. Rather than two collecting points for the tax contributions in close proximity, it would make sense that for the eastern diaspora as a whole there was one (Nehardea) in southern Mesopotamia and another (Nisibis) in northern Mesopotamia.[46] The latter would be the natural center where the exiles in Adiabene and northern Mesopotamia would send their tax and gather for making the journey to Jerusalem, but it would also serve the Median diaspora, being located on the main route from Media to Jerusalem.

Jewish leaders in Jerusalem kept in touch with the diaspora by means of circular letters.[47] One such letter, preserved in rabbinic sources, is ascribed to Gamaliel the Elder, the early-first-century Pharisee, and declares the intercalation of a month in that year. It is preserved with other letters of Gamaliel,[48] on different but similar subjects, to various parts of the land of Israel (*t. Sanh.* 2:6; *y. Sanh.* 1:2 [18d]; *y. Ma'as. Sh.* 5:4 [56c]; *b. Sanh.* 11a-b).[49] Since a calendrical

---

45. E.g., Schürer, *History*, 3/1:8; Oppenheimer, *Babylonia*, 333-34.

46. Neusner, *History*, 13-14, 47n.2.

47. See R. Bauckham, "James and the Jerusalem Church," in R. Bauckham, ed., *The Book of Acts in Its Palestinian Setting* (Grand Rapids: Eerdmans; Carlisle: Paternoster, 1995) 423-25; I. Taatz, *Frühjüdische Briefe: Die paulinischen Briefe im Rahman der offiziellen religiösen Briefe des Frühjudentums* (NTAC 16; Freiburg: Universitätsverlag; Göttingen: Vandenhoeck & Ruprecht, 1991).

48. Gamaliel the Elder, rather than his grandson Gamaliel II of Yavneh (as supposed in *b. Sanh.* 11a), is certainly intended: see S. D. Sperling, "Fragments of Tannaitic Letters Preserved in Rabbinic Literature," in D. Pardee, *Handbook of Ancient Hebrew Letters* (SBLSBS 15; Chico, Calif.: Scholars Press, 1982) 195-96.

49. Translations and discussion in Neusner, *Rabbinic Traditions*, 356-58, 360, 361, 368, 372-73; Sperling, "Fragments," 191-96. Letters of the same type are ascribed to Gamaliel's son Simeon, along with Yohanan ben Zakkai (including: "we have not begun to write to you, but our fa-

matter of this kind would have been the responsibility of the temple authorities, the letter is somewhat problematic, but there seems no reason for such a letter to have been invented[50] and good reasons for accepting the authenticity of the group of letters to which it belongs. Perhaps Gamaliel, as a Pharisaic member of the high priest's council (cf. Acts 5:34), writes to Jews of Pharisaic allegiance in the diaspora.[51] Whether or not the letter as it stands is authentic, we can be sure that such letters were regularly sent,[52] as more general references to communications from the temple authorities to the diaspora on calendrical and other matters confirm (*m. Rosh. HaSh.* 1:3-4; *m. Ohol.* 17:5; Acts 28:21). Gamaliel's letter is addressed to "our brothers belonging to the exile of Babylonia and belonging to the exile of Media and all the other exiles of Israel" (*t. Sanh.* 2:6; the version in *y. Sanh.* 1:2 [18d] adds "belonging to the exile of Greece"), a formula notable for its recognition of the distinct identity and importance of the Median diaspora. In the period after the destruction of the temple, the developing rabbinic movement took care to preserve and to consolidate its links with the diaspora, partly by means of journeys by leading Palestinian rabbis to major parts of the diaspora. Aqiba's travels are said to have included a visit to Ginzaq in Media (*b. 'Abod. Zar.* 34a, 39a; *b. Ta'an.* 11b; *b. Ber.* 8b; Gen. Rab. 33:5).[53]

All these references to the Median diaspora take for granted its allegiance to the Jerusalem temple and Jerusalem's version of the Torah, as does Josephus, *Ant.* 11.131-33 (discussed in §2 above). We do not know how and when these descendants of the northern tribes adopted this Jerusalem-centered version of

---

thers used to write to your fathers"), though not in this case to the diaspora: see Neusner, *Rabbinic Traditions*, 1:378-79; Sperling, "Fragments," 187-91.

50. Since the letter refers to sacrificial animals and its point is to warn diaspora Jews not to make the pilgrimage to Jerusalem a month too early, its subject matter would not be that of later letters from the rabbinic authorities to the diaspora.

51. Neusner, *Rabbinic Traditions*, 1:358-59, suggests this, but doubts there were Pharisees in Babylonia and Media (the named destinations in *t. Sanh.* 2:6), and concludes the letter must be authentic, "but I do not know who would have received it." He may be too skeptical about the presence of Pharisees in the eastern diaspora at this date; cf. Josephus, *Ant.* 20.43.

52. Cf. P. S. Alexander, "Epistolary Literature," in Stone, ed., *Jewish Writings*, 581n.14: "Whether or not the attributions are accurate, letters such as these were undoubtedly sent out by the religious authorities in Jerusalem, and it is very probable that the letters before us accurately reflect those letters' general formulae and style."

53. The skepticism expressed about Aqiba's alleged travels in the diaspora by P. Schäfer, "Rabbi Aqiva and Bar Kokhba," in W. S. Green, ed., *Approaches to Ancient Judaism*, vol. 2 (BJS 9; Chico, Calif.: Scholars Press, 1980) 114-17, is mainly directed at casting doubt on the theory that they were concerned with preparing for the Bar Kokhba revolt. Since Ginzaq is mentioned in only three other rabbinic traditions (Oppenheimer, *Babylonia*, 121), it seems likely that Aqiba's visit there is historical.

their religion, aligning them with their fellow exiles from Judah in Babylonia, but the probability is that they did so in the Persian period. The book of Tobit may offer some insight into their conversion to Jerusalem, and indeed may have been partly instrumental in securing it. The book is oriented to the situation of the northern Israelite exiles in Media[54] but also strongly advocates the cultic centrality of Jerusalem. Inspired both by Deuteronomy[55] and the prophets, it attributes the exile of the northern tribes to their apostasy from the house of David and the Jerusalem temple and their idolatrous worship at Dan and elsewhere (1:4-5), and sees their sufferings as fulfilling the prophecies that predicted the judgment of northern Israel for their sins (2:6; 3:4; 14:4); it offers the Jerusalem-centered piety of Tobit himself as a model (1:6-8); it expects the repentance of the Israelite exiles to lead to their return to the land, when Jerusalem will be restored and glorified, as predicted in Deutero- and Trito-Isaiah (13:3-17; 14:5-7); and it takes the fulfillment of Nahum's prophecy of the destruction of Assyria and Nineveh as the evidence that "everything that was spoken by the prophets of Israel, whom God sent, will occur" (14:4; cf. 14:15).[56] The whole amounts to an argument that, just as the northern Israelite exiles have seen the fulfillment of the prophecies of Moses and the prophets in their own punishment and in the punishment of their adversary Assyria, so, if they repent, they can expect the restoration of all the tribes in the land, as these same prophets predicted. But this interpretation of both past and future is tied up with the centrality of Jerusalem, as promoted by Deuteronomy and the prophets. We can well imagine Israelites in Media finding inspiration and hope in the book of Tobit and in its reading of the Law and the Prophets, and finding in Jerusalem a welcome symbolic focus both of national-religious identity in the diaspora and of hope for a better future. The Samaritan schism, occurring after these links with Jerusalem were well established, would have affected them no more than it did Galilee's attachment to Jerusalem.

In the light of the close contacts between the Median diaspora and Jerusa-

---

54. For an examination of alleged difficulties in the view that Tobit was written in the eastern diaspora, see Additional Note B at the end of this chapter.

55. For the decisive influence of Deuteronomy on the theology of Tobit, see A. A. di Lella, "The Deuteronomic Background of the Farewell Discourse in Tob 14:3-11," *CBQ* 41 (1979) 380-89; and cf. S. Weitzman, "Allusion, Artifice, and Exile in the Hymn of Tobit," *JBL* 115 (1996) 49-61, for the correspondence of Tob 12–13 with Deut 31–32.

56. Quotations from Tobit in this essay are usually from NRSV, which translates the Greek text in Codex Sinaiticus. I follow most recent scholars in accepting the superiority of the recension of Tobit represented by Sinaiticus and the Old Latin. The five fragmentary copies of Tobit from Qumran, four in Aramaic (4Q196-199) and one in Hebrew (4Q200), now strongly confirm this judgment.

lem that we have observed, and in the light of the cultic and eschatological centrality of Jerusalem in the religion Median exiles shared with the rest of the diaspora, we can readily suppose that in the later Second Temple period there were families and individuals who moved from Media to take up permanent residence in Jerusalem, just as there were many such who migrated to Jerusalem from all other parts of the western and eastern diasporas.[57] Once again, it is clear that to an informed contemporary reader there would be nothing at all "puzzling" about Anna's presence in Jerusalem.

4. Anna, Phanuel, and the Book of Tobit

Anna's name ("Αννα for חנה, Hannah) may be a further indication that she is more likely to be a returnee from the Median diaspora than a Galilean settled in Jerusalem. Only one woman in the Hebrew Bible/Old Testament bears this name (the mother of Samuel, 1 Sam 1–2), while epigraphic evidence yields one other example from preexilic Israel (a seal from Lachish, late eighth or early seventh century BCE).[58] Thereafter the name is unknown in Palestine until the third and fourth centuries CE, when four examples are found in Greek inscriptions from Beth She'arim (CIJ 1013, 1014, 1088) and Joppa (CIJ 907).[59] Of the 247 Jewish women in Palestine from the period 330 BCE–200 CE whose names are known, our Anna is the only one who bears this name.[60] Evidence for the diaspora supplies one or two examples of the name from the third-fourth century CE, from

57. For Jews originating from the western diaspora and resident in Jerusalem, see Acts 5:36-37; 6:1, 5, 9; 21:16; Mark 15:21; the Theodotus inscription (on which see now R. Riesner, "Synagogues in Jerusalem," in Bauckham, ed., Book of Acts, 192-200); J. P. Kane, "The Ossuary Inscriptions of Jerusalem," JSS 23 (1978) 276-82; E. Bammel, "Nicanor and his Gate," in E. Bammel, Judaica (WUNT 37; Tübingen: Mohr [Siebeck], 1986) 39-41. For immigrants from Babylonia see J. Jeremias, Jerusalem in the Time of Jesus, tr. F. H. and C. H. Cave (Philadelphia: Fortress; London: SCM, 1969) 66-67; and the Giv'at ha-Mivtar inscription (M. Sokoloff, "The Giv'at ha-Mivtar Aramaic Tomb Inscription in Paleo-Hebrew Script and its Historical Implications," Imm 10 [1980] 38-46). For members of the Adiabenian royal family, after their conversion to Judaism, residing in Jerusalem, see Josephus, Ant. 20.49-51, 71, 94-95; BJ 4.567; 5.252-53; 6.355; m. Naz. 3:6.

58. J. R. Bartlett, "The Seal of Ḥnh from the Neighbourhood of Tell ed-Duweir," PEQ 108 (1976) 59-61.

59. Also around the late fourth century lived Hannah, the wife of Rabbi Mani b. Yona (b. Ta'an. 24a), if her name can be considered historical. G. Mayer, Die jüdische Frau in der hellenistisch-römischen Antike (Stuttgart: Kohlhammer, 1987) 103, mistakenly locates her in Babylonia. Mani was a Palestinian rabbi who lived at Sepphoris.

60. T. Ilan, "Notes on the Distribution of Jewish Women's Names in Palestine in the Second Temple and Mishnaic Periods," JJS 40 (1989) 186, 193.

Rome (*CIJ* 411 = *JIWE*[61] 2:10; perhaps *CIJ* 211 = *JIWE* 2:245),[62] and two or three later examples from Italy (*CIJ* 614 = *JIWE* 1:90: sixth century; *CIJ* 634 = *JIWE* 1:195: eighth century; perhaps *CIJ* 575 = *JIWE* 1:72:[63] fifth century).

The absence of the name from Palestine in the period 330 BCE–200 CE is not surprising. Palestinian Jews generally did not use biblical names simply because they were the names of prominent biblical figures. For example, the many Palestinian Jewish women who were named Miriam (Mariamme, Maria) were named not after Moses' sister, but after Herod's wife, the Hasmonean princess Mariamne, just as the equally popular Palestinian woman's name Salome/Salomezion (not used in the diaspora) owed its popularity in Palestine to the Hasmonean queen of that name.[64] The only women's names in use because of their use in the Hebrew Bible/Old Testament seem to be Sarah (6 examples), Leah (2 examples), and perhaps Elizabeth (2 examples, including Luke 1:5).[65] These examples make it possible that Anna could have been a Palestinian woman's name in this period, but the possibility is stronger for the diaspora. The Jewish onomastica of Palestine and the diaspora differed markedly,[66] and there was a much stronger tendency in the diaspora to use biblical names because of their association with important figures in biblical history.[67] There parents were more likely to think of naming a daughter after Hannah the mother of Samuel — or perhaps, in the eastern diaspora, after Hannah the wife of Tobit.

There is more than this to be learned from the names of Anna and her father Phanuel. But first we must consider the name of the only other named person from the northern Israelite diaspora in the Second Temple period that we know (apart from the fictional characters in Tobit): Nahum the Mede. His

61. This abbreviation designates the two volumes of D. Noy, *Jewish Inscriptions of Western Europe,* vol. 1, *Italy (excluding the City of Rome), Spain and Gaul* (Cambridge: Cambridge University Press, 1993); vol. 2, *The City of Rome* (Cambridge: Cambridge University Press, 1995).

62. In this Latin inscription the name "Ann[. . .]" could be restored as Anna or as the Latin name Annia (borne by a Jewish woman in *CIJ* 300 = *JIWE* 2:15).

63. The name Ἄvα could be a spelling of Ἄννα, or it could be the male name חנא. In *CIJ* 598 = *JIWE* 1:65 (fifth-sixth century) Ἄνας could be the genitive of Ἄvα or the beginning of Ἀναστασίου.

64. Ilan, "Notes," 192. Most of the most popular male names among Palestinian Jews were also those borne by the Hasmoneans; see T. Ilan, "The Names of the Hasmoneans in the Second Temple Period," *ErIsr* 19 (1987) 238-41 (Hebrew).

65. Ilan, "Notes," 197, also gives one example each of Michal and Rachel, but these are in late rabbinic sources of dubious historicity.

66. See M. H. Williams, "Palestinian Jewish Personal Names in Acts," in Bauckham, ed., *Book of Acts,* 79-113.

67. For women's names see Mayer, *Jüdische Frau,* 39-40.

name is so appropriate that, were he not clearly historical (were he, for example, to be found in Luke's infancy narrative), we should probably consider him a fictional character named by his author for the sake of the significance of the name. This name, though common on preexilic seals,[68] occurs in the Hebrew Bible/Old Testament only as the name of the prophet Nahum, who prophesied God's judgment on Nineveh and whose prophecy therefore features significantly in Tobit (14:4, 15). Although Nineveh was destroyed six centuries before Nahum the Mede lived, the prophecy of Nahum would still have been of special significance for the Israelite exiles in Media, especially if they read it in the light of Tobit. The fulfillment of Nahum's prophecy of the downfall of Nineveh would be for them the guarantee of the fulfillment of prophecies still unfulfilled, notably the return of the Israelites Assyria had deported from their land (Tob 14:4-7). Moreover, the name Nahum refers to the hope of the regathering of the tribes also because of its meaning: "comfort, consolation" (נחום, from נחם). The verb נחם (in the Piel, "to comfort") is used repeatedly in Isaiah 40–66 with reference to God's salvific action to restore the exiles to the land and to restore Jerusalem to glory (Isa 40:1; 49:13; 51:3, 12; 52:9; 61:2; 66:13; cf. Jer 31:13; Zech 1:17; 2 Bar 44:7). Its opening repetition (Isa 40:1) forms virtually a rubric for the whole Deutero- and Trito-Isaianic prophecy of the restoration of Israel after exile. Consequently, in later rabbinic usage "comfort, consolation" (נחמה) is a comprehensive term for the messianic salvation,[69] and this usage can already be seen in Luke 2:25 (Simeon is "looking forward to the consolation [παράκλησιν] of Israel").[70] It would be difficult to think of a name more appropriate than Nahum to encapsulate the hopes of the exiles of Media. Perhaps for this reason it had become a common name among them. Or perhaps the parents of Nahum the Mede, pious Israelites who saw their own return to Jerusalem as a precursor of the return of all their fellow exiles, gave him this name as an indication of their hope that he would see the consolation of the exiles of Israel.

The names of Phanuel (Φανουηλ) and his daughter Anna (Luke 2:36) can be seen in the same light. The Hebrew name Penuel or Peniel, meaning "the face of God,"[71] occurs in the Hebrew Bible/Old Testament only in the genealo-

---

68. L. Y. Rahmani, *A Catalogue of Jewish Ossuaries in the Collections of the State of Israel* (Jerusalem: Israel Antiquities Authority, and Israel Academy of Sciences and Humanities, 1994) 200-201. The name also occurs on an ossuary from Mount Scopus: Rahmani no. 571 (p. 200).

69. Str-B 2:124-26; cf. also 2 Bar 44:7; 4 Ezra 10:20, 49.

70. Probably Luke 2:25 and 38 reflect Isa 52:9: "the Lord has comforted (נחם) his people, he has redeemed (גאל) Jerusalem." Luke (or his source) has apportioned these two descriptions of Israel's hope to Simeon and Anna, respectively. Note, however, that these verses in Luke do not reflect the LXX of Isa 52:9.

71. This is certainly the meaning that the name would have had in the Second Temple pe-

gies in 1 Chronicles 4:4 (פנואל, LXX Φανουηλ) and 8:25 (פניאל or פנואל,[72] LXX Φελιηλ or Φανουηλ). The only other occurrence in the biblical period is on an ostracon from Beersheba, from the end of the eighth century BCE (פנאל).[73] I have found no later occurrence other than Luke 2:36. But the "face" of God, often used in the Hebrew Bible/Old Testament as a metaphor for God's favor, appears in a number of key passages in connection with the theme of exile and return. In Deuteronomy 31:17-18 and 32:20, God's threat to judge the people if they turn to other gods is expressed as: "I will hide my face from them" (cf. also Mic 3:4; Isa 54:8). Conversely, in Psalm 80, a psalm that would be easily understood as a prayer for God to restore the northern tribes (cf. v 2 [MT 3]) to the land, this refrain occurs three times (vv 3, 7, 19 [MT 4, 8, 20]): "Restore us, O [Lord] God [of hosts]; let your face shine, that we may be saved." God's face shining on the exiles is his favor bringing them back from exile to the land of Israel. Similarly, Hezekiah's letter to the inhabitants of northern Israel who remain in the land after the Assyrian conquest (2 Chron 30:6-9) urges them to return to the Lord, so that he may return to them and so that their kinsfolk in exile may return to the land. It concludes: "For the Lord your God is gracious and merciful, and will not turn away his face from you, if you will return to him." Finally, Daniel's prayer for the restoration of Jerusalem asks: "let your face shine upon your desolated sanctuary" (Dan 9:17).

The positive use of the image of God's favor as his face shining (Ps 80:3, 7, 19 [MT 4, 8, 20]; Dan 9:17) recalls the priestly blessing: "The Lord make his face to shine upon you, and be gracious to you (ויחנך)" (Num 6:25; cf. Ps 67:1 [MT 2], which in the later Second Temple period would have been read as a prayer for eschatological salvation). Here the verb חנן ("to show favor, to be gracious") is used in parallel with the image of the face of God shining. Thus the name Penuel, used to evoke the image of God's face shining on the exiles to restore them to the land, can be easily linked with the name Hannah (חנה), which means "[God's] grace." As with the name Nahum, it could be that these two names were in common use in the Median diaspora because they expressed the hope of restoration, or it could be that they were chosen specifically and deliberately within this family of returnees.

Just as we connected the significance of the name Nahum, borne by Nahum the Mede, in part with the importance attached to Nahum's prophecy in the book of Tobit, it may be that we should also press the significance of the

---

riod. For other possibilities cf. R. Zadok, *The Pre-Hellenistic Israelite Anthroponymy and Prosopography* (Orientalia Lovanensia Analecta 28; Leuven: Peeters, 1988) 46.

72. Cf. the same variation in Gen 32:30-31 (MT 31-32), where it occurs as a place name.

73. Zadok, *Pre-Hellenistic Israelite Anthroponymy*, 282.

names Phanuel and Anna a little further by noticing their possible connection with Tobit. That Anna is the name of a major character in that book, the wife of Tobit, is only the starting point for observing this connection. We need to notice three relevant features of the book.

First, the two parallel personal stories of Tobit and his niece Sarah, which make up the plot of the book, function as parables of the national story of the exiled northern tribes.[74] Both Tobit and Sarah are afflicted and then delivered by God's mercy, but the parabolic significance of this pattern is made clear especially in Tobit's case. Tobit suffers not because of his own sins but because of the sins of his ancestors and kindred in northern Israel (3:3-5). The quotation of Amos's oracle "against Bethel" in 2:6 (Amos 8:10) is far from merely decorative; it indicates that Tobit suffers with his fellow exiles the sorrows that Amos predicted as judgment on the northern tribes for forsaking Jerusalem and worshiping at Bethel. The healing of Tobit's blindness occasions his prophetic psalm foretelling the restoration of the exiles and of Jerusalem (chap. 13) because he sees his affliction and deliverance as paradigmatic of God's dealings with his people.[75] The key to this lies in the statement that "God afflicts and he shows mercy" (13:2), modeled, like much in Tobit's theology, on the later chapters of Deuteronomy (32:39) and Deutero-Isaiah (Isa 54:7-8). This general statement of the pattern of God's activity is applied to Tobit himself (11:15: "Though he afflicted me, he has had mercy on me"), to "the children of Israel" (13:5a: "He afflicted you for your iniquities, but he will again show mercy on all of you"; cf. 14:5), with reference to the return from exile (13:5b), and to Jerusalem (13:9: "He afflicted you for the deeds of your hands, but will again have mercy on the children of the righteous").[76] This pattern therefore links Tobit's story with the promise of restoration of the northern Israelite exiles and the latter also with the restoration of Jerusalem.

Second, that the personal story of Tobit has national significance for the Israelite exiles means that the names of the characters, which, as has often been

74. The parallels are set out in Nickelsburg, "Stories," 42.

75. The theory of F. Zimmermann, *The Book of Tobit* (Jewish Apocryphal Literature; New York: Harper, 1958) that chaps. 13 and 14 are additions made to the book after 70 CE has now been disproved by the Qumran Aramaic and Hebrew fragments of Tobit (4Q196-200), which include fragments of these chapters. But, in any case, the theory was based on a failure to see that the parallel between Tobit's personal story and the destiny of the nation is integral to the design and message of the whole book. For the same reason, the complex redactional theory of Deselaers, *Tobit,* is redundant, as well as unverifiably speculative.

76. Perhaps Tobit's experience should be seen as parabolic of God's affliction of and mercy to the exiles, while Sarah's experience is parabolic of God's affliction of and mercy to Jerusalem. But 14:9-17 does not develop the feminine and nuptial imagery that could have been used of Jerusalem.

observed, have been chosen for their meaning, also have significance not just for the personal story but also for the eschatological hope for the exiles that is the book's overarching concern. Many of the names evoke ideas of God's favor and salvation. Tobias (טוביה)[77] and Tobit (טובי),[78] an abbreviated form of the same name,[79] not only mean "YHWH is good," but allude to Nahum 1:7 ("YHWH is good [טוב יהוה],[80] a stronghold in a day of trouble; he protects those who take refuge in him"), a verse that expresses the positive aspect, in relation to God's people, of Nahum's message of judgment on Nineveh. The name of the angel Raphael means "God has healed," while Azariah, the name he assumes when he takes part in the story incognito, means "YHWH has helped." Several names contain the root חנן ("to show favor, to be gracious"): Hananiel ("God is gracious," 1:1), Hananiah ("YHWH has shown favor," 5:13-14), Hanael ("the grace of God," 1:21), and, most notably, Hannah/Anna ("[God's] grace," 1:20; 2:1; etc.). Thus the name Anna is used in Tobit in this context of names expressing hope for God's gracious restoration of the repentant exiles, along with his restoration of Jerusalem, to which they will be gathered.

Third, the image of the face of God plays a significant part in Tobit, though this would not be apparent on rapid or superficial reading. In 13:6 ("If you turn to him . . . he will turn to you and will no longer hide his face from you") it relates closely to the passages in the Hebrew Bible/Old Testament cited above (Deut 31:17-18; 32:20; Isa 54:8; 2 Chron 30:9; Ps 80:3, 7, 19 [MT 4, 8, 20]) that connect the image with judgment, exile, and restoration. In Tobit's prayer in 3:6 ("do not, O Lord, turn your face away from me"), Tobit's personal affliction is by means of this image put in parallel to the affliction and salvation of the people. Finally, the image is used in the wisdom parenesis of chapter 4: "Do not turn your face away from anyone who is poor, and the face of God will not be turned away from you" (4:7b).[81] This relates it to another central theme of the book: the redemptive power of almsgiving (4:6-11, 16; 12:8-10; 14:8-11). This is not at all unconnected with the overarching theme of national redemption.

---

77. This name itself, of course, is common. For a prominent member of the Babylonian diaspora bearing this name, see Zadok, *Jews*, 54-55, 62-64.

78. That the Greek Τωβίτ represents טובי is now made certain by the Qumran fragments of Tobit.

79. Note also Tobiel ("God is good") (Tob 1:1): three generations of the family bear variants of the same name.

80. Note that the LXX renders: "The Lord is good to those who wait for him in the day of affliction. . . ."

81. Cf. Prov 21:13, which applies a comparable form of *lex talionis* to the same situation. If Tob 4:7b recasts Prov 21:13, then it is especially significant that it does so in terms of the image of turning away the face.

In Tobit's hope it is especially by practicing almsgiving that the Israelite exiles will turn to God and obey him, with the result that he will turn to them and restore them. If they do not turn their face from the poor, God will no longer turn his face from them.

It seems possible therefore that the names Anna and Phanuel belong to an exilic family deeply impressed by the eschatological piety of the book of Tobit. Such a suggestion coheres well with the rest of Luke's characterization of Anna. Indeed, it is precisely the theology and message of the book of Tobit that forges the closest connection between Anna's membership of a northern Israelite tribe, her temple-centered piety (Luke 2:37), and her association with those who were looking for the redemption of Jerusalem (2:38). No doubt the last group included others who have returned from the diaspora to await in Jerusalem the messianic redemption and the ingathering of the rest of the exiles.

5. Anna in Gospel and History

In terms of the contribution of Luke's account of Anna to the meaning of the larger narrative in which it occurs, Anna's membership of the tribe of Asher is by no means as insignificant as commentators usually suppose. A major purpose of the first two chapters of the Gospel is to embed the beginning of Jesus' story in the community of God's people Israel, whose own story reaches back to the patriarchs, and in particular to place the beginning of Jesus' story in the context of that community's hopes for messianic redemption. As a descendant of the exiles of the tribe of Asher, Anna ensures that the community represented in the narrative is Israel as a whole, northern tribes as well as southern, exiles as well as inhabitants of the land. She ensures that the messianic hopes represented include those of the northern tribes and the exiles.

As has often been observed, Simeon and Anna form one of the pairs of man and woman of which Luke is fond.[82] But Anna's role complements Simeon's in more respects than this. Simeon, presumably a native of Jerusalem, waiting for the consolation of Israel (2:25), hails the Messiah Jesus as the one who will fulfill Israel's destiny to be a light to the nations (2:31-32). He represents the hope of the centrifugal movement of salvation out from Jerusalem to the Gentiles. Anna, a returnee from the diaspora of the northern tribes, waiting for the redemption of Jerusalem (2:38),[83] recognizes the Messiah Jesus as the one

---

82. See T. K. Seim, *The Double Message: Patterns of Gender in Luke-Acts* (Nashville: Abindgon; Edinburgh: T. & T. Clark, 1994) 11-24, for a thorough discussion of this phenomenon.

83. For the probable derivation of the two phrases "the consolation of Israel" and "the re-

who will fulfill Jerusalem's destiny to be the center to which all the tribes of Israel are regathered. She represents the hope of the centripetal movement of salvation as the diaspora returns to Zion.[84] Thus together Simeon and Anna represent these two key aspects of the eschatological salvation predicted in Isaiah 40–66.

This much an informed contemporary reader of Luke, who recognized Anna as a returnee from the northern Israelite diaspora, would understand. The question remains whether the full significance of the names Anna and Phanuel and their relationship to the eschatological spirituality of the book of Tobit, which we have explored in §4, function on this literary level or belong to the historical reality behind the text. Should they be understood as a form of intertextuality giving literary depth to Luke's presentation of a literary character, or are they better understood as historical background illuminating the historical depth of a tradition Luke reports? The parallel with Nahum the Mede suggests that the latter is the case. As a prophet who devoted her long years of widowhood to religious devotion, who was always to be seen in the temple courts, Anna would have become a well-known figure in Jerusalem, easily remembered a few decades later in the time of the Jerusalem church. Some who in their youth had been impressed by her prophecies and shared her ardent hopes of the redemption of Jerusalem may have joined that church. There is nothing improbable in the idea that she appeared in traditions that reached Luke, directly or indirectly, from the Jerusalem church.

This proposal that Anna may be a historical person requires some consideration of her reputed age. Luke 2:37 probably means not that she was eighty-four years of age, but that she had been eighty-four years a widow, following her seven years of marriage.[85] In that case, it is likely that the tradition Luke follows schematized her life in periods of seven years: two weeks of years before marriage, one week of years married, twelve weeks of years as a widow. This

---

demption of Jerusalem" from Isa 52:9, see n. 70 above. With the phrase "the redemption (λύτρωσις = גאלה) of Jerusalem," cf. the phrase "the redemption (גאלה) of Israel," used in documents of the Bar Kokhba revolt, and the phrases "the redemption (גאלה) of Zion" and "the redemption (גאלה) of Israel" used on the coins of the two revolts: see Fitzmyer, *Luke I–IX*, 432; D. Flusser, "Jerusalem in the Literature of the Second Temple Period," *Imm* 6 (1976) 44; Schürer, *History,* 1:605-6; Wilcox, "Luke 2,36-38," 1575.

84. Perhaps the fact that Luke does not express the content of Anna's praise of God (2:38), as he does Simeon's (2:28-32), is connected to the fact that, although there are allusions later in his work to the hope of the regathering of all the tribes of Israel (Luke 22:30; Acts 26:7) and there are pilgrims from the diaspora of the northern tribes present at Pentecost (Acts 2:9), this theme does not feature in the rest of Luke's work in the way that the subject matter of Simeon's song does.

85. I. H. Marshall, *The Gospel of Luke* (NIGTC; Grand Rapids: Eerdmans; Exeter: Paternoster, 1978) 123; J. K. Elliott, "Anna's Age (Luke 2:36-37)," *NovT* 30 (1988) 100-102.

would make her age 105 years at the time of the event. This is the age at which Judith died (Jdt 16:23), after many years as a widow, in which she chose deliberately not to remarry (16:22). Since Judith is undoubtedly a fictional character, the parallel does not mean, as I. Howard Marshall infers, that "there is nothing impossible about Anna's great age."[86] In itself this statement is correct. One Jewish epitaph from Egypt at least claims that its subject lived to the age of 102,[87] while another from Rome records the age of 110 (*JIWE* 2:576). But the fifteen-weeks scheme suggests that Anna's life has been artificially schematized and its length deliberately conformed to that of Judith, not, indeed, in Luke's text, in which the parallel with Judith is far from clear, but in the tradition Luke used. But such artificiality does not throw doubt on the historicity of Anna herself. It is only to be expected that a revered figure, remembered for having lived to a great age, would in tradition be assigned a symbolically appropriate age. A good parallel is Simeon the son of Clopas, second leader of the Jerusalem church, martyred under Trajan, at the age of 120 years, according to Hegesippus (*apud* Eusebius, *Hist. Eccl.* 3.32.3, 6), who reports second-century Palestinian Jewish Christian tradition. Simeon's historicity is not in doubt, but the age of 120 years has been attributed to him in a tradition that wished to set him alongside Moses, just as in rabbinic tradition the same age was assigned to Hillel, Yohanan ben Zakkai, and Aqiba (Sifre Deut. 357).[88]

Finally, while Judith is not a historical figure, that the book of Judith evidently regards her refusal to remarry as praiseworthy and to be associated with her great piety (8:8; 16:22) is evidence of the esteem in which widowhood associated with religious devotion could be held, and in that respect illuminates the case of Anna. But we should also note that in the case of Anna's widowhood there is a relevant factor not involved in Judith's. Since having sex and bearing children are causes of impurity, remaining a widow would facilitate Anna's frequent attendance in the temple. Moreover, after menopause she would be able to maintain a continual state of purity, enabling the constant attendance in the temple that Luke depicts. Luke does not present Anna as a generalized example of "the single woman's possibility of singlemindedness, of living completely for God, without any interference from other obligations."[89] In keeping with the Jewish and temple setting of Luke's narrative, Anna is a much more historically particular Jewish figure than this: her singleness is related to the purity laws

---

86. Marshall, *Luke*, 124.

87. W. Horbury and D. Noy, *Jewish Inscriptions of Graeco-Roman Egypt* (Cambridge: Cambridge University Press, 1992) 114 (no. 47).

88. R. Bauckham, *Jude and the Relatives of Jesus in the Early Church* (Edinburgh: T. & T. Clark, 1990) 91-92.

89. Seim, *Double Message*, 244.

that governed attendance at the temple. She has been granted the psalmist's desire "to live in the house of YHWH all the days of my life" (Ps 27:4) so that she may await the Lord's coming to his temple (Mal 3:1).

Additional Note A: The Northern Tribes in Exile in 4 Ezra 13

I have stressed that in the Second Temple period the exiled northern tribes were not thought to be "lost." Those writers of the period who refer to them place them in concrete, identifiable geographical locations, especially in Media. Though Media was remote from most of the authors of the extant literature of this period, there was nothing mythical about it. Only in Josephus does an element of the legendary affect his account of the ten tribes, in that he considers them to have grown to numbers so vast as to be innumerable (*Ant.* 11.133), a claim that, as I have noted, has probably been influenced by the divine promise of innumerable descendants to the patriarchs (Gen 13:16; 15:5; 32:12 [MT 13]; Hos 1:10).[90] But Josephus still locates the tribes in Media. The contemporary Palestinian apocalypse 2 Baruch, from around the end of the first century CE, simply locates them across the Euphrates (77:22; 78:1), but in another apocalypse of the same period, 4 Ezra, which shares many traditions with 2 Baruch, we find a different, thoroughly legendary notion, which was to blossom in later Jewish and Christian legends about the ten "lost" tribes.[91]

In Ezra's vision in 4 Ezra 13:1-13a, which is interpreted for him in 13:21-55, he sees the Messiah defeat the innumerable multitude of the Gentile nations who gather to attack him on Mount Zion. The vision is clearly aimed against the kind of apocalyptic militarism that expected the Gentile oppressors to be destroyed in a war that Israel would fight under the Messiah's leadership. Ezra's Messiah acts single-handedly, and he destroys his attackers not with any weapon, but with his powerful word of judgment (vv 9-11, 37-38). Following the destruction of the Gentiles who oppose him, the Messiah calls to him "another multitude which was peaceable" (vv 12, 39). These are the nine and a half tribes returning from their exile.[92] That they are regathered to Zion only after the defeat of

90. The idea that the northern tribes in exile increased in numbers prodigiously may also be the meaning of TMos 4:9, but the extant Latin text is so hopelessly corrupt that it is impossible to be sure of the meaning of the verse.

91. For medieval Jewish legends, see A. Neubauer, "Where Are the Ten Tribes?" *JQR* 1 (1889) 14-28, 95-114, 185-201, 408-23.

92. The textual witnesses for 13:40 vary between ten, nine and a half, and nine tribes. M. E. Stone, *Fourth Ezra* (Hermeneia; Minneapolis: Fortress, 1990) 404, argues correctly that the less usual "nine and a half" (as in 2 Bar 77:17; 78:1) is probably original.

the Gentiles and that their peaceableness is stressed (13:12, 39, 47), by contrast with the warlike multitude of the Gentiles, is probably another element in the polemic against apocalyptic militarism. It is an alternative to an expectation that the northern tribes would return to take part in the messianic war.

Such an expectation is presupposed in the Qumran War Rule, where the messianic army comprises all twelve tribes (1QM 2:2-3, 7; 3:13-14; 4:16; 5:1-2; 6:10).[93] It is probably implied in Sibylline Oracles 2:170-76, where the return of the ten tribes seems responsible for reversing the Gentile domination of Israel. But it must have been expounded at length in a no longer extant Jewish source that the Christian Latin poet Commodian used (*Instr.* 1.42; *Carmen apol.* 941-86).[94] Commodian's account has sufficient links with 4 Ezra to make it likely that the latter knew the same tradition as Commodian records and is countering it.[95] In Commodian the exiled northern tribes are led back to Palestine by divine guidance and form an all-conquering army, irresistible because God is with them, coming to rescue Jerusalem from the Antichrist.

As to the place in which the tribes spend their exile until this eschatological return, in Commodian it is "enclosed beyond the Persian river" ("trans Persida flumine clausi," *Carmen apol.* 943), a river that God dried up for them to pass over on their way to their place of waiting and that he dries up again for them to return. This is clearly no longer the real geography of the historical diaspora of the northern Israelites, but a mythical place beyond the known world. It is the same tradition that 4 Ezra relates in an only slightly different form. 4 Ezra relates how King Shalmaneser of Assyria deported the tribes from Israel to "another land," but they subsequently decided to "leave the multitude of the nations and go to a more distant region, where no human beings had ever

93. 1QM 1:2-3 may indicate that the first six years of the war (in which the land of Israel is liberated) will be fought by the three tribes of Levi, Judah, and Benjamin, who will then be joined by the remaining tribes for the rest of the forty years of the war.

94. See M. R. James, *Apocrypha Anecdota* (TextsS 2/3; Cambridge: Cambridge University Press, 1893) 90-94; idem, *The Lost Apocrypha of the Old Testament* (London: SPCK, 1920) 103-6; F. Schmidt, "Une source esséniene chez Commodian," in M. Philonenko, et al., *Pseudépigraphes de l'Ancien Testament et Manuscrits de la Mer Morte 1* (CahRHPR 41; Paris: Presses Universitaires de France, 1967) 11-26; J. Daniélou, *A History of Early Christian Doctrine before the Council of Nicaea*, vol. 3, *The Origins of Latin Christianity*, tr. D. Smith and J. A. Baker (Philadelphia: Westminster; London: Darton, Longman & Todd, 1977) 116-19 (he oddly misunderstands Commodian as referring to the two and a half tribes in Babylon); J. H. Charlesworth, *The Pseudepigrapha and Modern Research with a Supplement* (SBLSCS 7S; Chico, Calif.: Scholars Press, 1981) 147-49, 295. The same source seems to have been used by the Ethiopic *Acts of Matthew*: see E. A. W. Budge, *The Contendings of the Apostles* (London: Oxford University Press, 1935) 94-95.

95. Cf. 4 Ezra 13:43-47 with Commodian, *Instr.* 1.42-30; *Carmen apol.* 940-44, 959-60.

lived" (13:42). Here it is the Euphrates (or perhaps its northern tributaries) that God dries up for them to cross (13:41-42), but then they travel for a year and a half to a land called Arzareth (13:45). The name is often explained as deriving from ארץ אחרת ("another land") in Deuteronomy 29:28, a text applied to the ten tribes in *m. Sanh.* 10:3.

That such a legend of the migration of the northern tribes to an extremely remote, inaccessible, and unknown place developed at the same time as other Jewish writers knew very well that the descendants of the northern exiles lived in Media is surprising. Two factors may help to explain it. First, as already noted, among the diaspora communities Media was especially remote from Palestine and even more remote from most parts of the western diaspora. After the destruction of the temple in 70, direct personal contact, such as would have occurred through pilgrims traveling from Media to Jerusalem, must have become much less frequent. The Median diaspora was not forgotten, but that it consisted of descendants of the northern tribes could now more easily fade from view. (However, we should note that the tradition in 4 Ezra evidently predates 4 Ezra, and so we cannot be sure that it developed only after 70.) Second, the belief, attested by Josephus, that the promise to the patriarchs that their descendants would be innumerable applied especially to the exiled northern tribes (which might well have been connected with the hope that they would return as an invincible army to defeat the Gentile oppressors) could have led to the further conclusion that these vast numbers of Israelites could not be the actually rather small communities in the Median diaspora. A clash of reality and legend led to further legend.[96]

Additional Note B: The Place of Origin of the Book of Tobit

I have argued that the book of Tobit not only reflects a diaspora situation, as most scholars agree, and more specifically the context of the eastern diaspora, as some scholars agree,[97] but that it addresses precisely the situation of the ex-

---

96. For the important theological function of the ten tribes and their return in 4 Ezra, where they solve the problem of contradiction between God's covenant promise to Abraham that he would be the ancestor of a multitude (Gen 17:4) and the small number (so far as Ezra can see) of the remnant of the righteous, see R. Bauckham, "Apocalypses," in D. A. Carson, ed., *Justification and Variegated Nomism: A Fresh Appraisal of Paul and Second Temple Judaism*, vol. 1 (Tübingen: Mohr [Siebeck], 2001) 161-69.

97. Listed in C. A. Moore, *Tobit* (AB 40A; New York: Doubleday, 1996) 42-43. Deselaers, *Tobit*, 322, summarizes the arguments that have been advanced for an origin in the eastern diaspora (which he does not accept), and in n. 24 lists those who have taken this view. To those he

iles of the northern tribes. On this view, it was either written in Media itself for the Median diaspora or written elsewhere in the eastern diaspora, most likely Babylonia, but with the Median diaspora as its intended audience.

The historical errors in Tobit 1, which are often cited in this connection, only exclude an origin close in time to the end of the Assyrian Empire. In the ancient world such errors are easily possible even a century after the events and even in areas geographically close to the events. They are no argument against the composition of Tobit in Media or Babylonia in the Persian period. More serious are the commonly alleged geographical errors, which are two.[98]

The first concerns the location of Nineveh. In 6:2 Tobias and Raphael, having set out from Tobit's home in Nineveh on their way to Ecbatana, camp for their first night beside the river Tigris. From Nineveh, which lay just east of the Tigris, the road to Ecbatana led east: it would not meet or cross the Tigris. One should note that it is not clear that the author thought Nineveh lay west of the Tigris, since he does not say that Tobit and Raphael had to cross it.[99] He may have thought only that their route ran beside the Tigris for some distance.[100] But that the relation of Nineveh to the Tigris was vague in his mind is not inconsistent with his living in Media or Babylonia three centuries, say, after Nineveh's destruction in 612 BCE.[101] Nineveh did not exist in his time. When Xenophon passed through the area in 401 BCE, he saw a ruined, uninhabited city, which he was told had been a Median city called Mespila (*Anabasis* 3.4.10-12).[102] It was certainly the ruins of Nineveh that he saw, but evidently his guides

---

lists, add Nickelsburg, "Stories," 45n.62. Deselaers, *Tobit*, 323, advances against the hypothesis of an origin in the eastern diaspora the remarkable argument that there is no hope for return from exile, so characteristic of the eastern diaspora, in the book. This argument is possible only because his theory of several stages of expansion of the book eliminates such a hope from the *Grunderzählung*.

98. C. C. Torrey, *The Apocryphal Literature* (1945; repr. Hamden, Conn.: Archon, 1963) 86; D. C. Simpson, "The Book of Tobit," in R. H. Charles, ed., *The Apocrypha and Pseudepigrapha of the Old Testament* (2 vols.; Oxford: Clarendon, 1913) 1:185; Zimmermann, *Tobit*, 16; C. A. Moore, "Tobit, Book of," *ABD* 6:587-88.

99. Nor is it clear, as Torrey, *Apocryphal Literature*, 86, claims, that 11:1 implies they have to cross the Tigris on their return journey.

100. It is even possible, though not likely, that he thought of the suburbs of Nineveh spreading across the Tigris to the west, as indeed they probably did (cf. D. Oates, *Studies in the Ancient History of Northern Iraq* [London: British Academy, 1968] 77), and, influenced by Jonah 3:3, supposed that from Tobit's house in these western suburbs it was a day's journey to the Tigris.

101. See Moore, *Tobit*, 40-42: c. 300 BCE is the earliest likely date for the composition of the book.

102. Oates, *Studies*, 60, supposes that Xenophon saw both the ruins of a Median city (Nineveh) and a nearby town called Mespila, but this is clearly a misunderstanding of the passage.

could not identify it as the famous capital of the Assyrian Empire (of which Xenophon would certainly have heard). The southern part of ancient Nineveh (Nebi Yunis) was later resettled and rebuilt as a Hellenistic city, but this was probably not before the second century BCE.[103]

The second, more serious error concerns the location of the two most important cities of Media: Ecbatana and Rhagae (Rages, Ragha).[104] According to Tobit 5:6b, "It is a distance of two regular days' journey from Ecbatana to Rhagae, for it lies in the mountains (ἐν τῷ ὄρει), while Ecbatana is in the middle of the plain."[105] Rhagae (modern Rai, about 5 miles southeast of Teheran) is in the plain, though a minor mountain ridge curves around it and the major range, the Elburz mountains, is close. Ecbatana is located in the Zagros mountains, far from the plain. Moreover, they are 180 miles apart, by the most direct route. Thus the whole statement is erroneous. No inhabitant of Media could have made it. It is possible, however, to question whether it is an original part of the text of Tobit.[106] It does not fit its context very happily. Raphael explains how far it is from Ecbatana to Rhagae, but has not explained how far it is from Nineveh to Ecbatana, even though Tobias has told him he does not know the roads to Media or how to get there (5:2). Even if the distance between the cities has some relevance to the conversation, it is not at all clear why their respective locations in the mountains and the plain should be added. The whole statement could easily be a later gloss, by someone, a scribe or the Greek translator, who thought the relation of the lesser-known city, Rhagae, to the better-known, Ecbatana, needed explanation.[107]

A better test of the author's knowledge of Median geography is whether the story, as told in 8:20–10:8, allows sufficient time for Raphael to travel from Ecbatana to Rhagae and back. The narrative assumes that, within a period of fourteen days, the period of the wedding celebration (8:20; 10:7), Raphael travels

---

103. Oppenheimer, *Babylonia*, 312-13.

104. For the information in ancient sources on Rhagae, see A. V. W. Jackson, "A Historical Sketch of Ragha, the Supposed Home of Zoroaster's Mother," in J. J. Modi, ed., *Spiegel Memorial Volume: Papers on Iranian Subjects* (F. Spiegel FS; Bombay: British India Press, 1908) 237-45.

105. My translation from the Greek text of Recension II (the recension represented by Sinaiticus and the Old Latin) in R. Hanhart, *Tobit* (Göttingen Septuagint 8/5; Göttingen: Vandenhoeck & Ruprecht, 1983) 99-100. There are many minor variations in the Old Latin manuscripts in this passage, but the text I have translated is nevertheless well supported.

106. Zimmermann, *Tobit*, 73, doubts that it is (but his statement that it is lacking in the Old Latin is mistaken), though, inconsistently, on p. 16 he treats it as evidence that the author of Tobit was ignorant of the geography of Media.

107. That the statement does not occur in the manuscripts of the abridged Greek recension (I) has little significance. Unfortunately neither this verse nor its context is represented among the Qumran fragments of Tobit.

from Raguel's home in Ecbatana to the home of Gabael in Rhagae, and Raphael and Gabael then travel to Ecbatana, arriving before the end of the wedding celebrations (9:6). Raphael travels with four servants and two camels, the latter for the purpose of transporting the money bags on the return journey. This means that, although Raphael is an angel in disguise and is capable of moving from place to place very rapidly indeed (8:3), we cannot suppose that here he travels faster than a human could. We can assume that both journeys are made with as much speed as possible, since Tobias has sent Raphael on this mission precisely so that he should not have to stay in Ecbatana longer than strictly necessary (9:4), while Gabael will be anxious to arrive in time to join at least the end of the wedding celebrations. Allowing for Sabbaths, when they could not travel, six days is the most that the journey in each direction could take.

Frank Zimmermann cites Arrian's account (3.20) of Alexander the Great's pursuit of Darius, in which it took ten (or eleven) days of forced marches for Alexander and his army to make the journey from Ecbatana to Rhagae.[108] But this is certainly not good evidence that this was the fastest possible time in which the distance could be covered, as the various discussions of Alexander's route in this area make clear. A. B. Bosworth argues that Arrian is incorrect in saying that Alexander traveled to Rhagae via Ecbatana, preferring Curtius's report that when Alexander heard that Darius had left Ecbatana, he broke off his march into Media and went in pursuit.[109] But those who accept Arrian's account have long pointed out that it could not have taken Alexander's army this long to cover the direct route from Ecbatana to Rhagae. J. Marquant pointed out in 1907 that the distances given in the Arabic itineraries make it no more than a nine days' journey, and concluded that Alexander must have made a detour.[110] A. F. von Stahl calculated that the direct route would take eight days, and argued for a detour to the south,[111] while Radet argued for a detour to the north.[112] J. Seibert suggests that Alexander could have been delayed by battles.[113]

Clearly Alexander's march provides no secure basis for calculating the

108. Zimmermann, *Tobit*, 16.

109. A. B. Bosworth, "Errors in Arrian," *CQ* 26 (1976) 132-36. The latest discussion of the issue, in J. Seibert, *Die Eroberung des Perserreiches durch Alexander d. Gr. auf kartographischer Grundlage* (Beihefte zur Tübinger Atlas des vorderen Orients B68; Wiesbaden: Reichert, 1985) 111-12n.46, notes Bosworth's view but finds difficulties with it.

110. J. Marquant, "Alexanders Marsch von Persepolis nach Herāt," *Philologus: Supplementband* 10 (1907) 21.

111. A. F. von Stahl, "Notes on the March of Alexander the Great from Ecbatana to Hyrcania," *Geographical Journal* 64 (1924) 317-18.

112. G. Radet, "La dernière campagne d'Alexandre contre Darius (juin-juillet 330 avant J.-C.)," in *Mélanges Gustav Glotz*, vol. 2 (Paris: Presses Universitaires de France, 1932) 767-71.

113. Seibert, *Eroberung*, 112.

time the same journey would take Raphael and Gabael. It is better to begin with the fact that the distance of 360 (180 × 2) miles would have to be covered in twelve days (the longest time available within the narrative), a rate of 30 miles per day. Reliable estimates of the distances foot travelers in the ancient world could cover per day are hard to come by. William Ramsey, discussing the Roman world, cites Friedländer's estimate of 26 or 27 Roman miles[114] per day, but thinks it too high, largely on pragmatic grounds of what modern people find possible, and the fact that people not in a hurry and traveling in the Mediterranean summer, when most travel was done, would probably travel only in the morning, a five-hour stage before noon. But he admits that people in a hurry would travel a second such stage in the evening.[115] These calculations seem to make 30 miles per day an extremely demanding but not impossible pace for people in a hurry, as Raphael and Gabael are. The camels could help on the outward journey, though not on the return.

If the author of Tobit knew the route from Ecbatana to Rhagae accurately, then he has allowed barely enough time for the journey. It is possible that this is precisely what he did, and in that case he could have lived in Media. But if it seems preferable to suppose that he must have thought the distance from Ecbatana to Rhagae a little shorter than it actually was, his error is not gross. In that case, probably he could not have lived in Media, but he could have lived in Babylonia.

---

114. The Roman mile was 1,618 English yards.
115. W. M. Ramsey, "Roads and Travel (in NT)," in J. Hastings, ed., *A Dictionary of the Bible: Extra Volume* (New York: Scribner's; Edinburgh: T. & T. Clark, 1904) 388.

CHAPTER 5

Joanna the Apostle

I read not that ever any man did give
unto Christ so much as one groat,
but the women followed him and
ministered to him of their substance.[1]

Elisabeth Moltmann-Wendel writes:

> Hardly anyone knows Joanna. Theologians in their studies never meet her,
> and they have ignored her in biblical texts. A journalist discussing a mod-
> ern biography of Jesus mocked the "fabrication" of a woman disciple called
> Joanna. She often does not appear at all in books about women of the Bible,
> and when she does, she is quickly passed over.[2]

Here, for once, we shall not pass quickly over Joanna, but take our time to un-
cover as much as can be known historically about her as well as to appreciate
her role in the Gospel of Luke. We shall see that there is more to be known than
has hitherto been realized and that her significance in Luke's Gospel is greater
than his two references to her might immediately suggest. The greatest surprise
will no doubt be to discover that Paul knew her and considered her an out-

1. John Bunyan, *The Pilgrim's Progress* (ed. R. Sharrock; Harmondsworth: Penguin, 1965)
316.
2. E. Moltmann-Wendel, *The Women Around Jesus* (tr. J. Bowden; New York: Crossroad;
London: SCM, 1982) 133.

standing apostle (see §6). Though not certain, this is a historical conjecture as probable as many that have classic status in biblical studies. But it is a conjecture confined to two sections (6 and 8) of this chapter so that it may not prejudice the argument of the other sections.

1. On the Road with Jesus and His Disciples

Joanna's name appears in the New Testament only in two passages of the Gospel of Luke: 8:3 and 24:10, but both are significant passages. The first (8:1-3) is usually treated as a "summary," often in the sense of a passage with a transitional role, both summing up what has preceded and providing "an interpretive heading for what is to come."[3] It differs from other kinds of pericopae in Luke's narrative of the Galilean ministry in that it does not relate a specific event but describes what was true from this point in the narrative onward. But we should not allow the term "summary" to downgrade its importance. It offers information not elsewhere provided in Luke's Gospel, especially with regard to the women disciples of Jesus. Maria Anicia Co's definition of a summary, referring to the summary passages in Acts, is appropriate and helpful also for this passage in Luke: "A summary may be defined as a relatively independent and concise narrative statement that describes a prolonged situation or portrays an event as happening repeatedly within an indefinite period of time."[4] So the relationship of the women disciples to Jesus that Luke here introduces is to be understood as continuing through the rest of Luke's narrative of Jesus' preaching ministry. The lack of other specific references to the women before the passion narrative is not an indication of their insignificance for Luke, but of the fact that he has highlighted their significance in his general description of the Galilean ministry (8:1-3) and can thereafter take it for granted.

Luke 8:1-3 (NRSV) reads:

> Soon afterwards he went on through cities and villages, proclaiming and bringing the good news of the kingdom of God. The twelve were with him, as well as some women who had been cured of evil spirits and infirmities: Mary, called Magdalene, from whom seven demons had gone out, and Joanna, the wife of Herod's steward Chuza, and Susanna, and many others, who provided for them out of their resources.

3. J. B. Green, *The Gospel of Luke* (NICNT; Grand Rapids: Eerdmans, 1997) 317.

4. M. A. Co, "The Major Summaries in Acts: Acts 2,42-47; 4,32-35; 5,12-16: Linguistic and Literary Relationship," *ETL* 68 (1992) 56-57; quoted in R. J. Karris, "Women and Discipleship in Luke," *CBQ* 56 (1994) 10.

While this is accurate enough, it necessarily obscures the rather loose syntax of the Greek, of which a literal rendering is: "he went on through cities and villages, proclaiming and bringing the good news of the kingdom of God and the twelve with him and certain women who . . ." (αὐτὸς διώδευεν κατὰ πόλιν καὶ κώμην κηρύσσων καὶ εὐαγγελιζόμενος τὴν βασιλείαν τοῦ θεοῦ καὶ οἱ δώδεκα σὺν αὐτῷ, καὶ γυναῖκές τινες αἳ . . .). The natural way to read this is to supply the verb "to be" with both "the twelve" and "certain women" as subjects. It would be more awkward to take both "the twelve" and "certain women" as subjects, with Jesus, of the main verb διώδευεν (singular to agree with the nearest subject).[5] Moreover, Luke has not portrayed any of the disciples as participating in Jesus' ministry of preaching, and does not do so until he explicitly recounts the sending of the twelve (9:1-6) and of the seventy-two (10:1-20). But it should be noted that, if the sentence is read in such a way as to include the twelve as additional subjects in the activity ascribed to Jesus, then this must also be true of the women. Grammatically, there is no way of attributing preaching to the twelve but not to the women. It is probably ascribed to neither. The twelve and the women are both said to be "with him." The paratactic structure places the twelve and the women alongside each other in the same relationship to Jesus, and the impression perhaps given by the NRSV that the women are something of an afterthought tagged onto the main statement about the twelve is misleading. We could translate: "There were with him the twelve and some women who. . . ."[6]

What is the relationship, then, of the women here to the twelve and the rest of the disciples? The twelve have already been adequately introduced in Luke's narrative, with the names of all twelve given (6:13-16), though 8:1 is the first subsequent reference to them. The women are here introduced for the first time, with three named and reference also made to "many others." But these two groups are not the only followers of Jesus. Luke makes quite clear that Jesus is constantly surrounded by a very large number of disciples (6:17; 19:37) and so

5. Q. Quesnell, "The Women at Luke's Supper," in R. J. Cassidy and P. Scharper, eds., *Political Issues in Luke-Acts* (Maryknoll, N.Y.: Orbis, 1983) 68.

6. J. Nolland, *Luke 1–9:20* (WBC 35A; Dallas: Word, 1989) 364, points out two further syntactical ambiguities: "it is unclear whether the final relative clause (v 3b) refers to all the women (vv 2-3a), or whether it forms a structural parallel to the relative clause of v 2a and refers only to the 'many others.' It is also possible, but not likely, that the 'many others' of v 3 are to be included in the 'certain women' of v 2 and are then to be included in the relative clause of v 2a." On the first point, it is hardly likely that the three named women are singled out as the only ones who did not "provide for them out of their resources." On the second, the "many others" (ἕτεραι πολλαί) would have no syntactical connection with the rest of the sentence if they were not understood as included in the "certain women" (γυναῖκές τινες). τινες need not refer to a few (e.g., Acts 17:5).

can commission no less than seventy-two disciples in addition to the twelve (9:1; 10:1). At 8:1-3 Luke singles out for special mention two groups within the larger body of disciples: the twelve and the women. Both groups have formed since his earlier summary statement about Jesus' ministry in 4:44. The order in which they occur here is not especially significant. Though there is no doubt that Luke does give the twelve a certain kind of priority over all other disciples, this passage is not designed to express that, except perhaps in the sense that the twelve have already been introduced earlier and have been specifically selected by Jesus. But the women in any case have to be mentioned after the twelve, because Luke has a good deal of detail to supply about them, and also because he needs to say that the women "provided for them" (i.e., Jesus and the twelve). In fact, the focus of the passage is very much on the women, matching in their case the kind of detail already provided about the twelve in 6:13-16.

It is important to notice that the last clause ("who provided for them out of their resources") is not the principal thing said about the women. The principal point is what is said equally of the twelve and of the women: that they were "with" Jesus as he traveled around proclaiming the good news of the kingdom of God. At this stage of Luke's narrative this is the essence of discipleship (cf. 6:17; 7:11; cf. Mark 3:14): to accompany Jesus and to witness his ministry. Only later will the disciples be ready for Jesus to delegate a form of his own ministry to them, albeit for a limited period of mission. Then it is not only the twelve he sends out (9:1-6) but also the seventy-two (10:1-20), among whom it is surely natural for readers to assume that the women are included.[7] Thus there is actually no differentiation here in what discipleship means for the twelve (men) and for the women: neither are yet actively participating in Jesus' mission, both are being prepared for doing so.[8] What Luke is indicating here, in this significant summary passage in his narrative, is that from an early period in the Galilean ministry the disciples accompanying Jesus included in particular two groups: the twelve and the women. Unlike Matthew and Mark, where it comes as something of a surprise to the reader to learn, during the passion narrative, that many women had accompanied Jesus from Galilee and had "provided for him" (Matt 27:55-56; Mark 15:40-41),[9] Luke makes clear that these

7. This would be required by the principle proposed by E. Schüssler Fiorenza, *In Memory of Her: A Feminist Theological Reconstruction of Christian Origins* (New York: Crossroad; London: SCM, 1983) 45: "any interpretation or translation claiming to be historically adequate to the language character of its sources must understand and translate New Testament language on the whole as inclusive of women unless proven otherwise."

8. See especially Green, *Luke,* 317.

9. Mark, but not Matthew, here makes clear that the women had been followers of Jesus and provided for him in Galilee, not just on the journey from Galilee to Jerusalem.

women disciples were constant companions of Jesus from an early stage of the Galilean ministry. At 8:1-3 Luke is identifying the two groups of disciples who will have an important role to play in the rest of his Gospel narrative. The women, of course, appear as distinctive actors in the story toward the end (23:49; 23:55–24:11), and the mention again in 24:10 of the first two names from the list in 8:2-3 forms a kind of *inclusio*, reminding the reader that the women's discipleship thus spans the whole narrative from chapter 8 to chapter 24. The women's presence among the disciples during the Galilean ministry is also recalled in 24:6, where the two angels in the empty tomb call on the women to "remember how he told you, while he was still in Galilee, that the Son of Man must be handed over to sinners, and be crucified, and on the third day rise again." The words here are closest to the those of the third of the three passion predictions in Luke (18:32-33), but that was explicitly given only to the twelve (18:31) and not in Galilee. The reference must be to the earlier passion predictions in 9:22 and 9:44, spoken to "only the disciples" (9:18) and to "his disciples" (9:43). This should remove any suspicion that Luke does not consider the women to be disciples.

Recognizing that the principal statement made about the women in 8:1-3 is that, just like the twelve, they accompany Jesus, and that this is what discipleship here means for both the twelve and the women, is essential to a proper understanding of the last clause of the passage, which has been considerably debated. This is an additional fact about the women. It is not the activity in which their discipleship consists, to be contrasted with something else (preaching?) that is reserved for the twelve. Nor is there a hierarchy in which the twelve assist Jesus, while the women minister to Jesus and the disciples. Rather, in addition to their essential discipleship role of accompanying Jesus, the women also supply the financial support for the whole group: they "provided for them[10] out of their own resources" (διηκόνουν αὐτοῖς ἐκ τῶν ὑπαρχόντων αὐταῖς). This is almost certainly what the words mean. Not only elsewhere in Luke's writings (11:21; 12:15, 33, 44; 14:33; 16:1; 19:8; Acts 4:32) but also throughout the New Testament and frequently outside the New Testament τὰ ὑπαρχοντά τινι/τινος refers to material possessions or economic means. In conjunction with that phrase the verb διακονέω here must mean that the women supplied the economic needs of Jesus and the twelve.[11] This is

---

10. There is a variant reading "for him" (αὐτῷ), which is best explained as assimilation to Matt 27:55 (par. Mark 15:41). A dissenter from the consensus on this view is C. Ricci, *Mary Magdalene and Many Others* (tr. P. Burns; Minneapolis: Fortress, 1994) 156-58, followed by Karris, "Women," 6-7.

11. L. Schottroff, *Lydia's Impatient Sisters: A Feminist Social History of Early Christianity* (tr. B. and M. Rumscheidt; Louisville: Westminster John Knox; London: SCM, 1995) 210, trans-

the sense of the verb in Romans 15:25 and of the cognate noun διακονία in Acts 6:1; 11:29; 12:25; and elsewhere.

It is therefore quite mistaken to suppose that the women are here assigned, within the community of Jesus' disciples, the kind of gender-specific roles that women played in the ordinary family situation.[12] Luke is not telling his readers that the women cooked the meals, washed the dishes, and mended the clothes. Perhaps they did (though cf. Luke 9:13; 22:8; John 4:8), but it is not what Luke says. The situation envisaged is not an ordinary one, but the special circumstances of Jesus and his followers, who lived without ordinary means of economic support. None of the members of Jesus' entourage, women or men, engaged in economically productive work. Sometimes they benefited from hospitality, but certainly not always (cf. Luke 10:58), while regular hospitality for all of the large following Luke envisages is unlikely to have been available. Luke 8:3 indicates that their financial needs were supplied by the women among them. Of course, this is a generalizing statement and need not indicate either that none of the male disciples made financial contributions to the common needs or that every one of the women did. But Luke indicates what he understood to be generally the case. The assumption commonly made that women did not have economic resources of which they were able to dispose at their own volition would make this a very surprising situation. But the situation is the unusual one in which the male disciples have left their homes and families. Leaving families to manage economically without them, no doubt in many cases with great difficulty,[13] did not leave them free to take significant funds with them. The women, on the other hand, were either independent people, without husbands or dependent relatives, or, if they left families, probably left male family members well able to support the family economically. Their own economic resources, such as they contributed to the support of Jesus and his disciples, would not have been the main economic resource of any families they left.

Thus the true male counterpart to the women's "service," as described in Luke 8:3, is not preaching or leadership but the abandonment of home and

---

lates: "provided for them according to what was possible for them in their circumstances." It is true that ἐκ τῶν ὑπαρχόντων can mean "under the circumstances" (LSJ s.v.), but with διακονέω and αὐταῖς a reference to financial resources seems required.

12. T. K. Seim, *The Double Message: Patterns of Gender in Luke-Acts* (Nashville: Abingdon; Edinburgh: T. & T. Clark, 1994) 71-74, summarizes interpretations along these lines. See also S. Heine, *Women and Early Christianity* (tr. J. Bowden; Minneapolis: Augsburg; London: SCM, 1987) 60-61.

13. On this see D. Sim, "What about the Wives and Children of the Disciples? The Cost of Discipleship from Another Perspective," *HeyJ* 35 (1994) 373-90.

family by the twelve (Luke 5:11; 18:28-29). In 18:28-29 Peter is, as usual, spokesman for the twelve when he says that "we have left our homes and followed you." Hence the specific terms of Jesus' response: "no one who has left house or wife or brothers or parents or children . . ." (where "wife" is peculiar to Luke, not in the Matthean and Markan parallels). The twelve who abandon everything and the women who give their material resources for the common support of the community of disciples exemplify in different ways the teaching of Luke's Jesus about possessions. The difference happens to coincide with gender, but not at all because the women disciples continue the same kind of women's role they were ordinarily expected to play. Both the men and the women among Jesus' disciples behave in a significantly countercultural way with regard to material resources. But the differing positions of men and women in the society from which they come mean that, perhaps rather surprisingly but entirely intelligibly, it is the women, rather than the men, who have disposable financial resources from which to supply the economic needs of the itinerant group. (It should be noticed that this difference between the men and the women corresponds to the situation in Jesus' ministry, not that of the churches Luke knew and addressed, and also that therefore this passage does not set up a model of discipleship to be literally imitated by Luke's readers.)

One might, however, question whether the women would have the financial resources to do this. Ben Witherington comments: "Probably, some of these women could give only their time and talents, perhaps in making meals or clothes."[14] But, as David Sim has rightly objected, this cannot be the *meaning* of διηκόνουν αὐτοῖς ἐκ τῶν ὑπαρχόντων αὐταῖς, which must refer to the use of economic resources.[15] Luke's statement is a generalization: no doubt there were some women who were not able to contribute financially, just as no doubt there were some women in the group who had not been healed of diseases or demons by Jesus. That too must be a generalization. But women who could not contribute financially are simply ignored by Luke's generalization, which is concerned only with material resources. Whatever other kind of contribution any of the women might have made is not something on which Luke comments at all. Insofar as any of the women are included in his generalization, it is with reference to their sharing of their possessions. Then what sort(s) of women would have

---

14. B. Witherington III, *Women in the Ministry of Jesus* (SNTSMS 51; Cambridge: Cambridge University Press, 1984) 195-96 (n. 238); cf. idem, "On the Road with Mary Magdalene, Joanna, Susanna, and Other Disciples — Luke 8 1-3," *ZNW* 70 (1979) 246n.18.

15. D. C. Sim, "The Women Followers of Jesus: The Implications of Luke 8:1-3," *HeyJ* 30 (1989) 57: "Luke 8:3 does *not* specify that the women who followed Jesus served him and the twelve from their own resources, either financial or physical. What the Greek text does suggest is that these women provided for Jesus and the others only in an economic sense."

disposable means of any kind? It has often been supposed that the passage must refer to a few wealthy women, presumably including the three named women, who had the resources to provide the economic support for Jesus and the disciples. Sim argues against this on two grounds: first, that Jesus' radical teaching on wealth implies that one could not be a disciple of Jesus and remain wealthy; second, that Jesus generally associated with nonelite people, so that it is unlikely that many of his women disciples would have had wealth at all. He therefore argues that "a general pooling of resources took place, each woman contributing what she could to a common fund."[16]

This last point is probably correct. In support of it Sim is able to appeal to the evidence of John 12:6, which depicts Judas as the keeper of the group's common funds (cf. also John 13:29), and to the practice of sharing of possessions in the early Jerusalem church (Acts 2:44-45; 4:32–5:11) as a continuation of the practice of Jesus' disciples during his ministry. But we should not too easily agree that all disciples simply abandoned any wealth they might have had. This was clearly not the case with those who did not travel around with Jesus, such as Zaccheus (Luke 19:8) or the sisters Martha and Mary of Bethany. Nor did this happen in the Jerusalem church according to Acts, where, for example, Mary the mother of Mark retained her rather grand house, while putting it at the disposal of the Christian community (Acts 12:12-13; cf. 2:46). As Barbara Reid comments, "The use of material possessions as related to discipleship is a constant Lukan theme, but there is no one model presented for disciples in Luke and Acts."[17] It is not impossible that, for example, some women who owned property and joined Jesus' band of traveling followers retained the property and put the income from it into the common fund.

No doubt many of Jesus' women followers were poor[18] and put what little they could spare into the common fund. But if we press this aspect exclusively, it becomes more difficult to understand the difference between the male disciples, who in general did not contribute financially, and the women who did. Moreover, while Jesus certainly did commonly associate with the ordinary people and made a habit of helping the destitute and the marginalized, the Gospels also depict him sometimes in contact with affluent people and healing them or converting them (e.g., Mark 5:22-24, 35-43; John 4:46-54; Luke 19:2-10). (Some of these, like Zaccheus, were both affluent and outcasts in the community.) It is not difficult to suppose that the women who followed Jesus included a few

---

16. Sim, "Women," 53.

17. B. E. Reid, *Women in the Gospel of Luke* (Collegeville, Minn.: Liturgical, 1996) 130.

18. On the attraction Jesus' movement might have had for poor Galilean women, see S. Freyne, "Jesus the Wine-Drinker: A Friend of Women," in I. R. Kitzberger, ed., *Transformative Encounters: Jesus and Women Re-viewed* (BibIntSer 43; Leiden: Brill, 2000) 177-79.

wealthy women and that these supplied the greater part of the economic resources of the group. From the story of the widow's offering to the temple
(Mark 12:41-44) we may infer that their contribution would not have been valued more highly than the meager contributions of the poorer women, but this
does not mean that there could not have been such major contributions from a
few wealthy women.

The passage has usually been thought to indicate that there was among
these women at least one wealthy woman who made a substantial financial contribution to the group: "Joanna, the wife of Herod's steward Chuza" (Luke 8:3).[19]
I shall later confirm her elite status and the probability that she was wealthy. But
Sim turns the usual inference from the passage around, arguing that Joanna was
probably one of the least likely of the women to have much to contribute, because as "a married woman the right to dispose of her goods lay not with her but
with her husband."[20] This is a statement I shall question, but I may note in passing that it is surprising that Sim does not consider the possibility that she was
widowed.[21] The reference to Chuza may not necessarily require that he be still
alive, especially if Luke's purpose in referring to him is to indicate Joanna's social
connections at the court of Herod and her access to wealth.[22]

Sim argues generally that most of the women followers of Jesus must have
been single (unmarried, widows, divorced, and perhaps former prostitutes),
"for only women of single status enjoyed some personal and economic independence." Those who were married (Joanna is the only certain case of this)
"braved public condemnation by leaving their husbands to follow Jesus."[23] That

19. J. M. Arlandson, *Women, Class, and Society in Early Christianity* (Peabody, Mass.:
Hendrickson, 1997) 130, argues that "Susanna was probably on the same socioeconomic level as
Joanna because retainers rarely associated closely in public with their superiors; likewise retainers did not associate publicly with underlings unless the retainer came from among the slaves,
which was often the case." But he then goes on to argue that "the presence of Mary Magdalene
and the 'many' who served argues in favor of a breakdown in class hierarchy" (132). This contradicts his earlier point about Susanna, since Luke 8:2-3 implies no less that Joanna associated
with the allegedly low-status Mary Magdalene than that she associated with Susanna. We cannot know the socioeconomic status of either Mary Magdalene or Susanna, but there is perhaps
some force in the argument that Mary Magdalene had to be named by Luke here, because she
was much the best-known woman disciple of Jesus, and so may not have been notable among
those who made financial contributions, whereas Joanna and Susanna are named as notable instances of women who were able to contribute substantially to the economic needs of Jesus and
the disciples.

20. Sim, "Women," 52.

21. This possibility is recognized by Ricci, *Mary Magdalene*, 154.

22. That this is the point of the reference to Chuza is argued, e.g., by Seim, *Double Message*, 36-37.

23. Sim, "Women," 55, followed by Green, *Luke*, 318-19.

single women (excluding, of course, young women still living in the family home under the authority of their father) would have a freedom to leave home and travel with Jesus that most married women did not have is certainly true. It is hard to imagine that even a husband who shared his wife's enthusiasm for Jesus would readily allow his wife to travel away from home with the band of Jesus' disciples. Mothers or wives of male disciples of Jesus would be an exception to this. The women who accompanied Jesus to Jerusalem, according to the Gospels, included such: Mary the wife of Clopas (John 19:15),[24] Mary the mother of James and Joses (Mark 15:40, 47; 16:1, etc.), and the mother of the sons of Zebedee (Matt 20:20; 26:56). While we cannot exclude the possibility that a son of Joanna was among Jesus' disciples, there is also no reason to conjecture this. But there is the possibility that a mature woman of aristocratic family, especially in the romanized court circles to which, as we shall see, Joanna belonged, might be used to more independence than most Jewish women of this time and place.[25] Against that we must place the greater scandal for such a woman in the eyes of her peers that would attach to her association with such a group as Jesus and his largely nonelite male and female followers.[26]

It is plausible that many of the women who traveled with Jesus did not have husbands. However, we cannot, as is sometimes suggested, conclude that Mary Magdalene and Susanna were in this category from the fact that Luke does not refer to their husbands, as he does to Joanna's.[27] When the Gospels elsewhere identify women among the disciples of Jesus by reference to their male relatives (Mary the mother of James the little and of Joses, Mary of Clopas, the mother of the sons of Zebedee, the mother of Jesus), the male relatives mentioned were themselves disciples, probably known as Christians in the early communities, and also, in three out of four of these cases, bore the extremely common name Mary and needed to be distinguished in some way from the other Marys among Jesus' disciples and kin. Susanna, like Salome (Mark 15:40; 16:1), needs no further identification because there were no other Susannas with whom Luke thought she could be confused. (The name Susanna

24. See chap. 6 below.

25. On the relative freedom of Roman women in society, see W. Cotter, "Women's Authoritative Roles in Paul's Churches: Countercultural or Conventional?" *NovT* 36 (1994) 362-66.

26. The Coptic *Book of the Resurrection by the Apostle Bartholomew* (fifth-sixth century) says that Joanna refused marital relations with Chuza (J.-D. Kaestli and P. Cherix, *L'évangile de Barthélemy d'après écrits apocryphes* [Turnhout: Brepols, 1993] 195 and n. 77): this is an application to Joanna of the theme common in the apocryphal acts of apostles, according to which upper-class women who converted to Christianity abandoned sexual relations with their husbands.

27. Contra Green, *Luke,* 318.

was not common.)[28] Mary Magdalene did need to be distinguished from other Marys, but if she had left a husband who was not a disciple of Jesus he would not have been mentioned because such relationships no longer had defining value among Jesus' disciples (cf. Mark 3:31-35; Luke 9:59-60; 11:27-28; 12:53; 14:26; 18:28-30).[29] That she is named from her town of origin cannot in itself tell us she had no husband. That she had been possessed by seven demons is more suggestive; such a woman might well never have married or have been rejected or divorced by a husband.

That Luke both names and describes Joanna's husband is therefore exceptional among all the Gospels' references to women disciples of Jesus.[30] It certainly does not mean that she alone had a husband. In order simply to be identified, she presumably needed only to be called Joanna, just as Susanna's name alone is sufficient to identify her. We cannot rule out the possibility that Chuza also became a disciple of Jesus and was known in the early communities. But his name, as we shall see, is extremely unusual. Simply for purposes of identification he need not have been described as Herod's steward. It is clear that Luke wishes to highlight Joanna's connection with the Herodian court, as he does also in the case of Manaen in Acts 13:1. There are five suggested reasons for him to have done so: (1) The reference indicates that Joanna was wealthy and so a major contributor to the disciples' expenses; (2) Joanna's high social status confers social legitimacy on Jesus' movement or the Christian movement;[31] (3) Luke makes a point of referring to people from the ruling elite because "there were members of his community who could identify with these early heroes of the faith by virtue of having a similar, or perhaps slightly inferior position in society";[32] (4) Luke is naming one of the sources of his Gospel traditions, who would especially account for his special material relating to Herod Antipas;[33] (5) the reference is part of Luke's larger narrative strategy, reminding

---

28. Only one other instance from Palestine in the Second Temple period is known: T. Ilan, "Notes on the Distribution of Jewish Women's Names in Palestine in the Second Temple and Mishnaic Periods," *JJS* 40 (1989) 199.

29. Cf. Seim, *Double Message*, 37: "To the extent that their identities are determined by relationships, this is now by reference to Jesus and the twelve."

30. Reid, *Women*, 126, thus misses completely the really interesting point when she comments: "Like most biblical women, [Joanna] is identified by her relationship to a man."

31. E.g., Nolland, *Luke 1–9:20*, 366: "Luke is quick to mention the fact that Christian influence has penetrated to high places"; K. E. Corley, *Private Women, Public Meals* (Peabody, Mass.: Hendrickson, 1993) 111: "Luke's overall interest in portraying a more highly placed movement."

32. P. F. Esler, *Community and Gospel in Luke-Acts* (SNTSMS 57; Cambridge: Cambridge University Press, 1987) 185.

33. E.g., C. F. Evans, *Saint Luke* (TPI NT Commentaries; Philadelphia: Trinity Press International; London: SCM, 1990) 366.

readers that Herod is still in power, suggesting, through Joanna's connection with his court, that Herod "knows or will soon know about Jesus," and so producing "suspense and speculation as to how Herod will react to Jesus."[34]

The fifth suggestion does not seem appropriate to this kind of reference, which is naturally read as saying something about Joanna, not about Herod. That it might also have this kind of effect on the reader is possible, but it is unlikely to be the major significance of the reference to Chuza as Herod's steward. The second suggestion is not very plausible, as Turid Karlsen Seim points out (following Gerd Theissen), because it is not at all clear that association with Herod would give a positive rather than a negative social signal:

> It has been claimed that, rather than bestowing social status on a person, a position at the court of the client king Herod would have engendered social suspicion and even contempt in the contemporary Jewish context, in other words a kind of dubious "tax-collector" status. Understood in this way, the presence of Joanna would not serve to enhance the social legitimacy of the group around Jesus; instead she fits in nicely with the other marginalised persons who join Jesus and/or support him.[35]

Moreover, Luke, who consistently portrays Herod in a bad light, would certainly have realized this. Neither Jesus nor his disciples could in Luke's eyes need legitimation from the man who put John the Baptist to death and pursued Jesus himself to death, earning the epithet "fox" from Jesus (Luke 13:31-32). The same objection does not necessarily apply to the third suggestion, but the reference to Joanna does differ from other Lukan references to believers from the ruling elite (Luke 7:1-10; Acts 8:26-39; 10:1-48; 13:1; 17:12; 19:31) in that Joanna's association with Jesus and his disciples should probably be understood as socially scandalous to the elite circles from which she comes. It is a curious feature of Luke-Acts (perhaps belonging to a more general difference between the Gospel and the Acts in their treatment of the theme of wealth) that wealthy believers are much more prominent in Acts than in the Gospel. Within the Gospel there does not seem to be much of a theme to which the reference to Joanna would belong. Luke is perhaps more interested in reflecting the range of persons attracted to Jesus according to the Jesus traditions he knew than in replicating the social composition of the churches he knew.

The first suggestion makes the most obvious sense in the context. Later in this chapter I shall take up the possibility that there may also be something in

---

34. J. A. Darr, *Herod the Fox: Audience Criticism and Lukan Characterization* (JSNTSup 163; Sheffield: Sheffield Academic Press, 1998) 162-63.

35. Seim, *Double Message*, 36.

the fourth suggestion, but I shall immediately pursue the plausibility of the first. For, despite its contextual appropriateness, it encounters Sim's objection that, however rich Joanna may have been, as a married woman she would not be free to dispose of this wealth herself. We need to look much more closely than Sim has done at the possibilities Jewish women had to own possessions of which they had free disposition.[36]

2. Jewish Women as Owners of Property

A Palestinian Jewish woman in this period had the following seven possible sources of independently disposable property: (1) inheritance from her father if he died without sons to inherit; (2) property acquired by a deed of gift from father, mother, husband, or other; (3) her ketubba money; (4) her dowry; (5) maintenance from her deceased husband's estate; (6) inheritance from her husband if their marriage and any previous marriage of the husband were childless; (7) money earned by working for payment. These various possibilities require some discussion. Our understanding of these issues will be considerably assisted by the relatively new evidence of the legal documents in the archives of two women, Babatha and Salome Komaïse, which were discovered in Naḥal Ḥever.[37]

(1) Inheritance by a Daughter

The right of a daughter to inherit if her father had no sons alive at the time of his death was established in the Torah itself (Num 27:1-11; 36) and must have

---

36. Sim, "Women," 54, refers briefly to laws in the Mishnah. Arlandson, *Women*, 131n.17, opposes Sim here on very general grounds, but does not address Sim's specific point that Palestinian Jewish married women were not free to dispose of property. Reid, *Women*, 128, similarly fails to address Sim's specific point. She also seriously misinterprets Sim when she says (with footnote reference to him): "Some scholars propose that Mary, Joanna, Susanna, and the other women were not using their own money, but were administering the common fund" (129). Sim says nothing about the women administering the common fund. His proposal is that the women did not retain the use of their economic resources but put them into the common fund.

37. For brief introductions to the texts, see R. Katzoff, "Babatha," in L. H. Schiffman and J. C. VanderKam, eds., *Encyclopedia of the Dead Sea Scrolls* (Oxford: Oxford University Press, 2000) 73-75; H. M. Cotton, "Ḥever, Naḥal: Written Material," in Schiffman and VanderKam, eds., *Encyclopedia*, 359-61; T. Ilan, "Women's Archives in the Judaean Desert," in L. H. Schiffman, E. Tov, and J. C. VanderKam, eds., *The Dead Sea Scrolls Fifty Years after Their Discovery* (Jerusalem: Israel Exploration Society, 2000) 755-60. Babatha's story is reconstructed by A. J. Saldarini, "Babatha's Story," *BAR* 24/2 (1998) 28-37, 72-74.

been recognized in Jewish courts in the late Second Temple period.[38] (According to H. M. Cotton and J. C. Greenfield, P. Yadin 23 and 24 indicate that the law observed among Jews in the province of Arabia early in the second century gave precedence to a man's brother or his brother's sons over the man's daughter,[39] though this cannot be regarded as certain.[40] If it is the case, these families must be following local Nabatean, not Jewish, custom. In Num 27:1-11 the precedence of daughters over brothers is unambiguous.) Later rabbinic interpretation (*m. B. Bat.* 8:2) understood the biblical law to mean that not only a son but also a deceased son's offspring (male or female) took precedence over a daughter, but the rabbis also ascribed to the Sadducees the contrary opinion that a daughter took precedence over a deceased son's offspring (*y. B. Bat.* 8:1, 16a; *t. Yad.* 2:20). Thus the circumstances in which a daughter might inherit may well have been debated in the New Testament period, and we cannot be sure which interpretation of the law would have prevailed in the courts. But it was undisputed that a daughter inherited from her father if no sons or offspring of sons were alive at the time of his death.[41]

38. A rather problematic instance of inheritance by daughters in early Jewish literature is the story of the daughters of Kenaz in *Bib. Ant.* 29. The usual interpretation (e.g., H. Jacobson, *A Commentary on Pseudo-Philo's Liber Antiquitatem Biblicarum* [AGAJU 31; Leiden: Brill, 1996] 823) takes the story to be a parallel to that of the daughters of Zelophehad (Num 27:1-11; 36), but this cannot be the case. As a result of Moses' decision in the case of the daughters of Zelophehad and his promulgation of a law on the inheritance of daughters, the daughters of Kenaz were legally entitled to inherit their father's property. If that were the issue, it makes no sense that Kenaz had refrained from giving them anything during his lifetime "lest he be called avaricious and greedy" (*Bib. Ant.* 29:1). He could not be called avaricious and greedy for disposing of his own property. The issue seems to be rather a matter of his ability, as ruler of Israel, to dispose of land that he had not inherited as his own family property. This is why the people want his daughters "to receive a *greater (ampliorem)* inheritance among the people" (*Bib. Ant.* 29:1), greater, that is, than their legal entitlement to the family property inherited from their father. Zebul, Kenaz's successor as ruler, is able to grant them considerable estates, which they would not have received by ordinary inheritance.

39. H. M. Cotton and J. C. Greenfield, "Babatha's Property and the Law of Succession in the Babatha Archive," *ZPE* 104 (1994) 219-20.

40. Cotton, "Greek Documentary Texts," in Cotton and A. Yardeni, *Aramaic, Hebrew and Greek Documentary Texts from Naḥal Ḥever and Other Sites* (DJD 27; Oxford: Clarendon, 1997) 204.

41. For some known cases of a daughter as an only child, see T. Ilan, *Jewish Women in Greco-Roman Palestine* (TSAJ 44; Tübingen: Mohr [Siebeck], 1995) 50-52.

(2) *Deeds of Gift*

Property could be conferred on a woman by deed of gift. She had full owner-ship and disposal of such property even when married. Deeds of gift seem to have been used to circumvent the laws of inheritance that otherwise prevented daughters and wives from inheriting in most circumstances. Instead of testamentary bequests, which would have directly contravened the Torah's laws of inheritance,[42] Jewish custom adopted the practice, also attested in Egyptian and Greek law, of using deeds of gift to confer property on persons other than the heirs, with various conditions attached, some of which could make the deed of gift functionally equivalent to a bequest in a will, even though technically distinguished from such a bequest.

Several documents in the Babatha and Salome Komaïse archives illustrate this. Papyrus Yadin 7 (120 CE) is a deed of gift from Babatha's father to her mother, giving her all he possesses in the town of Maḥoza, comprising four date groves, as a "gift forever." This was a gift in contemplation of death, a specific sort of gift in which the donor retained usufruct for life and in which the gift is finally irrevocable only on the donor's death.[43] Another deed of gift from the Babatha archive (P. Yadin 19, 128 CE) is by Babatha's second husband, Judah, in favor of his daughter Shelamzion immediately following her marriage: she receives half of a courtyard with its rooms and will receive the other half following his death. Babatha herself probably received from her father a gift of four date groves in Maḥoza (evidently not the groves that he had given to her mother) on the occasion of her first marriage, prior to her father's gift of all he then possessed to his wife. In this case the deed of gift has not survived, but it can be plausibly postulated from the evidence about Babatha's and her father's property.[44] In the Salome Komaïse archive there is a deed of gift in which Salome Gropte (Grapte)[45] gives a date grove in Maḥoza to her daughter Salome Komaïse (P. XḤev/Se 64, 129 CE). Salome Komaïse was Salome Grapte's daughter by her first marriage; by the time of the deed of gift she had remarried. In the case of both her gift to her daughter and of Judah's gift to his daughter Shelamzion, the parent had remarried, and so the motive for the gift may have

---

42. When Herod bequeathed territories to his sister Salome in his will (Josephus, *BJ* 1.646; 2.98; *Ant.* 17.147, 189, 321), he was following Roman, not local, legal practice.

43. See especially R. Yaron, *Gifts in Contemplation of Death in Jewish and Roman Law* (Oxford: Clarendon, 1960).

44. Cotton and Greenfield, "Babatha's Property," 211-18.

45. Cotton, "Greek Documentary Texts," DJD 27:163, notes that the name Grapte occurs as the name of a member of the royal house of Adiabene in Josephus, *BJ* 4.567, but not that it occurs also in Hermas, *Vis.* 2:4, as the name of a member of the Christian church in Rome.

been to ensure that the daughter by the first marriage received some of the parent's property even if the second marriage provided a male heir.

In Salome Gropte's case, it is of course noteworthy that she has property of her own of which she is entirely free to dispose as she wishes, even though she is married. The deed grants her daughter the gift "validly and securely for all time . . . to manage in whatever manner she chooses" (lines 16-17, 40-41).[46] In combination with the remnants of the same clause in Papyrus Yadin 19 (lines 23-25), Judah's deed of gift to his daughter, the clause in both texts can be restored as: "validly and securely for all time, to build, raise up, raise higher, excavate, deepen, possess, use, sell and manage in whatever manner she may choose, all valid and secure."[47] Clearly in each case the daughter's right to manage and dispose of her own property will be unaffected by marriage.

Another relevant document from the Salome Komaïse archive is a deed of renunciation of claims (XḤev/Se 63, probably 127 CE). This is evidently a case of settlement out of court of a controversy between Salome Komaïse and her mother, Salome Grapte. The controversy was about property left by Levi, Salome Grapte's husband and Salome Komaïse's father, and by his son, who was Salome Grapte's son and Salome Komaïse's brother. Salome Komaïse renounces her claims against her mother. No male heirs seem to have been involved. The dispute may have related to deeds of gift in consideration of death,[48] or alternatively it may have concerned the widow's claim on her dead husband's estate by virtue of her ketubba (see §[3] below). Perhaps Salome Komaïse was the sole heir to her father's estate following her brother's death and disputed her mother's claim on the estate, either as a beneficiary of a deed of gift or as a widow entitled to choose either maintenance from the estate or her ketubba in cash.

It is clear that in these two wealthy Jewish families the women owned considerable real estate, acquired from fathers, mothers, and husbands, perhaps in some cases as the heirs in the absence of male heirs with a prior claim, and certainly through deeds of gift, which seem to have been regularly used to ensure that property passed to wives and daughters as well as to sons. In the marriage contracts from Murabba'at and Naḥal Ḥever, real estate is never part of the ketubba or the dowry (see below),[49] which was in the control of a woman's husband while she was married to him. Rather, these women acquired, owned,

---

46. Translation of Cotton, DJD 27:213.

47. Translation of Cotton, DJD 27:219.

48. H. M. Cotton, "The Archive of Salome Komaïse Daughter of Levi: Another Archive from the 'Cave of Letters,'" ZPE 105 (1995) 177.

49. DJD 27:205. This is also true of the marriage contracts from Elephantine; see R. Yaron, *Introduction to the Law of the Aramaic Papyri* (Oxford: Clarendon, 1961) 50-51.

and disposed of real estate quite independently of their husbands.[50] It would not be at all surprising if an aristocratic woman such as Joanna the wife of Chuza did the same.

In addition to the evidence of these documents that are relatively close in time and place to the ministry of Jesus, we may also cite two other categories of evidence that cannot be considered direct evidence for Jewish practice in Palestine in the time of Jesus, but that become much more relevant for our interests when related to each other and when seen in the light of the evidence from the Babatha and Salome Komaïse archives.

First, there is the evidence from the Jewish community at Elephantine in Egypt in the fifth century BCE. In the archive of Anani (or Ananiah) son of Azariah there are four deeds of gift. In the earliest (Kraeling 4 = B3.5),[51] fifteen years after his marriage to his wife Tamut, he gives her half a house to belong to her and her children forever. The other three deeds confer property on Anani's daughter Yehoyishma.[52] In contemplation of her marriage, three months before it took place, he gave her restricted rights of usufruct to part of his house (Kraeling 6 = B3.7),[53] to which in a later deed, a deed in contemplation of death, he gave her full ownership, with the gift to become valid at his death (Kraeling 9 = B3.10).[54] In this case, Anani gives a reason for his gift: "because she supported me when I was old of days" (line 17).[55] Finally, he gave his daughter a house as a gift additional to her dowry (her original dowry having been given to her not by her father but by her adoptive brother) (Kraeling 10 = B3.11).[56] In this case she was given ownership, but her husband was to share rights of usufruct, as in the case of a dowry.[57] In these deeds of gift we see much the same practice as in those from the Babatha and Salome Komaïse archives. Anani uses them to en-

---

50. In this respect practice seems different from that prescribed by the Mishnah (*m. Ket.* 8:1), according to which a husband had the right to manage his wife's property, but even from the Mishnah it is clear that this right was not uncontroversial. See Ilan, *Jewish Women*, 168-69.

51. Papyrus 4 in E. G. Kraeling, *The Brooklyn Museum Aramaic Papyri* (New Haven: Yale University Press, 1953) 167-71; B3.5 in B. Porten and A. Yardeni, *Textbook of Aramaic Documents from Ancient Egypt*, vol. 2, *Contracts* (Jerusalem: Hebrew University Press, 1989) 68-71.

52. For a general account of them, see B. Porten, *Archives from Elephantine* (Berkeley: University of California Press, 1968) 225-30.

53. Kraeling, *Brooklyn Museum*, 191-93; Porten and Yardeni, *Textbook*, 74-77. For this interpretation see H. Z. Szubin and B. Porten, "A Life Estate of Usufruct: A New Interpretation of Kraeling 6," *BASOR* 269 (1988) 29-45.

54. Kraeling, *Brooklyn Museum*, 235-39; Porten and Yardeni, *Textbook*, 86-89.

55. Trans. Porten and Yardeni, *Textbook*.

56. Kraeling, *Brooklyn Museum*, 247-51; Porten and Yardeni, *Textbook*, 90-93.

57. For this interpretation see B. Porten and H. Z. Szubin, "A Dowry Addendum (Kraeling 10)," *JAOS* 107 (1987) 231-38.

able his wife and his daughter to inherit property from him, as they would not have been able to do by the laws of inheritance.[58] Another wealthy, property-owning Jewish woman of Elephantine, who was the beneficiary of deeds of gift by her father, was Mibtahiah, the daughter of Mahseiah.[59]

Second, the rabbinic literature, beginning with the Mishnah, recognizes the practice of deeds of gift, including those in contemplation of death (*m. B. Bat.* 8:5-7).[60] They are clearly regarded as a means of circumventing the laws of inheritance, avoiding disobedience to the Torah by speaking in terms of gift rather than inheritance. They are used to benefit relatives or friends who would not otherwise inherit and to prevent a son of whom a father disapproved from inheriting. The rabbis are not favorable to such distribution of property to the detriment of legitimate heirs, but they nevertheless recognize its legality. Still less were the rabbis favorable to female inheritance, and they do not explicitly mention wives, daughters, or other female relatives as the beneficiaries of deeds of gift. But the legal instruments they acknowledge could certainly be used in favor of women, as they were in the families of Babatha and Salome Komaïse. Indeed, the legal situation reflected in the Mishnah seems quite comparable to that obtaining in the courts used by those two families a hundred years earlier. The reason will not be that the rabbis' predecessors determined the law in such courts, but that Jewish customary law, itself owing much to the laws of other peoples, was in these respects, as in many others, adopted by the rabbis. In this case, that is, the use of deeds of gift to evade the laws of succession, there seems to be a continuity — though not a direct line of historical descent — from the practice of Egyptian Jews in the fifth century BCE, through that of Jews in Nabatea and Judea in the early second century CE, to the rabbinic law codified in the Mishnah at the end of the second century. We may reasonably assume that the same legal processes were available to Palestinian Jews in the time of Jesus.

The documents from the archives of Babatha and Salome Komaïse, especially in their evidence about the use of deeds of gift, illustrate what often seems to be the case: that detailed evidence and close examination show ancient Jewish (and other) societies to have been less thoroughly patriarchal than superficially they might seem to be. Ways and means for women to exercise a considerable degree of independence could be found within the broader patriarchal structures. Doubtless they could not challenge or disturb these structures in ordinary circumstances, but the structures did leave at least some women more

---

58. Cf. Yaron, *Introduction*, 68.

59. See Porten, *Archives*, 240-45.

60. T. Ilan, *Mine and Yours Are Hers: Retrieving Women's History from Rabbinic Literature* (AGAJU 41; Leiden: Brill, 1997) 144-46; Yaron, *Gifts*, 49-129.

room to maneuver than is generally recognized. It is also important (and a significant qualification of much of the older work on this subject) to realize that the hugely patriarchal bias of rabbinic laws is not necessarily fully representative of real life, even in the Jewish society of the periods in which the rabbis lived, still less of the first century CE.

(3) Ketubba, (4) Dowry, and (5) Maintenance of a Widow from Her Husband's Estate

The term *ketubba* refers both to a Jewish marriage contract and to the money or goods a husband pledges, in the contract, as due to his wife in the event of divorce or his death. It seems to have evolved from the bride-price (מהר), which in early Israel was paid by the bridegroom to his father-in-law as a compensation for the bride's family's loss of her labor. According to the rabbis (*b. Ket.* 10a, 82b), an enactment by Simeon ben Shetah in the early first century BCE required the bridegroom only to promise to provide the amount for his wife if he divorced her or when he died, with his whole property as guarantee for this payment. The ketubba, as it came to be called, was thus no longer compensation for the bride's family, but provision for a divorced or widowed wife. Whether the rabbinic account of the history of the ketubba is historical or not,[61] it does seem likely that in the New Testament period something like the practice of the ketubba as the rabbis later knew it existed. Marriage contracts from Elephantine already attest the treatment of the bride-price as only nominally given to the bride's father (or head of family) and its inclusion with the dowry in the payment the bride will receive if her husband divorces her.[62]

While the ketubba was a sum owed by the bridegroom to his wife, the dowry was paid by the bride's father to her husband. It functioned both to attract suitors and, like the ketubba, to provide for the woman in the event of divorce or widowhood, since, although the husband had the right to use the dowry during the period of the marriage, it had to be refunded in full to the wife if he divorced her or predeceased her.

In the Jewish marriage contracts from Murabbaʿat and Nahal Hever, which again provide our best evidence from a period close to the New Testa-

---

61. For an account that does not question its historicity, see L. J. Archer, *Her Price Is Beyond Rubies: The Jewish Woman in Graeco-Roman Palestine* (JSOTSup 66; Sheffield: JSOT Press, 1990) 159-65; for an account skeptical of its historicity, see M. Satlow, "Reconsidering the Rabbinic *ketubah* Payment," in S. J. D. Cohen, ed., *The Jewish Family in Antiquity* (BJS 289; Atlanta: Scholars Press, 1993) 133-51.

62. Yaron, *Introduction*, 47-48.

ment period, there is some difficulty in identifying and distinguishing dowries and ketubbot, and the issue has been disputed.[63] Of the five such contracts written in Greek (Mur 115, Mur 116, Yadin 18, XḤev/Se 65 [= Yadin 37], XḤev/Se 69), four refer unquestionably to a dowry, since the sum in question (silver, gold, clothing, etc., valued at sums from 96 to 500 denarii)[64] is brought with her by the bride, while the fifth (Mur 116) refers to a dowry (φερνή) amounting to 2,000 denarii that is probably to be understood in the same way. In one case (the marriage of Babatha's stepdaughter Shelamzion to Judah Cimber), however, there is reference to "another three hundred denarii that [Judah] promised to give [Shelamzion] in addition to the sum of her aforestated bridal gift [προσφορᾶς], all accounted toward her dowry [προι(ο)κός]" (Yadin 18, lines 46-49).[65] The full sum of 500 denarii (the bridal gift of 200 and Judah's addition of 300 denarii) is described as Shelamzion's dowry (פרכן[66] = φερνή) in the Aramaic subscription written by Judah himself (lines 70-71). This addition to the dowry by the husband functions just like the ketubba in rabbinic law,[67] and so, despite the contract's reference to "Greek law/custom" (line 51: ἑλλενικῷ νόμῳ), this contract seems to attest the Jewish practice of ketubba.[68] Moreover, the inclusion of the ketubba in the dowry is clearly paralleled in the much earlier marriage contracts from Elephantine.[69]

---

63. See R. Katzoff in N. Lewis, R. Katzoff, and J. C. Greenfield, "*Papyrus Yadin* 18," *IEJ* 37 (1987) 240-42; A. Wasserstein, "A Marriage Contract from the Province of Arabia Nova: Notes on Papyrus Yadin 18," *JQR* 80 (1989) 113-15; Y. Yadin, J. C. Greenfield, and A. Yardeni, "Babatha's *Ketubba*," *IEJ* 44 (1994) 87-98; M. A. Friedman, "Babatha's *Ketubba:* Some Preliminary Observations," *IEJ* 46 (1996) 55-76; Cotton, DJD 27:266-68; Satlow, "Reconsidering," 137-41.

64. On the monetary terms used, see Yadin, Greenfield, and Yardeni, "Babatha's *Ketubba*," 90-92.

65. Trans. N. Lewis in Lewis, Katzoff, and Greenfield, "*Papyrus Yadin* 18," 233; and in N. Lewis, *The Documents from the Bar Kochba Period in the Cave of Letters* (Jerusalem: Israel Exploration Society, and Hebrew University, 1989) 80.

66. On the term see Wasserstein, "Marriage Contract," 106-7n.44.

67. It is not clear to me why Satlow, "Reconsidering," 139, asserts that "it cannot be considered a *ketubah.*" On pp. 140-41 he seems to be distinguishing the rabbinic ketubba from a sum added to the dowry by the husband, which is "already transmitted to the bride and accounted as part of her dowry" (140). But the rabbinic ketubba too was notionally transmitted to the bride at the time of the marriage. In neither case did the sum actually pass into the wife's possession until divorce or widowhood.

68. The fragmentary text of Mur 116 also seems to refer to something additional to the dowry — "the dowry and the aforementioned things . . ." (line 6: τὴν φερνὴν καὶ τὰ πρ[ογε]γραμμένα . . .) — which may be the ketubba. The 2,000 denarii owed to the wife (line 12) may therefore include the ketubba as well as the dowry.

69. B2.6 (= Cowley 15) and B3.8 (= Kraeling 7) in Porten and Yardeni, *Textbook*, 30-33, 78-83.

There are also three marriage contracts in Aramaic (Mur 20, Mur 21, Yadin 10), two of which refer to "the laws of Moses and the Jews" (Mur 20, line 3; Yadin 10, line 5). Two of these use the word *ketubba* (Mur 21, lines 10, 13; Yadin 10, line 16). Unlike the dowry in the Greek contracts, it is not said in the surviving portions of the texts that this money has been brought by the bride, whereas one of the contracts refers, in addition to the ketubba, to what the bride has brought with her into the husband's house: "If I divorce you I will return [to you the money of] your *kethubah* and everything that is [yours that is with me]. . . . The sons which you shall have by me [will inherit] the money of your *kethubah* and [all] of you[rs that is with me and that is written above]" (Mur 21, lines 10, 13).[70] The word "return" (line 10: תוב) might suggest that the ketubba as well as the rest was brought by the bride, but may be used loosely. It looks as though the ketubba and the dowry ("all that is yours that is with me") are both acknowledged here, though it cannot be ruled out that "ketubba" in these Aramaic marriage contracts refers to the dowry.

It seems that at least some Jews combined traditional Jewish practice of ketubba with the Hellenistic practice of dowry, as seems already to have been the case four centuries earlier at Elephantine.[71] It may not be accidental that the contracts in Greek give priority to the dowry, while those in Aramaic give priority to the ketubba. The fragmentary state of the texts makes it impossible to tell whether all the contracts referred to both. It may be that practice varied.

In any case it is clear that, whereas a wife would not have the right to independent use of her dowry or ketubba while married, in the event of divorce[72] or her husband's death she was legally entitled to complete ownership of the full amount of her ketubba and dowry. Among the wealthy families from whom our marriage contracts come, this could be a considerable sum: 96 (but this was a case of second marriage: XHev/Se 65), 200 (Mur 115), 400 (Yadin 10), 500 (Yadin 18, XHev/Se 69), or even 2,000 (Mur 116) denarii. In the case of being widowed, the widow had the right either to remain in her husband's house and be maintained from his estate or to take her ketubba and/or dowry in full and leave. There might, of course, be disputes with the heirs and the need to go

70. Trans. Archer, *Her Price*, 294.

71. See B2.6 (= Cowley 15) and B3.8 (= Kraeling 7) in Porten and Yardeni, *Textbook*, 30-33, 78-83; and Yaron, *Introduction*, 47-48.

72. For the return of the dowry at the time of divorce, see Mur 19. It is debated whether XHev/Se 13 is a bill of divorce sent by a woman to her husband or a document in which a divorced woman renounces any claims on her husband's property, having presumably already received her ketubba and/or dowry from him (see T. Ilan, "Notes and Observations on a Newly Published Divorce Bill from the Judaean Desert," *HTR* 89 [1996] 195-202; A. Yardeni, "Aramaic and Hebrew Documentary Texts," DJD 27:65-70).

to law to secure her rights, as the widow in Jesus' parable found (Luke 18:1-5) and as Babatha herself seems to have found (see Yadin 21 and 22).

Because all of a man's property was lien and guarantee for the debt he owed his wife (e.g., Mur 20, lines 11-12), he could not sell any of it without his wife's consent. Papyrus Murabba'at 30 (134 CE) is a bill of sale of a house and land, and includes the seller's wife's renunciation of her claims on the property sold on condition of remaining in her husband's house after his death and receiving 30 denarii every year from the estate. Sapphira's part in the story of Ananias and Sapphira (Acts 5:1: he sold a piece of property with her consent) should probably be explained in this way: because of her claims on Ananias's estate in the event of his death before her, her consent is needed before he can sell. Since we do not have examples of joint ownership of property by husband and wife in any other sense, this is a plausible understanding of the passage,[73] too hastily dismissed by commentators who cannot be bothered with legal niceties.[74]

(6) Inheritance of a Widow

That the laws of succession allowed a widow to inherit her husband's estate if their marriage and any previous marriage of the husband were childless (or no heirs survived) is possible, though not proven.[75] The best evidence is the book of Judith. Judith's husband "had left her gold and silver, men and women slaves, livestock, and fields; and she maintained this estate" (8:7). Later we are told that before she died she distributed her property to her husband's nearest kin and her own nearest kin (16:24). It seems clear that readers are meant to suppose that she and her husband had no children. He may, of course, have bequeathed his property to her by a deed of gift in consideration of death (see §[2] above). That she herself used such deeds of gift to distribute her property at her death is

73. J. D. M. Derrett, "Ananias, Sapphira, and the Right of Property," *DRev* 89 (1971) 225-32.

74. E.g., J. A. Fitzmyer, *The Acts of the Apostles* (AB 31; New York: Doubleday, 1998) 322; B. Witherington III, *The Acts of the Apostles: A Socio-Rhetorical Commentary* (Grand Rapids: Eerdmans; Carlisle: Paternoster, 1998) 215. R. G. Maccini, *Her Testimony Is True: Women as Witnesses according to John* (JSNTSup 125; Sheffield: Sheffield Academic Press, 1996) 79, is wrong to say of Sapphira that "had she designated [the property] as part of her dowry or acquired it after their marriage, he could have sold it on his own."

75. Cf. F. S. Frick, "Widows in the Hebrew Bible: A Transactional Approach," in A. Brenner, ed., *A Feminist Companion to Exodus to Deuteronomy* (FCB 1/6; Sheffield: Sheffield Academic Press, 1994) 148-51. On the debatable evidence from the Elephantine marriage contracts, see Yaron, *Introduction*, 71-76; idem, *Gifts*, 14-16.

probably the implication of 16:24, but her own inheritance may have been by law of succession in the absence of other heirs, whether offspring of her husband or siblings of her husband or their offspring.[76]

In any case Judith, as a wealthy widow, is significant for our interests. She is of course a fictional character, but she is portrayed as a wealthy and childless widow because only such a woman could be easily envisaged as having the independence and respect to play the role she is given in the story. Such a woman would be in the relatively rare position of being wholly independent of father, husband, and sons, and yet with the resources to exercise her independence. A rich widow who was certainly a historical figure of the late Second Temple period, a younger contemporary of Jesus, is Martha the daughter of Boethus.[77] The stories told about her in rabbinic literature may have little historical value, but that she was an extremely wealthy woman, remembered as such in rabbinic tradition, seems highly probable. (In passages such as *b. Ket.* 104a and *Sifre Deut.* 281, she is treated as the proverbial example of the rich widow, the richest woman of whom the tradition knew.) She belonged to the aristocratic priestly family of Boethus, which supplied many of the high priests of the period. Widowed by her first husband, she was later married again to the high priest Joshua son of Gamla; but the rabbinic traditions, such as the story that she secured her second husband's nomination to the high priesthood by bribery (*b. Yoma* 18a), take for granted that her wealth was her own, not her husband's.[78]

These examples suggest the possibility that Jesus' women disciples included widows with independent means. Such women would have had both the independence to travel with Jesus and the financial resources to support him.

---

76. The Mishnah later denies that a wife can inherit from her husband (*m. B. Bat.* 8:1), but does not explain who inherits if neither a man nor his siblings have descendants. If it was possible for a widow to inherit from her husband, we should probably assume that the estate would revert to her husband's family if she married, since otherwise the property would be permanently alienated from the man's family. Cf. Yaron, *Introduction*, 74.

77. See Ilan, *Mine*, 88-97.

78. A case of a property-owning widow in the NT is Mary the mother of John Mark, who owned a house in Jerusalem (Acts 12:12). Since her son is alive and presumably of age, however, she cannot have inherited the house from her husband. If it were his, it would have passed to John Mark, not Mary. So the house may be property she had inherited from her father or received by deed of gift, or it may be her ketubbah or dowry.

(7) Money Earned by Working for Payment

Tal Ilan has collected the information in early rabbinic literature about women's work.[79] Though later than our period, this evidence is likely to reflect a relatively unchanging social situation, and, given the rabbis' bias toward the subordination of women to their husbands and the confining of women to the home, we can assume that possibilities of independent work for women, usually mentioned only incidentally in rabbinic literature, were, if anything, greater than the rabbis acknowledge.

We must, of course, leave aside the work done by female slaves and the work done by a woman for the benefit of her family members. Such work, while entitling the woman to provision for her basic needs, could not provide her with payment of which she was free to dispose as she wished. But it was possible for a woman to earn money by performing the same tasks for others as she would normally perform for her family. She could sell, whether at her home or in the market,[80] such things as bread, clothes, and farm produce. In most cases this would probably be only as an augmentation of the family income, especially in poorer families, while full-time "professional" bakers and shopkeepers would commonly be male.[81] But a woman needing to make a living for herself — an unmarried or divorced woman not part of her father's household, or a poor widow without male relatives — might well attempt to do so by these means. We do know of one group of "professional" and doubtless highly skilled, unmarried[82] women: those who wove the curtains of the temple were members of the temple staff, on the temple treasury's payroll, like the families (including their women?) who baked the shewbread and made the incense for the temple.[83] This high-profile example suggests that there would have been other women who either augmented the family income or who supported themselves independently by the skilled production of cloth and garments. Whether it was possible for a woman to build up a sizable business, as Lydia did (Acts 16:14) in a social context in Asia Minor that probably allowed more opportunity for women than Palestine at this time, is less likely, though our evidence is not such as to rule it out.

Other occupations that were normally those of women included innkeeping, that is, taking paying guests in the home, a natural extension of women's customary work into a way of earning money from nonfamily mem-

79. Ilan, *Jewish Women*, 184-90.
80. For women selling in the markets, see Ilan, *Mine*, 171-74.
81. See Ilan, *Mine*, 229-30.
82. That they were unmarried virgins is clear from 2 Bar 10:19.
83. Ilan, *Mine*, 139-43.

bers. (The innkeepers of Bethlehem, implied though not actually mentioned in Luke 2:7, are likely to have been female, not the male figures portrayed in many a modern nativity play.) Other female occupations, recognized as such in the rabbinic literature, were hairdresser, midwife, and professional mourner. In all these cases, the women's work in question could either be an addition to the family income or, more plausibly in some cases than others, a means for an independent woman to make a living. Women who did not live with adult male relatives must have been relatively rare, and the fact that charitable help for the widow and the orphan (who might well be living with a widowed mother) was a well-recognized duty in Judaism implies that it cannot have been easy for women without able-bodied male relatives to make a living. Nevertheless, the possibilities for wage earning that I have noted show that there may well have been some who managed such a life without dependence on charity. Some prostitutes were probably also in this category.[84]

A married woman or a woman who lived in her father's household could make money in these ways but could not dispose of it freely. It would be a contribution to the family income and controlled by her husband or father. Only women (unmarried, divorced, or widowed) who were not under the authority of father or husband could earn money for themselves.

In the light of this discussion of the ways in which women could acquire and own property, we must now consider which of these ways were open to women of different marital status. Every adult woman belonged to one of four categories: (a) unmarried; (b) married; (c) divorced and not remarried; (d) widowed and not remarried. The possibilities of owning property are for each category thus:

(a) An unmarried woman might have property in categories (1), (2), and (7).
(b) A married woman's only freely disposable property would be in categories (1) and (2). Any money she earned (7) would be her husband's, while her ketubba (3) and dowry (4) were not at her disposal unless and until her husband divorced her or died.
(c) A divorced woman, as well as categories (1), (2), and (7), which an unmarried woman might also possess, would have (3) and (4).
(d) A widow could have property in any of the seven categories, though she could only have (3) and (4) if she renounced (5), while (6) would replace (3), (4), and (5).

---

84. On prostitutes see Ilan, *Jewish Women*, 214-21.

Women in any of these categories could therefore have been among the women who followed Jesus in Galilee and supported his ministry from their own economic resources. It is unlikely that many women remained unmarried much beyond puberty, since fathers would usually be concerned to get their daughters married as soon as possible (cf. Sir 42:9-10),[85] and marriages were often already arranged before puberty.[86] But some women whom Jesus had healed of diseases or delivered from demons (Luke 8:2) might well have been mature women who had not been able to marry because of their condition. A demon-possessed woman might also be someone who had been married and then divorced by her husband when she became useless and unmanageable. Mary Magdalene, a former demoniac, may have been a woman who had never married or who had been divorced.[87] Of the four categories, a married woman was the least likely to have financial resources with the power to dispose of them as she wished, but the documents from the archives of Babatha and Salome Komaïse show that at least in wealthier families it would not be unusual for married women to have property of their own with full ownership rights.

This last point is the most important qualification to be made of David Sim's assertion, based only on the rabbinic statements about wives and property, that "Joanna, despite her apparently wealthy background, was probably not in a position to contribute financially to the ministry of Jesus."[88] This statement, like others in Sim's discussion, takes no account of deeds of gift and the way, as we can now see, in which they were used to circumvent the laws of inheritance that normally prevented women from inheriting. Joanna's wealthy background would make it quite likely that she did own property received, if not by inheritance, then by deed of gift, as Babatha and others in the scrolls from the Judean desert did. Even as a married woman she could very plausibly have economic resources of her own from which to support Jesus and his band of followers. Sim assumes that she was married. But it is not clear that she could not be called "the wife of Chuza" even if her husband had died, especially since

85. Cf. Archer, *Her Price*, 125-26.

86. Cf. Archer, *Her Price*, 151-53. But note the discussion by Ilan, *Jewish Women*, 65-69, who adduces some evidence to qualify this generalization. On the almost complete lack of evidence for women remaining unmarried throughout life, see Ilan, *Jewish Women*, 62-65.

87. I mean that her state of demon possession could have prevented marriage or led to her being divorced; but C. B. Unieta, "Mary Magdalene and the Seven Demons in Social-Scientific Perspective," in Kitzberger, ed., *Transformative Encounters*, 221, thinks the demon possession could have been the result of her being widowed or divorced: "The symptoms of possession in such a society seem to indicate a feeling of inadequacy, and at the same time a mute and ineffective protest."

88. Sim, "Women Followers," 52.

this description was the easiest way in which Luke could indicate her connection with the Herodian court and her elite status. If she was a wealthy widow her independence, financial and otherwise, might be even greater than those of a married woman with private means.

3. Wife of Herod's "Steward"

Joanna's husband Chuza was the ἐπίτροπος of Herod Antipas (Luke 8:3). The word refers to the administrator of a household or estate, as in Matthew 20:8. Josephus and Philo use it as a translation of the Latin *procurator* and apply it to Roman governors, both those properly called *procuratores* and those more properly called *praefecti*.[89] But more relevant to Chuza's case are Thaumastus, the ἐπίτροπος of King Agrippa I; Ptolemy, the ἐπίτροπος of Agrippa II; and Syllaeus, the ἐπίτροπος of the Nabatean king Obodas. Josephus tells us that Thaumastus had been a slave of the emperor Gaius.[90] He had done Agrippa a favor when Agrippa was arrested in Rome, and so when Agrippa became king and Gaius sent him Thaumastus, Agrippa freed him and appointed him steward of his estate (τῆς οὐσίας ἐπίτροπον). When he died he left Thaumastus to his son Agrippa II and his daughter Berenice "to serve them in the same capacity," and he remained in that position until he died (*Ant.* 18.194).[91] Another ἐπίτροπος of Agrippa II and his sister was called "Ptolemy" (*BJ* 2.595; *Vita* 126-28), a Greek name often used by Jews. He may be the same person to whom the Babylonian Talmud referred as the steward (ἐπίτροπος used as a loanword — אפיטרופוס — in *b. Shab.* 121a; *b. Suk.* 27a) of Agrippa II.[92] In the case of a king, the manager of his estate was in effect also the finance minister of the kingdom, administering all the revenues of the realm as well as the royal domains and

---

89. Josephus, *BJ* 2.117, 169, 223, 247, 252, 271, 273; *Ant.* 15.406; 20.2, 14, 97, 99, 107, 132, 142, 162; Philo, *Leg.* 299. In this sense Josephus uses ἔπαρχος synonymously: *BJ* 6.305; *Ant.* 18:33, 237; 19.363; 20.197. In Josephus, *BJ* 1.199; *Ant.* 14.143, where Herod the Great's father Antipater is made ἐπίτροπος of Judea, the word probably refers more strictly to financial affairs. For these usages see E. Schürer, *The History of the Jewish People in the Age of Jesus Christ (175 B.C.–A.D. 135)*, ed. G. Vermes and F. Millar, vol. 1 (Edinburgh: T. & T. Clark, 1973) 358-60; E. M. Smallwood, *The Jews under Roman Rule* (Leiden: Brill, 1981) 39, 145; N. Kokkinos, *The Herodian Dynasty* (JSPSup 30; Sheffield: Sheffield Academic Press, 1998) 98n.52.

90. Thaumastus is a Greek name known to have been borne by other slaves in Rome. It is unlikely that Thaumastus was Jewish.

91. For the suggestion that Thaumastus was Josephus's source for much of his material about Tiberius and Agrippa I, see D. R. Schwartz, *Agrippa I: The Last King of Judaea* (TSAJ 23; Tübingen: Mohr [Siebeck], 1990) 10n.13.

92. Cf. Schwartz, *Agrippa I*, 168-69.

household. While this highly responsible position was occupied in Agrippa I's realm by a favored freedman, in the Nabatean kingdom the aristocratic Syllaeus was the ἐπίτροπος of King Obodas (Josephus, *BJ* 1.487).[93] That Syllaeus was of noble birth would seem required by the fact that he was considered eligible to marry Herod the Great's sister Salome (*Ant.* 6.224-25), as well as by the fact that, on a votive tablet he left at the temple of Apollo near Miletus, he called himself "Syllaeus, the brother of the king,"[94] evidently not a family relationship but a title indicating the highest position at court. So powerful was his position as ἐπίτροπος that Syllaeus was able to take advantage of the weakness of the elderly and idle King Obodas and effectively to rule the kingdom (*Ant.* 16.220, 280), even making a bid for the succession to the throne (*Ant.* 16.295-96).

These three parallels suggest that Herod Antipas's ἐπίτροπος would have been a very high ranking official at Herod's court. But, before concluding this about Chuza, we should consider the possibility that he was not "*the* [unique] steward of Herod," but merely "*a* steward," that is, the manager of one of the royal estates. Luke's phrasing is ambiguous and the latter translation is possible. We might then compare the ἐπίτροπος of the imperial estate at Jamnia (Yavneh). This part of the royal estates had been bequeathed by Herod the Great to the empress Livia, and, after passing to the emperors Tiberius and Gaius, was managed by C. Herennius Capito,[95] whom Josephus calls "the procurator of Jamnia" (ὁ τῆς Ἰαμνείας ἐπίτροπος) (*Ant.* 18.158). According to Philo he was an originally poor man who enriched himself considerably by abusing his position (*Leg.* 199; cf. 203). One other procurator of Jamnia (probably during Livia's ownership of the estate), known from an inscription, was a freedman of the emperor Augustus.[96] But, by contrast with Judea and Samaria, where there seem to have been extensive royal estates, there is no evidence that Antipas owned royal estates in Galilee.[97] He proba-

---

93. Smallwood, *Jews*, 95, calls him "a Nabataean plenipotentiary."

94. P. Richardson, *Herod: King of the Jews and Friend of the Romans* (Columbia, S.C.: University of South Carolina Press, 1996) 280n.73.

95. Smallwood, *Jews*, 158, 175, 189; Z. Safrai, *The Economy of Roman Palestine* (London: Routledge, 1994) 323-24.

96. Smallwood, *Jews*, 159n.56.

97. R. A. Horsley, *Galilee: History, Politics, People* (Valley Forge, Pa.: Trinity Press International, 1995) 210-14; D. A. Fiensy, *The Social History of Palestine in the Herodian Period* (Lewiston, N.Y.: Mellen, 1991) 24-48. The suggestion that Antipas built the city of Tiberias on royal land (J. Pastor, *Land and Economy in Ancient Palestine* [London: Routledge, 1997] 133-34, following Avi-Yonah) is rejected by Horsley, *Galilee*, 212. But note the reference to a royal estate at Shikhin in *t. Shab.* 13(14).9, to which Horsley, *Galilee*, 214, himself refers. We also know from Josephus, *Vita* 119, that there was a royal estate (at that time belonging to Queen Berenice) near Besara (Beth She'arim) in Lower Galilee, on the border of Antipas's territory.

bly did in Perea,[98] but the attachment of Chuza's wife to Jesus in Galilee is easier to understand if Chuza lived and worked in Galilee. Thus, while we cannot rule out the possibility that Chuza was manager of one of Antipas's royal estates in Galilee or Perea, it is more likely that he was in charge of Antipas's property and revenues generally. This would be a highly important position, especially in the early years of Antipas's reign, when large amounts of money needed to be raised, no doubt from taxation, in order to finance the building of three new cities (Sepphoris, Livias, and Tiberias).[99] But whether Chuza merely administered one of Antipas's estates or was finance minister of the realm, but especially in the latter case, and whatever his social origins, Chuza would be well rewarded for his services and a man of some wealth. As such, and however he came by it (inheritance, gift of the king,[100] purchase, exploitation of peasant indebtedness),[101] he would certainly have owned land. He and his wife Joanna would have been members of the Herodian court at Tiberias, the city that Herod Antipas had founded (probably c. 18 CE)[102] and that was his capital for most of his reign.

This is an appropriate point at which to mention the suggestion, made by some scholars,[103] that Chuza was the "royal official" (βασιλικός)[104] of John 4:46, who was evidently resident in Capernaum and whose whole household came to believe in Jesus (4:53). The healing of his son (on this hypothesis Joanna's son) would then explain Joanna's devotion to Jesus' ministry. The βασιλικός of John 4:46 is unlikely to be the ἐπίτροπος of a royal estate, since we know of none in the

---

98. Fiensy, *Social History,* 48.

99. Cf. R. A. Horsley, *Archaeology, History, and Society in Galilee* (Valley Forge, Pa.: Trinity Press International, 1996) 34.

100. He could have been granted land from the royal estates in Perea. Josephus, *Vita* 33, refers to Crispus son of Compsus, who had been ἔπαρχος (military commander?) under Agrippa I, and who, as well as being associated with Tiberias, owned estates in Perea. Cf. Kokkinos, *Herodian Dynasty,* 293; and, differing from this view of Crispus, cf. Schwartz, *Agrippa I,* 114n.27, 136n.124. S. Schwartz, "Josephus in Galilee: Rural Patronage and Social Breakdown," in F. Parente and J. Sievers, eds., *Josephus and the History of the Greco-Roman Period* (SPB 41; Leiden: Brill, 1994) 304, thinks of courtiers being rewarded with land in Galilee, but does not note the lack of evidence for royal domains in Galilee.

101. On this as a means by which royal officials could acquire land, see Horsley, *Galilee,* 215-16; and cf. Schwartz, "Josephus in Galilee," 302, for possible evidence in Josephus (*Vita* 177, 392) of Tiberian aristocrats gaining land through defrauding peasants.

102. This date was proposed by M. Avi-Yonah, rejected by H. W. Hoehner, *Herod Antipas* (SNTSMS 17; Cambridge: Cambridge University Press, 1972) 93-95, but vindicated by S. Freyne, *Galilee: From Alexander the Great to Hadrian 323 BCE to 135 CE* (2d ed.; Wilmington, Del.: Glazier; Edinburgh: T. & T. Clark, 1998) 149n.65; and Kokkinos, *Herodian Dynasty,* 234-35.

103. E.g., V. R. L. Fry, "Chuza," *ABD* 1:1022.

104. For the term cf. Josephus, *Vita* 112, 149.

vicinity of Capernaum. If Chuza were the ἐπίτροπος of Herod's realm, he might have owned property in Capernaum. But the βασιλικός might be the head of one of the toparchies of Galilee,[105] or a lesser official. We cannot consider his identity with Chuza more than a possibility. He does, however, provide corroborative evidence of Jesus' reputation as a healer among the Herodian elite to which Chuza and Joanna belonged. Further such evidence is probably provided by the figure of Manaen (Greek form of Menahem), later a prominent leader in the church of Antioch, who had been σύντροφος of Herod Antipas (Acts 13:1). Although the word could mean "foster brother" or more generally "boyhood friend, companion in education," it acquired a broader meaning of "close companion."[106] More specifically and most relevantly, the term "σύντροφος of the king" had become, in the Hellenistic kingdoms of the Near East, a court title, designating a courtier as the intimate friend of the king.[107] So we should not speculate that Manaen was brought up together with Herod Antipas, possible though this is,[108] but we do know that Manaen was a trusted member of the king's inner circle of courtiers. He is almost certainly the same person to whom Papias later refers as Manaim (Μαναιμ). Papias knew a story, which unfortunately has not survived, about the raising of his mother from the dead.[109] It is not entirely clear whether the miracle was performed by Jesus or by an apostle, but the context in Philip of Side's report of Papias's words suggests the former. It is therefore not improbable that Manaen, like Joanna and the royal official of Capernaum, first believed in Jesus through experience of Jesus' healing ministry in Galilee. These associations also give special resonance to Herod's reported interest in Jesus and desire to see him perform miracles (Luke 9:7-9; 23:8; cf. Mark 6:14-16).[110]

---

105. For these see Hoehner, *Herod,* 102. We do not know that Capernaum was the capital of a toparchy, though it may have been. The nearest such capital was Tarichaeae: Hoehner, *Herod,* 45-46; Freyne, *Galilee: From Alexander,* 55n.52, 69.

106. In *BJ* 1.215; *Ant.* 14.183, Josephus has Antipater refer to Hyrcanus II as king and σύντροφος of Antipater's son Herod. Hyrcanus was a close friend of the family while Herod was growing up, but he must have been at least twenty years older than Herod. So the meaning cannot be "companion in education" or "friend since they were boys."

107. Cf. 2 Macc 9:29; other references in BAGD s.v. (793); and G. A. Deissmann, *Bible Studies* (tr. A. Grieve; 2d ed.; Edinburgh: T. & T. Clark, 1903) 310-12.

108. Antipas spent his mid-teens being educated in Rome, in the care of "a certain Jew" (Josephus, *Ant.* 17.20). He must have been provided with Jewish companions of his own age.

109. Reported by Philip of Side: J. B. Lightfoot, *The Apostolic Fathers* (ed. J. R. Harmer; London: Macmillan, 1891) 519. J. Chapman proposed that Manaen's mother (also in his view Antipas's own foster mother) was Joanna (reported by A. Hastings, *Prophet and Witness in Jerusalem* [London: Longmans Green, 1958] 49). On the view argued later in this chapter, Joanna could not be old enough to be Manaen's mother.

110. Given these strong Christian associations with the court of Herod Antipas, it is also

We have little more information, from the time of Antipas, about this elite of Herodian courtiers and officials to which Joanna belonged. There is Mark's reference, in his story of Herod's birthday party, to "his courtiers and officers and the leaders of Galilee" (τοῖς μεγιστᾶσιν αὐτοῦ καὶ τοῖς χιλιάρχοις καὶ τοῖς πρώτοις τῆς Γαλιλαίας, Mark 6:21).[111] The difference between the courtiers or nobles (μεγιστᾶνες)[112] and the leaders (πρῶτοι) of Galilee is not clear, but it may be that the former are the members of Antipas's court, high officials of his government resident in Tiberias, while the latter are the traditional aristocracy of Galilee, who, whatever their real sympathies, would be obliged to honor the tetrarch by attending his birthday celebration. Chuza and Joanna would belong to the former group, though it is possible that Joanna's own family was one of the prominent local families of Galilee.[113] One more piece of information from this period takes the form of a lead weight from Tiberias, dated to the year 29/30, bearing the name of one of the city magistrates: one of the two *agoronomoi* of the city bore the conspicuously Roman imperial name Gaius Julius.[114] If one assumes he was Jewish (and he need not have been), the name is a striking indi-

---

possible that Herodion (Rom 16:11) was a former courtier of the tetrarch. Others have suggested that he was a freedman of one of the Herods, which is certainly possible, but the analogy with known Jews called Herod who were not actual members of the family (*Vita* 33, 96) favors my suggestion. Kokkinos, *Herodian Dynasty*, 270, 313, even suggests that the Aristobulus of Rom 16:10 may be Aristobulus (III) son of Herod (V) of Chalcis, and the Herodion of Rom 10:11 Aristobulus's son Herod (VII), who is probably the Herod to whom Josephus, *Ap.* 1.51, refers. As a mere boy at the time of Paul's writing of Romans, he is there called by the diminutive Herodion. On the possible reading of the name Herodion in a synagogue inscription from Rome, proposed by D. Noy, *Jewish Inscriptions of Western Europe* (2 vols.; Cambridge: Cambridge University Press, 1995) 2:252-54 (no. 292), see Kokkinos, *Herodian Dynasty,* 313n.169.

111. On these terms see Hoehner, *Herod,* 102; S. Freyne, "Urban-Rural Relations in First-Century Galilee: Some Suggestions from the Literary Sources," in Freyne, *Galilee and Gospel: Collected Essays* (WUNT 125; Tübingen: Mohr [Siebeck], 2000) 51. At a somewhat later date, in the reign of Agrippa I, Josephus refers to the "leaders" (οἱ πρῶτοι) of Tiberias (*Ant.* 18.273), and later still, during the revolt, to the leaders (οἱ πρῶτοι) of Galilee (*Vita* 220, 266, 305); cf. S. J. D. Cohen, *Josephus in Galilee and Rome* (Columbia Studies in the Classical Tradition 8; Leiden: Brill, 1979) 208 and n. 52.

112. That this term refers to Gentile nobles in Josephus, *Vita* 112, 149, is no good reason for distinguishing the two groups here as Gentile and Jewish, as Freyne, "Urban-Rural," does.

113. On the Jewish elite of Galilee and their relationship with Jerusalem, see Ch. Safrai, "The Role of the Jerusalem Elite in National Leadership in the Late Second Temple Era," in M. Poorhuis and Ch. Safrai, eds., *The Centrality of Jerusalem: Historical Perspectives* (Kampen: Kok Pharos, 1996) 65-72.

114. A. Stein, "Gaius Julius, an Agoronomos from Tiberias," *ZPE* 93 (1992) 144-48, argues that Gaius Julius here is Agrippa I; but Kokkinos, *Herodian Dynasty,* 233n.100, 272n.26, 277, argues that the year when Agrippa I was *agoronomos* of Tiberias was 34/35, and that his full name must have been the same as that of his son Agrippa II: Marcus Julius Agrippa.

cation of the identification of the Jewish elite in the city with the Roman over-lordship. Latin names were very rare among Palestinian Jews, most of whom would surely have seen them as unpatriotic. Finally, the term "Herodians" ('Ηρῳδιανοί) is used in the Gospels (Mark 3:6; 12:13; Matt 22:16) for partisans of Herod Antipas, probably the very group of high officials and courtiers to which Chuza and Joanna belonged. It is very significant that the Greek word 'Ηρῳδιανοί is a Latin formation *(Herodiani)*, like Καισαριανοί and Χριστιανοί, which must derive from the romanized and even partially Latin-speaking court of Antipas itself (whereas Josephus, by contrast, uses the proper Greek form 'Ηρωδεῖοι, *BJ* 1.319).[115]

Fortunately, we can also learn something about the Tiberian aristocracy in Joanna's time from the information Josephus provides about the next gener-ation of Tiberian notables, at the time of the Jewish revolt (66 CE). At that time the aristocracy of the city of Tiberias included Julius Capella (or Capellus) son of Antyllus (*Vita* 32, 65, 69, 296), Herod son of Miarus, Herod son of Gamalus, Compsus and Crispus, the two sons of Compsus (*Vita* 33),[116] Justus son of Pistus,[117] and Jesus son of Sapphias.[118] The high proportion of Latin names among these Tiberian aristocrats (Julius Capella, Crispus, Justus)[119] is very no-table. As just noted, Latin names were rare among first-century Jews in Palestine[120] and would presumably constitute a kind of pro-Roman statement

115. J. P. Meier, "The Historical Jesus and the Historical Herodians," *JBL* 119 (2000) 740-46.

116. During the events narrated by Josephus, Crispus, formerly prefect of Agrippa I, was away from Tiberias on his estate in Perea (*Vita* 33). This Crispus is surely not the same person as Agrippa II's groom of the bedchamber (*Vita* 382, 388-89, 393) (against A. Schalit, *Namen-wörterbuch zu Flavius Josephus [A Complete Concordance to Flavius Josephus*, ed. K. H. Rengstorf, Supplement 1; Leiden: Brill, 1968] 76), though the latter might be his son or other rel-ative. Kokkinos, *Herodian Dynasty*, 293-94, argues that the Crispus of *Vita* 32 may be the ances-tor of the wealthy Julia Crispina (early second century CE), known from the Babatha archive and as an absentee owner of property in Egypt.

117. Pistus himself was still active at this time: *Vita* 34, 87, 175.

118. Jesus was magistrate (ἄρχων) of Tiberias (*Vita* 134) and clearly a wealthy man (*Vita* 246), and so he must be classified with the elite, even though he was also leader of the poor in the faction fighting in the city. On Josephus's disdain for this Jesus, see J. Pastor, "Josephus and Social Strata: An Analysis of Social Attitudes," *Henoch* 19 (1997) 308-9.

119. The name Justus ('Ιοῦστος) was a favorite among Jews in the diaspora, because it could be regarded as equivalent to the Hebrew name Joseph, a common Jewish name of the pe-riod: G. Mussies, "Jewish Personal Names in Some Non-Literary Sources," in J. W. van Henten and P. W. van der Horst, eds., *Studies in Early Jewish Epigraphy* (AGAJU 21; Leiden: Brill, 1994) 240.

120. See R. Bauckham, "Paul and Other Jews with Latin Names," forthcoming in the Festschrift for A. J. M. Wedderburn (2002).

in many cases. Julius Capella, with his two Latin names, *nomen* and *cognomen*, was presumably a Roman citizen, though his father Antyllus (a Greek name) would seem not to have been. In fact, it is noteworthy that all the Roman names in this group belong to the second generation.[121] We should probably think of the fathers, most of whom have Greek names,[122] as those who were settled in the new city of Tiberius by Antipas and who honored their association with his Roman patrons by giving their sons Roman names. (Similarly, a Tiberian magistrate, one of the two *agoronomoi* of the city, whose name appears on a lead weight apparently dating from the year 97/98, is called Animus the son of Monimus.[123] The son's name is Latin, the father's Greek [Μόνιμος].)[124] We should suppose a comparable phenomenon in the case of the two Herods among the aristocracy of Tiberias in 66. Their patronyms show that they cannot have been members of the Herodian family itself unless their mothers were members of it. More likely, Antipas's courtiers and aristocratic clients named their sons after him (cf. also the "Herod of Tiberias" to whom Josephus refers in *Vita* 96, and who does not seem to be one of these two). The sons remained pro-Roman and pro-Herodian in 66 CE.

After the founding of Tiberias it became the site of Antipas's palace and the center of the administration of his realm. His highest-ranking officials would have lived there, most probably including Chuza with his wife, Joanna. Not all the aristocratic families of Tiberias mentioned by Josephus need have been Jewish, since certainly not all the population of the city was. Antyllus and Compsus (both rather uncommon Greek names) need not have been Jewish. We cannot conclude too much from the names. Although few Palestinian Jews bore Latin names, most of those who did would probably have both a Semitic and a Latin name, and would use either in different contexts, just as many more would use their Semitic or their Greek name in appropriate contexts. From this point of view it is at least notable that the Tiberians to whom Josephus referred, the pro-Roman and pro-Herodian elite of the city, were

---

121. Pistus (Πίστος) is a Greek, not a Latin name, pace Horsley, *Galilee*, 78. N. G. Cohen, "Jewish Names as Cultural Indicators in Antiquity," *JSJ* 7 (1976) 121, suggests that the otherwise unattested name Miarus (Μιαρός) is a corruption of the Latin name Marius, but this must remain uncertain. Against Cohen, "Jewish Names," 120, Compsus (Κομψός) is not a Latin but a Greek name, though the feminine form Κόμψη is attested as in Latin use; see the examples from Latin inscriptions from Pompeii and Lucania in P. M. Fraser and E. Matthews, eds., *A Lexicon of Greek Personal Names*, 3 vols. (Oxford: Clarendon, 1987-97) III.A:254.

122. The names Miarus and Gamalus are unknown, but the latter is probably a Greek form of the Jewish name Gamla or Gamaliel (Josephus, *Ant.* 20.213, 222; *m. Yeb.* 6:4; etc.).

123. Kokkinos, *Herodian Dynasty*, 397-98. The other *agoronomos* bears a Jewish name and patronym: Iaesaius son of Mathias (Ἰαεσαίου Μαθίου).

124. For a Jew named Herod son of Monimus, see *CIJ* 983 (Capernaum).

known in the city by their non-Jewish names (Greek or Latin), even if they also had Semitic ones. (The exception is Jesus son of Sapphias or Saphat,[125] and the fact that he was the leader of the popular faction in Tiberius may not be unconnected.) These Herodian courtiers and officials must have been (like Antipas himself) somewhat flexible in their attitude to Jewish religion, since Antipas had built Tiberias on the site of a cemetery (*Ant.* 18.38). Strictly Torah-observant Jews would not live there for fear of contracting corpse impurity (the most serious kind of impurity, which took considerably more trouble to remove than other kinds). Richard Horsley's comment that, while Antipas was thus violating the laws and traditions of Judean Jews, he was not necessarily offending "Galilean religious sensibilities" is mistaken.[126] The many *miqva'ot* (ritual immersion pools) that have been found in Galilee[127] show that Galileans, both the rich and the ordinary people, were concerned to observe the purity laws of the Torah, though not necessarily the Pharisaic interpretations of them.[128] We can nevertheless agree with Horsley that the prominent Jewish members of the Herodian court at Tiberias were "well-Hellenized Herodian clients,"[129] but cannot, as he does, rule out the possibility that some of them may have been from prominent local Galilean families.[130] Joanna herself (certainly Jewish, as her name shows: see below) was most likely a member of one of these leading families of Tiberias, or of another powerful Galilean family of Herodian supporters. Representative of such families at the time of

125. Jesus's father's name appears as (in the genitive) Σαπφια (*Vita* 66; *BJ* 2.599), Σαπιθα (*Vita* 134), Σαφατου (*BJ* 3.450) (but in most of these cases there are variant readings). The last reveals the Hebrew form of the name, Shaphat (שׁפט), which has been conformed to Greek names in the forms that have πφ. Jesus the son of Sapphas (Σαπφα and variants: *BJ* 2.566), one of the chief priests, appointed one of the generals for Idumea, cannot be the same person, pace Schalit, *Namenwörterbuch*, 107 (contrast 60). The problem of these two persons with the same name and almost identical patronymics is discussed (though not resolved) by T. Ilan and J. J. Price, "Seven Onomastic Problems in Josephus' *Bellum Judaicum*," *JQR* 84 (1994) 198-200.

126. Horsley, *Galilee*, 170.

127. E. P. Sanders, *Judaism: Practice and Belief 63 BCE–66 CE* (Philadelphia: Trinity Press International; London: SCM, 1992) 223; E. Regev, "Pure Individualism: The Idea of Non-Priestly Purity in Ancient Israel," *JSJ* 31 (2000) 181-86.

128. It is odd that Josephus himself, a priest bound by the Torah not to contract corpse impurity (Lev 21:1-4), seems quite freely to enter Tiberias. He must have thought that the law was overridden (like the Sabbath law) by the requirements of war. He could also not have fought in battle without contracting corpse impurity.

129. Cf. Freyne, *Galilee: From Alexander*, 133: Tiberias "was built initially because Herod Antipas did not feel comfortable in an old Jewish city, even an aristocratic one, and the character given it then was likely to remain with it subsequently, producing a type of Jew that differed both from the older priestly aristocracy and the peasant people alike."

130. Horsley, *Galilee*, 170.

the Jewish revolt were, for example, Janneus[131] son of Levi and Dassion, friends of Agrippa II and leading citizens of Tarichaeae (Magdala) (*Vita* 131; *BJ* 2.597). Although at that time many of the leading men of Galilee outside the cities seem to have supported the revolt,[132] we cannot ignore Josephus's statement (even though part of a rhetorical strategy and plausibly exaggerated) that "many of the most eminent men in Galilee" were pro-Herodian and pro-Roman and opposed the revolt (*Vita* 386).

Joanna's name tells us little about her family except that they were Jewish. The name (variously spelled יחנה, יוחנה, יהוחנא, יהוחנה) was used both as the hypocoristic form of the masculine name John (יהוחנן or יוחנן) and as the feminine equivalent of John.[133] Including Luke's Joanna, we know of six or seven Palestinian Jewish women who bore the name.[134] (Elsewhere we have only two examples from Egypt.)[135] This makes it the fifth most popular woman's name in Jewish Palestine. The masculine equivalent John happens to be the fifth most popular man's name, but the comparison is not very instructive because of the excessive popularity of the two most popular women's names, Salome and Mary (Mariamme), which together account for about half the women,[136] whereas the most popular male names are more evenly distributed.[137] Nevertheless, it seems

131. He is called Ἰανναῖος in *Vita* 131, Ἀνναῖος in *BJ* 2.597. The former is certainly preferable, representing the Hebrew Yannai, the short form of Jonathan.

132. Cohen, *Josephus*, 208-9.

133. G. Mussies, "Jewish Personal Names in Some Non-Literary Sources," in van Henten and van der Horst, eds., *Studies in Early Jewish Epigraphy*, 252 (with examples from the Babatha archive), 261-68 (on Hebrew names used for both men and women).

134. L. Y. Rahmani, *A Catalogue of Jewish Ossuaries in the Collections of the State of Israel* (Jerusalem: Israel Antiquities Authority/Israel Academy of Sciences and Humanities, 1994) nos. 31 (= *CIJ* no. 1281), 202 (here the name, written in Latin characters as IOHANA, could be either male or female), 270, 871; P. Benoit, J. T. Milik, and R. de Vaux, *Les Grottes de Murabba'at* (DJD 2; Oxford: Clarendon, 1961) no. 10; *CPJ* no. 7, lines 160, 166 (this slave girl Ἰωάναι probably came from Palestine); Luke 8:3 and 24:10. Ilan, "Notes on the Distribution," 195; idem, *Jewish Women*, 54, counts eight instances, but she includes Benoit, Milik, and de Vaux, *Grottes*, no. 18, line 11, where the name is almost certainly that of a man.

135. W. Horbury and D. Noy, *Jewish Inscriptions of Graeco-Roman Egypt* (Cambridge: Cambridge University Press, 1992) no. 6; *CPJ* no. 133, lines 35, 39.

136. Of the 15 women named in the four Gospels, 5 are called Mary and 1 Salome.

137. The figures (top nine names for each gender) are, for women: Salome 218, Mary (Mariamme) 131, Martha 15, Shappira 10, Joanna 7 (figure adjusted from Ilan's 8), Sarah 6, Amma 5, Cypros 4, Bernice 4 (Ilan, "Notes on the Distribution"); and, for men: Simeon 173, Joseph 150, Judah 128, Eleazar 124, John 90, Joshua 71, Hananiah 55, Jonathan 51, Mattathiah 46 (T. Ilan, "The Names of the Hasmoneans in the Second Temple Period" [Hebrew], *ErIsr* 19 [1987], Hebrew section 238-41). No doubt these figures need some updating from more recently published evidence, but the general patterns revealed will not be greatly affected.

clear that the popularity of the woman's name Joanna was a consequence of the popularity of John, and therefore of the popularity of the names of the Hasmoneans, which in large part probably account for at least six of the most popular masculine names (Simeon/Simon, Judah, Eleazar, John, Jonathan, Mattathiah)[138] and the two most popular feminine names (Salome, Mariamme). Therefore Marianne Sawicki can write, with reference to Luke's Joanna:

> But "Joanna" is a nationalistic Hasmonean name. . . . The betrothal of Joanna to Chuza may have been arranged with the same sort of political intentions as the betrothal of the Judean Mariamme to the Idumean Herod one generation earlier. Joanna's marriage may have been intended to forge an alliance between an elite Judean family and one of the first families of neighboring Idumea or Perea.[139] [Sawicki uses "Judean" in the sense of "Jewish," hence including Galilean Jews. Herod's wife Mariamme was from the Hasmonean royal family.]

This intriguing analogy is unfortunately not valid, for Sawicki is certainly mistaken in conjecturing that Chuza is an Idumean name. As we shall see in the next section, Chuza was almost certainly a Nabatean. The marriage was rather an alliance between an elite Jewish family, probably Galilean, and the Herodian court, where Chuza held one of the most important offices. The name Joanna probably does not indicate that her family were anti-Roman (and therefore anti-Herodian) Jewish nationalists, which would make the marriage a little difficult to explain. The masculine name John was popular because it had been a Hasmonean name, but, once popular, it would not have been used only by families wishing thereby to proclaim their nationalist loyalties. It is, for example, hardly likely that the high priest Theophilus, appointed by the Roman governor Vitellius in 37 CE, named his son John (Yehoḥanan)[140] for nationalistic reasons, even though his family were later involved in the Jewish revolt. We should also remember that the meaning of the name ("the LORD has shown favor") must have played its part in its popularity, since other names of the same meaning (Hananiah, Hanan — respectively, sixth and eleventh in order of popularity among men's names) were also popular.[141]

138. Ilan, "Names." She also gives the same reason for the popularity of the name Joseph, relying rather perilously on 2 Macc 8:22.

139. M. Sawicki, *Crossing Galilee* (Harrisburg: Trinity Press International, 2000) 147.

140. For this Yehoḥanan, see D. Barag and D. Flusser, "The Ossuary of Yehoḥanah Granddaughter of the High Priest Theophilus," *IEJ* 36 (1986) 39-44.

141. Cf. M. H. Williams, "Palestinian Jewish Personal Names in Acts," in R. Bauckham, ed., *The Book of Acts in its Palestinian Setting*, vol. 4 of *The Book of Acts in Its First Century Setting* (Grand Rapids: Eerdmans; Carlisle: Paternoster, 1995) 85.

Joanna may have been named after her father. For the practice of giving a daughter the feminine form of her father's name, known in Rome and Greece, there is limited evidence from elite families in Jewish Palestine, at least of women bearing the feminine form of a family name (the Hasmonean Alexandra; Herodias in the Herod family)[142] and in one case of a daughter named after her father: John (Yehoḥanan) son of the high priest Theophilus, just mentioned above, gave his daughter the name Joanna (Yehoḥanah), as we now know from her ossuary.[143] We have so little evidence of the names of daughters and their fathers that we cannot tell how common this practice was, but it seems likely that Joanna was so named for no better reason than that John was a name used in her family.

Whatever her own family origins, Joanna's marriage to Chuza identified her with the Herodian upper class of Tiberias. In order to grasp the significance of the social gulf she crossed in becoming a follower of Jesus, we need to understand something of, first, the relationship between Tiberias and rural Galilee, and, second, Jesus' own attitude to Tiberias.

On the first point, several factors will have combined to sustain feelings of anger and resentment by the ordinary people of Galilee against the city of Tiberias, as also against the city of Sepphoris, which had been rebuilt by Antipas and served as his administrative capital until he built Tiberias. These were the first real cities built in Galilee, and Tiberias had stood for less than ten years at the time of Jesus' ministry. Although Horsley stresses that, compared with Hellenistic-Roman cities in other parts of Palestine such as Scythopolis and Caesarea Maritima, there was only a "limited degree of Roman urbanization and cosmopolitan culture" in first-century Sepphoris and Tiberias,[144] the two cities must nevertheless have seemed a culturally alien intrusion into Galilee,[145] "aggressive acts of Romanization by Antipas," as Sean Freyne calls them.[146] Tiberias's location on a cemetery, in defiance of Jewish religious concerns, merely increased the hostility that the typical buildings of a Roman city,

142. Ilan, *Jewish Women*, 53-54.

143. Barag and Flusser, "Ossuary."

144. Horsley, *Archaeology*, 59. Horsley is evaluating J. F. Strange's thesis of a "Roman cultural overlay" in Sepphoris and Tiberias, and accepts it with this strong qualification. He is particularly concerned to refute the picture of Lower Galilee as generally urbanized and culturally cosmopolitan. Also accepting Strange's thesis only in a strongly qualified form (economic links and architectural styles are not necessarily evidence of cultural continuity) is S. Freyne, "Town and Country Once More: The Case of Roman Galilee," in Freyne, *Galilee and Gospel*, 59-72.

145. Cf. S. Freyne, *Galilee, Jesus, and the Gospels* (Philadelphia: Fortress; Dublin: Gill and Macmillan, 1988) 147.

146. Freyne, "Town," 69.

however few, and the luxurious lifestyle of its wealthier inhabitants would have provoked. Gerd Theissen suggests that the siting of the city on a cemetery may have been not merely careless disregard of Jewish religious sensibilities, but a deliberate move by Antipas designed to assemble around him people who put their loyalty to him before their loyalty to Jewish traditions.[147] But he had difficulty populating Tiberias with Galileans willing to settle there and had to import people, including Gentiles, from his other territories. Economically, these cities were surely no exception to the general rule that ancient cities were less a marketing opportunity for the surrounding villages than an economic burden, living off their surrounding territories by way of taxes and rents.[148] Taxation must have been heavy in order to fund the building of Tiberias, a burden on the peasantry that would still be fresh in the memory, and now replaced only by the burden of taxes required to finance the life of the palace and the city.[149] As Horsley puts it,

> The decor on the Herodian palace in Tiberias [which included depictions of animals despite the Torah's prohibition: *Vita* 65] symbolized the alien culture that had suddenly intruded upon the Galilean landscape along with the "in-your-face" city built so visibly from revenues regularly taken from the threshing floors and olive presses of Galilean villages by officers who lived lavishly near the palace.[150]

Of course, Tiberias represented not only economic exploitation but also, as its basis, political dominion, which had alienating features of its own. It was, in effect, the rule of the hated pagan empire of Rome by means of Rome's client-ruler and friend, the highly romanized Herod Antipas. The association with Rome was inescapably symbolized in the very name of the city, expressing Antipas's policy of integration of his domain into the sphere of Roman imperial rule. The cultural, economic, and religious feelings against Antipas's rule and the city that symbolized and implemented it can scarcely be separated out. Neither Herodian-Roman rule nor Herodian-Roman taxation was new to Galilee, but Sepphoris and then Tiberias brought the Herodian-Roman power threateningly and offensively close to home.

---

147. G. Theissen, "Jésus et la crise sociale de son temps: Aspects socio-historiques de la recherche du Jésus historique," in D. Marguerat, E. Norelli, and J.-M. Poffet, eds., *Jésus de Nazareth: Nouvelles approches d'une énigme* (Le Monde de la Bible 38; Geneva: Labor et Fides, 1998) 139.

148. Horsley, *Archaeology*, 76-85.

149. On taxation under Antipas, see Hoehner, *Herod*, 73-79.

150. Horsley, *Archaeology*, 57.

We can see something of the tensions and dynamics of the situation, as they must have been already during Jesus' ministry, by looking again at what happened in Tiberias at the beginning of the great revolt in 66. Through Josephus's strongly biased and not always coherent accounts, some things are clear.[151] When Josephus arrived in Tiberias, the city was split into two[152] main factions.[153] There was the aristocratic group led by Julius Capellus together with the two Herods and Compsus, all apparently members of the body of ten principal men of the city (*Vita* 32-34, 66; cf. *BJ* 2.639). This group was pro-Roman and pro-Herodian (i.e., pro–Agrippa II). Supporting war against Rome was a party led by Jesus son of Sapphias and consisting of the poorest members of the populace (*Vita* 35, 66). This Jesus was the city magistrate (ἄρχων) and cannot himself have been one of the poor.[154] On a later encounter with Josephus in Tarichaeae he brandished a Torah scroll while exhorting the crowds to take action in accordance with it (*Vita* 134-35). He seems to represent an anti-Roman, anti-Herodian ideology that was religiously motivated as well as appealing to the economic and political interests of the poorest people in Tiberias along with the ordinary people of Galilee outside the city. Some of the latter joined him and his party in Tiberias in destroying and looting the royal palace, at the same time massacring the "Greek" citizens of Tiberias (*Vita* 66-67). Of the attack on the palace, Horsley comments: "We can surmise whether the motives were political-economic or cultural hostility or both."[155] No doubt both the ostentatious wealth of the palace and the images prohibited by the Torah combined with the palace's obvious status as the symbol of political and economic dominance, associated as the latter was with exploitation and irreligion.

Did Jesus of Nazareth share this hostile view of Tiberias and its Herodian elite that was no doubt common to the ordinary people from whom he and most of his followers came? That he did is suggested by the conspicuous absence of Tiberias from the Gospel traditions. In fact, neither of the two cities of Galilee, Sepphoris and Tiberias, appears in the Gospel traditions at all (except Tiberias at John 6:23). Several cities around Galilee — Gadara (or Gerasa), Caesarea Philippi, Tyre, and Sidon — are mentioned, though Jesus only travels near them, not into them. But these were Gentile cities, which Jesus' limitation

---

151. On the obscurities in the history of Tiberias during the revolt, see Horsley, *Galilee*, 271-75.

152. Josephus's account of a third party led by Justus is problematic, but unimportant for our purposes.

153. Cf. Horsley, *Galilee*, 78-79.

154. Freyne, *Galilee: From Alexander*, 234, thinks "he was a member of the destitute classes."

155. Horsley, *Archaeology*, 59.

of his mission to Israel placed outside his orbit. This cannot explain his apparent avoidance of Tiberias and Sepphoris.

Several inadequate reasons have been offered: (a) These cities go unmentioned in the traditions because Jesus' ministry in them was a failure.[156] But Nazareth, Chorazin, and Bethsaida appear in the Gospel traditions precisely because they rejected Jesus' message (Matt 11:21; Mark 6:1-6). (b) Jesus avoided Tiberias for fear of contracting corpse impurity, since it was built on a cemetery.[157] But, although Jesus did not go out of his way to break the purity laws, he certainly subordinated them to more important concerns of the Mosaic law[158] and would not have allowed them to prevent him going where he understood himself to be called by God to go. If even the Jerusalem priest Josephus incurred the risk of impurity presumably because his political and military mission required him to enter Tiberias,[159] we can scarcely suppose that Jesus would have allowed his own mission to be impeded in this way. But in any case, this reason could explain Jesus' avoidance of Tiberias only, not Sepphoris. (c) Mindful of the fate of John the Baptist, Jesus avoided confrontation with the political authorities in Galilee.[160] This may be part of the truth, since, although Jesus certainly did not shrink from the eventual confrontation with the authorities in Jerusalem that his mission required, he does seem to have avoided the danger that his mission be brought to an end prematurely.[161] (If the reference to Antipas as "that fox" in Luke 13:32 goes back to Jesus, it would indicate that Jesus saw Antipas, the murderer of John the Baptist, as a malevolent predator.)[162] As Gerd Theissen and Annette Merz point out, however: "Antipas had had John arrested in southern Peraea; he could also have seized Jesus anywhere."[163] That Tiberias might be especially dangerous for Jesus presupposes that he was known to take a critical attitude to the regime, as John did.

Jesus certainly denounced the rich (Luke 6:24-25). While the rich man condemned in the parable (Luke 16:19) could be imagined inhabiting, for example, the castle at Gabara (*Vita* 246), his purple and fine linen clothes and his

---

156. W. Bösen, quoted in G. Theissen and A. Merz, *The Historical Jesus* (tr. J. Bowden; Minneapolis: Fortress; London: SCM, 1998) 182-83.

157. J. J. Rousseau and R. Arav, *Jesus and His World* (Minneapolis: Fortress, 1995) 318.

158. See R. Bauckham, "The Scrupulous Priest and the Good Samaritan: Jesus' Parabolic Interpretation of the Law of Moses," *NTS* 44 (1998) 475-89.

159. Cf. the more general statement by Freyne, *Galilee, Jesus,* 138.

160. Freyne, *Galilee: From Alexander,* 139-40.

161. Richardson, *Herod,* 308-10.

162. J. A. Darr, *On Character Building: The Reader and the Rhetoric of Characterization in Luke-Acts* (Louisville: Westminster/John Knox, 1992) chap. 5.

163. Theissen and Merz, *Historical Jesus,* 587.

daily banqueting associate him most obviously with the Herodian elite of Sepphoris and Tiberias. They also recall another saying of Jesus that points more explicitly in the direction of Tiberias. In connection with John the Baptist, Jesus addresses the crowds:

> What did you go out into the wilderness to look at?
> A reed shaken by the wind?
>
> What then did you go out to see?
> Someone dressed in soft robes?
> Look, those who put on fine clothing and live in luxury are
>   in the royal palace (ἐν τοῖς βασιλείοις).[164]
>
> What then did you go out to see?
> A prophet?
> Yes, I tell you, and more than a prophet.
>
> (Luke 7:24-25 par. Matt 11:7-9)

Theissen has argued that, because a reed appears on Herod Antipas's coinage, minted for the founding of Tiberias, the first stanza of this saying alludes to Herod himself. The reed emblem appears on the coins where a head of the ruler would normally appear on non-Jewish coins, and the image of the reed in Jesus' saying could suggest Herod's wavering policies, adapting to every circumstance like a reed blown in the wind.[165] Whether or not this is correct, the allusion to Herod's court is unambiguous in the second stanza, both because for Jesus' Galilean hearers there was only one royal court worth mentioning and because it was Herod who had put John in prison. The implicit contrast is between John's ascetic clothing and lifestyle, on the one hand, and the luxury of the ruler he criticized, on the other. But even though Jesus' own nonascetic lifestyle was contrasted with John's (Luke 7:33-34), his reference to the luxury of the Tiberian ruling elite is not neutral. It takes John's side in the clash of values between the prophet and the court. Moreover, it speaks of a luxury not to be found elsewhere in his Galilean hearers' experience. It shares something of the cultural as well as political and economic alienation with which ordinary Galileans viewed Antipas, his courtiers, and his officers.[166] As Freyne puts it, Jesus' "opposition is

---

164. The plural βασιλείοις does not mean "palaces" but "palace." The plural is in fact more commonly used in this sense than the singular (BAGD s.v. [136]).

165. G. Theissen, *The Gospels in Context* (tr. L. M. Maloney; Minneapolis: Fortress, 1991) 26-42.

166. This is also argued in more detail by S. Freyne, "Jesus and the Urban Culture of Galilee," in T. Fornberg and D. Hellholm, eds., *Texts and Contexts* (L. Hartman FS; Oslo: Scandinavian University Press, 1995) 597-622.

not to places as such, but to certain values that are associated with city dwellers, especially among the elites who shaped and dominated their ethos, especially as this was viewed from the distance of the peasant."[167]

Jesus' saying in Luke 7:24-25 provides, in Luke's narrative, an immediate background for his reference, very soon afterward, to the wife of Herod's ἐπίτροπος as one of the women disciples of Jesus (8:3). Joanna is not just an illustration of the fact that Jesus attracted followers from the social elite as well as from the ordinary people and the poor. In deciding not only to support Jesus but also to take part in his ministry by traveling with him and his itinerant disciples, Joanna may well have been motivated initially mainly by the healing she had experienced, but it was a radical step right outside the Herodian establishment to which she had belonged and into the life of the ordinary people of Galilee and of the marginalized and rejected of society whom Jesus often attracted and sought out. The kind of people she would now come to know (probably as never before) were accustomed to resenting the luxury of her former lifestyle, the burden of taxation that financed it, and the pagan domination of their land that the Herodian court she belonged to represented for them. In a certain sense her following of Jesus was also a conversion to the poor. She may have seen her financial contribution to Jesus' ministry as putting to rights some of the economic wrongs in which she had been involved as Chuza's wife.

When Josephus, the priestly aristocrat, writes of the rabble of Tiberias who found a spokesman and leader in Jesus son of Sapphias, his contempt is undisguised (*Vita* 35, 134). Jesus son of Sapphias probably himself belonged to an aristocratic family and certainly was of higher social status than most of those who rallied to his cause. The interests served by his movement were not those of his own social class. Similarly, Joanna set aside the interests of her own social circle when she joined a movement that brought good news to the poor and liberation to the oppressed (Luke 4:18). The way in which it did so was different from that of the Galilean popular revolt against Rome in the late 60s, but in both cases joining the movement required of members of the elite a radical conversion to the poor.

4. Wife of Chuza the Nabatean

It is remarkable to find it still said that the name Chuza is not known to us outside Luke 8:3.[168] In fact, scholars, including even commentators on the Gospel

167. Freyne, "Town and Country Once More: The Case of Roman Galilee," in *Galilee and Gospel: Collected Essays* (Tübingen: Mohr [Siebeck], 2000) 71.

168. Sawicki, *Crossing Galilee*, 146.

of Luke, have long known of other occurrences of the name, though only two or three such have usually been noted.[169] The following five or six (since one of them is no more than a conjectural restoration) occurrences of the name Chuza[170] are assembled here for (to my knowledge) the first time.[171]

(1) A Nabatean inscription from Mada'in Salih (ancient Hegra) was first recorded by the British explorer Charles Doughty on his travels in Arabia in 1876-77. It was published several times before being incorporated in the *Corpus Inscriptionum Semiticarum* in 1889.[172] F. C. Burkitt, writing in 1899, was the first to recognize that it contained the same name as that of Joanna's husband.[173] The latest edition of the text by John Healey appeared in 1993.[174]

Hegra, in northwest Arabia, was the southernmost major settlement of the Nabatean kingdom, from the late first century BCE "the most important Nabatean commercial centre in the Indo-Arabian trade."[175] There are about

---

169. H. J. Cadbury, "Some Semitic Personal Names in Luke-Acts," in H. G. Wood, ed., *Amicitiae Corolla* (J. R. Harris FS; London: University of London Press, 1933) 53-54, assembled the three occurrences in inscriptions that had been published before he wrote (i.e., nos. 1, 3, and 4 below), though he reached the odd conclusion: "But I see no reason to suppose the bearer [of the name] was a Nabatean." But commentators on Luke seem not to know Cadbury's article, and, if they say anything at all on the subject, depend on BAGD, which gives references to the two inscriptions numbered 1 and 4 below. Thus, e.g., J. A. Fitzmyer, *The Gospel according to Luke I–IX* (AB 28; Garden City, N.Y.: Doubleday, 1981) 698, merely borrows the two references from BAGD, repeating the latter's erroneous dating of Littmann's 1912 article to 1913. Fry, "Chuza," *ABD* 1:1022, refers for evidence about the name only to Fitzmyer's commentary! Where should one expect to find the available historical evidence about a biblical name if not in an up-to-date six-volume Bible dictionary? Assembling such evidence seems to be something the reference works consider a commentator's job and the commentators consider the role of the reference works.

170. The name is not listed in M. Maraqten, *Die semitischen Personennamen in der alt- und reichsaramäischen Inschriften aus Vorderasien* (Texte und Studien zur Orientalistik 5; Hildersheim: Olms, 1988), which covers Aramaic inscriptions from the tenth to the third centuries BCE; or in J. K. Stark, *Personal Names in Palmyrene Inscriptions* (Oxford: Clarendon, 1971).

171. I am grateful to Philip Alexander and John Healey for advice on what follows.

172. *CIS*, 2/1:266 (no. 227).

173. F. C. Burkitt, "Chuza," *Expositor* 9 (1899) 118-22. Burkitt first came across the Aramaic name in S. A. Cook, *A Glossary of Aramaic Inscriptions* (Cambridge: Cambridge University Press, 1898) 63, but Cook was merely indexing its occurrence in *CIS* 227 and did not connect it with Luke 8:3.

174. J. F. Healey, *The Nabataean Tomb Inscriptions of Mada'in Salih* (*JSS* Sup 1; Oxford: Oxford University Press, 1993) 174-75 (no. H21), with copy and plate toward the end of the volume.

175. A. Negev, "The Nabatean Necropolis at Egra," *RB* 83 (1976) 203-36, quotation 205. On Hegra see also A. Negev, *Nabatean Archeology Today* (New York: New York University Press, 1986) 25-27, 73-75; D. F. Graf, "Hegra," *ABD* 3:113-14; Healey, *Nabataean Tomb Inscrip-*

eighty rock-cut monumental tombs in the necropolis, resembling those at Petra. Thirty-six bear inscriptions, not only naming owners but also imposing curses and fines on any who might misuse the tombs. The tombs plainly belonged to wealthy families, and many inscriptions identify their owners as high-ranking military officers or government officials. Most inscriptions are dated, the earliest to the year 1 BCE/1 CE, the latest to the year 74/75 CE.[176] The presence also of some unfinished tombs suggests there was a rather rapid change of circumstances around that time, such that wealthy Nabatean families no longer resided there.[177]

Inscription H21 is on the exterior of an unfinished tomb that would have been one of the grandest had it been completed. The inscription is undated and is clearly not the formal lengthy inscription, in the style known from the other tombs, for which the cartouche was designed. It occupies only about a quarter of the space provided for lettering, and the size of the lettering is larger than usual. It is evidently in some sense a makeshift inscription placed on a tomb that was being left, for the time being at least, unfinished. It can be read as either: לחין בר כוזא אחרה, or: לחין בר כוזא אחדה, allowing two possible translations: (a) "For Hayyan son of Kuza [and] his descendants";[178] or (b) "Lihyan son of Kuza took possession of it."[179] The latter seems preferable, partly because the same kind of formula occurs in other inscriptions placed not on tomb facades but on rock faces. For example, one inscription reads, "Rabibel, the governor, has taken possession of this place," and high above it a new tomb has been begun but not finished.[180] The inscription makes Rabibel's legal claim to ownership of the section of rock where he intended his tomb to be built. It looks as though, around the year 75/76 CE, many of the Nabatean ruling elite were obliged for reasons unknown to leave Hegra. Lihyan son of Kuza's tomb was unfinished, but before leaving he had the inscription making clear his ownership of it inscribed on the cartouche. His father Kuza was therefore a contemporary of Joanna's husband, though not likely to be the same man.

---

tions, 1-48. Jews seem to have associated Hegra with Hagar, which perhaps accounts for Paul's identification of Hagar with Mount Sinai in Arabia (Gal 4:25): M. Hengel and A. M. Schwemer, *Paul Between Damascus and Antioch* (tr. J. Bowden; Louisville; Westminster John Knox; London: SCM, 1997) 113-14.

176. Healey, *Nabataean Tomb Inscriptions,* 288-89; Negev, "Nabatean Necropolis," 207-8. Inscription H18 may provide a date in the following year: 75/76: see Healey, *Nabataean Tomb Inscriptions,* 165.

177. Cf. Healey, *Nabataean Tomb Inscriptions,* 27-28, 175.

178. Burkitt, "Chuza," 122, following Euting, preferred: "To Hayyan, son of Kuza, his posterity [have erected this tomb]."

179. See the discussion in Healey, *Nabataean Tomb Inscriptions,* 174-75.

180. Healey, *Nabataean Tomb Inscriptions,* 7.

Since Hegra was a commercial center on a major trade route, some of the people buried there came from elsewhere and not all were Nabateans. One of the tombs (H4), constructed in 42 CE, was owned by a Jew, Shubaytu the son of Aliu, who called himself "the Jew" in the inscription.[181] But Lihyan is not a plausibly Jewish name,[182] and Lihyan son of Kuza was almost certainly Nabatean, like the owners of almost all of the inscribed tombs.

(2) The second inscription, published in 1953, is among the brief inscriptions in Nabatean Aramaic carved on rocks in the eastern desert of Egypt. Like the similar inscriptions in the Sinai, they must have been left by traveling Nabatean traders. This inscription reads: (א)מ(ל)ך מחיל כוז.[183] (The last word could be כוזא or כוזה.) The editors offer the translations: "Muhaiyal got possession of a [or: his] jug"; or: "Muhaiyal overpowered Kuza."[184] Though neither translation seems entirely satisfactory, it is more in keeping with the tenor of these inscriptions (as well as less banal) to suppose this one refers to a person, Kuza, than to the acquisition of a jug (which is the meaning of the name). Muhaiyal, we may suppose, at last got the better of his old enemy Kuza in a fight, and proudly recorded the event on a rock.

A large majority of the names found in the more than fifteen hundred Nabatean inscriptions are unique,[185] and so it should not surprise us that these are the only two certain occurrences of Kuza in such inscriptions. In fact, it is striking to find its two occurrences in parts of the Nabatean world so distant from each other. Avraham Negev calculates that of the 545 names in Nabatean inscriptions from north Arabia and the 468 names in inscriptions from Egypt, Sinai, and the Negev (treated together as a region), only 34 are common to the two regions.[186] The occurrence of the name Kuza just once in each region might indicate members of the same family in which this rather uncomplimentary name ("jug" in Aramaic)[187] was a recurring family name.

(3) Among many Nabatean inscriptions from Petra first published by Gustav Dalman in 1912 was a two-line inscription (no. 84) of which Dalman

---

181. Healey, *Nabataean Tomb Inscriptions*, 95; and cf. 97 for other evidence of Jews in Hegra.

182. It is otherwise known only as the name of the nearby Lihyanite kingdom (at Dedan); see Healey, *Nabataean Tomb Inscriptions*, 175.

183. E. Littmann and D. Meredith, "Nabataean Inscriptions from Egypt," *BSOAS* 15 (1953) 15 (no. 44).

184. Littmann and Meredith, "Nabataean Inscriptions," 16.

185. A. Negev, *Personal Names in the Nabatean Realm* (Qedem 32; Jerusalem: Institute of Archaeology of the Hebrew University, 1991) 179-80.

186. Negev, *Personal Names*, 78-79.

187. E. Littmann, "Eine altsyrische Inschrift," *ZA* 27 (1912) 381, compares the German name Krug.

was able to read only six letters in the first line.[188] Two years later Enno Littmann, rereading the inscription, read many more letters and attempted a restoration, according to which the second line reads: שלם (כוזא)כוזא בני ("the sons of
Kuza, peace"). But Littmann himself confessed that his restoration of the name
Kuza was very doubtful.[189] So this possible occurrence of the name can be given
hardly any weight.

(4) Our fourth and fifth occurrences of the name are from inscriptions in
Old Syriac from the area of Urfa (ancient Edessa) in eastern Syria. One was first
published by Giron in 1911[190] and has been edited most recently by Han J. W.
Drijvers and John F. Healey in 1999.[191] It is evidently a rock relief from a cave-
tomb but had already been cut from the rock when first recorded. There are two
busts, of a man and a woman, and a partly damaged inscription beside the female figure, referring to her. Presumably there was originally another inscription referring to the male figure. Giron dated the inscription to 150-250 CE on
grounds of script and style of dress,[192] though Littmann preferred, on grounds
of script, the first century CE.[193]

Drijvers and Healey translate: "[Th]is [the im]age of Qaymi [dau]ghter
of Arku [or: Adku], which ['A]bdallat son of Kuza, our . . . , made. Ala[s!]" The
name 'Abdallat refers to the Arab goddess 'Allat, who was worshiped by
Nabateans as well as other Arab tribes in the first century CE.[194] Drijvers and
Healey agree with Giron's observation that "there is a distinctively Nabatean
flavour to the names in this inscription."[195]

(5) This inscription was first published by J. B. Segal in 1954[196] and has
been most recently edited by Drijvers and Healey.[197] It is one of thirteen in-

---

188. G. Dalman, *Neue Petra-Forschungen und der heilige Felsen von Jerusalem* (Paläs-
tinische Forschungen zur Archäologie und Topographie 2; Leipzig: Hinrichs, 1912) 96 (no. 84).
Dalman's reading was republished as part of *CIS* 1430.

189. E. Littmann, "Zu den nabatäischen Inschriften von Petra," *ZA* 28 (1914) 275. Another
Nabatean name that could be restored here, if Littmann's reading of the other letters is correct,
is כומי (Negev, *Personal Names*, 35).

190. N. Giron, "Notes épigraphiques," *Mélanges de l'Université St. Joseph* 5 (1911) 77-78;
see also Littmann, "Eine altsyrische Inschrift," 379-83.

191. H. J. W. Drijvers and J. F. Healey, *The Old Syriac Inscriptions of Edessa and Osrhoene*
(Leiden: Brill, 1999) 57-58 (no. As6), with plate 4.

192. Giron, "Notes," 78.

193. Littmann, "Eine altsyrische Inschrift," 381-82.

194. Healey, *Nabataean Tomb Inscriptions*, 33.

195. Drijvers and Healey, *Old Syriac Inscriptions*, 58; cf. Giron, "Notes," 78. For Qaymi see
Stark, *Personal Names*, 110; Negev, *Personal Names*, 58; for 'Abdallat see Stark, *Personal Names*, 102.

196. J. B. Segal, "Some Syriac Inscriptions of the 2nd-3rd Centuries A.D.," *BASOR* 16
(1954) 16-17.

197. Drijvers and Healey, *Old Syriac Inscriptions*, 87-88 (no. As26).

scriptions on the rock face of a hill at Sumatar Harabesi, sixty kilometers south-east of Urfa. Three of the inscriptions are dated to 164 CE,[198] and so the others may be confidently assigned also to the mid–second century CE. Our inscription is placed beside a relief bust. Drijvers and Healey, who prefer Drijvers's reading "Zakkai" to Segal's "Zabbai," translate: "Remembered be Zakkai son of Kuza and his children, before the god."[199] In the context of the cult at Sumatar Harabesi, the god is undoubtedly the moon deity Maralahe/Sin,[200] and Zakkai must have been one of the ruling officials of the area who were closely associated with the cult of Sin. The name Zakkai occurs in Hebrew, Palmyrene,[201] and Nabatean.[202]

Whether or not the persons named Kuza in these two Syriac inscriptions were actually themselves Nabateans who had settled in Osrhoene (and this seems likely at least in the first case), it is plausible to ascribe the use of the name to Nabatean influence.

(6) The final source in which we find the name Chuza is literary rather than epigraphic. The two Targums to Esther provide Haman, the villain of the book, with an extensive genealogy (Tg I to Est 5:1; Tg II to Est 3:1), which is also found in tractate *Soferim* 13:6 and *Aggadat Esther* 3:1 (13b/14a). Theodor Zahn in 1913 noted in his commentary on Luke that this genealogy includes the name Chuza (כוזא) as that of Haman's great-grandfather,[203] but this does not seem to have been noticed subsequently by any New Testament scholar. The genealogy depends on the supposition that the term "Agagite" links Haman with the Amalekites (cf. 1 Sam 15:8), and so traces his descent from Amalek the grandson of Esau (cf. Gen 36:15-16). Between Amalek and Haman's father Hammedatha (Est 3:1) some fourteen to sixteen largely nonbiblical names[204] are given (the number varies in different versions of the list). Chuza or an equivalent occurs in almost all versions of the list as the name of Haman's great-grandfather, but

198. Segal, "Some Syriac Inscriptions," 14.

199. Drijvers and Healey, *Old Syriac Inscriptions,* 87.

200. On the cult of Sin at Sumatar Harabesi, see H. J. W. Drijvers, *Cults and Beliefs at Edessa* (Études Préliminaires aux Religions Orientales dans l'Empire Romain 92; Leiden: Brill, 1980) chap. 5.

201. Negev, *Personal Names,* 26.

202. Stark, *Personal Names,* 19.

203. T. Zahn, *Das Evangelium des Lukas* (Kommentar zum Neuen Testament 3; Leipzig: Deichert, 1913) 339-40n.8. He was dependent on H. L. Strack, *Jesus die Häretiker und die Christen nach den ältesten jüdischen Angaben* (Schriften des Institutum Judaicum in Berlin 37; Leipzig: Hinrichs, 1910) 45*-47*.

204. The names Parmashta and Vayezata are taken from the list of Haman's sons in Est 9:9. The version of the genealogy in Targum I includes the name Agag, but surprisingly the others do not.

the name varies considerably in the manuscripts of the two Targums.[205] As well as כוזא, כוזה, כיזא, כוזנאי, and כיזנאי, similar forms with initial ב also occur. There is some probability that כוזא is the original form of the name, at least in the manuscript tradition of Targum II, but this must remain somewhat doubtful.

Many names in the list are unparalleled, as well as probably corrupt in many cases, and difficult to interpret. But the name of Chuza's father 'Apolitus (אפוליטוס and variants) seems to be clearly a reference to Pontius Pilate, and this has led to suggestions that other names conceal those of other Roman governors of Judea (Felix, Fadus, Florus, Flaccus, Vitellius, Rufus) as well as Antipater and Herod.[206] There is no doubt that many of the names are intended to be Latin (with the ס ending), and enough of the specific suggestions are plausible to make it likely that the bulk of the list is of the Roman enemies of the Jews in the pre–70 CE period, more specifically (since there are no emperors) the local Roman rulers of Palestine (including the Herodian family as clients of Rome). Anachronism notwithstanding, it is not surprising that Jews in the Roman period should have wished to associate Haman, the paradigmatic enemy of the Jews in the Hebrew Bible, with Rome. That there are no identifiable names from the time of the Jewish revolt of 66 CE onward might indicate that, though the sources in which we find the genealogy are much later, the genealogy itself has its origin in first-century Palestine.[207]

This date would make the occurrence of the name Chuza (if that is the name) potentially interesting for our purposes. Neither this name[208] nor that of Haman's grandfather (which varies considerably: 'Ana', 'Ada', Serah, Sira', Kido, etc.) have been satisfactorily explained, though H. L. Strack and S. Krauss suggested for Chuza the procurator Gessius Florus (64-66), who was the Roman governor at the time of the revolt and would be the latest identified name in the

---

205. For the six manuscripts of Targum I (as well as tractate *Soferim* and *Aggadat Esther*), see the table in B. Grossfeld, *The First Targum to Esther: According to the MS Paris Hebrew 110 of the Bibliothèque Nationale* (New York: Sepher-Hermon, 1983) 144; for the fifteen manuscripts of Targum II, see the table in B. Grossfeld, *The Two Targums of Esther* (Aramaic Bible 18; Collegeville, Minn.: Liturgical; Edinburgh: T. & T. Clark, 1991) 211.

206. The suggestions are collected in B. Ego, *Targum Scheni zu Ester* (Tübingen: Mohr [Siebeck], 1996) 234n.411; and cf. Strack, *Jesus*, 46*-47*.

207. The haggadic traditions in both Targums to Esther are thought to derive from a larger and older, no longer extant work, Targum Rabbati: see Grossfeld, *Two Targums*, 14-16, 23-24.

208. Zahn, *Lukas*, 339-40n.8, attempted to explain how a reader of Luke's Gospel could think Chuza (Luke 8:3) was the son of Pontius Pilate. But it seems very unlikely that the genealogy derived the name Chuza from Luke. Zahn was not aware of the epigraphic evidence for the name.

list. However, Chuza (or any of its variant forms) does not have the Latin **ɔ̃** ending that characterizes the other names that can be plausibly identified as those of Roman governors, even if corrupted. There are no evident grounds for considering it a corruption of a Latin name, other than consistency with the rest of the list. It may well be that, like the names at the end of the list (Parmashta, Vayezata [Est 9:9], Agag [1 Sam 15:8] . . . Amalek, Eliphaz, Esau [Gen 36:15-16]), the two at the beginning after Hammedatha are to be distinguished from the list of first-century Roman enemies that has been inserted after them in the genealogy. The names ʿAnah and ʿAdah, two versions of the name of Chuza's son in the genealogy, in fact occur in close proximity to Amalek, Eliphaz, and Esau in Genesis 36:16 and 18. Either could have been considered an appropriately Edomite name. The old Edomite area south of the Dead Sea was by the first century CE the heartland of the Nabatean kingdom, and so it is possible that the use of the Nabatean name Kuza in Haman's genealogy could have seemed appropriate. Whoever first included it in Haman's genealogy may have known it as a Nabatean name. But this suggestion can be no more than a possibility.

Our reliable evidence for the name Chuza, outside the Gospel of Luke, must therefore be reduced to four occurrences: numbers 1, 2, 4, and 5 above. This evidence is sufficient to make it highly probable that Joanna's husband Chuza was a Nabatean by birth. But is Herod Antipas likely to have appointed a Nabatean as his ἐπίτροπος? The Nabatean kingdom was the foreign power of most importance, after Rome, to the Herods, owing to proximity, to economic relationships,[209] and to the policies of expansion in the direction of Herodian territories that the Nabateans occasionally pursued. But there were also family connections. Herod the Great's mother, Antipas's grandmother, was Nabatean, probably related to the Nabatean royal house, giving Antipas himself a distant family relationship to the Nabatean kings. Good relationships in Herod the Great's early years turned to conflict in the later years of his reign.[210] But early in his son Herod Antipas's reign over Galilee and Perea (the latter sharing a frontier with the Nabatean realm) Antipas probably saw the importance of repairing relationships and sought to cement a political peace by marrying the daughter of the Nabatean king Aretas IV.[211] After a long period of marriage,

209. I. Shatzman, *The Armies of the Hasmonaeans and Herod* (TSAJ 25: Tübingen: Mohr [Siebeck], 1991) 305-7.

210. On Herod the Great's relationships with the Nabateans, see A. Kasher, *Jews, Idumaeans, and Ancient Arabs* (TSAJ 18: Tübingen: Mohr [Siebeck], 1988) 126-74; Shatzman, *Armies,* chap. 7; Richardson, *Herod,* 62-67, 101-3, 166-69, 238-39, 279-81.

211. Kokkinos, *Herodian Dynasty,* 229-32 (and cf. 376-77), argues that this daughter was Aretas's eldest daughter Phasaelis, known from coins and inscriptions, and that the marriage took place in 7/6 BCE.

Herod decided to marry his sister-in-law and niece Herodias and to divorce Aretas's daughter. This was apparently one of the causes of worsening relationships that eventually led to war in 36 CE,[212] but the remarriage and divorce occurred only just before or early in the ministry of Jesus. It was in the long period of peaceful relations with Nabatea, while Antipas was married to Aretas's daughter, that Chuza must have been appointed ἐπίτροπος in Antipas's administration. He might have been a Nabatean courtier who came to Herod's court as part of the young princess's entourage.

An incident related by Josephus, occurring near the end of the reign of Herod the Great, is interesting evidence about the presence of Nabateans at a Herodian court. One of Herod's bodyguards was a man called Corinthus, "brought up within [Herod's] dominion, but an Arab [i.e., Nabatean] by birth" (*BJ* 1.576). It was discovered that this man had been bribed by the Nabatean ἐπίτροπος Syllaeus (whom we have met earlier) to assassinate Herod. Two Nabateans of high rank who were visiting Corinthus — one a friend of Syllaeus, the other a tribal chief — were found to be implicated in the plot (*BJ* 1.577; *Ant.* 17.56-57).[213] Although the incident illustrates the dangers that Nabateans at court could present, it also shows that, until the plot was discovered, it was quite acceptable for a man of Nabatean birth to be a bodyguard of the king and for members of the Nabatean aristocracy to be visiting the court. Such relationships are even more likely at the court of Herod Antipas while he was married to the daughter of the Nabatean king.

If Chuza was a Nabatean serving Herod Antipas, was he also a convert to Judaism? Would Joanna's family have contemplated her marrying him unless he were a proselyte? There was certainly a strong Jewish taboo against marrying Gentiles, dating from the reforms of Ezra and Nehemiah in the postexilic period. It is well represented in the literature of Palestinian Judaism in the first century CE by the *Biblical Antiquities* of Pseudo-Philo, which polemicizes against mixed marriages, associating the practice with idolatry and its serious consequences for the people of God.[214] Opposition to marrying Gentiles was

---

212. The considerable difficulties, not least chronological, raised by the accounts in Josephus and the Gospels (both of which involve John the Baptist in the events), need not concern us here: see Hoehner, *Herod,* chap. 7; Kasher, *Jews,* 177-81; Kokkinos, *Herodian Dynasty,* 265-69. Hoehner proposes to date Antipas's marriage to Herodias in either 27/28 or 29/30 CE, Kasher in 28 at the latest, Kokkinos in 34/35 (his revisionist chronology entails dating the crucifixion of Jesus in 36).

213. The details of how the three were involved in the plot differ in Josephus's two accounts.

214. The theme emerges clearly in the study of M. T. DesCamp, "Why Are These Women Here? An Examination of the Sociological Setting of Pseudo-Philo Through Comparative Read-

part of Palestinian Judaism's strong antipathy to the presence of pagan idolaters in the land of Israel, defiling the land and usurping the role of Israel's God.

However, perhaps this would not have inhibited the Tiberian aristocracy who frequented the court of Herod. One parallel case that may be instructive concerns Syllaeus again. This ambitious politician, who had the throne of Nabatea itself in his sights, sought to further his ambitions by marriage to Herod the Great's widowed sister Salome, who was herself strongly inclined to this offer and perhaps even signed an illegal contract. But Syllaeus could not agree to the condition on which Herod insisted: that he convert to Judaism.[215] It would have made him too unpopular among his own people (Josephus, *Ant.* 16.220-25; cf. *BJ* 1.487). Nikos Kokkinos judges the condition to have been no more than a pretext of Herod's to prevent the marriage, which he thought undesirable for other reasons.[216] But it had to be at least a credible pretext, not one that would surprise people.

A similar, later case in the Herodian family was that of Agrippa II's sister Drusilla, who was promised to the son of the king of Commagene until the intended bridegroom refused to convert to Judaism. She was married instead to the king of Emesa, who agreed to be circumcised (Josephus, *Ant.* 20.139). Similarly, the king of Cilicia was circumcised in order to become the second husband of Agrippa II's sister Berenice (*Ant.* 20.145).[217] Marriages to Gentiles were not infrequent in the Herodian family, mainly for political reasons, and there are certainly cases in which conversion of the Gentile partner is hardly likely. But the examples cited by Kokkinos are obviously exceptional ones, involving a Herodian who had himself abandoned Judaism and another (Drusilla again)

---

ing," *JSP* 16 (1997) 53-80; cf. her summary on this point: "intermarriage is linked irrevocably with idolatry, and intermarriage and idolatry are connected to the destruction of children and community. The stories of Amram, Kenaz, and Micah all link idolatry with the destruction of children. References to the intermarriage of prominent characters — Abraham, Moses, Joseph, Samson — are deleted and the negative character of foreign women is heightened." For the polemic against intermarriage in Jubilees, see B. Halpern-Amaru, *The Empowerment of Women in the Book of Jubilees* (SJSJ 60; Leiden: Brill, 1999), especially 147-59. She argues that in Jubilees the concern is with pollution rather than idolatry.

215. Syllaeus, as a Nabatean, would have been already circumcised.

216. Kokkinos, *Herodian Dynasty*, 183.

217. These examples are impressive testimony to the prestige that attached to marrying into the Herodian dynasty. The Herods could insist on circumcision (to non-Jews generally unpopular, even abhorrent practice) of men marrying their sisters and daughters because the political advantage lay mainly with the husbands: cf. Kokkinos, *Herodian Dynasty*, 356. This is why we can reasonably extrapolate to other cases in which there is no explicit evidence of conversion.

who was seduced by the man who became her second husband while she was still married to the first.[218] There are enough clear examples to indicate that the general practice in the Herodian family was to insist that Gentile spouses be proselytes.[219] (It may well be significant that the instances of which we know involve a Gentile man and his circumcision. It may be that in the case of a Gentile woman it was simply taken for granted that marriage to a Jewish man entailed her conversion to Judaism. Shaye Cohen argues that there was at this time no ritual of conversion for a woman and that "the act of marriage to a Jewish husband was *de facto* an act of conversion.")[220]

This Herodian practice of requiring non-Jewish spouses to convert was part of the general Herodian policy of not gratuitously offending their Jewish subjects. We could compare the way that Herod Antipas, though decorating the walls of his palace in Tiberias with pictures of animals, avoided the normal, non-Jewish practice of putting a ruler's head on his coins, using only plant forms on them.[221] Clearly he felt no personal obligation to the Torah's commandment, but outside the walls of his palace it was politic to represent himself as an observant Jew to his subjects. Such a policy would be the more advisable (as well as practicable) in Antipas's case, in that most of his subjects were Jews, which was not true for many of the Herodian rulers. It is true Antipas was prepared in his own case to ignore the law by marrying his sister-in-law (when her husband was still living),[222] but he was denounced for doing so by John the Baptist and risked strongly antagonizing his subjects. In this case he was pursuing his own desires, not the political policy that governed most Herodian marriages. Marriages, like coins, were very public statements.

If this was the practice of the Herodian family itself, it is likely to have been that of the Herodian Jewish aristocracy, despite their tendency to adopt features of a hellenized and romanized lifestyle. In Jewish Palestine the Jewish taboo against mixed marriages was simply too strong to be ignored.[223] We must

218. Kokkinos, *Herodian Dynasty,* 355.

219. Smallwood, *Jews,* 96n.128, doubts this, but does not take full account of all the evidence. Kokkinos, *Herodian Dynasty,* 355, adds one other case (Alexas) in which conversion, though not mentioned explicitly by Josephus, certainly occurred.

220. S. J. D. Cohen, "Crossing the Boundary and Becoming a Jew," *HTR* 82 (1989) 25.

221. Theissen, *Gospels,* 29.

222. Kokkinos, *Herodian Dynasty,* 268n.13, thinks Antipas married Herodias after the death of her previous husband Philip, but since Philip died childless, such a marriage was not forbidden in Jewish law. Kokkinos's view does not provide a sufficient basis for John the Baptist's criticism of Antipas.

223. In the diaspora, where Timothy's Jewish mother was married to a Gentile husband (Acts 16:1), this might not always be the case. But even in the diaspora, clear cases of mixed marriage are not easy to find; cf. M. H. Williams, *The Jews among the Greeks and Romans* (Baltimore:

conclude that in all probability Chuza had become fully Jewish. Since, as a Nabatean, he would have been already circumcised,[224] conversion to Judaism would have been considerably easier and more acceptable for him than for many Gentile men.

This rather extensive treatment of Joanna's husband may seem to have distracted us from Joanna herself, but it has been important for establishing and confirming Joanna's social status and affiliations, against the claim that as "a steward or manager of an estate [Chuza] would still be a slave or freedman. . . . Such a person would still be deprived of real status."[225] On the contrary, Chuza and Joanna were members of the Herodian aristocracy of Tiberias, and the sheer rarity of the name Chuza, together with the plausibility of its bearer as a Nabatean at the court of Herod, assures us that Luke's information about Joanna is historically reliable.

5. Patron or Servant?

The previous two sections have enabled us to place Joanna in the romanized Herodian court at Tiberias, and to gauge the remarkable nature of the step she took in associating herself so closely with a group of people, Jesus' disciples, who were, in the eyes of her social circle, almost despicably inferior, while at the same time in their eyes she deserved not the esteem given to social superiors but the contempt given to this particular ruling elite by ordinary Galilean people. With this background we can return to the question of the role Luke 8:2-3 gives her in helping to finance Jesus' mission, quite probably contributing the lion's share of the economic support for Jesus and his itinerant disciples. We can mention at once that there are other known cases of the association of aristocratic women with Jewish religious movements, in particular the Pharisees, and cases where such women provided financial support for the leaders and teachers of the movement.[226]

Johns Hopkins University Press, 1998) 131. For the strength of opposition to mixed marriage in the diaspora, see J. Barclay, *Jews in the Mediterranean Diaspora from Alexander to Trajan (323 BCE–117 CE)* (Edinburgh: T. & T. Clark, 1996) 410-12.

224. According to Josephus, *Ant.* 1.124, Arab boys were circumcised at the age of thirteen. Circumcision was abolished in Nabatea only after it became the Roman province of Arabia in 106 CE; see F. Millar, *The Roman Near East 31 BC–AD 337* (Cambridge: Harvard University Press, 1993) 11-12.

225. Corley, *Private Women*, 111n.13.

226. T. Ilan, "The Attraction of Aristocratic Women to Pharisaism During the Second Temple Period," *HTR* 88 (1995) 1-33.

Queen Salome Alexandra's favor to the Pharisees is the most historically significant instance, but more relevant for comparison with Joanna is the wife of Pheroras, Herod the Great's younger brother. Josephus places her among a group of women at the court of Herod who followed the teachings of the Pharisees. When over six thousand Pharisees refused to take the oath of allegiance to Caesar and the king and were punished with a fine, Pheroras's wife paid the fine for them (*Ant.* 17.41-42). As Tal Ilan comments, like the case of Queen Salome Alexandra, this "story is a second clear example of a woman's support of the Pharisees in opposition to the expressed political leanings of her family. Pheroras's wife, therefore, is another woman who took an independent religious-political position by adopting Pharisaism."[227] Like the Pharisees in the time of Herod the Great, Jesus' movement may well have been regarded in the court of Herod Antipas as politically subversive, especially in the light of Jesus' connection with John the Baptist. Joanna's courageous independence in supporting the movement evidently stands in a tradition of Herodian aristocratic women who exercised remarkable independence in their religious allegiance and their financial support for religious movements. What is unprecedented in Joanna's case, however, is that she not only financed Jesus' mission but herself joined his itinerant followers in their countercultural lifestyle. Pheroras's wife and the other Herodian women who supported the Pharisees did not cross the social gulf in the way that Joanna did.

When we turn to scholarly comments on Joanna's economic support for Jesus and the disciples, we find that they take two apparently contradictory directions, one of which casts Joanna in the social role of patron,[228] the other focusing on the word διακονέω, with its connotation of demeaning service given by the socially inferior to their superiors. There is little evidence that the patron-client model of social relationships was generally recognized in ordinary Palestinian Jewish society of the first century,[229] but it would certainly have been known in the romanized circles of the Herods. The type of patronage ap-

---

227. Ilan, "Attraction," 14.

228. Reid, *Women,* 129; H. Moxnes, *The Economy of the Kingdom: Social Conflict and Economic Relations in Luke's Gospel* (OBT; Philadelphia: Fortress, 1988) 161; idem, "Patron-Client Relations and the New Community in Luke-Acts," in J. H. Neyrey, ed., *The Social World of Luke-Acts* (Peabody, Mass.: Hendrickson, 1991) 263; Seim, *Double Message,* 64-66; Corley, *Private Women,* 111, 118-19.

229. E.g., the evidence supplied in K. C. Hanson and D. E. Oakman, *Palestine in the Time of Jesus* (Minneapolis: Fortress, 1998) 70-80, relates solely to the Roman and Herodian ruling elites in Palestine. Luke 7:1-10 falls into this category, but is unlikely in any case to constitute reliable evidence for Palestine, since the theme of patronage is here peculiarly Lukan, missing from the parallel in Matt 8:5-13.

parently relevant in Joanna's case is that of the benefactor, a wealthy person who spent money on provision for a community in return for status and honor.[230]

Writers on Luke-Acts put Joanna in a category of women benefactors that also includes Lydia (Acts 16:14-15) in her provision of hospitality to Paul,[231] as well as other "relatively well-off, independent women whom [*sic*], as *patronae* accommodate the community and/or sustain it": Martha in Luke 10:38, Tabitha in Acts 9:36 and 39, Mary the mother of Mark in Acts 12:12, and Priscilla in Acts 18:2.[232] It has to be said once again, however, that Joanna differs from all these women in actually joining the itinerant disciples as one of them. (This alone is sufficient to show that Luke's account of Joanna is not based on the female benefactors of the churches he knew in his own time but on historical reality.) Moreover, Joanna cannot have been regarded in the company of the disciples of Jesus as a patron-benefactor in the usual sense. We have already observed that the Herodian aristocracy of Tiberias would not have been regarded with respect by ordinary Galileans such as most of Jesus' disciples, but as collaborators with an exploitative and idolatrous foreign power. But, more decisively still, the radical reversal of status taught by Jesus and practiced in the community of his disciples is incompatible with the honor and status attributed to a wealthy benefactor by her beneficiaries. Luke's version of one of Jesus' most distinctive sayings about status reversal is particularly illuminating on this point:

> The kings of the Gentiles lord it over them; and those in authority over them are called benefactors. But not so with you; rather the greatest among you must become like the youngest, and the leader like one who serves. For who is greater, the one who is at the table or the one who serves? Is it not the one at the table? But I am among you as one who serves. (Luke 22:25-27)

This brings us to the use of the verb διακονέω in the phrase "provided for them out of their own resources" (διηκόνουν αὐτοῖς ἐκ τῶν ὑπαρχόντων αὐταῖς). The word commonly refers to serving at table (e.g., Luke 4:39; 10:40; 12:37; 17:8; 22:27; Mark 1:31; John 12:2) and by extension to other household tasks (John 2:5, 9; Matt 22:13). As Luise Schottroff rightly insists, it is not a word easily separated from connotations of social subordination. It "refers almost exclusively to the menial labor of women and slaves, performed for the people of

---

230. Moxnes, "Patron-Client Relations," 249-50; cf. Seim, *Double Message*, 65, for women in this role.

231. Moxnes, "Patron-Client Relations," 262-63.

232. Seim, *Double Message*, 64.

higher rank on whom they are economically dependent."[233] All the Gospel texts just cited refer to the activity of women or servants.

Two Lukan texts have been cited especially as parallels to Luke 8:3. First, 4:39 says of Peter's mother-in-law, when Jesus has healed her of a fever, that "immediately she got up and began to serve (διηκόνει) them," meaning that she prepared and served a meal for Jesus and the disciples. The relationship between healing and service is similar to 8:2-3. Second, in 10:40 διακονία and διακονεῖν refer to the household tasks, primarily the preparation of meals, with which Martha was busy, on the occasion of having Jesus as a guest in the home. However, the fact that in these two Lukan texts (as also in 12:37; 17:8; 22:27) the words refer to the serving of meals does not mean that we must find this sense in 8:3, as though the women not only provided the money but actually bought the food with it and prepared the meals.[234] The context in 8:3 must determine the particular nuance of the verb there. A different parallel, closer to the meaning in 8:3, is Acts 6:1-2, where the daily διακονία (v 1) is not the actual cooking and serving of meals, but the provision for them, and the "serving of tables" (διακονεῖν τραπέζαις: v 2), for which the seven are appointed can also not be understood literally, but refers to the administration of the common fund for the provision of food to the widows and others in need. This use of διακονία also occurs in references to the famine relief provided by the church of Antioch for the Jerusalem church (Acts 11:29; 12:25). Schottroff exposes the patriarchal bias of the scholarly tradition that gives the words διακονία and διακονεῖν different meanings in texts about women and texts about men: leadership functions when men are in question, cooking and serving at table when women (and slaves) are concerned.[235] We need to recognize that neither for women nor for men do these words always refer to the menial tasks of serving meals, but nor do they ever lose the connotation of the kind of service women and slaves performed.

The use of these words in the New Testament frequently reflects the transformation in ideas of status within the group of Jesus' disciples and in the early church. In sayings such as Luke 22:25-27, quoted above, and in his parabolic action of washing the disciples' feet (John 13:1-20),[236] Jesus made the de-

---

233. Schottroff, *Lydia's Impatient Sisters*, 205.

234. E. J. Via, "Women, the Discipleship of Service, and the Early Christian Ritual Meal in the Gospel of Luke," *SLJT* 29 (1985) 38.

235. Schottroff, *Lydia's Impatient Sisters*, 218-20. Curiously, this patriarchal bias appears in Corley, *Private Women*, 113, 116-17, 140-43. Her distinction between διακονέω as women's service and διακονία as leadership exercised by men is not valid, as Acts 6:1-2 clearly shows.

236. See R. Bauckham, "Did Jesus Wash His Disciples' Feet?" in B. D. Chilton and C. A. Evans, eds., *Authenticating the Activities of Jesus* (NTTS 28/2; Leiden: Brill, 1999) 411-29.

meaning service of women and slaves to their social superiors characteristic and therefore also emblematic of the role of leaders in the new kind of social group he was fashioning among his followers. And what should be especially characteristic of leaders must also be characteristic of all. The reversal of status in effect abolishes distinctions of status between slaves, women, and free men, such that διακονία becomes the service that any do for any others in the community (John 13:14).[237]

Halvor Moxnes recognizes that the combination of the verb διακονέω with a benefactor-like role for Joanna and the other women in Luke 8:3 is paradoxical, and he rightly finds a clue to the paradox in 22:27. Of these women, together with Lydia and some others in Luke-Acts, he says that they "exemplify in their lives the model of Jesus as 'the patron who serves' (22:27). . . . The usual pattern of patronage with its unequal relationship of patron and client is now put within the structure of the new community and transformed."[238] But perhaps even this does not go far enough with reference to 8:3. It might be better to say that the role of patron or benefactor is subverted within a community where the usual forms of social status and honor are reversed. In contributing her wealth to the group around Jesus, Joanna crosses the vast social gulf between the aristocratic lady and the serving woman, as do the others who accept her solidarity and welcome her among them.

One other aspect of the discarded patronage model must also be removed from our reading of Luke 8:2-3: the suggestion that the generosity of the women is returning the favor done them by Jesus in healing them. This kind of social reciprocity is contradicted by Jesus' vision of the free generosity of God and its imitation by God's people (6:30-36). As Joel Green puts it: "In Jesus' ministry debts are canceled. His mission is to release persons from evil in all of its guises, including the evil of the never-ending cycle of gifts leading to obligations. His graciousness toward these women is not repaid by their benefactions; rather, his graciousness is mirrored in theirs."[239]

6. Joanna Also Known as Junia

The aim of this section is to suggest the probability that Luke's Joanna is the same person as the apostle Junia to whom Paul refers in Romans 16:7: "Greet Andronicus and Junia, my relatives and fellow prisoners, who are prominent

---

237. Schottroff, *Lydia's Impatient Sisters*, 209-11.
238. Moxnes, "Patron-Client Relations," 263.
239. Green, *Luke*, 319.

among the apostles and were in Christ before me." Before we consider the possible identity of Junia with Joanna, several aspects of what Paul says about Andronicus and Junia require attention.

a. The Name Junia

The case for reading the female name Junia rather than the male name Junias in Romans 16:7 has been made adequately in scholarship since the 1970s and has been widely accepted, while the REB and NRSV are, I believe, the first English translations to place "Junia" in the text and to relegate "Junias" to a footnote.[240] The history of the matter is a sad story of prejudice making bad translation. Most commentators from the patristic period onward have taken Paul's phrase "prominent among the apostles" (ἐπίσημοι ἐν τοῖς ἀποστόλοις) to mean that he includes Andronicus and Junia(s) in the category of apostles. (Whether this interpretation is correct will be discussed in §d below.) On this view, to read the female name Junia entails recognizing that Paul acknowledges a woman as an apostle (in some sense). Yet those of the fathers who commented on this matter, most of whom understood the two names in the verse to be those of apostles, seem to have been unanimous in taking for granted that one apostle's name was the female Junia, despite their views about male authority in the church. Joseph Fitzmyer lists Origen, Ambrosiaster, Jerome, John Chrysostom, Theodoret, Pseudo-Primasius, John of Damascus, and some later commentators down to the twelfth century.[241] (Epiphanius of Salamis would be a significant exception among the fathers, if a recent claim to this effect were justified, but it is probably mistaken.)[242] Not until the medieval period did scribes, assuming that only

240. B. J. Brooten, "Junia . . . Outstanding among the Apostles (Romans 16:7)," in L. and A. Swidler, eds., *Women Priests* (New York: Paulist, 1977) 141-44; P. Lampe, "Iunia/Iunias: Sklavenherkunft im Kreise der vorpaulinischen Apostel (Röm 16,7)," *ZNW* 76 (1985) 132-34; idem, *Die Städtrömischen Christen in den ersten beiden Jahrhundert* (WUNT 2/18; Tübingen: Mohr [Siebeck], 1987) 137n.40, 139-40; R. S. Cervin, "A Note Regarding the Name 'Junia(s)' in Romans 16.7," *NTS* 40 (1994) 464-70; J. Thorley, "Junia, a Woman Apostle," *NovT* 38 (1996) 18-29.

241. J. A. Fitzmyer, *Romans* (AB 33; New York: Doubleday, 1993) 737-38.

242. M. H. Burer and D. B. Wallace, "Was Junia Really an Apostle? A Re-examination of Rom 16.7," *NTS* 47 (2001) 77, following J. Piper and W. Grudem, refer to Epiphanius, *Index discipulorum*: "Junias, whom Paul also mentions, became bishop of Apamea in Syria" (where the masculine pronoun οὗ makes it incontestable that Junias is here understood to be a man). The same passage takes Prisca (Rom 16:3) to be a man, Priscas, who became bishop of Colopho. The work in question was apparently attributed to Epiphanius by the ninth-century monk Epiphanius and is also ascribed to Epiphanius in a thirteenth-century manuscript that is one of

a man could have been an apostle, introduce the form Junias, while Giles (Aegidius) of Rome (thirteenth century) seems to have been the first commentator to take both Andronicus and Julian (*sic!* — he followed the variant reading Ἰουλιᾶν in Rom 16:7) to be men. The assumption that only men could be apostles and that therefore the name must be male was thereafter dominant down to the 1970s. For example, A. C. Headlam, writing in 1899, maintains that the name could be either Junia or Junias, but that the fact that the name is borne by an apostle is decisive: "In that case it is hardly likely that the name is feminine."[243] However, the contrary opinion has been also at least suggested, sometimes advocated, during the modern period. For example, C. H. Dodd, writing in 1932, commented that "Chrysostom, preaching on this passage, saw no difficulty in a woman-apostle; nor need we," although he thought the name could "equally well" be Junias or Junia.[244] But it is much to the credit of Père A. Lagrange that, writing in 1914, he saw the force of the argument from name usage: that, whereas Junia is a well-attested name, Junias is not attested at all, and therefore the only prudent course for the exegete is to accept that there was indeed a female apostle called Junia.[245] Only relatively recently has this argument been as generally recognized as it deserves.

In the text of Romans 16:7 the name is in the accusative: Ἰουνιαν, and only accentuation (not, of course, in the most ancient manuscripts) can distinguish the male name (Ἰουνιᾶν) from the female (Ἰουνίαν). The latter would be the common Latin name *(nomen gentilicium)* Junia, the feminine equivalent to Junius. Peter Lampe counts more than 250 recorded instances of the name

---

the nine manuscripts containing the work; the others do not ascribe it to Epiphanius and it is unlikely to be a genuine work of the fourth-century bishop of Salamis. In that case its date is unknown, with the ninth century as the terminus ad quem. In this light, it is scarcely true that "one patristic writer is inexplicably overlooked" (Burer and Wallace, "Was Junia," 77). See T. Schermann, *Prophetarum Vitae Fabulosae Indices Apostolorum Discipulorumque Domini Dorotheo, Epiphanio, Hippolyto Aliisque Vindicata* (Leipzig: Teubner, 1907) XXXV (discussion), 125 (text).

243. A. C. Headlam, "Junias (or Junia)," in J. Hastings, ed., *A Dictionary of the Bible*, vol. 2 (New York: Charles Scribner's Sons; Edinburgh: T. & T. Clark, 1899) 825. Comparison of Headlam's article with W. Sanday and A. C. Headlam, *A Critical and Exegetical Commentary on the Epistle to the Romans* (5th ed.; ICC; Edinburgh: T. & T. Clark, 1902) 422-23, shows that in the 1st ed. (1895) Headlam put this view a little less strongly: "it is more probable that the name is masculine" (423).

244. C. H. Dodd, *The Epistle of Paul to the Romans* (MNTC; New York: Harper & Row; London: Collins, 1959) 241 (1st ed. 1932). For a survey of the options taken in English translations, commentaries, and Greek NT reference works, see Cervin, "Note," 464-66.

245. M.-J. Lagrange, *Saint Paul: Épitre aux Romains* (Ebib; Paris: Gabalda, 1931) 366 (1st ed. 1915).

Junia in Rome alone.[246] The male name Junius would, of course, according to the standard way of representing Latin names in Greek, appear in Greek as Ἰούνιος, as indeed it does in known examples.[247] But the case for a male name in Romans 16:7 is not refuted simply by this observation,[248] since the proposal is that Ἰουνιαν is here the accusative of Ἰουνιᾶς, which would be a Greek hypocoristic form of the Latin name Junianus. This name is one of many *cog-nomina* ending in *-anus* and derived from *gentilicia*.[249] Kajanto notes more than eighty recorded instances of it,[250] and Solin and Salomies note one example of its use in Greek (apparently as a *nomen*).[251] Male names in Greek were often abbreviated with the ending -ᾶς[252] (NT examples include Epaphras for Epaphroditos, Antipas for Antipatros), and such names include Latin names borne by Greek-speakers (e.g., Λουκᾶς [Col 4:14; Phlm 24; 2 Tim 4:11] for Lucius or Lucanus). However, the name Junias is not attested among the thousands of Greek names preserved from antiquity. Even examples of the names Junius and Junianus borne by Greek-speakers are rare.[253] This is significant because the abbreviated form presupposes the currency of the nonabbreviated form. In the case of Λουκᾶς, the Latin form Lucius is common in Greek (Λούκιος or Λεύκιος).[254] The rarity of Junius and Junianus in Greek use makes the occurrence of the Greek form Junias less likely, although in a predominantly Greek-speaking community in Rome, such as the early Christians in Rome seem to have been, it is possible that the Greek form Junias could be adopted as a result of familiarity with the use of Junianus by Latin-speakers. (The Junia/s of Rom 16:7 was not a native of Rome, but came from the eastern

246. Lampe, *Städrömischen,* 139. Cervin, "Note," 468 gives some literary and epigraphic examples.

247. There are nine instances in Fraser and Matthews, eds., *Lexicon,* vols. 1-3. For one example of a Jew with this name, see Noy, *Jewish Inscriptions,* vol. 2, no. 71 (from Monteverdi): Ἰούνιος Ἰοῦστος.

248. Cervin, "Note," comes close to giving this impression, although he knows that the proposal is the male name Junianus, not Junius. It is hardly necessary to refute the view that the name is Junius, since, so far as I am aware, this has not been argued. Cervin is surely mistaken in saying, "Few commentators seem to realize that *Iunia* is a Latin name" (467).

249. See I. Kajanto, *The Latin Cognomen* (Societas Scientiarum Fennica: Commentationes Humanarum Litterarum 36/2; Helsinki: Helsingfors, 1965) 32-35.

250. Kajanto, *Latin Cognomen,* 148.

251. H. Solin and O. Salomies, *Repertorium nominum gentilicium et cognominum Latinorum* (2d ed.; Alpha-Omega A50; Hildersheim: Olms/Weidmann, 1994) 99.

252. See BDF §125 (1), (2).

253. I have found only one instance of Ἰουνιανός (Solin and Salomies, *Repertorium,* 99). There are no instances in Fraser and Matthews, eds., *Lexicon,* vols. 1-3.

254. There are 248 instances in Fraser and Matthews, eds., *Lexicon,* vols. 1-3. There are also five instances of Λουκιανός, and one each of Λευκῖνος and Λουκάνιος.

Mediterranean, and so the question arises whether this person already bore the name Junia/s before coming to Rome or adopted it when living in Rome.) Moreover, there are many Greek names of which we know only one instance, and so the possibility that the person in Romans 16:7 bore the name Ἰουνιᾶς cannot be ruled out. But it remains the case that the name is unattested in our evidence, whereas the name Junia is well attested. There would have to be overwhelming reasons for preferring "Junias" to "Junia" here.

We certainly cannot presuppose, as such overwhelming reasons, that there could not have been a woman apostle or that Paul would not have recognized a woman apostle. This would be to beg the question. If Paul does here include the two persons he mentions among the apostles (a question we have yet to resolve: see §d below), then precisely our text is evidence that there was a woman apostle and that Paul did recognize a woman apostle. But nor can we give any real weight to the analogy between the pair of names (Andronicus and Junia) in Romans 16:7 and the pair in 16:3 (Prisca and Aquila), who are certainly wife and husband, because Paul does also pair two sisters or other relatives (Tryphaena and Tryphosa) in 16:12.[255] The evidence of name usage must count as the only significant argument, and it points strongly to the female name.

Unlike Roman men, who bore three names, Roman women usually had only two, *nomen gentilicium* and *cognomen,* and were often known by the former. An example among those Paul greets in Romans is Julia (16:15), whereas Urbanus (16:9) is doubtless this man's *cognomen.* The name Junius/Junia was that of a prestigious Roman family (including Marcus Junius Brutus, one of Julius Caesar's assassins), but it is scarcely possible that our Junia could be a member of the *gens Junia,* in view of her Jewishness and her history, as Paul alludes to it in Romans 16:7. Freedmen and freedwomen often adopted the *nomen gentilicium* of their patron, and Lampe therefore argues that Junia was probably of slave origin (either a freedwoman herself or descended from a freedman).[256] This is possible but not a necessary conclusion. It was not unusual for Jews and other non-Romans to use a Roman *nomen gentilicium* as their sole name or sole Latin name. In explaining Junia's name we need to take full account of the fact that she was a Palestinian Jew and a Christian missionary. The issue will be taken up further below (see §f).

---

255. The use of such similar names probably indicates members of the same family.
256. Lampe, "Iunia/Iunias," 133-34; Lampe, *Städrömischen,* 147, 152-53.

b. Paul's Relatives

Junia and her husband Andronicus are two of six persons in Romans 16 whom Paul designates his relatives (συγγενεῖς μου). The others are Herodion (16:11), Lucius, Jason, and Sosipater (16:21). Some have suggested that these people were literally relatives of Paul, members of his extended family,[257] which is not impossible. But it seems more likely that Paul means "fellow Jews." This usage would be unusual, but Paul in this same letter speaks of his fellow Jews in general as "my brothers and sisters, my relatives according to the flesh" (τῶν ἀδελφῶν μου τῶν συγγενῶν μου κατὰ σάρκα). We should note that he could not have used the terms "brother" or "sister" to designate fellow Jews in Romans 16, as other Jews might have done, since for Paul these terms have come to mean "Christian" (Jewish or Gentile). It is true that there are other Jews in Romans 16 whom Paul does not call relatives: Prisca and Aquila (16:3), probably Rufus and his mother (16:13; Jews often used the Latin name Rufus as a sound-equivalent of the Hebrew name Reuben), and perhaps Mary (16:6; Μαρία could be the Hebrew Miriam, but it could also be the Latin name Maria borne by a Gentile Christian). But the explanation is probably that Paul simply has other things to say about these other Jews.

c. Paul's Fellow Prisoners

Paul's reference to Andronicus and Junia as "fellow prisoners of mine" (συναιχμαλώτους μου) is rather surprising, since this word for "prisoner" (αἰχμάλωτος) refers to a captive taken in war (cf. the verb αἰχμαλωτεύω in Rom 7:23; 2 Cor 10:5; Luke 21:24). The terminology appears again in the two closely related passages Philemon 23, where Paul calls Epaphras his fellow prisoner,[258] and Colossians 4:10, where it is Aristarchus who receives this designation. At first sight it is odd that Aristarchus is mentioned in Philemon 24 without being called fellow prisoner, and the same is true of Epaphras in Colossians 4:12. If the language is purely figurative ("captive to Christ"?), allied to the term "fellow soldier" (συστρατιώτης) that Paul applies both to Epaphroditus (Phil 2:25) and Archippus (Phlm 2),[259] then it is strange that Paul applies it so selectively, only

257. E.g., E. E. Ellis, "Coworkers, Paul and His," in G. F. Hawthorne and R. P. Martin, eds., *Dictionary of Paul and His Letters* (Downers Grove, Ill./Leicester: InterVarsity Press, 1993) 186; cf. also Lagrange, *Saint Paul*, 366, who thinks of a sort of clan consisting of hundreds of people.

258. This probably rules out the possibility that in Rom 16:7 Paul could mean "fellow members of the Jewish diaspora," following the Jewish use of αἰχμαλωσία in this sense.

259. Cf. C. S. Wansink, *Chained in Christ: The Experience and Rhetoric of Paul's Imprisonments* (JSNTSup 130; Sheffield: Sheffield Academic Press, 1996) chap. 4.

to these four persons. In any case, it is clear from Colossians 4:3, 18; Philemon 1, 10, and 13 that Paul really was in prison. If Colossians is an authentic Pauline letter, these two letters were written during the same imprisonment. The variation between Philemon 23, where Epaphras is singled out from the group as the one designated Paul's fellow prisoner, and Colossians 4:10, where Aristarchus has this honor, is best explained by the hypothesis that Paul's friends took turns to share his imprisonment.[260] But, while referring to literal incarceration, Paul uses a word that also interprets this fate as an event in the battle in which he and his coworkers are fighting as fellow soldiers of Christ. He has been taken captive by the forces of darkness. The shame associated with imprisonment in the ancient world is transformed into the honor of a soldier who had stood his ground, refusing to retreat, and had been captured.[261]

If Paul's usage is consistent, he would mean that Andronicus and Junia had at some time when Paul was in prison opted to share his confinement in order to bring him encouragement and care. But Romans was not written at the same time as Philemon and Colossians,[262] and so there is no need to insist that Paul uses the term "fellow prisoners" in exactly the same way as he does in those letters. He may therefore mean that Andronicus and Junia were taken captive at the same time as he, on the occasion of one of his imprisonments, and were held in prison with him.[263] But it is also by no means impossible that he means

260. J. D. G. Dunn, *The Epistles to the Colossians and to Philemon* (NIGTC; Grand Rapids: Eerdmans; Carlisle: Paternoster, 1996) 275-76 (citing Abbott, Dibelius, and Scott) 347-48. For the general context in which this might be possible, see B. Rapske, *The Book of Acts and Paul in Roman Custody* (Grand Rapids: Eerdmans; Carlisle: Paternoster, 1994) (vol. 3 of *The Book of Acts in Its First-Century Setting*) chap. 14, especially the quotation from Lucian, *Peregr.* 12, on p. 379 (church leaders sleep inside the prison with a Christian prisoner). On pp. 372-78, Rapske argues against the notion that in Acts 27:2 Aristarchus is literally a prisoner along with Paul. The suggestion I endorse is not that Epaphras and Aristarchus were condemned prisoners, but that they voluntarily spent time with Paul in his prison cell.

261. Wansink, *Chained*, 171-73. Might Paul have noticed the appropriateness of this image to the name Andronicus?

262. It is a slip when Dunn suggests that "all three letters were written during the same imprisonment" (*Epistles*, 276). Romans was almost certainly written from Corinth, as Dunn, *Romans 1–8* (WBC 38A; Dallas: Word, 1988) xliv, agrees.

263. G. S. Duncan, *St. Paul's Ephesian Ministry* (London: Hodder & Stoughton, 1929) 68; and R. Riesner, *Paul's Early Period* (tr. D. Stott; Grand Rapids: Eerdmans, 1998) 213, suggest Paul's putative imprisonment in Ephesus, to which they think Rom 16:4a also refers. But since Andronicus and Junia were members of the early Jerusalem church, an earlier period is more likely: perhaps during the early mission in Antioch (Dodd, *Epistle*, 241) or even perhaps during Paul's first missionary enterprise in Arabia (Nabatea), where Junia and Andronicus might have gone because of their Nabatean connections (if Andronicus is Chuza). (This anticipates the argument about the identity of Junia and Joanna that will be pursued below.)

that they had been in prison, but not at the same time and place as himself.[264] They are his "fellow prisoners" in the sense that they too had suffered imprisonment for their allegiance to the gospel. The first of these three possibilities is especially consistent with the warm regard in which Paul evidently holds them, while the first or second would explain why he singles out their prison experience for special mention. But the third could be explicable if their imprisonment was an especially notable fact about them. Were they actually in prison in Rome when Paul wrote the letter? Though I am not aware that commentators have suggested this, it seems entirely possible. But we simply do not have sufficient evidence to decide among the possibilities.

d. "Prominent among the Apostles"

In this phrase (ἐπίσημοι ἐν τοῖς ἀποστόλοις), the adjective ἐπίσημος means: "marked out, distinguished, outstanding, prominent."[265] It has sometimes been taken to mean that Andronicus and Junia were well known to or well regarded by the apostolic body, not themselves belonging to it, but much more often it has been understood to mean that they were outstanding members of the apostolic body, distinguished as apostles among the apostles. This was the view of most of the fathers who express an opinion,[266] and has also been much the most common view among modern commentators, endorsed by most modern translations.[267] It has often been stated that, while the first interpretation is grammatically possible, the second is a much more natural reading of the Greek and can be regarded as "virtually certain."[268] But this consensus has been strongly challenged in a recent article by Michael Burer and Daniel Wallace, who offer new evidence in favor of the first interpretation. Reversing the judgment of other recent scholars, they claim that the phrase "*almost certainly*

Moreover, since they were clearly significant people in the early Christian movement, of whom Paul himself evidently thought highly, we should expect them to be mentioned in other Pauline letters or in Acts if they had been associated with Paul at the time of Paul's ministry in Ephesus.

264. Sanday and Headlam, *Romans*, 423; C. E. B. Cranfield, *A Critical and Exegetical Commentary on the Epistle to the Romans*, vol. 2 (ICC; Edinburgh: T. & T. Clark, 1979) 788-89.

265. I am grateful to Professors C. F. D. Moule and C. E. B. Cranfield for comments on this section.

266. See, e.g., Origen and Chrysostom quoted in J. B. Lightfoot, *Saint Paul's Epistle to the Galatians* (7th ed.; London: Macmillan, 1881) 96.

267. See the detailed survey in Burer and Wallace, "Was Junia," 78-84.

268. E.g., Cranfield, *Romans*, 2:789; cf. Dunn, *Romans 1–8*, 849 ("almost certainly").

means 'well known *to* the apostles.'"[269] Since this article presents itself as rather conclusive, I shall have to go to some lengths to show that it is not.

Burer and Wallace, who are prepared to accept the case for the female name Junia, rightly point out that discussion of this verse has focused largely on the question of the gender of the name, whereas the meaning of the phrase ἐπίσημοι ἐν τοῖς ἀποστόλοις — whether Junia(s) is included in the apostolic body or not — "has been the object of almost no substantive discussion."[270] The issue they address is that of "the syntax of ἐπίσημος with adjuncts,"[271] that is, what is the meaning of ἐπίσημος + ἐν + a noun in the dative (the construction used in Rom 16:7)? They usefully distinguish the two interpretations of the phrase as "inclusive" and "exclusive": the inclusive meaning makes Andronicus and Junia members of the category of apostles ("prominent among the apostles"), while the exclusive meaning places them outside that category ("well known to the apostles"). In the first case, the word ἐπίσημος has an "*implied* comparative sense":[272] Andronicus and Junia are prominent in comparison with some other, less prominent apostles (not necessarily, of course, more prominent than all other apostles). In the second case, the word has an elative sense: Andronicus and Junia are famous, but no comparison with the apostles is implied. It is clear that the word ἐπίσημος can be used with or without a comparative implication. The question is which meaning is conveyed by the construction with ἐν and the dative. Since the dative can scarcely be one of agency, most commentators have felt it more natural to read the phrase in the inclusive sense. Burer and Wallace approach the issue from the observation that this sense implies comparison and from the fact that comparative adjectives are usually followed by the genitive:

> As a working hypothesis, we would suggest the following: Since a noun in the genitive is typically used with comparative adjectives, we might expect such with an implied comparison too. Thus, if in Rom 16.7 Paul meant to say that Andronicus and Junia were outstanding *among* the apostles, we might have expected him to use the genitive (τῶν) ἀποστόλων. On the other hand, if an elative sense is suggested — i.e. where no comparison is even hinted at — we might expect ἐν + the dative.[273]

This is merely a working hypothesis. They go on to give the results of a *Thesaurus Linguae Graecae* search for comparable passages including ἐπίσημος and

---

269. Burer and Wallace, "Was Junia," 90.
270. Burer and Wallace, "Was Junia," 76.
271. Burer and Wallace, "Was Junia," 82.
272. Burer and Wallace, "Was Junia," 84.
273. Burer and Wallace, "Was Junia," 84.

reach the conclusion: "Repeatedly in biblical Greek, patristic Greek, papyri, in-scriptions, classical and Hellenistic texts, our working hypothesis was borne out. The genitive personal modifier was consistently used for an inclusive idea, while the (ἐν plus) dative personal adjunct was almost never so used."[274] Unfortu-nately, as we shall see, their evidence does not actually support this conclusion.

Burer's and Wallace's work is clearly significant as the first attempt to col-lect and to evaluate syntactical parallels to our phrase. But it must be treated as opening a discussion, not closing one, since it has serious defects. The presenta-tion of the evidence is unsatisfactory in several ways: (1) Not all the evidence discovered is presented. There are footnote references (nn. 63, 65) to evidently highly relevant texts that are not discussed, and we are not told whether there are other relevant texts that are not mentioned at all. It seems likely there are, since the authors say that the search (after elimination of obviously irrelevant texts) yielded "a few dozen passages, containing illuminating information and definite patterns."[275] By my count, twenty-two passages are discussed in the ar-ticle, and seven more are mentioned in footnotes. Twenty-nine is considerably short of "a few dozen," vague though this phrase is. (2) As a result there is no statistical information and attempts to compile it from the article are frustrated by the fact that the evidence is not sufficiently described or revealed. This is a grave weakness in the argument, since it is clear that there is some evidence to support both of the interpretations of our phrase in Romans 16:7, and the argu-ment thus hangs on the claim that one sort of evidence is rare and the other comparatively frequent. For such an argument to carry conviction it is essential that all available evidence be brought into the discussion and be explicitly counted. (3) This vagueness about the amount of evidence makes the conclu-sions drawn from it highly tendentious, even misleading. The two most impor-tant examples are these. First, the authors summarize the biblical and patristic evidence thus:

> To sum up the evidence of biblical and patristic Greek: although the inclu-sive view is aided in some *impersonal* constructions that involve ἐν plus the dative, every instance of *personal* inclusiveness used a genitive rather than ἐν. On the other hand, every instance of ἐν plus *personal* nouns supported the exclusive view.[276]

The phrase "some *impersonal* constructions" actually refers to just one passage that has been discussed (AddEst 16:22), and the repeated phrase "every in-

274. Burer and Wallace, "Was Junia," 90.
275. Burer and Wallace, "Was Junia," 86.
276. Burer and Wallace, "Was Junia," 87.

stance" in both cases refers to only one text (3 Macc 6:1; PsSol 2:6, respectively). Only five texts have been discussed in all, and no indication has been given that there are others not mentioned that support the conclusions. This seems an extraordinary way to draw conclusions from such minimal evidence.

The second example is from the conclusion to the whole argument: "The genitive personal modifier was consistently used for an inclusive idea, while the (ἐν plus) dative personal adjunct was almost never so used."[277] Here the first clause rests on just two instances discussed (with one other reference given in n. 63), while the second clause refers to two instances (of ἐν + dative personal adjunct for the inclusive sense) as against seven (of the same construction for the exclusive sense).[278] It is surely misleading to call two out of nine cases "almost never." The sentence also hides the fact that, in the evidence actually quoted, the inclusive idea is conveyed as often by the ἐν + dative personal adjunct construction as by the genitive personal modifier: twice in both cases. We are meant to infer that, in cases referring to persons, the genitive modifier is the usual way of conveying the inclusive idea, while the ἐν + dative construction only rarely has this sense, and so Paul's use of the latter "almost certainly" conveys the exclusive sense. But this is not at all what the evidence reveals.

There are other major problems in the interpretation of the evidence presented. In the category of biblical and patristic Greek, the authors make much of Psalms of Solomon 2:6, which is the sole evidence for this part of the summary: "every instance of ἐν plus *personal* nouns supported the exclusive view, with Pss. Sol. 2.6 providing a very close parallel to Rom 16.7."[279] On closer examination this "very close parallel" turns out to be not a parallel at all. Here is the complete text:

υἱοὶ καὶ θυγατέρες ἐν αἰχμαλωσίᾳ πονηρᾷ
ἐν σφραγῖδι ὁ τράχηλος αὐτῶν, ἐν ἐπισήμῳ ἐν τοῖς ἔθνεσιν.[280]

It is hard to make sense of the second line, which means literally: "their neck in [or: with] a seal, in [or: with] a mark among the nations." R. B. Wright translates the verse:

---

277. Burer and Wallace, "Was Junia," 90.

278. In these figures I accept, for the sake of argument so far, Burer's and Wallace's understanding and classification of all the texts they cite. But I have not included cases of the dative not preceded by ἐν.

279. Burer and Wallace, "Was Junia," 87.

280. J. Viteau, *Les Psaumes de Salomon* (Documents pour l'Étude de la Bible; Paris: Letouzey & Ané, 1911) 258.

> The sons and the daughters (were) in harsh captivity,
> their neck in a seal, a spectacle among the gentiles.[281]

Sebastian Brock offers probably the best that can be done with the Greek as it stands:

> Her sons and her daughters were in grievous captivity,
> There [*sic*] neck bears a seal-ring, a mark among the nations.[282]

The Greek is probably corrupt,[283] but what is indubitably obvious is that ἐπισήμῳ is a substantive, not an adjective qualifying υἱοὶ καὶ θυγατέρες. Burer and Wallace claim that the construction (they quote just ἐπισήμῳ ἐν τοῖς ἔθνεσιν without the preceding ἐν) is close to Romans 16:7, because "the parallels include (a) people as the referent of the adjective ἐπίσημος, (b) followed by ἐν plus the dative plural, (c) the dative plural referring to people as well. All the key elements are here."[284] But the fact is that the essential element (a) is not present at all. This passage must be dropped from the evidence altogether. A few other passages (1 Macc 11:37; 14:48;[285] 2 Macc 15:36;[286] P. Oxy. 1408 and 2108;[287] *Mart. Pol.* 14:1;[288] *Peloponnesos* 1.G.5.2.8[289]) must also be dropped as not relevant.[290]

The remaining passages quoted or mentioned by Burer and Wallace (I have placed those mentioned, but not quoted, in parentheses) can be classified

---

281. Wright, "Psalms of Solomon," in J. H. Charlesworth, ed., *The Old Testament Pseudepigrapha* (2 vols.; Garden City, N.Y.: Doubleday; London: Darton, Longman & Todd, 1983-85) 2:652.

282. H. F. D. Sparks, ed., *The Apocryphal Old Testament* (Oxford: Clarendon, 1984) 655.

283. The Syriac has: "Her sons and her daughters were in bitter captivity, / And upon their neck was placed the sealed yoke of the nations." The second line is probably an attempt to make sense of an obscure or already corrupt Greek text; cf. J. L. Trafton, *The Syriac Version of the Psalms of Solomon* (SBLSCSS 11; Atlanta: Scholars Press, 1985) 29, 35.

284. Burer and Wallace, "Was Junia," 87.

285. The syntax in these two texts, quoted in Burer and Wallace, "Was Junia," 87-88n.52, is significantly different.

286. Despite Burer and Wallace, "Was Junia," 87n.52, it is impossible to see how this verse could be relevant.

287. These texts (quoted in Burer and Wallace, "Was Junia," 77) use the superlative, ἐπισημότατος. There can be no question that the superlative should be followed by the genitive, but this is not evidence for the meaning of constructions with ἐπίσημος itself.

288. The construction here is ἐπίσημος + ἐκ + genitive.

289. The construction here is ἐπίσημος + παρά + dative.

290. I have also had to omit from the following table Lucian, *Peregr.* 22.2, to which Burer and Wallace, "Was Junia," 90n.65, refer, because it is not clear from this reference in which category it should be placed, and because their reference is a mistake and I have not been able to trace the passage intended.

thus, according to the three different syntactical constructions used and the distinction they stress between reference to persons and reference to animals and inanimate things:

personal	*nonpersonal*

(a) ἐπίσημος + genitive
inclusive meaning

3 Macc 6:1	PsSol 17:30
Lucian, *Peregr.* 6.1(?)[291]	P. Oxy. 2705
(Herodian 1.7)	

(b) ἐπίσημος + dative
exclusive meaning

    Lycurgus, *Against Leocrates* 129
    Euripides, *Bacch.* 967

(c) ἐπίσημος + ἐν + dative
inclusive meaning

Lucian, *Merc. Cond.* 28	AddEst 16:22
Josephus, *BJ* 2.418[292]	Lucian, *DMeretr.* 1.2
	(Rufus Medicus, *Quaest. Medic.* 20)
	Philo, *Fug.* 10
	Galen, *De Methodo Medendi* 14.10.242

exclusive meaning

    TAM 2.905.1
    (TAM 2.1–3.838)
    (TAM 2.1–3.905)
    (Fd Xanth 7.76.1.1.1.4)[293]
    Euripides, *Hipp.* 103
    Lucian, *Harm.* 1.17

The issue is whether Romans 16:7 belongs in category (c) *inclusive meaning* or (c) *exclusive meaning*. Even if we accept Burer's and Wallace's opinion

291. This reference (Burer and Wallace, "Was Junia," 89n.63) is incorrect and the passage quoted does not seem to occur anywhere in *Peregrinus*. I have been unable to trace its origin.

292. Burer and Wallace, "Was Junia," 88-89, claim this text is "not a clear parallel," but they have probably been misled by Thackeray's translation. The meaning is surely: "[ambassadors] among whom Saul and Antipas and Costobar were eminent."

293. Burer and Wallace, "Was Junia," 88, say that these three inscriptions contain "similar idioms" to that which they quote from *TAM* 2.905.1 *west wall coll.* 2.15.18.

that the texts with personal referents are more relevant to the case of Romans 16:7 and should be given more weight, it is clear that the examples are so few that they cannot require us to align Romans 16:7 with the six texts in category (c) *exclusive meaning* rather than with the two personal texts in category (c) *inclusive meaning*. Nor can the mere three texts in category (a) (personal), compared with the two personal texts in category (c) *inclusive meaning*, justify the argument that, if Paul intended to include Andronicus and Junia among the apostles, he would be more likely to have used construction (a) than construction (c). But we should also question the priority given to the "personal" texts: it is not at all clear why these should be grammatically different from those with impersonal referents. If we include all the evidence cited, personal and impersonal cases alike, the implications are even less decisive for Paul's usage.

It may be helpful to ask why the evidence falls as it does. That construction (a) has inclusive meaning and construction (b) has exclusive meaning is only to be expected. It would be extraordinary for the Greek in these cases to mean anything else. Construction (c) seems to be used in both the inclusive and the exclusive senses (though most particular uses of it are not ambiguous). It should be noted that Burer and Wallace are mistaken when they seem to suggest that construction (b) and construction (c) are much the same.[294] Construction (b) has to have the exclusive meaning, but there is nothing in the character of construction (c) that requires the exclusive meaning.

To a large extent the usage this evidence displays may be explained by the fact that, as Burer and Wallace are aware, ἐπίσημος is not a comparative adjective[295] but in some instances carries "*implied* comparative sense."[296] If it were a comparative adjective, construction (a) would probably be more or less obligatory. But since it is not, usage in which it has a comparative sense takes either the form of construction (a), by analogy with true comparative adjectives, or the form of construction (b), by analogy with many other cases where ἐν in the sense of "among" is followed by reference to the group to which an individual belongs. A convenient example, which has both comparative and inclusive meaning, is Matthew 2:6: σὺ Βηθλέεμ, γῆ Ἰούδα, οὐδαμῶς ἐλαχίστη εἶ ἐν τοῖς ἡγεμόσιν Ἰούδα ("you, Bethlehem in the land of Judah, are by no means least among the rulers of Judah"). It is more surprising that construction (c) is also used in the exclusive sense, but it should be noted that the instances seem to be completely unambiguous, except for that in Euripides, who might have been

294. Burer and Wallace, "Was Junia," 85.

295. An example of the true comparative is in Lucian, *Peregr.* 4: τὸν τοῦ Ἡλίου ἐπισημότερον.

296. Burer and Wallace, "Was Junia," 84.

writing at a time when ἐπίσημος had not yet acquired a comparative sense. The main reason the other texts in this category are unambiguous is that the nouns after ἐν are collective nouns (ἐν τῷ ἔθνει, ἐν πλήθεσι). By contrast, in the two "personal" examples of category (c) *inclusive sense,* the noun after ἐν is a plural referring to persons of whom the individual in question could be one (ἐν τοῖς ἐπαινοῦσι, πρεσβεῖς). If this is a pertinent observation, it would suggest that the sense in Romans 16:7 is more likely to be inclusive.

Finally, it is necessary to add that it is a major error when Burer and Wallace dismiss the evidence of patristic interpreters of Romans 16:7, who understood Paul to be including Andronicus and Junia among the apostles. They complain that these fathers "seem to assume a particular view, without interacting over the force of the Greek."[297] But writers such as Origen and John Chrysostom were educated native speakers of Greek. They had no reason for thinking Andronicus and Junia to be apostles other than supposing this to be the meaning of Paul's Greek. If Burer and Wallace's conclusion is right, then it is inexplicable that these Greek patristic interpreters should have read the Greek of Romans in the way they did. At the very least they demonstrate that the inclusive meaning is possible. But it would be fair to give even more weight to their evidence, making the inclusive interpretation the more probable of the two. Since the comparative evidence adduced by Burer and Wallace, though valuable, is too sparse to be of statistical significance, the weight of the patristic readings of Romans is all the more to be taken seriously.

It remains to ask whether it is plausible that Paul should have considered Andronicus and Junia to be apostles. Some have thought this could only be possible if "apostle" were used in a broader sense than the strict sense referring to a closed group of persons of whom Paul counted himself one.[298] Others have opted for the exclusive sense of the phrase in Romans 16:7 precisely because they do not think "the apostles" here can be intended other than in the strict sense and consider Andronicus and Junia cannot have been apostles in that sense. Zahn thought it incredible that Andronicus and Junia could have been well-known apostles when they apparently go completely unmentioned in the whole of the rest of early Christian literature.[299] The issue has certainly been confused by a lack of accurate understanding of precisely Paul's use of the term "apostle" in the so-called strict sense.[300]

---

297. Burer and Wallace, "Was Junia," 78n.12. Accordingly, they also blame Lightfoot and Cranfield for relying on this patristic interpretation.

298. E.g., Ellis, "Coworkers," 186; G. Edmundson, *The Church in Rome in the First Century* (London: Longmans, Green, 1913) 25.

299. Quoted in Burer and Wallace, "Was Junia," 81.

300. Thus Burer and Wallace, "Was Junia," 90n.68, are quite wrong to maintain that

There is a nontechnical sense of the term "apostle" that Paul uses twice (2 Cor 8:23; Phil 2:25) to designate official messengers of the churches. But this cannot be the meaning in Romans 16:7. Such people are clearly designated "apostles of the churches" (2 Cor 8:23) and "your [i.e., the Philippian Christians'] apostle" (Phil 2:25). It is hard to see how they could form a known body of people among whom Andronicus and Junia could be said to be outstanding. The unqualified "the apostles" of Romans 16:7 must refer to the apostles of Christ, whom Paul generally refers to simply as "apostles." But Paul's use of the term in this sense is broader than that of Matthew, Mark, and Luke, who restrict it to the twelve. For Paul the apostles of Christ included not only the twelve but also Barnabas (1 Cor 9:6), the brothers of the Lord (Gal 1:19; 1 Cor 9:5), probably Silvanus/Silas (1 Thess 2:7), and perhaps Apollos (1 Cor 4:9), as well as Paul himself. Paul speaks of "all the apostles" alongside the narrower category of "the twelve" (1 Cor 15:5, 7). These are those who had been commissioned by the risen Christ himself in resurrection appearances, since it is in this sense that Paul can regard himself, the last to be so commissioned, as the least of the apostles (1 Cor 15:9; cf. 9:1). It is important to realize that this category could have been considerably larger than the few names we know, and so there is no difficulty in supposing that Andronicus and Junia belonged to it, especially as Paul says specifically that they were Christians before him (see the next section).[301] It is true that they could not have been apostles in Paul's eyes unless they had been Christians before him, and so the latter information might seem redundant after they have been called apostles, but probably Paul wishes to underscore the special status of these two. That we hear nothing of either of them elsewhere in early Christian literature may not, as we shall see, be entirely true, but even if it were it need not be especially puzzling. Our knowledge of the earliest churches is extremely patchy. We know next to nothing about the spread of the Christian movement outside Palestine and outside the limited area of Paul's missionary work. Andronicus and Junia could have spent two or three decades as extremely important Christian missionaries in Rome and neighboring areas: if that were the case, there is no early Christian literature other than Romans in which we could expect to hear about it.

"Those who hold to the inclusive view for this passage have to ascribe a broader semantic range to ἀπόστολος, when used without adjuncts, than is normally accepted for the *corpus Paulinum.*" There is no convincing reason why Andronicus and Junia should not have been apostles in this normally accepted Pauline sense.

301. Maccini, *Her Testimony,* 230, asserts: "Junia was not a resurrection witness." How does he know?

e. "In Christ" before Paul

That Andronicus and Junia were Christians before Paul tells us that they were almost certainly Palestinian Jews (unless they were diaspora Jews converted while visiting Jerusalem)[302] and probably members of the early Jerusalem church. In that case we can put them in the context of other evidence of close contact between the church in Rome and the early Jerusalem church. Other members of the Jerusalem church who at some time are found in Rome are Peter, Silvanus/Silas (1 Pet 5:13), John Mark (1 Pet 5:13), and perhaps Rufus and his mother (Rom 16:13; cf. Mark 15:21). The Mary (Μαρία) of Romans 16:6 seems to be someone whose identity would be well known just through the use of this name. If she is a Jewish Christian with the Hebrew name Miriam, rather than a Gentile Christian with the Latin name Maria, then she too may have come from Jerusalem, and could be identified with Mary the mother of James and Joses, whom the Synoptic evangelists evidently expect to be someone their readers will know by repute (Matt 27:56, 61; 28:1; Mark 15:40, 47; 16:1; Luke 24:10). We should probably suppose that it was from Jerusalem that the Christian gospel first reached the Jewish community in Rome.

Andronicus and Junia may well have been involved in the founding or early growth of the Christian community in Rome. As "outstanding among the apostles" they must certainly have been leaders of considerable significance among the Roman Christians. No one else to whom Paul refers in Romans 16 has comparable standing. One way in which one might detect a logic in the order in which Paul names the people who occupy the earlier places in his long list is that he first of all names those of special personal significance to himself, owing to their role in his Aegean mission (Prisca and Aquila, Epaenetus), and then those who had pioneered and led the Christian mission in Rome: Mary "who has worked [ἐκοπίασεν, a term Paul often uses of his own apostolic labors] very hard among you," and Andronicus and Junia, "prominent among the apostles." Paul then goes on to some others with whom he was personally acquainted: Ampliatus, Urbanus, Stachys. After this there may be no special significance in the order.

f. The Names Junia and Joanna as Sound-Equivalents

Why should a Palestinian Jewish woman bear the Latin name Junia? We have already noticed that it was rare for first-century Palestinian Jews to have Latin

---

302. Edmundson, *Church*, 26n.1.

names. It is not difficult to explain this. For Jews who wished to add a non-Semitic name to or substitute one for their Semitic name, the practice of adopting Greek names was well established before the Roman occupation. Moreover, adopting a Latin name would not imply culture, as a Greek name might, but alignment with Roman political rule. Few Palestinian Jews would have wanted a name that proclaimed allegiance to Rome. Thus it is not surprising that the majority of those who are known to have had Latin names are found within the sphere of the Herods and the Herodians: members of the Herodian family itself; close friends, court officials, army officers, and other members of the Herodian households; the romanized, Herodian aristocracy of Tiberias and Sepphoris.[303] Junia may have belonged to this Herodian elite, but before taking up that possibility we should attend to another aspect of her name.

When Jews adopted Greek or Latin names, it was evidently quite common[304] for them to choose names that sounded similar to Semitic names (even though the meaning was quite different).[305] Perhaps some diaspora Jews used only the Greek or Latin name, but many, along with some Palestinian Jews, would seem to have used either name according to context. Probably the commonest, as well as the neatest, example is the Greek name Simon used as equivalent to the Hebrew name Simeon.[306] In pronunciation these two names

303. The evidence is presented in Bauckham, "Paul and Other Jews."

304. The evidence is underestimated by G. H. R. Horsley, "Names, Double," *ABD* 4:1015, who calls the practice "not especially common." This is partly because he distinguishes it from what he calls "substitute name" (1016). But his examples of the latter do not differ from the former: Simon (Peter) did not discontinue the use of Semitic form of his name Simeon (Acts 15:14; 2 Pet 1:1), nor did Silas simply replace this name with the Latin Silvanus. As is clear from Acts, the alternatives names were used in different, appropriate contexts. Horsley's mistake was earlier made by Deissmann, *Bible Studies*, 315n.2.

305. For evidence of the same practice among non-Jews, see Horsley, "Names, Double," 1015; Deissmann, *Bible Studies*, 315; C. J. Hemer, "The Name of Paul," *TynB* 36 (1985) 179-83, citing the interesting case of a native of Cilicia called both Lucius Antonius Leo and Neon son of Zoilus (*CIL* 10.3377).

306. See N. G. Cohen, "Jewish Names as Cultural Indicators in Antiquity," *JSJ* 7 (1976) 112-17; but she does not take account of the fact that the popularity of Simon/Simeon in later Second Temple Judaism was to a large extent due to the fact that it was a Hasmonean name. Ilan, "Names," 238-41, shows that the most popular male names among Palestinian Jews were all those of the Maccabees: Simeon, Joseph, Judah, Eleazar, John. (For Joseph as one of the Maccabee brothers, Ilan relies rather perilously on 2 Macc 8:22.) A nice example of the equivalence of Simon and Simeon is N. Lewis, Y. Yadin, and J. C. Greenfield, eds., *The Documents from the Bar Kokhba Period in the Cave of Letters* (Jerusalem: Israel Exploration Society, 1989) nos. 21-22, where two Jews are called Σίμων in the Greek parts of the documents, but Shimeon in the Aramaic and Nabatean of the attestations.

would have sounded very similar indeed. Other Greek names we know to have been used by Jews because of their assonance with Hebrew names include

Alkimos — Jakim/Eliakim[307]
Aster — Esther [308]
Cleopas — Clopas[309]
Jason — Jesus (Yeshuʿa)[310]
Mnason/Mnaseas — Manasseh[311]
Mousaios — Moses.[312]

Latin names used in this way as sound-equivalents include

Annia — Hannah?[313]
Annianus — Hanina/Hananiah[314]
Julius/Julianus — Judah[315]

307. Josephus, *Ant.* 12.385.

308. Ἀστήρ is a fairly uncommon Greek name, but popular with Jews in both Greek (Ἀστήρ or Ἀσθήρ) and Latin (Aster) (for the Greek spellings see Noy, *Jewish Inscriptions*, 1:66-67; M. Schwabe and B. Lifshitz, *Beth Sheʿarim*, vol. 2 [New Brunswick, N.J.: Rutgers University Press, 1974] 64: Ἀσθήρ assimilated the Greek name to the Hebrew): e.g., Williams, ed., *Jews among Greeks and Romans*, 47 (no. II.70) (= *CIL* VIII.8499), 77 (no. III.55) (*CIJ* 874); Noy, *Jewish Inscriptions*, vol. 1, nos. 26, 47, 130, 192; vol. 2, nos. 91, 140, 278, 552, 596; Schwabe and Lifshitz, *Beth Sheʿarim*, nos. 147, 176. The possible derivation of Esther from the Persian word for "star" would probably not have been known to Jews of this period.

309. Luke 24:18; Deissmann, *Bible Studies*, 315n.2; chap. 6 below.

310. Josephus, *Ant.* 12.239; Rom 16:21. See also N. G. Cohen, "The Names of the Translators in the Letter of Aristeas: A Study in the Dynamics of Cultural Transition," *JSJ* 15 (1984) 46-48.

311. Acts 21:16; *CPJ* 28 1.17; Noy, *Jewish Inscriptions*, vol. 2, no. 544. See also Cadbury, "Some Semitic Personal Names," in Wood, ed., *Amicitiae Corolla*, 51-53.

312. *CPJ* 20; Noy, *Jewish Inscriptions*, vol. 2, no. 74.

313. Noy, *Jewish Inscriptions*, vol. 2, no. 15.

314. Schwabe and Lifshitz, *Beth Sheʿarim*, 147-48; see nos. 166, 175; Noy, *Jewish Inscriptions*, vol. 2, nos. 120, 288, 466 (?); Noy, *Jewish Inscriptions*, vol. 1, no. 176.

315. For the three male names in this list, see *Lev. Rab.* 32:5 (and the same tradition in *Cant. Rab.* 56:6 to Cant. 4.12): "R. Huna stated in the name of Bar Kappara: Israel were redeemed from Egypt on account of four things, viz. because they did not change their names. . . . They did not change their name[s], having gone down as Reuben and Simeon, and having come up as Reuben and Simeon. They did not call Judah 'Leon,' nor Reuben 'Rufus,' nor Joseph 'Lestes' [corrected: Justus], nor Benjamin 'Alexander.'" The form of the text in *Cant. Rab.* 56:6 has: "They did not call Reuben 'Rufus,' Judah 'Julianus,' Joseph 'Justus,' or Benjamin 'Alexander'" (adapted from J. Neusner, *Song of Songs Rabbah: An Analytical Translation*, vol. 2 [BJS 196; Atlanta: Scholars Press, 1989] 73).

Justus — Joseph[316]
Justus — Jesus (Yeshuʿa)[317]
Lea — Leah?[318]
Maria — Mary (Miriam)?[319]
Paulus — Saul[320]
Rufus — Reuben[321]
Silvanus — Silas.[322]

The prevalence of this practice of adopting a Greek or Latin name for the sake of its assonance with a commonly used Semitic name makes it plausible that this might also be the case with Junia. The similarity in sound of Junia to the Hebrew name Joanna (Yehohannah or Yohannah) is quite close, as close as many of the known equivalences listed above. This opens the way to the suggestion that the Junia of Romans 16:7 is the same person as Luke's Joanna. That both were founding members of the Jerusalem church gives this suggestion considerable plausibility. It has always seemed remarkable that Paul could call two apostles of whom we never hear anywhere else in early Christian literature "prominent among the apostles" (Rom 16:7). Perhaps we do in fact hear of at least one of these in Luke's Gospel, where she is already prominent among the women followers of Jesus.

With regard to her acquisition of the Latin name Junia, two considerations are relevant. First, we know of other early Christian missionaries, of whom Paul is the best known, who had a Greek or Latin sound-equivalent to their Semitic name and evidently preferred to use the former when working in the diaspora, since it was more culturally appropriate and user-friendly for non-Semitic speakers. Among these are several Jews of Palestinian origin, members of the early Jerusalem church who later traveled elsewhere as missionaries: Silas/Silvanus, John Mark, and Joseph/Justus Barsabbas. Silvanus, who like Paul was a Roman citizen (Acts 16:37) and like Paul seems to have used

316. Acts 1:23; Josephus *Vita* 5, 427.

317. Col 4:11.

318. Noy, *Jewish Inscriptions*, vol. 2, no. 377.

319. If Μαρία (Rom 16:6) is Jewish, then the Latin form (Maria) of her Hebrew name Miriam would be an exact sound-equivalent of the Roman name Maria, the feminine form of Marius. Whether Jews exploited this particular sound-equivalence is not certain.

320. On the disputed issue whether Paul's Latin name would have been chosen as a sound-equivalent of his Hebrew name, see Bauckham, "Paul and Other Jews."

321. Mark 15:21; Rom 16:13. On this equivalence, see Cohen, "Jewish Names," 117-28. She also discusses the equivalence between Reuben and the Semitic name Roubel.

322. It is generally accepted that Silvanus (2 Cor 1:19; 1 Thess 1:1; 2 Thess 1:1; 1 Pet 5:12) is the same person as Silas (Acts 15:22, 27, 32, 34, 40; 16:19, 25, 29; 17:4, 10, 14, 15; 18:5).

his Latin name exclusively when in the diaspora, would presumably have borne this Latin name (one of the three Latin names a Roman citizen had) from birth. But in view of the general rarity of Latin names among Palestinian Jews, it is not likely that John Mark and Joseph/Justus Barsabbas had Latin names in early life (the latter already had the byname Barsabbas to distinguish him from other Josephs), much more likely that they adopted them when they became traveling missionaries in the diaspora. Outside Acts and so also outside Palestine, Mark is always called simply Mark (Col 4:10; 2 Tim 4:11; Phlm 24; 1 Pet 5:13). John (Yehohanan or Yohanan) was little used in the diaspora, and Marcus was one of the commonest of Latin *praenomina*. As Margaret Williams suggests: "The Gentiles he was seeking to convert would have found Mark a far easier name to cope with than the outlandish and unfamiliar Yehohanan."[323] In other words, he probably adopted the name Marcus when he started traveling in the diaspora, and Luke merely identifies him retrospectively "as John whose other name was Mark" in Acts 12:12 and 25, perhaps even intending to indicate the chronological point at which he adopted his Latin name in Acts 15:37-39.

That Luke can call John Mark retrospectively, "John whose other name was Mark," when in Luke's narrative he is still in Jerusalem (Acts 12:12, 25), is a valuable clue to the significance of the Latin name of "Joseph called Barsabbas, who was also called Justus" (Acts 1:23). As we have noticed already, Justus is the sound-equivalent of Joseph. To qualify for the position for which he was proposed, Joseph must almost certainly have been a Galilean (Acts 1:21-22). Williams suggests he acquired the name Justus in the environment of Tiberias,[324] but it is more likely that his case is parallel to Mark's: he later became a missionary in the diaspora and adopted an appropriate Latin name for the purpose. The only information about him other than Luke's one reference in Acts 1:23 is in Papias, who heard from the daughters of Philip (who settled in Papias's home town Hierapolis) that he had once drunk deadly poison without ill effects (cf. Mark 16:18).[325] That Papias knew such a story suggests that Joseph/Justus was later known as a traveling missionary. Significantly, Papias calls him "Justus who was also called Barsabbas," as he would have been known in the diaspora, substituting his Latin name for its Hebrew sound-equivalent.

The case of Joanna/Junia may be parallel to those of John Mark and Joseph/Justus Barsabbas. Like its masculine equivalent John, her Hebrew name was an awkward one for Greek- or Latin-speakers. She may have adopted the Latin sound-equivalent of her Hebrew name when she began to travel in the di-

323. Williams, "Palestinian," in Bauckham, ed., *Book of Acts*, 105.
324. Williams, "Palestinian," 104.
325. *Apud* Eusebius, *Hist. Eccl.* 3.39.9.

aspora, if this was before she went to Rome, or when she became a Christian missionary in Rome, where Junia was a common female name. But there is another possibility, since our second consideration is that one of the few circles in which one could find Palestinian Jews bearing Latin names was, as already noted, the Herodian aristocracy of Tiberias. Joanna, as we know, belonged with her husband Chuza to that elite. Perhaps she already called herself Junia in that context, where it would have the appropriateness not only of being a sound-equivalent of her Hebrew name but also of being a distinguished, aristocratic Roman name.

I cannot decide between these two possibilities, but the second alerts us also to consider how appropriate it would have been for Joanna, the wife of Herod's steward, member of the romanized Herodian elite of Tiberias, to become a Christian missionary specifically in Rome. She would have known some Latin, doubtless a rare accomplishment among the first Jewish Christians of Jerusalem. She had the means to support herself and a degree of acculturation to Roman ways.

What of her husband? The Greek name Andronicus could be the name adopted by Chuza for the same reasons that Joanna adopted the name Joanna.[326] But it is also possible, as noted above, that Joanna was already widowed at the time of Jesus' ministry. Andronicus would then be her second husband. Again I can do no more than state these possibilities.

7. Joanna as Apostolic Witness

In §1 above, I suggested that Luke 24:10, where Luke names Mary Magdalene and Joanna for the second time in his Gospel, forms an *inclusio* with his first reference to them in 8:2-3, reminding readers that the discipleship of these two women and the others spans the whole of his narrative from the time of the Galilean ministry to the resurrection, and that this impression is reinforced by the fact that the angels at the tomb remind the women of what Jesus had said to them in Galilee (24:6). The women have in fact already reappeared in Luke's narrative at the cross (23:49) and at the burial of Jesus (23:55-56), where, as in the other Synoptics, their presence is emphasized for the sake of their role as the witnesses to the death and burial of Jesus as well as to the empty tomb. Unlike Matthew and Mark, who give names for the women at these points (Matt 27:56, 61; Mark 15:40, 47), Luke assumes his readers will be able to identify the women

---

326. For Jews with the name Andronicus, see Josephus, *Ant.* 13.75, 78, 79; *CPJ* 18; Horbury and Noy, *Jewish Inscriptions,* 322; Noy, *Jewish Inscriptions,* vol. 1, no. 85.

as those to whom they were introduced in 8:2-3, and only names them again at the point when they report the news of the empty tomb and the message of the angels to the male disciples (24:9-10). As in 8:2-3, three women are named and nameless others mentioned, but in addition to Mary Magdalene and Joanna, the third named woman is not Susanna, as in 8:3, but the Mary (called by Luke "Mary [mother] of James") who appears in all six lists of women at the cross, the burial, and the empty tomb in Matthew (Matt 27:56, 61; 28:1) and Mark (Mark 15:40, 47; 16:1) but occurs in Luke only at 24:10. As I shall argue in detail in chapter 9 below (§8), all three Synoptic evangelists take noticeable care in their naming of the women in these passages, naming only those known as witnesses of the events. Luke's omission of Susanna and naming of Mary the mother of James instead shows that he shares this concern. The corollary is that Joanna does not appear in Luke as a witness to the empty tomb only because she is a prominent member of the band of disciples already in Luke 8:3, but because Luke had reason to think she was a witness to the empty tomb, just as he had in the cases of Mary Magdalene and Mary the mother of James. From his own special sources of Gospel traditions Luke knew not only that Joanna was a disciple of Jesus but also that she was among the women at the tomb.

In all the Synoptic lists of women disciples, including Luke's two (8:2-3; 24:10), Mary Magdalene is placed first, as Peter is always first in the trio of prominent male disciples (Peter, James, and John). She must have been of special importance in the early Christian communities. But, although Luke 24:10 gives this usual primacy to Mary of Magdala, it has been argued that it also suggests the special importance Joanna had for Luke by means of the chiastic structure of 24:9b-10:

A   ἀπήγγειλαν ταῦτα πάντα τοῖς ἕνδεκα

B   καὶ πᾶσιν τοῖς λοιποῖς.

C   ἦσαν δὲ ἡ Μαγδαληνὴ Μαρία

D   καὶ Ἰωάννα

C′   καὶ Μαρία ἡ Ἰακώβου

B′   καὶ αἱ λοιπαὶ σὺν αὐταῖς.

A′   ἔλεγον πρὸς τοὺς ἀποστόλους ταῦτα[327]

It is not possible to be sure that Luke created this structure in order to suggest a central significance for Joanna, but even without it we can be sure that Joanna has some kind of special importance for Luke. I shall shortly ask what this was.

<hr>

327. L. Dussaut, "Le triptyque des apparitions en Luc 24 (Analyse structurelle)," *RB* 94 (1987) 168, followed by J. Nolland, *Luke 18:35–24:53* (WBC 35C; Dallas: Word, 1993) 1191.

The role of the women in the resurrection narratives of Luke 24 is discussed in detail in chapter 9 (§5), where I shall argue that Luke's emphasis on a body of Jesus' disciples, male and female, which is considerably larger than the twelve, continues through chapter 24, and that the women disciples are included in the gathering of "the eleven and those with him" (24:33), to whom the risen Christ appears and whom he commissions to be witnesses of his resurrection (24:36-49). This means that, according to Luke's Gospel, Joanna, Mary Magdalene, and other women disciples fulfill the conditions Peter specifies in Acts 1:21-22: they have "accompanied us [the eleven] during all the time that the Lord Jesus went in and out among us, beginning from the baptism of John until the day when he was taken up from us." These are the conditions to be fulfilled by the person who is to replace Judas among the twelve, and clearly they are designed to describe one who is qualified to be an authoritative witness to Jesus (cf. Acts 13:31). However, Peter's words also make clear that any candidate for this position must be male (1:21). Presumably because the twelve are the symbolic heads of the new Israel, corresponding to the twelve phylarchs of Israel's founding generation (Num 1:4-16), it is taken for granted that they must be male. But this does not preclude the role of other witnesses, including the women, who in the nascent Christian community still have their place alongside the twelve (cf. Acts 1:14) just as they did during the ministry of Jesus (Luke 8:1-3). Like Matthew (10:2) and Mark (3:14; 6:30), Luke uses the word "apostle" only of the twelve (Luke 6:13; 9:10; 17:5; 22:14; 24:10; Acts 1:1; etc.).[328] In Luke's terminology Joanna and the other women cannot be called apostles, but Luke's account of them makes them apostles according to Paul's use of the term, which includes himself, Barnabas, and the brothers of Jesus (alongside whom Luke places the women in Acts 1:14).

In chapter 9 (§8) I shall also discuss the role that the women who, according to the Gospels, witnessed the empty tomb and the risen Lord must have played in the early church. Their witness had a unique role because they alone witnessed the burial as well as the empty tomb, and so could vouch for the fact that the tomb they found empty was the one in which the body of Jesus had been laid. But, according to Matthew, Luke, and John, they were also qualified to testify, "I have seen the Lord" (John 20:18), just as the male eyewitnesses to the resurrection were. Using the word "apostolic" in this Pauline sense (1 Cor 9:1), the women were apostolic eyewitness guarantors of the traditions about Jesus, and the Gospel stories about their visit to the tomb and encounters with

---

328. Acts 14:14 uses the term of Paul and Barnabas, presumably in the nontechnical sense of missionaries sent out by the church of Antioch. It is not likely that the term refers to the twelve alone in Luke 11:49, a Q passage where Matthew does not have the term.

the risen Jesus are the textual form eventually given to the witness that they must have given orally during the early decades of Christian life and mission. The names so precisely preserved by the Gospels show that the witness of the women was not known simply in a generalized form as that of an anonymous group, nor was it attached solely to the most prominent of these women disciples of Jesus, Mary Magdalene. Rather each of these named women, some better known to some of the evangelists, others to others, were prominent figures in the early communities, active traditioners with recognized eyewitness authority. It is to their witness to the death, burial, and empty tomb of Jesus that the Gospels especially appeal, because in this respect their witness was of unparalleled importance for these key events of the history of Jesus; but it is unlikely that the traditions they passed on were limited to these events. They would surely also have been sources and guarantors of traditions from the ministry of Jesus: stories and dominical sayings.

It is quite plausible that this is the special significance of Joanna for Luke, especially as there are several other places in the Gospel and Acts where Luke appears to be naming people who were available to him as eyewitness sources for his history (Luke 24:18; Acts 13:1; 21:8-9, 16).[329] In previous scholarly discussion, two significant suggestions have been made with regard to traditions Luke may have had (immediately or ultimately) from Joanna. One is that Luke's special knowledge of Herod Antipas (9:9b; 23:4-12; cf. 13:1-3, 31-32)[330] has Joanna as its source,[331] but there is also Manaen, who had also been a member of Herod's court (Acts 13:1), to be considered in this role. We do not know what Joanna's standing among the Herodian courtiers was or what contacts with them she retained after becoming a disciple of Jesus. On the other hand, information that, if reliable, must have come from inside Herod's court (Luke 9:9b; 23:4-12) relates closely to traditions that must derive from the circle of Jesus' disciples (13:1-5,[332] 31-32). This suggests that Joanna is likely to have played some role in the origins of these traditions.

329. Cf. C. J. Hemer, *The Book of Acts in the Setting of Hellenistic History* (ed. C. H. Gempf; WUNT 49; Tübingen: Mohr [Siebeck], 1989) 350-51. Note the role of the daughters of Philip for Papias: Eusebius, *Hist. Eccl.* 3.39.9.

330. Luke's omission of Mark's story of the death of John the Baptist (Mark 6:17-29) might be due to his awareness of its legendary character.

331. B. H. Streeter, "On the Trial of Our Lord before Herod — a Suggestion," in W. Sanday, ed., *Studies in the Synoptic Problem* (Oxford: Clarendon, 1911) 231; A. Hastings, *Prophet,* 42-49. Both also refer to Manaen.

332. This passage explains the enmity between Pilate and Herod to which 23:12 refers. See Streeter, "Trial," 229-31, who argues that this relationship is good evidence for the historicity of Luke's account of Jesus' appearance before Herod; Hoehner, *Herod,* 236-37.

Thorlief Boman argued that the whole of Luke's special material (so-called L) derives from a circle of women disciples, including Joanna, who were the eyewitnesses, traditioners, and custodians of a cycle of Gospel traditions.[333] Following earlier scholars, he argued that Luke's special source, comprising material from Luke 1:5 to the end of the Gospel, is a coherent and consistent collection and redaction of Gospel traditions. He associates it with the women disciples because of the prominence of women in it. It is certainly true that the special prominence of women in Luke's Gospel results from his inclusion of this special material along with most of the Markan pericopae about women. Apart from Luke's infancy narrative, in which Elizabeth, Mary, and Anna are prominent,[334] and the story of the empty tomb, which is often considered merely Luke's redaction of Mark, L material accounts for two of the only four parables of Jesus that feature women (Luke 15:8-10; 18:1-14)[335] and seven other pericopae in which women are central (Luke 7:11-17, 36-50;[336] 8:1-3; 10:38-42; 11:27-28;[337] 13:10-17; 23:27-31; cf. also 4:25-26). It is also true, however, that women are prominent in Acts, though to a lesser extent; and so, judging by this criterion alone, it could be that Luke's interest in women led him to collect Gospel traditions with female characters from several sources besides Mark.

It is a pity that the most recent study of Luke's special material, a study by Kim Paffenroth that argues for a single coherent source comprising less material than Boman assigned to L,[338] does not refer at all to Boman's work, though Paffenroth mentions Leonard Swidler's suggestion that the author of L was a woman[339] and, since stories about women do not predominate in L, declines to speculate that L's community might have been a community of widows.[340] Since he denies that Luke's infancy narratives derive from this source or that it included a passion narrative or resurrection narratives, women are certainly less prominent in his reconstruction of L than in Boman's more capacious hy-

---

333. T. Boman, *Die Jesus-Überlieferung im Lichte der neuen Volkskunde* (Göttingen: Vandenhoeck & Ruprecht, 1967) 123-37. A. Hastings, *Prophet*, 40, thinks of the women as a source for Luke 9:51–18:14.

334. Cf. chap. 3 above for the predominantly gynocentric nature of Luke 1–2.

335. The others are Luke 13:20-21 = Matt 13:33 (Q); Matt 25:1-12 (M).

336. A few scholars consider this Luke's redaction of Mark 14:3-10, but most think it must represent a distinct source even if both derive ultimately from a common tradition.

337. Some scholars assign this passage to Q, though it has no parallel in Matthew.

338. K. Paffenroth, *The Story of Jesus according to L* (JSNTSup 147; Sheffield: Sheffield Academic Press, 1997).

339. Paffenroth, *Story*, 124n.45.

340. Paffenroth, *Story*, 157n.70. He is referring to Davies's theory about the origins of the apocryphal Acts: S. L. Davies, *The Revolt of the Widows: The Social World of the Apocryphal Acts* (Carbondale: Southern Illinois University Press; London: Feffer & Simons, 1980).

pothetical source. Paffenroth assigns to L only six of the nine pericopae mentioned above as featuring women (Luke 7:11-17, 36-50; 10:38-42; 13:10-17; 15:8-10; 18:1-14). This is fewer such pericopae than Mark has (see Mark 1:29-32; 3:31-35 [?]; 5:21-43; 7:24-30; 12:41-44; 14:3-9; 15:40-41, 47; 16:1-8), and so Boman's case for women's tradition is not strong for this version of the L hypothesis.

It is also rather disappointing to find that Boman's hypothesis has not (so far as I know) been discussed by feminist biblical scholars, among whom only Carla Ricci mentions it in a survey of scholarly treatments of Luke 8:1-3.[341] This may be because much feminist scholarship on the Gospels subsequent to Elisabeth Schüssler Fiorenza's *In Memory of Her* has been much more concerned with redactional and literary approaches to the Gospels than with source-critical or more historically oriented approaches. This is true, for example, of the best book on women in Luke-Acts: Turid Karlsen Seim's *The Double Message*. Schüssler Fiorenza herself, mentioning Swidler's suggestion that a woman wrote L, along with other proposals for female authorship of parts of the New Testament, thinks such conjectures helpful insofar as they "challenge the androcentric dogmatism that ascribes apostolic authorship only to man."[342] But she also correctly points out that "a look at writings attributed to women in antiquity or written by women today indicates that these works are not necessarily written differently and do not always espouse different values from those written by men. Women as well as men are socialized into the same androcentric mind-set and culture."[343]

It also true that stories about women need not derive from women (just as stories about men could derive from women). Joanna Dewey, one feminist scholar who has discussed the question whether some Gospel traditions can be attributed to women tradents, argues primarily on form-critical grounds that, whereas other Gospel stories of women's healing are close to the oral tradition and were plausibly transmitted orally by women, the two stories of women's healing peculiar to Luke (7:11-17; 13:10-17) lack the countercultural features that would have appealed to oral storytellers and probably derive from written compositions by men (Luke himself at least in the latter case).[344] In both cases the

---

341. Ricci, *Mary Magdalene*, 44.

342. Schüssler Fiorenza, *In Memory*, 60-61; cf. also idem, *Jesus and the Politics of Interpretation* (New York/London: Continuum, 2000) 50.

343. Schüssler Fiorenza, *In Memory*, 61. The point is also made by R. S. Kraemer, "Women's Authorship of Jewish and Christian Literature in the Greco-Roman Period," in A.-J. Levine, ed., *"Women Like This": New Perspectives on Jewish Women in the Greco-Roman World* (SBLEJIL 01; Atlanta: Scholars Press, 1991) 232-33.

344. J. Dewey, "Jesus' Healings of Women: Conformity and Non-conformity to Dominant Cultural Values as Clues for Historical Reconstruction," *BTB* 24 (1994) 122-31.

woman is entirely passive and the story reinforces the restricted role for women upheld by the culture.[345] This coheres with what Dewey, like some other feminist scholars, considers "Luke's general pattern of rendering women visible in his narrative, but at the same time restricting them to subordinate roles."[346] We have seen that this is a reading of Luke only possible if one ignores the way Luke includes the women in the wider group of disciples with whom his narrative is at least as much concerned as with the twelve. It is not consistent, for example, with a reading of the mission of the seventy-two disciples (10:1-20) as including women. Moreover, Dewey seems in conflict with Schüssler Fiorenza's observation just quoted. It is not obvious why stories that put women in passive and culturally conforming roles could not have been transmitted by women.

However, Dewey's work shows that, while on general grounds it must be virtually certain that women did function as sources and tradents of Gospel traditions that have subsequently reached textual form in the Gospels, the identification of such traditions is highly problematic. Moreover, since the question of women's traditions or, more specifically, traditions from Joanna in Luke's Gospel could be adequately addressed only in the context of a wider discussion of Luke's special material in general, this is not the place for more than some suggestions toward a theory.

I begin with two observations about Luke's resurrection narratives. First, it is important to establish, against most recent scholars, that Luke 24:1-11, the context of Luke's second reference to Joanna, is not merely Luke's redaction of Mark 16:1-8.[347] The detail of the two "men" (24:4; contrast Mark's one "young man") is one of a series of resemblances between Luke 24 and John 20.[348] Unless John is dependent on Luke or Luke on John, neither of which can be entirely ruled out but neither of which is held by the majority of scholars today, there must be common tradition behind Luke's and John's resurrection narratives. In that case, the two angels in Luke's story of the empty tomb derive from a version of this tradition different from Mark's. But, furthermore and in any case, verbal agreement between Luke 24:1-11 and Mark 16:1-8 is minimal, far too little to prove a literary connection at all and much less than is characteristic of Luke's redaction of Mark. There do not seem to be plausible special reasons why Luke should have treated Mark's narrative so much more freely in this in-

345. Dewey, "Jesus' Healings," 125.

346. Dewey, "Jesus' Healings," 124. The full discussion by Seim, *Double Message*, reaches a more nuanced conclusion, recognizing the active roles of women in the Gospel as well as their subordinated position in Acts.

347. See Fitzmyer, *Gospel according to Luke X–XXIV* (AB 28A; New York: Doubleday, 1985) 1541, for references to scholars on both sides of this issue.

348. See, e.g., Nolland, *Luke 18:35–24:53*, 1184-85.

stance than usually.[349] If, then, Luke draws on a source other than Mark for his story of the women and the empty tomb, it is notable that he evidently *prefers* this source to Mark. When we recall the importance the Synoptic evangelists clearly attached to the women's eyewitness testimony to this tradition (as evidenced by the careful recording of their names), it is hard to see why Luke should have preferred his alternative source to Mark unless he thought this source had at least as good a claim to be based on the eyewitness testimony of the women as Mark's version. Then it becomes clear that by naming Joanna, as Mark did not, Luke indicates the source of his tradition about the empty tomb.

It is also noteworthy that Luke's account of the appearance of Jesus to the travelers on the way to Emmaus (24:13-32), which is unique to him,[350] contains the name of a disciple, Cleopas (24:18), otherwise unknown in the Synoptic traditions.[351] There is no narratological reason for Luke to name either of the travelers, and it is curious that he names only one.[352] It seems likely that he names the source of this tradition, just as Joanna is named as the source of the previous tradition. But then it is noteworthy that both are disciples who do not belong to the circle of the twelve. I have noted that Luke, in contrast to Mark's and Matthew's emphasis on the twelve, characteristically envisages a much larger group of itinerant disciples, including especially the women but also other male disciples (Luke 6:17; 8:1-3; 10:1-20; 19:37; 23:29; 24:9, 33; Acts 1:15, 21-23). The references in Luke's Gospel to the twelve (or the synonymous "the apostles") are all in material derived from Mark,[353] with the exception of 8:1-3 (the twelve and

349. It is often supposed that Luke mentions Galilee in 24:6 because Mark does in 16:7, but that Luke had to change the significance of Galilee because he does not have the disciples meeting the risen Christ there. But this is a very odd explanation. Galilee functions quite differently in the two narratives. Luke mentions Galilee because it takes the women and the reader back to the earliest phase of Jesus' ministry. There is no need to suppose he took it from a sentence of Mark that he otherwise could not have taken over and does not take over.

350. The brief summary of this tradition in the Longer Ending of Mark (16:12-13) is most probably dependent on Luke.

351. He is almost certainly the same person as the Clopas of John 19:25: see chap. 6 below. But Cleopas is the Greek sound-equivalent to the Semitic name Clopas. That either of these references to him is dependent on the other is very implausible. As suggested in chap. 6 below, they corroborate each other as historical references.

352. Fitzmyer, *Luke,* 2:1564, thinks that therefore "the best explanation is that [the name Cleopas] was already part of the pre-Lukan tradition." But this only raises the same question one stage back: why was the name in the pre-Lukan tradition?

353. Luke 6:13; 9:1, 10, 12; 17:5; 18:31; 22:3, 14, 47. In 9:12 and 17:5 Luke clarifies his Markan source by substituting "the twelve" or "the apostles" for Mark's "disciples" (meaning the twelve). On the one occasion where Mark clearly speaks of a body larger than the twelve (4:10: "those about him with the twelve") Luke substitutes "his disciples" (Luke 8:9), confirming that for him this term has a wider reference than to the twelve.

the women); 11:49 (Q) ("prophets and apostles," where a broader meaning of "apostles" is likely); 24:10; and the two postresurrection references to "the eleven and all the rest" (24:9) and "the eleven and those with them" (24:33). Whereas readers of Mark reasonably assume that his frequent references to the disciples are to the twelve, there is no need to assume this in Luke. That Luke's special traditions derive from disciples of Jesus other than the twelve seems plausible.[354] To consider whether his contact with them was firsthand would involve other considerations of Lukan authorship that I cannot enter here. But this should not be prejudicially ruled out. Chronological factors make it unlikely that Luke could have known Cleopas, who was Joseph's brother, but he could easily have known his son, who succeeded James as leader of the Jerusalem church.[355] There is no reason why Luke could not have known Joanna. But in whatever form, oral or written, firsthand or indirectly, Luke's special traditions reached him, it seems likely some of them had the names of Joanna and Cleopas associated with them, while perhaps some were linked with Susanna. (Mary Magdalene and Mary the mother of James are so generally prominent in the Gospels they are less likely to be sources of traditions peculiar to Luke.)

8. The Historical Joanna — A Sketch

No historical reconstruction is possible without the exercise of historical imagination. What follows is my attempt to draw historical findings together into a sketch of the life of Joanna, using historically informed imagination to draw possible inferences from the evidence but stopping short of the kind of imaginative speculation that goes far beyond the evidence. Inevitably, gaps have to be filled and other reconstructions are possible[356] (and this statement exempts me from tedious repetition of "probably" and "perhaps" in the sketch: readers may judge the degrees of probability for themselves); but, so long as we are aware of

354. This was suggested by J. V. Bartlett, "The Sources of St. Luke's Gospel," in Sanday, ed., *Oxford Studies*, 344-45. He supposed that Luke received his special traditions from Philip the evangelist (Acts 21:8) who had gathered traditions from members of the seventy disciples (Bartlett does not seem to think these included the women) as well as from the apostle John.

355. See chap. 6 below.

356. My reconstruction differs considerably from the historical hypotheses about Joanna and Mary Magdalene developed by Sawicki, *Crossing Galilee*, chap. 7. I find her ideas too speculative and not sufficiently restrained by the most probable conclusions that can be drawn from the evidence about Joanna. According to Sawicki, Mary Magdalene, who was a businesswoman in the fish salting trade in Magdala, and Joanna, who organized entertainment for the tourists who visited Herod's court, were business partners. They first got to know Jesus as a faith healer employed at the healing spa in the tourist resort of Tiberias.

the limitations of the evidence, historical reconstruction of this kind is a valuable aid to historical understanding. We enter another time and place by understanding both the facts, more or less probably established, and the possibilities they suggest. Even the unrealized possibilities are part of history. It is the possibilities of history, realized and unrealized, that make it relevant to the present.

Joanna was born into one of the prominent and wealthy Jewish families of Galilee and grew up in one of the small castles that dotted the Galilean hills. Her parents arranged her marriage for her at an early age, and, like most Jewish girls, she was married when she reached puberty. The marriage was made for political advantage, to promote her family's alliance with Herod Antipas's rule in Galilee. Her husband was the Nabatean nobleman Chuza, who had recently come to Herod's court in the entourage of the young Nabatean princess who became Herod's wife. Herod had soon promoted him to finance minister of his realm. To marry Joanna he adopted Jewish religion, though this was to his advantage in any case if he was to make his career in Herod's administration.

As Chuza's wife Joanna lived in a magnificent house in the new city of Tiberias, with estates elsewhere in Galilee. She became part of the would-be romanized culture of the Tiberian aristocracy and court officials, who aped the life and manners of the Roman aristocracy known to Herod and his close companions from his time in Rome. Wealth was conspicuous, and the political maneuvering and sycophancy of the court were inescapable. This aristocratic and romanizing environment probably allowed Joanna, as a woman, more independence of mind and activity than were available to most Jewish women. This was all the more true in that she had wealth of her own, given her by her father by deed of gift at the time of her marriage, and available for her use quite independently of her husband.

In these mixed Jewish and Gentile circles, with their romanizing aspirations, the practice of Jewish religion was not taken very seriously, except as a politically necessary appearance of Jewish identity. This was a difference from Joanna's upbringing. She may have been part of a circle of devout Jewish women at the court who practiced their religion more strictly and took an interest in the movements of religious renewal in the Palestinian Judaism of their time, while acutely aware from the case of John the Baptist that such movements were politically dangerous in Herodian eyes. Joanna must also have been aware of the hatred and resentment with which the ordinary people of Galilee viewed Tiberias and all it represented, in political, economic, and (because these aspects of life were inseparable) religious terms.

It was as a healer and exorcist that Jesus of Nazareth first became known among the courtiers and officials of Tiberias. His activities in the area immediately north of Tiberias could not be ignored. He was a popular sensation, with crowds pouring into the area in the expectation of healing for them and theirs. Extraordinary tales of healing were circulating. Jesus and his disciples kept clear of Tiberias, frustrating even Herod's own curiosity and suspicion, but members of the court went to Jesus. The most remarkable story was that the mother of Manaen, one of Herod's closest circle of friends and advisers, had died and been brought back to life by Jesus. Joanna was also one of those who went to Jesus not out of curiosity but in urgent need of healing. Whatever her illness was, her healing encounter with Jesus was an experience that changed the whole direction of her life.

Joanna knew that Jesus was no mere charismatic healer, but that his healings were integral to a vision of the coming kingdom of God. Her own healing brought her into growing participation in this vision, which included an uncompromising call to repentance, a corresponding enactment of God's transformative forgiveness, and the inclusion of all kinds of marginal and excluded people in the Jewish people of God as Jesus was beginning to reconstitute it. Jesus' practice of the coming kingdom drew together a community of disciples among whom the life of the kingdom was taking form in the renunciation of all status and wealth. This was the particular challenge for Joanna, who could have remained, as others did, a sympathizer with Jesus' movement without leaving her home and social location. But Joanna took the step of discipleship, for her a step across the whole of the social gulf that separated the Tiberian elite from the ordinary people, not to mention the beggars, the prostitutes, and other outcasts with whom Jesus habitually associated. But she herself was an outcast of a sort, one of the oppressors, in her identification with Rome and its Herodian clients a traitor to the Jewish national and religious cause. Throwing in her lot with Jesus was a radical conversion to the poor, but it must have been the nondiscriminating acceptance with which the community of Jesus' disciples welcomed all who joined them, even tax collectors, that gave her the confidence to risk her reputation among her peers, burning her bridges behind her, in order to identify herself as fully as possible with Jesus and his movement. Among these people, her status brought her no honor; not even her substantial donations to the common fund gave her a place above others. But instead she found a place in what Jesus called his new family of those who were practicing the will of God, his sisters and brothers and mothers, who were therefore also sisters and brothers and mothers to each other.

As a devout Jewish woman, Joanna had always made a practice of charitable giving to the poor, but joining the disciples of Jesus required a more radical step. She sold some of her property and gave the proceeds to the needy. She retained ownership of the rest, but put all of the income from it into the common fund on which Jesus and his disciples drew for the necessities of life. Most of the male disciples had left dependent relatives at home and had nothing to spare, and so the women provided the bulk of the economic support of the group, the poorer women contributing what little they could, Joanna and other wealthier women providing much more.

There followed two years or so in which Joanna was in the constant company of Jesus and his many disciples. Sometimes as many as a hundred were traveling with him, sometimes far fewer, but Joanna, with other women and the twelve men, belonged to the inner circle of those in constant attendance. Following Jesus took them to most parts of Jewish Palestine. For disciples like Joanna it was an extraordinary learning experience, witnessing Jesus' miraculous deeds, by which he manifested the coming kingdom as God's grace for the needy, and the turning around of the lives of those who encountered him, imbibing Jesus' teaching and deliberately remembering the parables and aphorisms in which he encapsulated his teaching in memorable form.

From time to time Jesus would send his disciples out in pairs to visit the towns and villages to which he would come himself later. This was active participation in Jesus' mission, preaching the kingdom as he did, healing and exorcising as he did. Traveling without money or provisions, utterly dependent on those who took them in, the disciples made obvious their solidarity with the poorest of the poor in the villages they stayed in. For Joanna, this was the point of deepest immersion in the life of ordinary people, to whom she made known the good news and made it effective in deliverance from disease and demons. She and the other women did not scandalize the people by preaching in public places, but she would talk to the women where they gathered at the well or the market stalls, visit them in their homes, relating some of Jesus' parables and sayings. She would be available for the people to bring the sick to her, as they were used to going to village women with healing skills. But there was also the bitter experience of rejection in villages that wanted nothing to do with Jesus' disciples.

When Jesus arrived in Jerusalem for what was to be his last visit to the city and for the first time publicly acted out his messianic vocation by riding into Jerusalem amid the acclamation of his Galilean followers, the danger was palpable, and Joanna knew the Jewish and Roman political world well enough to sense it more than most. A few days later she was one of the first to hear the news that Jesus had been sentenced to death by crucifixion. She still had contacts in high places and so was able to find out what had become of Jesus after his arrest. With some of the other women she made her way to the place of crucifixion and watched Jesus' agonizing death. It took some courage to be associated with Jesus at that time, and many of the male disciples had gone into hiding. But she and some of the other women were concerned that Jesus' body be properly treated, and so, after waiting for the Sabbath to pass, they went with spices and ointments to the tomb. The discovery and the revelation that followed formed a story she would tell a thousand times in the rest of her life.

Joanna's husband Chuza took a favorable view of Jesus and could not but be impressed by his wife's healing, but he stopped short of approving her behavior thereafter, and his high position in Herod's government made association with Jesus problematic. But he was in Jerusalem, with Herod, for the Passover when Jesus was crucified. He was deeply disturbed by what happened and easily drawn by his wife into the company of the disciples. Both he and Joanna were among the quite large number of disciples who were gathered when the risen Jesus appeared to them and commissioned them as his witnesses.

This commission determined Joanna and Chuza's life thereafter. Like Jesus' uncle Clopas/Cleopas and his wife Mary, they became one of the husband-and-wife teams of traveling missionaries in the early days when the gospel of the crucified and risen Jesus the Messiah was being spread through Jewish Palestine. But it was not long before they were called further afield. The Christian message first reached the Jewish community in Rome when pilgrims visiting Jerusalem for the festivals heard it preached by the leaders of the Jerusalem church in the temple forecourt. But apostles from Jerusalem were needed, and Joanna and Chuza were an obvious choice. Through Herod's court they had contacts with Rome and the Jewish community there. They were used to Roman ways to some degree and spoke a little Latin. Joanna even had a Latin sound-equivalent to her Hebrew name: Junia. She had adopted this in Tiberias, where it seemed a suitably aristocratic Roman name to signal her identification with Roman culture and Herodian loyalties. Now it acquired fresh usefulness when she moved to Rome. Chuza adopted the Greek name Andronicus, popular among Jews, as a name more familiar to the Roman Jews than his Nabatean name.

It was because of their apostolic labors in Rome for more than a decade, while Paul was founding churches in Asia Minor and Greece, that Paul, writing to the Christians of Rome in the mid-50s, was able to call Junia and her husband "outstanding among the apostles." Christians in Rome were often suspected of being politically subversive, and from time to time their leaders were arrested. When Paul wrote his letter, Junia and Andronicus were imprisoned. We know no more of them, but perhaps, some years later, the evangelist Luke spent many hours with Junia, hearing from her the versions of the Gospel traditions as she had long been telling them.

9. Readers on the Road with Joanna

From historical reconstruction we return to the text of Luke's Gospel, and to the literary function of 8:1-3, the summary passage in which Joanna first appears. As a forward-looking summary it provides a general characterization of Jesus' activities (v 1a), within which the stories and teaching of the following chapters can be placed. Readers are to understand that these took place within the context of a wide-ranging preaching ministry in many cities and villages. The summary also places with Jesus two groups within the wider body of disciples: the twelve and the women. It is with this inner circle, close to Jesus, witnessing all he does and says, that readers now follow the rest of Luke's narrative. Luke does not introduce the women at 8:2-3 so that readers may forget them again until 23:50, but so that readers may journey with them in Jesus' company all the way to the cross. There are occasions when readers must leave the women: when Jesus ascends the mountain with Peter, James, and John (9:28), leaving behind the rest of the twelve as well; and when Jesus takes the twelve aside to speak to them alone (18:31). But such occasions are explicitly marked and they are rare. For the most part readers view Jesus' activities and hear his teaching from among the broad circle of those who are close to him, including the women as well as the twelve.

Thus the placing of both the twelve and the women with Jesus in 8:1-3 guides readers as to the perspective from which they should view the narrative that follows. The various stories themselves offer a variety of perspectives. Sometimes they invite readers to adopt the perspective of someone who encounters or is healed by Jesus. The story of the hemorrhaging woman (8:43-48) is a good example: since Luke recounts her unobserved actions and unvoiced thoughts, readers find themselves in her shoes. But in many instances there is no clear alignment of readers with the perspective of one or a group of the characters. In these cases, it is the disciples, who move with Jesus from scene to scene, observing everything, who provide the obvious perspective for readers to view and to listen in. Therefore it is of considerable importance for the literary strategy of his whole narrative that in 8:1-3 Luke has defined the inner circle of the disciples as both men and women. These verses authorize readers to read on with the eyes of the women or with the eyes of the men. They may adopt either sex's perspective (no more in the Gospels than in any other literature is it expected that men will adopt only the perspective of male characters and women only the perspective of female characters). They may see more if sometimes they read from one, sometimes from the other perspective. Confirmation that this is the strategy of the text comes at 23:49, the first point at which the women disciples are again explicitly mentioned, as well as explicitly identified with those in 8:2-3 ("who had followed him from Galilee"). Here readers find, if they had forgotten, that their view of the cross is that of the group of both male and female disciples (though Luke leaves it unclear whether specifically the twelve are still among the former).

If we read on from 8:1-3 in the company of Joanna and the other women, it will not be possible to read 10:1-20, where Jesus sends out seventy-two disciples to participate actively in his own mission of preaching and healing, without assuming that the women are included among these disciples. Here, as often elsewhere, it is clear that the grammatical masculinity of the language is an androcentric bias of the Greek language, not of the narrative. The masculine forms are used, quite normally and naturally, to include women. But beyond the androcentrism of language, we may become conscious of a degree of androcentrism in the narrative. Despite the relative prominence of women in Luke, the majority of individual characters in stories and parables are male. Joanna Dewey has attempted to compare the "mimetic vividness" of male and female minor characters (i.e., individual characters who appear in only one pericope) in the Synoptic healing stories and some other narratives. Mimetic vividness is measured by such things as length of story, detail not strictly necessary to the narrative, direct discourse by the character, internal views of the character's thoughts and feelings. Dewey concludes:

> Considering the healing narratives and other stories combined, the stories about male characters are longer than the stories about female characters. The male characters speak more than the female ones, and Jesus speaks to men more than to women. The synoptic evangelists have encouraged their audiences to remember the men more than the women by means of their differential use of mimetic techniques.[357]

In evaluating these conclusions one should remember that almost all these stories take place in public spaces where women were expected on the whole to be silent, at least not to initiate conversation with male strangers.[358] Thus the social realism of the stories biases them toward less vivid representations of their female characters. The story of the hemorrhaging woman is an exception in the

---

357. J. Dewey, "Women in the Synoptic Gospels: Seen but Not Heard?" *BTB* 27 (1997) 58.

358. Dewey, "Women," 58-59, dismisses this consideration on inadequate grounds: she fails to note that most of exceptions in the Gospels that she notes (including those in John) fall outside this specific requirement that women should not initiate conversation with a male stranger in a public place, which does apply in most of the stories, while, whatever the truth of her assumption that in the egalitarian Jesus movement women must have spoken as much as men, it is not relevant to these stories, where (with one or two exceptions) the women are not disciples but are meeting Jesus for the first time.

mimetic vividness with which the woman is portrayed (even in Luke's version, shorter than Mark's) because it adopts her perspective. But from the disciples'-eye view (whether male or female) from which most of the stories are told, the relative silence of women in public impedes vivid portrayal of them. This is not invariably the case: in the story of the woman who anoints Jesus (Luke 7:36-50) she says nothing, while Jesus and Simon the Pharisee talk about her at some length. But her action is more eloquent than words, and therefore described in considerable detail by the narrator and then redescribed by Jesus later. We do not need to be told her feelings by an inside view: as in many biblical stories, actions convey feelings to readers. This story is not therefore to be considered androcentric simply because the woman does not speak.[359] The conditions that constrain the woman from speaking are androcentric; but the story, while realistically abiding by the androcentric social conventions, brilliantly foregrounds the woman who shows her love for Jesus in her unconventional performance of an act conventionally reserved for women and slaves. Such stories, where a woman steps vividly out of the androcentric frame of social conventions without breaking them, may well have been told by women, and it may be that a woman's oral version stands close behind the textual form in the Gospels.

These remarks go some way to meeting the charge of androcentric narration, but they do not fully answer it. There is a degree of androcentrism in the selection and narration of the traditions, doubtless due to the unthinking operation of male perspectives in the transmission and redaction.[360] But Luke's Gospel's own authorization of its readers to see with the eyes of the women disciples and to hear with their ears (8:2-3) goes a long way to authorizing the correction of androcentric bias in the narrative. Readers who read in this way may supply what is lacking, for example by imagining a female character with a vividness the text itself does not provide or supplying female characters who must have been present but are ignored by the text.

359. So Dewey, "Women," 57-58.

360. J. Dewey, "From Storytelling to Written Texts: The Loss of Early Christian Women's Voices," *BTB* 26 (1996) 71-78, draws on the example of European women's folk tales which became much more androcentric when edited by men for printed versions, and argues that in early Christianity women's voices were lost in the shift from an oral to a manuscript medium. An interesting example of androcentric editing of a previously more gynocentric literary text is the three versions (LXX, 4QSam[a], MT) of 1 Sam 1:24-28; 2:11. E. Tov, "Different Editions of the Song of Hannah and of Its Narrative Framework," in M. Cogan, B. L. Eichler, and J. H. Tigay, eds., *Tehillah le-Moshe* (M. Greenberg FS; Winona Lake, Ind.: Eisenbrauns, 1997) 151-57, shows that probably actions assigned to Hannah in an earlier version of the text (represented by LXX, 4QSam[a]) have been reassigned to Elkanah in MT: "The impression is created that the MT did not wish to assign these actions to Hannah since she was a woman, and it would not be appropriate that a woman should play such a central role in the story" (156).

There are two further reasons why such a reading strategy should not be considered to run against the grain of the text. One is that stories as spare as those of the Gospel narratives work by appealing to the imagination of readers/hearers. For the most part they are reduced to essentials, leaving the inessentials to readers/hearers to supply for themselves. Ancient readers/hearers were adept at doing this, whereas modern readers, used to the greater detail of modern novels or the visuality of films, are not used to it. By requiring readers to enter imaginatively into the story and to fill out the outline provided, narratives of the kind we have in the Gospels are designedly and intentionally open to interpretation.

The second reason is that when the Gospels give textual form to oral traditions, they in effect give permanence to one performance of the oral tradition. But in their ancient context they were used — and designed to be used — in oral contexts in which they would be continually re-oralized. They provided permanence for traditions, but without inhibiting the expected degree of freedom allowed to the oral storyteller. Retellings that, working from a female perspective on the events, correct the androcentric bias of the Gospel versions need not be regarded as deconstructive, but could be fulfilling the Gospel's own literary strategy of authorizing reading from the perspective of the women disciples. Of course, the perspective must be credibly that of first-century women who both know the social world of the text and bring to it expectations formed by the teaching and practice of Jesus. But as Schüssler Fiorenza observes, "Imaginatively adopting the perspective of biblical wo/men rather than just looking at them as fixed objects in texts in a fixed context yields a different world and set of possibilities."[361] This is intended as more than a reading strategy, but it is at least a reading strategy and one that (and here I differ from Schüssler Fiorenza) Luke's Gospel positively encourages.

361. Schüssler Fiorenza, *Jesus,* 36.

CHAPTER 6

Mary of Clopas

The three Maries beneath the cross. . . .
The same veil wrapped around them,
the same name, the same weeping.[1]

The aim of this chapter is a straightforwardly historical one: to discover what may be known about one of the women disciples of Jesus, Mary of Clopas. Since she is mentioned in early Christian literature only in John 19:25, as one of a group of women who were present at the crucifixion of Jesus, the reader may be forgiven for wondering whether we can know anything more about her than her name and that she was present at the crucifixion. When read in the light of other relevant evidence, however, this verse will prove capable of yielding a surprising amount of reliable historical information about her. Such historical information about people who played a part in the origins of Christianity should not be despised. It is on the accumulation and interpretation of such information that accurate understanding of the early church as a historical movement depends. In the case of Mary of Clopas, what we can know about her will contribute to our understanding both of the roles that relatives of Jesus played in the early church[2] and of the roles that women played.

1. L. Santucci, *Wrestling with Christ* (tr. B. Wall; London: Collins, 1972) 200.
2. In this respect, the present chapter is a supplement to my book, *Jude and the Relatives of Jesus in the Early Church* (Edinburgh: T. & T. Clark, 1990). For the women relatives, see pp. 15-16, 37-44, 130; and also chap. 7 below.

1. Who Was She?

John 19:25 reads: εἱστήκεισαν δὲ παρὰ τῷ σταυρῷ τοῦ Ἰησοῦ ἡ μήτηρ αὐτοῦ καὶ ἡ ἀδελφὴ τῆς μητρὸς αὐτοῦ, Μαρία ἡ τοῦ Κλωπᾶ καὶ Μαρία ἡ Μαγδαληνή (literally: "standing by the cross of Jesus were his mother and his mother's sister, Mary of Clopas and Mary Magdalene"). Unfortunately, this statement contains two ambiguities concerning the identity of Mary of Clopas. First, how many women are listed? Grammatically, there are three possibilities. The one that has attracted little support[3] and is the least likely is that only two women are mentioned. The list should in this case be read as: "his mother and his mother's sister, that is, Mary of Clopas and Mary Magdalene." In this case Jesus' mother is Mary of Clopas and his aunt is Mary Magdalene. This interpretation has perhaps one advantage: it would mean that John refers only to the two women who subsequently play a part in his narrative, whereas it is hard to see any real point, narratological or theological, in reference to one or two other women. But the decisive objection to this interpretation is that it is inconceivable that the mother of Jesus should be called "Mary of Clopas." Even if this were an appropriate way of referring to her, it would be very odd for John to use it at this point in his Gospel, when he is not introducing the mother of Jesus for the first time (as he is Mary Magdalene) but has already referred to her simply as "the mother of Jesus" (2:1, 3, 12). But, furthermore, it would be very odd for anyone ever to refer to the mother of Jesus as Mary of Clopas. Since her husband was Joseph (John 6:42) and no brother of Jesus called Clopas is known (cf. Matt 13:55; Mark 6:3), the only possible explanation could be that Clopas was her father. But, since the point of mentioning Clopas at all is to distinguish this Mary from other women of the same name, there would be no need to add this distinguishing feature to a reference to the mother of Jesus. It is inconceivable that Mary the mother of Jesus, who could always and most obviously be distinguished from other women called Mary by calling her "the mother of Jesus," could ever have been known in the early church as Mary of Clopas.

It is harder to decide between the other two possibilities: does John 19:25 refer to three or to four women? Either ἡ ἀδελφὴ τῆς μητρὸς αὐτοῦ is in apposition to Μαρία ἡ τοῦ Κλωπᾶ, meaning that Jesus' aunt was called Mary of Clopas, or there are two pairs of women, the first pair unnamed (his mother and his mother's sister), the second pair named (Mary of Clopas and Mary Magdalene). The considerations that have been urged to decide between these

3. See J. Blinzler, *Die Brüder und Schwestern Jesu* (2d ed.; SBS 21; Stuttgart: Katholischer Bibelwerk, 1967) 111.

two possibilities are largely inconclusive: (1) If Mary of Clopas was Jesus' aunt, then the two sisters were both called Mary.[4] It is certainly unlikely that two full sisters should bear the same name, though evidence from antiquity shows that this is not impossible.[5] But ἀδελφή need not mean full sister. The two Marys could be half-sisters, stepsisters, sisters-in-law, or even in some other family relationship for which modern English would not use the word "sister" at all. (2) Interpreting the list as two pairs of women, one pair unnamed and one pair named, produces a stylistic symmetry.[6] But this cannot be decisive, especially since, if Mary of Clopas were the sister of Jesus' mother, it would be natural, in a list in which she accompanies Jesus' mother, to mention the fact. (3) That in other lists of people John places καί between each item (2:12; 21:2) can scarcely be decisive for his meaning here. (4) The women at the cross are contrasted with the soldiers who cast lots for Jesus' clothes (19:24-25: μὲν . . . δέ).[7] Since there are four soldiers (19:23), it would be appropriate for there to be four women. But again this cannot be decisive. Moreover, even if there are only three women, there could still be a contrast between the four soldiers and the four faithful disciples of Jesus, including the beloved disciple (19:26). On the basis of these arguments we must leave open the question whether Mary of Clopas is here described as Jesus' aunt. We shall return to the question later.

The second ambiguity concerning Mary of Clopas is her relationship to Clopas. No one seems to have collected and studied the contemporary evidence of this usage in which a woman is designated as related to a man by the use simply of the genitive.[8] When men are so described, the relationship is usually that

---

4. This argument is frequently held to decide the issue: e.g., Blinzler, *Brüder*, 113; R. Bultmann, *The Gospel of John* (tr. G. R. Beasley-Murray; Philadelphia: Westminster; Oxford: Blackwell, 1971) 672n.1; R. E. Brown, *The Gospel according to John (xiii–xxi)* (AB 29A; Garden City, N.Y.: Doubleday, 1966; London: Chapman, 1971) 904; G. R. Beasley-Murray, *John* (WBC 36; Waco: Word, 1987) 348; D. A. Carson, *The Gospel according to John* (Leicester: Inter-Varsity Press; Grand Rapids: Eerdmans, 1991) 615.

5. BAGD 437; Blinzler, *Brüder*, 116n.20.

6. Blinzler, *Brüder*, 112-13.

7. C. K. Barrett, *The Gospel according to St John* (2d ed.; Philadelphia: Westminster; London: SPCK, 1978) 551.

8. For the use and nonuse of the article with this "genitive of relationship," see BDF §162 (1)-(4); K. Meisterhans, *Grammatik der attischen Inschriften* (3d ed.; Berlin: Weidmann, 1900) 223-24; F. Eakin, "The Greek Article in First and Second Century Papyri," *AJP* 37 (1916) 337; C. W. E. Miller, "Note on the Use of the Article before the Genitive of the Father's Name in Greek Papyri," *AJP* 37 (1916) 341-42; E. Mayser, *Grammatik der griechischen Papyri aus der Ptolemäerzeit* (Berlin/Leipzig: de Gruyter, 1933) 2/2.7; B. L. Gildersleeve, *Syntax of Classical Greek from Homer to Demosthenes* (repr. Groningen: Bouma, 1980) 266. Classical usage would be Μαρία ἡ Κλωπᾶ (where θυγάτηρ, γυνή or μήτηρ must be understood) (so also Mark 15:47; 16:1; Luke 24:10), but official documents (and so generally the papyri and inscriptions) omit the arti-

of son to father (Matt 4:21; 10:2, 3; Mark 3:17, 18; Luke 6:15, 16; John 6:71; 13:2, 26; 21:15, 16, 17; Acts 1:13; 20:4; 1 Clem 12:2; Josephus, BJ 5.5, 6, 11, 249, 250, 398). Apparently the relationship may also be that of brothers,[9] but presumably only in cases where the persons were known to the readers to be related in this way. But it does not necessarily follow that when the usage applies to women, the relationship may be expected to be that of daughter to father.[10] No doubt, an unmarried daughter would be described by reference to her father, but might not a married woman be more likely to be described by reference to her husband, at any rate in a Jewish context, where a woman was regarded as being transferred, at marriage, from her father's to her husband's authority?[11]

Other New Testament evidence is not conclusive. In Matthew 1:6 Bathsheba is designated τῆς τοῦ Οὐρίου, where the genitive suffices for the meaning "the wife of Uriah."[12] This is not a precise parallel to Mary of Clopas, because Bathsheba is not named, but it shows that Μαρία ἡ τοῦ Κλωπᾶ could mean "Mary the wife of Clopas." In the New Testament the usage can also mean "mother of."[13] The woman who is most fully described, in Mark 15:40, as "Mary the mother of James the little and Joses" (cf. Matt 27:56), is also called simply "Mary of Joses" (Μαρία ἡ Ἰωσῆτος, 15:47) and "Mary of James" (Μαρία ἡ Ἰακώβου, Mark 16:1; Luke 24:10). She is presumably so called because her sons were her male relatives best known in the early Christian community. There is also some epigraphical evidence from Jewish Palestine of women designated by reference to their sons,[14] though none that I have found use this idiom (simply the genitive, without μήτηρ).

A preliminary survey of epigraphical evidence from Jewish Palestine

---

cle (except, for clarity, when the first name is in the genitive) (so also Luke 6:16; John 6:71; Acts 1:15; 20:4). In adding a second article in the genitive with the second name (Μαρία ἡ τοῦ Κλωπᾶ), John 19:25 follows common later literary usage (e.g., Plutarch, Mor. 205A: ἡ τοῦ Μετέλλου [scil. μήτηρ]; Matt 1:6; 4:21; 10:2-3; Acts 13:22).

9. Alciphro 2.2 is cited by BDF §162 (4), but this is not at all a certain instance: the manuscripts indicate a lacuna after ὁ.

10. According to J. Robert and L. Robert, Bulletin épigraphique 4 (1959-63) 1960: p. 168 (no. 216), this is normally the case. But, contrary to R. S. Kraemer, "Hellenistic Jewish Women: The Epigraphical Evidence," SBLSP 1986 (Atlanta: Scholars Press) 197n.51, Robert does not "demonstrate" this point at all.

11. L. J. Archer, Her Price Is Beyond Rubies: The Jewish Woman in Graeco-Roman Palestine (JSOTSup 66; Sheffield: JSOT Press, 1990) 207-8 (citing m. Ket. 4:5). This did not mean, however, that she lost all ties with her father's house: Archer, Her Price, 164 and n. 1.

12. Cf. also Aristophanes, Eccl. 727: τὸν τῆς στρατηγοῦ (scil. ἄνδρα), meaning "the [female] captain's husband."

13. Cf. also Plutarch, Mor. 205A.

14. CIJ nos. 948, 1000, 1007, 1061, 1160.

yields the following information.[15] Most occurrences of the Greek idiom are as ambiguous to us as the phrase Μαρία ἡ τοῦ Κλωπᾶ is. I found ten such instances,[16] alongside one in which clearly a married woman is designated by reference to her father.[17] In addition, we should note cases where the relationship is specified by the use of γυνή (two cases),[18] θυγάτηρ (three cases,[19] one these certainly a married daughter),[20] or μήτηρ (five cases).[21] Some of these, at least, are evidence of Semitic influence on the use of Greek, since in Hebrew or Aramaic the relationship has to be specified. Hebrew and Aramaic inscriptions surveyed provide sixteen cases of designating a woman by reference to her husband,[22] and nineteen cases of designating a woman by reference to her father,[23] of which two are certainly cases of married women.[24] While this evidence shows that a married woman could be described either as a wife of her husband or as the daughter of her father,[25] it seems to indicate that the former was the more common usage, since some (perhaps most) of those described as daughters must have been unmarried. Therefore Palestinian Jews using the Greek idiom in which the relationship is expressed by the genitive alone would probably be more likely to use it to designate a married woman by reference to her husband than to designate her by reference to her father.

Thus the purely linguistic evidence suggests that Mary of Clopas was most probably either the wife of Clopas or an unmarried daughter of Clopas. That she was a married daughter of Clopas is unlikely, though possible. She could be the mother of Clopas if both were well known in early Christian cir-

15. Jewish insciptions from Asia Minor are probably more likely to conform to pagan usage.

16. *CIJ* nos. 909, 937, 946, 1107, 1108, 1147, 1169, 1172, 1237, 1387.

17. *CIJ* no. 964.

18. *CIJ* nos. 949, 1284.

19. *CIJ* nos. 888, 1007, 1035.

20. *CIJ* no. 1007.

21. *CIJ* nos. 948, 1000, 1007, 1061, 1160.

22. *CIJ* nos. 1198 (= J. A. Fitzmyer and D. J. Harrington, *A Manual of Palestinian Aramaic Texts (Second Century B.C.–Second Century A.D.)* [BibOr 34; Rome: Biblical Institute Press, 1978] [henceforth FH] no. A2), 1294, 1295, 1313, 1314, 1338 (= FH no. 104), 1341 (= FH no. 103), 1353 (= FH no. 94), 1356 (= FH no. 98), 1362 (= FH no. 97), 1384 (= FH no. 147), FH nos. 84, 122, Masada ostraca nos. 399, 400, 402 (in *Masada I: The Yigael Yadin Excavations 1963-1965: Final Reports:* Y. Yadin and J. Naveh, *The Aramaic and Hebrew Ostraca and Jar Inscriptions* [Jerusalem: Israel Exploration Society/Hebrew University of Jerusalem, 1989]).

23. *CIJ* nos. 1144, 1145, 1199 (= FH no. A3), 1245 (= FH no. 134), 1253, 1265, 1296, 1297 (= FH no. 111), 1311, 1317, 1353, FH nos. 74, 88, 119, A51, A52, Masada ostraca nos. 401, 403, 405.

24. *CIJ* nos. 1145, 1353.

25. For this usage, see also FH no. 51, lines 12, 16; no. 62, line 1; and Mur 29 verso line 3; Mur 30 lines 25-26, 33.

cles, so that readers would know this to be the relationship. However, the possibility that she was an unmarried daughter of Clopas can be rejected on the grounds that Jewish custom would not have permitted an unmarried young woman to be in such a public place.[26] Further progress in specifying Mary's relationship to Clopas can be made only by identifying Clopas himself.

This is not difficult to do. From the second-century writer Hegesippus, who transmits early second-century Palestinian Jewish Christian traditions, we know that the successor to James the Lord's brother as head of the Jerusalem church was Simon or Symeon the son of Clopas (Hegesippus *apud* Eusebius, *Hist. Eccl.* 3.11; 3.32.6; 4.22.4). This Clopas was the brother of Jesus' putative father Joseph. His son's succession to James is part of the pattern of dominance of relatives of Jesus in the leadership of Palestinian Jewish Christianity down to the early second century at least.[27] That this Clopas, the brother of Joseph, is the same person as the Clopas of John 19:25 can be considered certain, because the name Clopas is extremely rare. The Greek form of the name occurs only in these passages of Hegesippus and the Fourth Gospel. Its Semitic original, which used to be uncertain, has now been found in an Aramaic document of the early second century CE from Muraba'at (Mur 33, line 5: קלופו).[28] This shows conclusively that the name is a quite different one from that of which Ἀλφαῖος is the Greek form (חלפי), and so disproves speculations that John's Clopas is the same person as the Alphaeus who was the father of James, one of the twelve (Matt 10:3; Mark 3:18; Luke 6:15; Acts 1:13).[29] But it also shows that Clopas was a rare name (whereas חלפי [Alphaeus] was relatively common).

If Mary's Clopas was Joseph's brother, she can hardly have been his

---

26. Cf. Archer, *Her Price*, 110-22. The point has even more force if, as we shall show, Mary of Clopas was a Galilean disciple of Jesus who must have traveled from Galilee to Jerusalem with the other woman disciples.

27. See Bauckham, *Jude*, chap. 2 passim.

28. J. T. Milik in P. Benoit, Milik, and R. de Vaux, *Les Grottes de Murabba'at* (DJD 2; Oxford: Clarendon, 1961) 151. The name probably also occurs in a Nabatean inscription from Palmyra (J. B. Chabot, "Notes d'épigraphie et d'archéologie orientale," *JA* 10 [1897] 328), though it is not certain that קלופי rather than מלופי should be read. The name is not listed in J. K. Stark, *Personal Names in Palmyrene Inscriptions* (Oxford: Clarendon, 1971).

29. Still maintained by J. Wenham, "The Relatives of Jesus," *EvQ* 47 (1975) 13-14; cf. Blinzler, *Brüder*, 135-36n.40, for other references. The alleged identity of the names Ἀλφαῖος and Κλωπᾶς has always been doubtful on philological grounds: see Blinzler, *Brüder*, 120-21; J. J. Gunther, "The Family of Jesus," *EvQ* 46 (1974) 25-26. See the many Greek forms of חלפי attested in H. Wuthnow, *Die semitischen Menschennamen in griechischen Inschriften und Papyri des vorderen Orients* (Studien zur Epigraphik und Papyruskunde 1/4; Leipzig: Dieterich, 1950) 16-18, 61-62, 119, 141: all lack the long first vowel of Κλωπᾶς.

mother. Since we have already considered it unlikely that she was an unmarried daughter, she was most likely the wife of Clopas. In that case, we can return to the problem of the number of women in John's list. Mary of Clopas, who was in fact Jesus' mother's husband's brother's wife, could well be described as Jesus' mother's sister. To state the exact relationship would have been impossibly cumbersome. Greek does have a word for "sister-in-law" (γάλοως), but it does not seem to have been commonly used, and since ἀδελφός is attested in the sense of "brother-in-law,"[30] there is no difficulty in supposing that ἀδελφή here means "sister-in-law." That the list refers to three relatives of Jesus — his mother, his mother's sister, and his uncle's wife — is less likely, because there would then be an odd difference between the second woman, whose relationship to Jesus is stated but who is not named, and the third, who is named but whose relationship to Jesus is not stated.

Mary of Clopas had a very famous son:[31] Simon or Symeon the son of Clopas, always designated by the patronymic because Simon/Symeon was the most common Jewish male name at the time, succeeded his cousin James either (most probably) following the latter's martyrdom in 62, or perhaps only after the fall of Jerusalem, and remained the leader of the Jerusalem church until his own martyrdom in the reign of Trajan. He was the most important Christian leader in Palestine for half a century. He had already been the most important Christian leader in Palestine for some considerable time when the Fourth Gospel was written. Though we know little else about him, the extreme reverence in which he was held in Palestinian Jewish Christian tradition can be inferred from Hegesippus's account of his martyrdom (*apud* Eusebius, *Hist. Eccl.* 3.32.3, 6). His supposed age of one hundred and twenty at death corresponds to the biblical limit on human life, according to Genesis 6:3 (cf. Josephus, *Ant.* 1.152; Pseudo-Philo, *Bib. Ant.* 9:8), which the most righteous people could be expected to attain. It places him in the same category as Moses (Deut 34:7). Although the influence of the Jerusalem church leadership outside Palestine and the links between Palestinian Jewish Christianity and churches elsewhere must have been declining in the later first century, Symeon the son of Clopas must nevertheless have been known by reputation throughout the churches. So the first readers of the Fourth Gospel would have had no difficulty in identifying Mary of Clopas as his mother.

It has frequently been suggested that Mary of Clopas was the same person as Mary the mother of James the little and Joses, who appears in the Synoptic Gospels as one of the women at the cross, the burial, and the empty tomb (Matt

---

30. BAGD s.v.

31. For this paragraph see Bauckham, *Jude*, 79-84.

27:56, 61; 28:1; Mark 15:40, 47; 16:1; Luke 24:10).[32] This identification has always had a very tenuous basis, since the Synoptic evangelists all state that many women who followed Jesus from Galilee were present at the cross (Matt 27:55-56; Mark 15:40-41; Luke 23:49) and themselves name women unique to each (Matthew: the mother of the sons of Zebedee; Mark: Salome; Luke: Joanna). Since Mary, along with Salome, was one of the two most common names among Palestinian Jewish women,[33] there is no reason why a Mary named in the Johannine tradition of the women at the cross should be the same person as a Mary named in the Synoptic traditions.[34] But if Mary of Clopas was the mother of Symeon the son of Clopas, her identity with Mary the mother of James and Joses is not only unproven but very improbable. We do not know who James the little[35] and Joses were, since they are not to be identified with the Lord's brothers of those names.[36] They must have been well enough known in the early church for their mother to be identified by reference to them, but they cannot have been as well known as Symeon the son of Clopas, at least when Matthew and Luke were writing. If their mother was also the mother of Symeon, it would therefore be odd to identify her by reference to them and not to him.

However, this may raise the question why John identifies Mary of Clopas by reference to her husband rather than by reference to her son. The answer may be that Simon/Symeon was too common a name to identify her. He himself had to be identified as Simon or Symeon the son of Clopas. But it may also be that Mary of Clopas had long been so called, and that this was her usual designation dating from a time when it was her husband, rather than her son, who was well known as a Christian leader. Since Jesus' relatives as a group — known

32. References to scholars making this identification are in Blinzler, *Brüder*, 113n.11; L. Oberlinner, *Historische Überlieferung und christologische Aussage: Zur Frage "Brüder Jesu" in der Synopse* (FB 19; Stuttgart: Katholisches Bibelwerk, 1975) 121-22; and add Beasley-Murray, *John*, 348.

33. T. Ilan, "Notes on the Distribution of Jewish Women's Names in Palestine in the Second Temple and Mishnaic Periods," *JJS* 40 (1989) 186-200; cf. Bauckham, *Jude*, 43; and chap. 7 §1 below.

34. Bauckham, *Jude*, 12-13.

35. For Palestinian Jewish parallels to this designation, see *CIJ* nos. 1038 (Joseph the little: Ἰωσήφ [. . .] μικκός), 1039 (Judah the little: יהודה הקטן), as well as Rabbi Samuel the Small (שמויל הקטן) and Honi the Small (חוני הקטן), grandson of Honi the Circle-drawer. Cf. also L. Y. Rahmani, *A Catalogue of Jewish Ossuaries in the Collections of the State of Israel* (Jerusalem: Israel Antiquities Authority/Israel Academy of Sciences and Humanities, 1994) 172, no. 421: a Jerusalem ossuary inscribed גאיס נניס, "Gaius the small," where נניס derives from Greek νᾶνος, "dwarf."

36. Bauckham, *Jude*, 13-15.

as the *desposynoi* (Julius Africanus, *apud* Eusebius, *Hist. Eccl.* 1.7.14) — were prominent in the leadership of the early Christian movement in Palestine,[37] it is likely enough that his uncle Clopas was one of these. Moreover, this probability is strengthened by the probability that Clopas is the same person as the Cleopas (Κλεοπᾶς) of Luke 24:18.[38]

Κλεοπᾶς is an abbreviated form of the Greek name Κλεόπατρος. It is not the same name as the Semitic name Clopas,[39] but could easily have been used as its Greek equivalent. Jews of this period often adopted Greek names that sounded similar to their Semitic names; thus Simon was used as the equivalent of Symeon and Jason as the equivalent of Jesus (Joshua).[40] The Greek names were not simply substituted for the Semitic (so that a Jew called Simon would never be called Symeon). Rather, even in Greek, both the transliterated form of the Semitic name and the genuinely Greek name that was regarded as its equivalent could be used of the same person. Thus in the New Testament Simon Peter is normally called Simon but could occasionally be called Symeon (Acts 15:14; 2 Pet 1:1 — both perhaps intending to reflect what he would have been called among his fellow Palestinian Jews). Clopas's son is called both Simon and Symeon. (It seems that Hegesippus preferred the Greek name, which therefore usually appears when Eusebius quotes directly from Hegesippus, but that Eusebius himself preferred Symeon, which he uses when paraphrasing Hegesippus or writing freely.[41] But Symeon is also the form used in the Jerusalem bishops list, which derives from Palestinian Jewish Christian sources.)[42]

Thus it is entirely possible that, like his son, Clopas was known both by his Semitic name and by a Greek equivalent, Cleopas. That he is the same person as the Cleopas of Luke 24:18 is rendered probable by the consideration that the latter must have been a disciple of Jesus sufficiently known in the early church for his name to have been preserved in this tradition and for Luke to think it worth giving in a context where a name is not required by the narrative. It is a good general rule, capable of explaining most occurrences of personal

---

37. Bauckham, *Jude*, 61-62, and chap. 2 passim.

38. Cf. Gunther, "Family of Jesus," 26-30.

39. In Mur 29 the Greek name Κλεοπος (verso line 1) is transliterated in Hebrew as קלבוס (recto line 10). That Cleopos signed this Hebrew legal document in Greek probably indicates that Greek was his native language. P. J. Sijpesteijn, "A Note on P. Murabba'at 29," *IEJ* 34 (1984) 49, concludes from his name that Cleopos was "of Greek origin," but since his wife (Sapphira the daughter of Joshua) was undoubtedly Jewish, he was most probably a Jew of diaspora origin.

40. Cf. also Silas (Acts 15:22 etc) = Silvanus (e.g., 1 Thess 1:1); see C. J. Hemer, *The Book of Acts in the Setting of Hellenistic History* (WUNT 49; Tübingen: Mohr [Siebeck], 1989) 230.

41. Bauckham, *Jude*, 83.

42. Bauckham, *Jude*, 70-71.

names in the Gospels, that when characters in the Gospels (other than public figures such as Pilate or Caiaphas) are named, it is because they were Christians well known in the early church and of whom the first readers of the Gospel in question would already have heard.[43]

Of course, the extent of tradition and redaction in Luke's story of the appearance to the two disciples on the road to Emmaus is debated,[44] and even if it is substantially dependent on a pre-Lukan tradition, this tradition is widely regarded as legendary, rather than historical. These questions need not be discussed here. Even if the story as such is a pre-Lukan legend or a Lukan creation, it is probable that the story has been created on the basis of a very early tradition that ascribed a resurrection appearance to a disciple named Cleopas (or to two disciples, one of whom was Cleopas).[45] The case would be comparable to the account of the resurrection appearance to James the Lord's brother in the *Gospel of the Hebrews*. The account itself is no doubt legendary, but it has not been created ex nihilo. It is based on the very early and doubtless historical tradition that the Lord appeared to James (1 Cor 15:7). Just as Paul knew of this appearance in tradition he received from the Jerusalem church, so the Jerusalem church may also have preserved a tradition that another relative of Jesus, his uncle Clopas/Cleopas, was the recipient of a resurrection appearance. Provided we do not dismiss as unhistorical the whole notion, common to Luke and John, of resurrection appearances in Jerusalem, then there is an interesting convergence between John's tradition that Mary of Clopas was one of the women disciples of Jesus present at the cross and Luke's that Cleopas was a disciple of Jesus who was present in Jerusalem at the time of the crucifixion. The traditions are clearly independent, and allow us to conclude that both Clopas and his wife Mary were disciples of Jesus who traveled with him from Galilee on his final journey to Jerusalem, and subsequently became prominent members of the early Jewish Christian community in Palestine.

---

43. Cf. Bauckham, *Jude*, 9n.14; and chap. 7 n. 48 below.

44. See, e.g., J. E. Alsup, *The Post-Resurrection Appearance Stories of the Gospel Tradition* (CTM 5; Stuttgart: Calwer; London: SPCK, 1975) 190-200; I. H. Marshall, *The Gospel of Luke* (NIGTC; Grand Rapids: Eerdmans; Exeter: Paternoster, 1978) 890-91.

45. It has sometimes been suggested (cf. Marshall, *Luke,* 894) that Cleopas's companion was his wife, who in my view was Mary of Clopas. Nothing in Luke's account is inconsistent with this suggestion, whereas if the other disciple were known to Luke to be such a well-known early Christian leader as James the Lord's brother or Symeon the son of Clopas (for these suggestions, see Bauckham, *Jude,* 17-18), it is incredible that he should not have named him.

2. Her Role in the Mission of the Church in Palestine

Finally, one may ask whether it is possible to make any reasonable conjectures about the role Mary herself may have played in the early church. Since the focus of the discussion so far has shifted from Mary to her husband, some readers may suspect an androcentric bias. But the shift has been necessitated by the fact that John 19:25 identifies Mary by reference to her husband, and the surviving evidence allows us to identify her only by reference to her husband and son. Only by examining this evidence have we been able to conclude that John 19:25 also identifies her by relating her to her sister-in-law, the mother of Jesus. No doubt, "Mary of Clopas" was how she was generally known in the early church. But this form of identification by no means implies that she was not a figure of significance in her own right. Her name necessitated a way of distinguishing her from other Marys, including other Marys among the disciples of Jesus and members of the early Jerusalem church. To distinguish her by reference to her husband was a common practice of a patriarchal society. But it is worth comparing the way the other Marys in the first Christian community are identified. Three are identified by reference to their sons: Mary the mother of Jesus (it is, of course, inconceivable that this Mary could have been identified in any other way), Mary the mother of James the little and Joses, and Mary the mother of John Mark (Acts 12:12). In the last two cases we may assume that the husbands of these Marys were either dead or not members of the church or were much less prominent than the sons. But two other Marys are not identified by reference to male relatives. Mary Magdalene is always identified simply by reference to her home village, while Mary of Bethany, the sister of Martha, seems to have been known always as one of the pair of sisters who were sufficiently identified by reference to each other. Luke introduces her as Martha's sister (Luke 10:39).[46] John first refers to the sisters in a way that indicates that "Mary and her sister Martha" were already well known as such to his readers, whereas it was necessary to explain that Lazarus, whose name John never uses to identify either sister, was their brother (John 11:1-2; cf. 12:2-3).

Since there were clearly other ways in which our Mary could have been identified to distinguish her from other Marys (by reference to her son Simon, by reference to her relationship with Jesus or his mother, by reference to her home village), it may be that she was called Mary of Clopas because she and her husband were naturally associated in the minds of early Christians, just as

---

46. M. R. D'Angelo, "Women Partners in the New Testament," *JFSR* 6 (1990) 79-80, implausibly tries to link this with the use of ἀδελφός and ἀδελφή to refer to missionary partners (on which, see below).

Prisca or Priscilla is always mentioned in association with her husband Aquila, even though, contrary to normal custom, she is usually placed first in the pair (Acts 18:26; Rom 16:3; 1 Cor 16:19; 2 Tim 4:19), probably because she was the more prominent in Christian activity. To confirm this possibility we have some minimal information about the role of women in the early Christian mission in Palestine. In 1 Corinthians 9:5 Paul, who is in the process of claiming for himself and Barnabas the right to material support from the churches they founded, argues that it was generally accepted that the apostles had this right and that it included also the right to such provision for their wives who accompanied them on their missionary travels. Giving well-known instances of this practice to support his case, Paul mentions, along with Peter (Cephas), the brothers of the Lord. This indication that Jesus' brothers were well known for their missionary travels correlates with the later information that Julius Africanus, drawing on Palestinian Jewish Christian tradition, gives: that the relatives of Jesus (the *desposynoi*), a category that includes not only the brothers of Jesus but also other relatives such as Clopas, traveled throughout Palestine from their Galilean home villages of Nazareth and nearby Kokhaba (*apud* Eusebius, *Hist. Eccl.* 1.7.14). Though there is no need to exclude some missionary activity by the *desposynoi* outside Palestine, we should probably think of them primarily as engaged in the spread of the Christian gospel in Jewish Palestine.[47] In this activity, we learn from Paul, the men of the family were commonly accompanied by their wives. What role did the wives play?

On the usual reading of 1 Corinthians 9:5, they appear there only as adjuncts to their husbands, to be supported by the churches for their husbands' sake, not as Christian workers in their own right. But Elisabeth Schüssler Fiorenza has suggested that the difficult double accusative ἀδελφὴν γυναῖκα, usually understood to mean "a fellow Christian as a wife," should instead be rendered "a coworker as a wife."[48] Certainly Paul commonly uses ἀδελφός to mean simply fellow Christian (in the plural usually to include both men and women), and in 1 Corinthians 7:12-16 uses ἀδελφός and ἀδελφή specifically in the context of marriage between Christians. There are at least two occasions on which ἀδελφοί must refer more specifically to Paul's missionary colleagues (Gal 1:2; Phil 4:21), though in both cases the word is given this sense by the phrase in which it occurs: οἱ σὺν ἐμοὶ ἀδελφοί. It is less clear whether the words ἀδελφός and ἀδελφή have this more specific sense of "coworker" when Paul refers to specific people as "our brother" (e.g., 1 Cor 1:1; 16:12; 2 Cor 1:1; 8:22; 1 Thess 3:2),

---

47. Bauckham, *Jude*, 57-68.

48. E. Schüssler Fiorenza, *In Memory of Her: A Feminist Theological Reconstruction of Christian Origins* (New York: Crossroad; London: SCM, 1983) 172.

"our sister" (Rom 16:1; Phlm 2), "our brothers" (e.g., 2 Cor 8:23), or "the brothers" (e.g., 1 Cor 16:11-12; 2 Cor 9:3). In virtually all these cases (only Phlm 2 is ambiguous) the persons in question are certainly Christian workers who share in Paul's missionary work, but it does not necessarily follow that the term itself means more than "fellow Christian" (cf. Phil 2:25).[49] However, even if the term is only customarily used of colleagues in the Christian missionary enterprise, without strictly designating them such, it could still be the case that in 1 Corinthians 9:5, where it is a matter precisely of people traveling together on behalf of the gospel, the word ἀδελφή indicates that the wives of the apostles are being considered as coworkers in the mission. Certainly, this would give more relevance to the expression ἀδελφὴν γυναῖκα περιάγειν. Did Paul need to specify that the wives apostles had the right to take with them on their missionary travels would be fellow Christians? It would be more relevant to indicate that they shared in the missionary task and therefore should also be supported by the churches.

The perspective from which Paul refers to the wives in 1 Corinthians 9:5 is, admittedly, androcentric. Even if the wives are envisaged as coworkers, it is the male apostles who have the right to be accompanied by them. But after all, Paul is arguing his own case and that of Barnabas, as male apostles. In other contexts Paul is certainly capable of fully acknowledging the roles of women as Christian workers in their own right. The case that is most germane to the present argument is that of Junia, mentioned along with her husband Andronicus in Romans 16:7.[50] In this verse Paul almost certainly refers to two apostles, husband and wife, who engaged in traveling missionary work together as a two-person team.[51] That they had at some point been in jail with Paul and were in Rome when Paul wrote shows that they were traveling missionaries, like Paul. As "apostles," which in Paul's usage must mean that they had both been commissioned by the risen Christ in a resurrection appearance,[52] they had of course been Christians before Paul, as he says. They were probably among the original members of the Jerusalem church. By calling Junia an apostle, Paul attributes to her the same authority as her husband and other male apostles, in-

---

49. For an argument that ἀδελφοί in Paul frequently refers to Paul's missionary colleagues, see E. E. Ellis, "Paul and His Co-Workers," in Ellis, *Prophecy and Hermeneutic in Early Christianity* (WUNT 18; Tübingen: Mohr [Siebeck]; Grand Rapids: Eerdmans, 1978) 13-22.

50. Here I take for granted the interpretation of this verse that is persuasively argued by J. D. G. Dunn, *Romans 9–16* (WBC 38B; Dallas: Word, 1988) 894-95, following other recent scholars; see also chap. 5 §6 above..

51. Schüssler Fiorenza, *In Memory*, 172.

52. Cf. J. D. G. Dunn, *Jesus and the Spirit* (Philadelphia: Westminster; London: SCM, 1975) 273.

cluding Paul himself, and by indicating that she and her husband were "outstanding (ἐπίσημοι) among the apostles" he makes clear that her apostolic authority and function were fully acknowledged in the church at large. There is no reason why Andronicus and Junia should be unique. Rather, we may take them as a model for understanding how other couples engaged together in Christian missionary work could have been viewed.[53] For my present purpose, it is significant that they take the notion of a husband-and-wife missionary team back to the earliest Palestinian church. This means that the brothers of Jesus and their wives could have formed such teams, as we have seen 1 Corinthians 9:5 may indicate. It means that Jesus' uncle Clopas and his wife Mary could also have formed such a team. Indeed, it is likely that Mary, like her husband and like some other women disciples of Jesus (Matt 28:9-10; John 20:14-17), was present at one of the appearances of the risen Jesus, and so, like Junia, could be considered an apostle in her own right. (Perhaps the two disciples in the tradition on which Luke's Emmaus story is based were Clopas and Mary.)[54]

Schüssler Fiorenza connects the existence of husband-and-wife missionary pairs in the early church with the Gospel traditions in which Jesus sends out the disciples in pairs (Mark 6:7; Luke 10:1).[55] Although Mark applies this concept to the mission of the twelve and therefore obviously envisages pairs of men, Luke applies it to the mission of the seventy (or seventy-two). Commentators unanimously take it for granted that the seventy are to be understood as male disciples, but this is not required by the text. Indeed, the reader of Luke who knows, from Luke 8:3, that Jesus was accompanied by a large number of women disciples, would more naturally assume that the seventy include women as well as men. This mission of the seventy certainly need not be a Lukan creation. It may well represent a traditional way of grounding in the Gospel tradition the mission of the wider circle of apostles, besides the twelve, and applying to them the tradition of Jesus' instructions to missionaries, which Mark and Matthew restrict to the twelve. If the concept of mission in pairs was applied in the early Palestinian church,[56] there seems no reason why some of

---

53. Cf. Schüssler Fiorenza, *In Memory*, 172-73, 178-79. D'Angelo, "Women Partners," 73-74, suggests that Philologus and Julia, and Nereus and his "sister" (= missionary colleague; Rom 16:15) were also husband-and-wife missionary teams. The main point of her article is to argue that there were also pairs of women working as missionaries in the early church: Tryphaena and Tryphosa (Rom 16:12), and Martha and Mary.

54. See n. 44 above.

55. Schüssler Fiorenza, *In Memory*, 169.

56. For further evidence of this, see J. Jeremias, "Paarweise Sendung im Neuen Testament," in A. J. B. Higgins, ed., *New Testament Essays: Studies in Memory of Thomas Walter Manson* (Manchester: Manchester University Press, 1959) 136-43.

the pairs should not have been husband and wife, like Andronicus and Junia, Clopas and Mary.

Commenting on 1 Corinthians 9:5 and wishing, for reasons of asceticism, to avoid the idea that the apostles took their wives with them for the sake of conjugal relations, Clement of Alexandria supposes that the wives accompanied them "as co-ministers (συνδιακόνους) in dealing with housewives. It was through them that the Lord's teaching penetrated also the women's quarters without any scandal being aroused" (*Strom.* 3.6.53.3).[57] Of course, this comment is not based on historical information, but it does reflect contemporary social conditions and is too quickly dismissed by Schüssler Fiorenza.[58] While Clement is probably thinking of Gentile society, his comments are even more plausible with reference to the Palestinian Jewish society in which Mary of Clopas would have worked as a missionary. The segregation of the sexes in much of life and the confining of many women to the women's quarters of the house, at least in well-to-do families,[59] would limit the extent to which male missionaries could speak to women, except when preaching in synagogue, and would also severely limit the possibilities of missionary work by women to men. It seems plausible that, within these social restrictions, a husband-and-wife missionary team would find it easier to reach both sexes with the gospel.

Investigating the role of women in the early Christian mission, Schüssler Fiorenza focuses exclusively on the Hellenists and the Gentile mission,[60] as most scholars discussing the early Christian mission do. This is to ignore the fact that Paul, in 1 Corinthians 9:5, takes as signal examples of traveling missionaries, well known as such even to Christians in Corinth, not only Peter but also the brothers of Jesus. While Peter's missionary work had by then extended beyond Palestine, Paul's reference to the Lord's brothers points to the importance of the mission of the *desposynoi* to their fellow Jews primarily within Palestine. This study of Mary of Clopas enables us to glimpse, even if faintly, the role that women relatives of Jesus also played in that mission.

---

57. Translation from Schüssler Fiorenza, *In Memory,* 201n.43. Note also Syriac *Didascalia* 16 and *Apostolic Constitutions* 3.15, where instructions are given to send a woman deacon to a house when a male deacon cannot be sent for fear of scandal in the view of unbelievers.

58. Schüssler Fiorenza, *In Memory,* 173.

59. Archer, *Her Price,* 113-20. Although Archer's work has been criticized for its use of rabbinic evidence (which is not necessarily reliable for the period before 200 CE, and which may reflect what the rabbis wished were the case rather than what was always actually the case), for this point she provides good early evidence.

60. Schüssler Fiorenza, *In Memory,* chap. 5.

Additional Note on Tradition in John 19:25-27

In the preceding discussion I have assumed that the reference to Mary of Clopas in John 19:25 reflects good tradition, independent of the Synoptics. If the verse were purely dependent on the Synoptics, it would be incomprehensible why John has transformed their Mary into "Mary of Clopas." Moreover, while one could argue that Jesus' mother occurs in John 19:25 to prepare for the episode in verses 26-27 and Mary Magdalene to prepare for her role in 20:1-18, there could be no narrative or theological reason for the sheer invention of the figure of Mary of Clopas.

It is possible to maintain that John drew the presence of Mary of Clopas at the cross, along with Mary Magdalene, from tradition, without regarding anything else in verses 25-27 as traditional. In his speculative reconstruction of a pre-Johannine narrative source, Robert Fortna supposes that it contained John 19:25 without the reference to Jesus' mother, and that the evangelist added Jesus' mother to the list of women, in order to prepare for verses 26-27, which are his own creation.[61] This accords with the rather common opinion that the presence of Jesus' mother at the cross is Johannine fiction, but it disrupts what would otherwise seem to be the quite natural association of the two sisters-in-law. It would also be possible to maintain that the whole of verse 25 is in substance traditional, and that the evangelist has taken advantage of the already traditional presence of the mother of Jesus at the cross to create the episode involving her and the beloved disciple in verses 26-27.[62] Of course, for those who consider the beloved disciple to be a purely ideal figure created by the evangelist, the question of tradition in verses 26-27 does not arise. But those who rightly find this view incompatible with the clear implication of John 21:23-24 that to the editor and first readers of the Gospel the beloved disciple was a specific, known person, and who therefore see the beloved disciple as an historical figure whose authority as a witness to the Gospel tradition in some sense stands behind the Gospel,[63] ought to be more cautious than they often are about taking verses 26-27 to be Johannine fiction with no basis in tradition. It is hard to see what the Gospel's appeal to the beloved disciple's witness means if all refer-

---

61. R. T. Fortna, *The Fourth Gospel and Its Predecessor* (Philadelphia: Fortress; Edinburgh: T. & T. Clark, 1988) 177, 181, 185.

62. Brown, *John*, 922, though he allows that the evangelist's addition of the beloved disciple in vv 26-27 might have a historical basis.

63. For my own view of the beloved disciple as author of the Gospel, see my two articles: "The Beloved Disciple as Ideal Author," *JSNT* 49 (1993) 21-44; "Papias and Polycrates on the Origin of the Fourth Gospel," *JTS* 44 (1993) 24-69. The present argument is intended to accommodate a variety of views as to the relation of the beloved disciple to the Gospel.

ences to his role in the Gospel narrative are attributed to the evangelist's free invention, and since there are rather few of these references a verdict of fiction on any one of them is from this point of view a serious matter. If the Gospel's claim to incorporate the beloved disciple's witness is to be given even a chance of credibility, we ought not to dismiss without serious consideration the possibility that he was present at the cross. That the evangelist intends verses 26-27 to convey symbolic theological significance is not to be doubted, though we need not here enter the debate as to exactly what this significance is;[64] but it is the evangelist's habit to tell already traditional Gospel narratives in such a way as to invest them with an additional level of symbolic meaning. Thus the Johannine symbolism intended by the beloved disciple's new relationship with the mother of Jesus may not contradict, but on the contrary may presuppose an authentic tradition that the beloved disciple was present at the cross along with a group of Jesus' women relatives and disciples, and was entrusted by Jesus with the care of his mother.

The usual reason for summarily discounting the historicity of both the presence of the mother of Jesus and the presence of the beloved disciple at the cross is that both are in contradiction to traditions common to Mark and Matthew.[65] This is at least superficially accurate. What is not accurate is the broader claim sometimes made that on both points John contradicts the Synoptics.[66] On the contrary, on both points Luke may be claimed to support John. This contact between Luke and John is of particular interest for two reasons. First, we have already noticed a point of contact between Luke and John in these very verses of John, viz. the probable identity of John's Clopas with Luke's Cleopas. Second, there is a well-known series of major and minor correspondences between Luke and John, in distinction from Matthew and Mark, especially in the passion and resurrection narratives.[67] The question of the relationship between Luke and John is usually discussed in terms either of dependence by John on Luke or, more frequently, of common tradition. But the link between John's reference to Mary of Clopas and Luke's reference to Cleopas is not really a case of common tradition. It is a case of quite different and independent traditions that happen to correlate at one point. It is comparable to the appearance of Martha and Mary in both Gospels, but in quite different traditions. It may indi-

---

64. Cf. Brown, *John*, 923-27; J. McHugh, *The Mother of Jesus in the New Testament* (London: Darton, Longman & Todd, 1975) 399-403; R. E. Brown, et al., *Mary in the New Testament* (Philadelphia: Fortress, 1978) 212-14; Beasley-Murray, *John*, 349-50; Carson, *John*, 617-18.

65. Cf. Brown, et al., *Mary in the New Testament*, 209-10.

66. Bultmann, *John*, 672; Brown, *John*, 922 (but more carefully: 906).

67. See especially F. L. Cribbs, "St. Luke and the Johannine Tradition," *JBL* 90 (1971) 422-50.

cate a common origin for Lukan and Johannine traditions that are not as such common traditions. This suggests that the question of the relationship between Luke and John should not be too narrowly posed. The point will be relevant to the points of contact we shall now consider.

The presence of the mother of Jesus at the cross in John can be said to be contradicted by Mark in two respects. First, Mark paints a wholly negative picture of the relationship between Jesus and his relatives (his mother and his brothers): they misunderstand his mission, seek to curtail it, and are in effect disowned by him (Mark 3:21-35). There is no hint in Mark that the breach was ever healed. Second, Mark names three of the women at the cross (15:40), but does not mention the mother of Jesus. However, to take this contrast between Mark and John as settling the historical question is clearly naive. It ignores both the inevitable selectivity of all Gospel traditions and Mark's own redactional intentions. On the first point, it is arguable that, although the breach between Jesus and his relatives was probably in Mark's tradition, he himself has played up the theme, either, as some have argued, by way of polemic against the Jerusalem church whose leaders were relatives of Jesus, or, as I think more probable, to present Jesus as the model for Christians whose Christian discipleship involves breaking with their close relatives (cf. Mark 10:28-30).[68] In any case, even Mark's readers would know perfectly well that Jesus' brothers eventually became some of his most ardent followers. They could not have taken Mark 3:21-35 to portray a final breach. On the second point, in the tradition Mark followed the women were surely named primarily as witnesses to the burial of Jesus (Mark 15:47) and the empty tomb (16:1). The difference between 15:47 (two women named) and 16:1 (three women named) shows that the tradition attached importance to precisely which women could be cited as witnesses to these events. Mark names the three women in 15:40 in order to prepare for their role as witnesses in 15:47 and 16:1. Therefore if the mother of Jesus was not known in the tradition as a witness to the burial or the empty tomb, she would not have been named in Mark's tradition, even if she had been present at the cross. The tradition was not concerned to name women who were merely present at the cross.

Thus, on the presence of the mother of Jesus at the cross, Mark cannot be cited as conclusive evidence against John. Luke, on the other hand, can be read as positively supporting John. Of course, Luke, no more than Mark, specifically refers to the mother of Jesus in his passion narrative, but the reason is the same as in Mark and even more obviously so. Luke names none of the women when he refers to their presence at the cross (23:49), but only with reference to the dis-

68. Bauckham, *Jude*, 46-49.

covery of the empty tomb (24:10). However, the attentive reader of Luke-Acts could well infer that Mary the mother of Jesus was with the other women at the cross. In Acts 1:14, with the eleven apostles in Jerusalem after the ascension are "the women and Mary the mother of Jesus and his brothers." Since, in Luke's narrative, all the disciples have simply stayed in Jerusalem since arriving with Jesus for the Passover, the natural assumption is that the mother of Jesus has all along been with the women who followed Jesus from Galilee (23:49). The assumption is aided by the fact that, unlike Matthew and Mark, Luke's Gospel contains no indication of a breach between Jesus and his family.

It is noteworthy that on the general question of Jesus' relationship with his family, John stands, as it were, between Matthew and Mark, on the one hand, and Luke on the other. Matthew[69] and Mark give the impression of a complete rift, Luke of complete harmony between Jesus and his relatives.[70] John has a more complex picture: Jesus' mother and brothers at first accompany him as disciples (2:1-2, 12); later his brothers do not believe in him (7:5); but finally his mother and his aunt are among the few who stand by him at the cross (19:25). The probability is that, after an early breach, on which Mark and John agree, the relatives of Jesus — his mother, his brothers, Clopas, and Mary — had by the end of Jesus' ministry joined the circle of his disciples. This is suggested not only by the agreement of Luke and John, but also by the tradition of the resurrection appearance to James (1 Cor 15:7), which most probably presupposes that James was already a follower of his brother.[71]

On the presence of the beloved disciple at the cross, the relevant Markan assertions are that all the disciples deserted Jesus in Gethsemane (14:50), as Jesus had foretold (according to Mark 14:27), and that accordingly only women disciples are mentioned as present at the cross (15:40-41). But again it is relevant to ask both about Mark's redactional interests and about the selectivity of his traditions. This material clearly belongs to Mark's portrayal of the failure of the disciples (or at least of the male disciples), whose literary impact he had no reason to spoil by noting exceptions. Moreover, Mark's traditions about the disciples are primarily about the twelve. With disciples of Jesus who were not members of the twelve but residents of Jerusalem, such as we should suppose the beloved disciple to have been, Mark is concerned only incidentally (14:14-15). His tradition may be reliable in indicating that none of the twelve was present at the cross. Indeed, it is confirmed by the Johannine parallel (John 16:32) to Mark's version of Jesus' prediction of the scattering of the disciples (Mark

---

69. Against the view that Matthew plays this down, see Bauckham, *Jude*, 49-50.
70. Bauckham, *Jude*, 50-52.
71. Bauckham, *Jude*, 56.

14:27). But it does not follow that male disciples other than the twelve, in whom Mark's tradition was simply not interested, were not present at the cross.

Luke's position on this matter is curiously parallel to his position on the mother of Jesus. He has no indication that any of the disciples other than Peter deserted Jesus. Together with the women at the cross are all Jesus' "friends" (γνωστοί, 23:49). The verse certainly reflects the influence of Psalm 38:11 (LXX 37:11; cf. also Ps 88:8 [LXX 87:8]), which may explain the use of γνωστοί rather than μαθηταί. But Mark 15:40, referring only to the women, also reflects this text, so that we should beware of supposing that the prophecy simply determined the narrative.

Again it is noteworthy that, as on the question of Jesus' relation to his relatives, so on that of the disciples at the cross, John stands between Mark and Luke.[72] Unlike Luke, he has a parallel to the Markan tradition of Jesus' prediction that the disciples will desert him, but he also knows of at least one male disciple who was present at the cross.

Of course, there is a considerable difference between Luke's reference to all the disciples at the cross and the presence of just one disciple, the beloved disciple in John 19:26-27. But there is an interesting parallel case that also concerns the beloved disciple. If Luke 24:12 (Peter's visit to the empty tomb) belongs to the original text of Luke, as it probably does,[73] it is one of the most striking instances of tradition common to Luke and John. That only Peter goes to the tomb in Luke 24:12 is often taken to prove that John's addition of the beloved disciple (20:3-10) is sheer Johannine fiction with no basis in tradition. What this argument overlooks is that in Luke 24:24, where Cleopas reports the visit of some (τινες) of the disciples to the tomb, Luke indicates that at this point his tradition spoke of more disciples than Peter.[74] Similarly, in John 20:2, Mary Magdalene's "we" shows that, in the tradition behind the chapter, not just Mary Magdalene but a group of women visited the tomb. In both cases the evangelist has retold a narrative about a group of disciples with reference to

72. A further case of this phenomenon in the passion-resurrection narratives should also be noticed. On the question of the location of the resurrection appearances to the male disciples, John agrees with both, on the one hand, Matthew and Mark (Galilee), and, on the other hand, Luke (Jerusalem).

73. On the authenticity of this verse, see Marshall, *Luke*, 888 (references to other literature); R. J. Dillon, *From Eye-Witnesses to Ministers of the Word: Tradition and Composition in Luke 24* (AnBib 82; Rome: Biblical Institute Press, 1978) 59-62; F. Neirynck, "Lc xxiv.12: Les témoins du texte occidental," in idem, *Evangelica* (BETL 60; Leuven: Peeters/Leuven University Press, 1982) 313-28.

74. So Dillon, *From Eye-Witnesses*, 63-65, although J. Muddiman, "A Note on Reading Luke xxiv,12," *ETL* 48 (1972) 547, takes the generalizing τινες as deliberate vagueness, intended to play down the importance of the visits to the tomb.

only one disciple, no doubt in both cases for reasons of literary effect. Thus Luke's tradition knew that Peter and other disciples visited the tomb; John specifies Peter and the beloved disciple. As in the case of the disciples at the cross, only Johannine tradition was interested in marking out this particular disciple from the anonymous plural of the Lukan tradition.

CHAPTER 7

The Two Salomes
and the *Secret Gospel of Mark*

Salome built a tower upon the rock of truth and mercy.
The builders that built it are the righteous,
the masons that hew stones for it are the angels. . . .
They that go into it rejoice,
they that come out of it, — their heart seeks after gladness.
She built it and gave it a roof, Salome gave a parapet to the tower.[1]

The name Salome occurs in the New Testament only twice, in Mark 15:40; 16:1, where it designates the third of three women disciples of Jesus. Perhaps it is not surprising that this disciple of Jesus has received very little attention, even in recent studies of the women disciples of Jesus.[2] But she is not infrequently named in extracanonical Gospel traditions and other early Christian literature. Because she appears in one of the two quotations from the *Secret Gospel of Mark* that Clement of Alexandria gives in his *Letter to Theodorus*,[3] the fullest previous

1. *Psalms of Thomas* 16, translated in C. R. C. Allberry, ed., *A Manichaean Psalm-Book Part II* (Stuttgart: Kohlhammer, 1938) 222. For the full text of this psalm, see the appendix to this chapter.
2. See E. Schüssler Fiorenza, *In Memory of Her: A Feminist Theological Reconstruction of Christian Origins* (New York: Crossroad; London: SCM, 1983) 320; B. Witherington III, *Women in the Ministry of Jesus* (SNTSMS 51; Cambridge: Cambridge University Press, 1984) 120; J. A. Grassi, *The Hidden Heroes of the Gospels: Female Counterparts of Jesus* (Collegeville, Minn.: Liturgical, 1989) 40-44; C. Ricci, *Mary Magdalene and Many Others* (tr. P. Burns; Minneapolis: Fortress, 1994) 174-77.
3. Morton Smith's argument for the authenticity of the *Letter to Theodorus* has been

study of the figure of Salome in early Christian literature is the two pages that Morton Smith devotes to her in his exhaustive study of Clement's *Letter* and *Secret Mark*.[4] Smith assembles most, though not quite all, of the significant references to Salome, but closer study of these references shows his interpretation of the evidence to be seriously deficient. In particular, (1) he does not distinguish the disciple Salome from a sister of Jesus who was also known by the name Salome in some early Christian traditions; (2) partly for this reason, he mistakenly sees in references to Salome by orthodox writers evidence of polemic against her status as an authority for unorthodox or Gnostic groups.

The aims of this chapter are to recover the tradition about Salome the sister of Jesus and to disentangle it from the traditions about her namesake the disciple of Jesus; to provide a detailed study of the role of Salome the disciple of Jesus in early Christian traditions; and, in the light of the latter, to criticize Smith's interpretation of the passage of *Secret Mark* in which Salome the disciple of Jesus appears and to suggest a more probable interpretation. While this chapter will certainly not solve the whole of the puzzle of *Secret Mark*, it may help to explain one of its most enigmatic parts.

1. Salome the Sister of Jesus

The best-attested names that postcanonical Christian tradition attributed to the sisters of Jesus are Mary and Salome.[5] These are given by Epiphanius (*Pan.* 78.8.1; 78.9.6; cf. *Ancoratus* 60.1)[6] as the names of the two daughters of Joseph by

---

widely accepted and will be assumed in this chapter. But A. H. Criddle, "On the Mar Saba Letter Attributed to Clement of Alexandria," *Journal of Early Christian Studies* 3 (1995) 216-20, argues that the letter contains too high a ratio of Clementine to non-Clementine traits to be authentic and that it should be recognized as a deliberate imitation of Clement's style. Moreover, it remains the case that no scholar other than Smith has seen the original document, and so some doubt must persist. For the state of the discussion on this question, see M. Smith, "Clement of Alexandria and Secret Mark: The Score at the End of the First Decade," *HTR* 75 (1982) 449-61; S. Levin, "The Early History of Christianity, in Light of the 'Secret Gospel' of Mark," *ANRW* 25/6 (Berlin/New York: de Gruyter, 1988) 4272-75.

4. M. Smith, *Clement of Alexandria and a Secret Gospel of Mark* (Cambridge: Harvard University Press, 1973) 189-92.

5. In *Pan.* 78.8.1 the order is Mary, Salome; in *Pan.* 78.9.6 the order is Salome, Mary. For other names, see J. Blinzler, *Die Brüder und Schwestern Jesu* (2d ed.; SBS 21; Stuttgart: Katholisches Bibelwerk, 1967) 36-38.

6. The text of *Ancoratus* 60.1 gives the names Anna and Salome (Ἄνναν καὶ Σαλώμην). Ἄνναν may be a textual error for Μαρίαν (so K. Holl, *Epiphanius: 1: Ancoratus und Panarion Haer. 1-33* [GCS 25; Leipzig: Hinrichs, 1915] 70n.), but if so it was an early error known to

his first wife.[7] Although Hugh Lawlor argued that in *Panarion* 78.8.1 Epiphanius was dependent on Hegesippus,[8] it seems more likely that he drew these names, along with other information about Joseph's first marriage, from some apocryphal source that is no longer extant, probably one that bore some relation to the *Protevangelium of James,* on which Epiphanius seems also to be dependent (directly or indirectly) in this context.[9] These names for the sisters of Jesus are not found often in early Christian literature. References to them in later patristic and early Byzantine writers (Sophronius of Jerusalem, Anastasius of Sinai, Theophylact, Euthymius Zigabenus, Nicephorus Callistus) are probably dependent on Epiphanius.[10] But the names can probably also be traced in two writings prior to Epiphanius: the *Gospel of Philip* and the *Protevangelium of James.*

The *Gospel of Philip* is a Valentinian work of probably the third century. It contains the following statement: "There were three who always walked with the Lord: Mary his mother[11] and her sister and Magdalene, the one who was called his companion.[12] His sister and his mother and his companion were each a Mary" (59:6-11).[13]

If the two lists of three women are to be made consistent,[14] then "her sis-

---

Sophronius of Jerusalem, who knew of three daughters of Joseph: Mary, Anna, and Salome (Blinzler, *Brüder,* 36-37).

7. The extant text of Epiphanius gives no name to Joseph's first wife, but Anastasius of Sinai, *Quaest.* 153 (*PG* 89:812), purporting to quote Epiphanius (*Pan.* 78.8.6), calls her Salome. Other late writers identify her with Mary the mother of James and Joses (Mark 15:40).

8. H. J. Lawlor, *Eusebiana: Essays on the Ecclesiastical History of Eusebius Pamphili* (1912; reprinted Amsterdam: Philo Press, 1973) 11-12.

9. *Pan.* 78.7.2; *Protevangelium of James* 9. The references to Joseph's age in *Pan.* 78.8.1-2, which do not derive from the *Protevangelium of James,* correspond roughly, but not exactly, to *History of Joseph* 14.

10. For references see Blinzler, *Brüder,* 36-37.

11. For Mary the mother of Jesus as his constant companion, see Epiphanius, *Pan.* 78.13.1. Differently, Tertullian, *Carn.* 7.9.

12. For Mary Magdalene as Jesus' consort, see also *Gos. Phil.* 63:32-36.

13. Translation by W. W. Isenberg in J. M. Robinson, ed., *The Nag Hammadi Library in English* (New York: Harper & Row; Leiden: Brill, 1977) 135-36.

14. H. J. Klauck, "Die dreifache Maria: Zur Reception von Joh 19,25 in EvPhil 32," in F. Van Segbroeck, et al., eds., *The Four Gospels 1992,* vol. 3 (F. Neirynck FS; Leuven: Leuven University Press/Peeters, 1992) 2352-58, argues that they are deliberately inconsistent. He understands the first list to be taken from John 19:25, with the variation in the second list signaling an allegorical interpretation. In the author's free interpretation of John 19:25-27, Mary Magdalene takes the place of the Beloved Disciple (cf. *Gos. Phil.* 63:34-35). It is Mary Magdalene, therefore, who adopts Jesus' mother as her own mother, and is thus entitled to be called Jesus' sister. So in the second list she, as Jesus' best-loved disciple, takes the prominent first place as well as the description "his sister." However, this explanation does not, as seems to be its intention, account

ter" in the first list must be corrected to "his sister," as in the second list. The scribal error may be due to the fact that Jesus' mother's sister is mentioned in John 19:25, and on the most probable reading of that verse could be thought to be named Mary.[15] This fact has also misled some modern scholars into supposing the original text of the *Gospel of Philip* referred to Jesus' mother's sister,[16] but this is impossible: if "his sister" in the second list were corrected to "her sister" the reference would be to Mary Magdalene's sister, not Jesus' mother's sister. The original reference must have been to Jesus' sister Mary.[17] The notion that she was a constant companion of Jesus might be the result of identifying her with one of those Marys (other than Mary Magdalene)[18] who appear in the Gospels as disciples of Jesus (Matt 27:56, 61; 28:1; Mark 15:40, 47; 16:1; Luke 24:10; John 19:25).[19] But it is worth noting that the *Apostolic Constitutions* (3:6), which certainly did not make this identification, supposed the sisters of Jesus to have been among his women disciples.

The significance of the statement is probably allegorical, in accordance with a common Valentinian manner of allegorizing the Gospel narratives.[20] The three Marys are no doubt seen as symbolizing feminine spiritual powers

---

for the discrepancy between the two lists by distinguishing the literal sense of the Johannine text from its allegorical interpretation. The discrepancy remains at the literal level.

15. See chap. 6 above. The ancient versions differ on this point; see T. Zahn, *Forschungen zur Geschichte des neutestamentliche Kanons und der altkirchen Literatur* 6 (Leipzig: Deichert, 1900) 338n.1; Blinzler, *Brüder*, 112. According to L. Oberlinner, *Historische Überlieferung und christologische Aussage: Zur Frage der "Brüder Jesu" in der Synopse* (FzB 19; Stuttgart; Katholisches Bibelwerk, 1975) 124n.391, the majority of exegetes think Jesus' mother's sister and Mary of Clopas are distinct persons.

16. Cf. J. J. Buckley, *Female Fault and Fulfilment in Gnosticism* (Chapel Hill/London: University of North Carolina Press, 1986) 108.

17. Cf. R. M. Wilson, *The Gospel of Philip* (London: Mowbray, 1962) 97-98.

18. For the constant attendance of "the other Marys" (including Mary Magdalene) on Jesus, see Tertullian, *Carn.* 7.9.

19. For some later writers who identified Mary the sister of Jesus with Mary the mother of James and Joses (Mark 15:40), see Blinzler, *Brüder*, 36. According to Anastasius of Sinai, *Quaest.* 153 (*PG* 89:812), Mary the sister of Jesus, Joseph's daughter, married her uncle, Joseph's brother Clopas, and was therefore known as the sister of Mary the mother of Jesus (John 19:25) (so also Hippolytus of Thebes, quoted by Blinzler, *Brüder*, 36). This information purports to come from Epiphanius, *Panarion*, but is not in the extant text of *Pan.* 78.7-8, and probably represents a later elaboration of Epiphanius, perhaps on the basis of Epiphanius's claim that the Gospels of Mark and John are evidence that Joseph had six sons and two daughters (*Pan.* 78.7.6). It would make sense of the extant text of *Gos. Phil.* 59:6-11: Mary the sister of Jesus was, on this view, also Jesus' mother's sister! But it is unlikely that this view was presupposed by the *Gospel of Philip.*

20. Cf. B. Layton, *The Gnostic Scriptures* (Garden City, N.Y.: Doubleday; London: SCM, 1987) 272-74; and the examples in Irenaeus, *Adv. Haer.* 1.2.3-4; 1.8.1.

(such as the Holy Spirit and Sophia), who are related to Jesus as his mother, his sister, and his consort.[21] Or perhaps they are understood as three manifestations of the Holy Spirit. (The last sentence of the passage might be better translated as reducing the three Marys to a single Mary, one and the same person related to Jesus in three different ways: "For Mary is his sister, his mother, and his companion.")[22] The allegorical significance of these three relationships (mother, sister, consort) can explain why specifically these three Marys are mentioned, while other Marys who appear in the Gospel narratives as disciples of Jesus are not mentioned. But the sister of Jesus is not likely to have been invented for the sake of the allegory. Rather, the allegory is possible because Jesus' mother, sister, and closest female disciple were known to share the same name, Mary. The *Gospel of Philip* is therefore evidence of the same tradition as we find later in Epiphanius. Of course, we cannot tell whether the tradition behind this Gospel also knew of a sister of Jesus called Salome, since this particular passage provides no occasion for her to be mentioned. In favor of dependence by the *Gospel of Philip* on an apocryphal tradition about the relatives of Jesus, like that known to Epiphanius, is the fact that apocryphal traditions about the family and the childhood of Jesus are also used elsewhere in this Gospel (63:25-30; 73:9-15).[23]

If Jesus' sister Mary appears in the *Gospel of Philip*, it is arguable that the other sister Salome appears in the *Protevangelium of James*. This late-second-century, probably Syrian account of the family background and birth of Jesus treats the brothers of Jesus as sons of Joseph by his first marriage (9:2; 17:1-2; 18:1; 25:1).[24] The narrative tells how Joseph leaves Mary, who is about to give birth, in a cave, in the care of his sons, while he goes to find a midwife (18:1).

21. Cf. the discussion of feminine symbolism in the *Gospel of Philip* in Buckley, *Female Fault*, 105-25.

22. Klauck, "Dreifache Maria," 2356-58.

23. The tradition in 73:9-15 is otherwise unknown. The tradition in 63:25-30 is a variant of a story about the child Jesus that is found in some Infancy Gospels; see M. R. James, *The Apocryphal New Testament* (Oxford: Clarendon, 1924) 66-67; O. Cullmann, "Infancy Gospels," in W. Schneemelcher, ed., *New Testament Apocrypha*, vol. 1 (tr. and ed. R. M. Wilson; rev. ed.; Cambridge: James Clarke; Louisville: Westminster/John Knox, 1991) 453.

24. For the date see E. De Stryker, *La Forme la plus ancienne du Protévangile de Jacques* (Subsidia Hagiographica 33; Brussels: Société des Bollandistes, 1961) 412-18; H. R. Smid, *Protevangelium Jacobi: A Commentary* (Assen: Van Gorcum, 1965) 22-24; Cullmann, "Infancy Gospels," in Schneemelcher, ed., *New Testament Apocrypha*, 1:423-24. De Stryker, *La Forme*, followed by Smith, *Clement*, 191, located the *Protevangelium of James* in Egypt; but against De Strycker's evidence for this, see Smid, *Protevangelium*, 20-22. Its affinities with other second-century Christian works from Syria makes a Syrian original probable; see Bauckham, *Jude*, 26-28.

When he returns with a midwife, they witness the miraculous birth of Jesus.[25] Leaving the cave, the midwife meets Salome (19:3), who appears at this point in the narrative without any explanation of who she is. Salome refuses to believe that a virgin has given birth unless she can test Mary's condition with her finger and find her to be still a virgin. When she goes to do so, her hand is burned (20:1). When she prays, an angel appears and tells her that if she touches the child she will be healed. She does so, is healed, and is told not to tell of the miracle she has seen (20:4). This story is clearly modeled on that of Thomas, who refuses to believe in the resurrection until he can put his fingers in the wounds of the risen Christ (John 20:24-29). Salome's role is that of a witness of the miracle of the virgin birth.[26]

This may in part account for the fact that Salome is named, by contrast with the midwife, whose witness is less dramatic. But the abrupt introduction of Salome in 19:3, not even as "a woman called Salome," but simply as "Salome," requires that the writer expected his readers to know who she was. The best explanation is that she is Salome the daughter of Joseph, who would naturally have accompanied her father and brothers on their journey to Bethlehem. This is much more plausible than Morton Smith's assumption that she must be Salome the disciple of Jesus (Mark 15:40; 16:1),[27] whom the *Protevangelium's* readers would hardly expect to find loitering outside a cave on the road from Jerusalem to Bethlehem at the time of the birth of Jesus. The introduction of Salome without identification would be similar to the abrupt appearance of James, as the writer of the work, in 25:1, with no explanation that he is the son of Joseph. In these cases, and probably also in 17:2, where the name of Samuel is most likely a corruption of Simeon, the writer takes for granted his readers know the names of Joseph's children.

If the name of Salome the sister of Jesus was well known in the circle from which the *Protevangelium* comes, it was evidently not well known in the early church as a whole. The unexplained appearance of Salome therefore caused difficulty for later readers of the work, and the Greek textual tradition of the *Protevangelium of James* already shows attempts to identify her with the midwife or as another midwife.[28] Later birth narratives dependent on the

---

25. In chaps. 19–20, in which Salome appears, the text in the earliest manuscript (P. Bodmer V) is considerably shorter than that in other manuscripts. De Stryker, *La Forme*, 377-89, and Smid, *Protevangelium*, 7, 131, agree that here the text of P. Bodmer V is not the more original form, but is an abridgment of the longer text. The issue makes no decisive difference to my argument.

26. Smid, *Protevangelium*, 139, points out that the midwife and Salome together fulfill the Deuteronomic requirement of two witnesses (Deut 19:15; cf. Matt 18:17).

27. Smith, *Clement*, 190-91.

28. The abridged version of chap. 20 in P. Bodmer V calls her the midwife (ἡ μαῖα) at

Protevangelium solve the problem by one or other of these options. In the Latin *Infancy Gospel of Pseudo-Matthew,* which tells basically the same story about Salome (13), she is a second midwife, while the first is called Zelomi (a variant of her name). In two closely related Coptic narratives — a Sahidic fragment on the birth of Jesus and the *Discourse by Demetrius of Antioch on the Birth of Our Lord*[29] — there is just one midwife who is Salome. In these narratives the story of Salome's unbelief, testing, and healing is omitted. As soon as she arrives with Joseph and sees the mother and child, she believes the miracle of the virgin birth. Both accounts say that she became a follower of Mary and Jesus from that moment until after his resurrection. According to the *Discourse by Demetrius,*

> this woman Salome was the first who recognized the Christ, and who worshipped Him, and believed in Him when He came upon the earth; and she did not return to her own house until the day of her death. Whithersoever Christ went to preach, with His mother the Virgin, there she followed Him with His disciples until the day when they crucified Him and (the day of) His holy resurrection. She saw them all, with His mother the Virgin.[30]

The *Coptic History of Joseph,* which gives the two daughters of Joseph the names of Lysia and Lydia (2:3), briefly alludes to the same Coptic tradition about Salome when it says that Salome followed Mary, Joseph, and Jesus on the flight into Egypt (8:3).[31]

This Coptic tradition has evidently identified Salome the midwife with Salome the disciple of Jesus known from the Gospel traditions (Mark 15:40; 17:1). Another trace of this identification is probably to be found in another late Coptic work, the *Book of the Resurrection by Bartholomew,* which includes in its

---

20:2. Most manuscripts of the longer text conclude Salome's prayer in 20:2 with a reference to her performance of her duties as a midwife (τὰς θεραπείας), but this is missing in C. These are clearly two alternative attempts by scribes to identify Salome as a midwife and so to explain her appearance in the narrative. Smith's view (*Clement,* 191) that the reading of P. Bodmer V at 20:2 shows that in an older form of the text Salome was the (one and only) midwife is quite implausible.

29. Sahidic fragment translated by F. Robinson, *Coptic Apocryphal Gospels* (TextsS 4/2; Cambridge: Cambridge University Press, 1896) 196-97; *Discourse by Demetrius* translated by E. A. W. Budge, *Miscellaneous Coptic Texts in the Dialect of Upper Egypt* (London: Trustees of the British Museum, 1915) 652-98.

30. Budge, *Miscellaneous Coptic Texts,* 674.

31. No doubt as a result of this Coptic tradition, in Arabic and Ethiopic literature about the infancy Salome later appears in this role as the constant companion of the holy family. James, *Apocryphal New Testament,* 88n.1, refers to "a Coptic text not yet printed in full" that tells the whole life story of Salome, but I have not been able to trace this.

list of women who went to the tomb on Easter morning "Salome who tempted him [Jesus]" (8:1).[32] The same list includes "Mary of James whom he [Jesus] delivered from the hands of Satan" — evidently an identification of Mary the mother of James (Matt 27:56; Mark 15:40; Luke 24:10) with the woman of Luke 13:16. But there is no woman in the canonical Gospels who is said to tempt Jesus. The reference is probably to Salome's confession in *Protevangelium of James* 20:1: "I have tempted the living God."[33] The *Book of the Resurrection* is therefore evidence that the *Protevangelium's* story of Salome's unbelief and healing was not always suppressed when she was identified with Salome the disciple of Jesus. The reason why it was suppressed in the texts mentioned above was probably not that it was considered derogatory to Salome the disciple of Jesus. Most likely it was suppressed because it was associated with the *Protevangelium's* account of the birth of Jesus, which could be considered too close to Docetism. Both the Sahidic fragment and the *Discourse of Demetrius*[34] describe the birth in the words of Luke 2:7, avoiding the account of the miraculous appearance of the child in *Protevangelium of James* 19:2.

It seems that the identification of Salome the midwife with Salome the disciple of Jesus is found only in the Coptic tradition[35] and in works that can be dated no earlier than the fourth century. Smith's claim that the story of Salome's refusal to believe in the virgin birth originated as polemic against the role of Salome the disciple of Jesus in Gnostic tradition appears quite unfounded.[36] The stages of tradition seem to be rather: (1) In the *Protevangelium*

32. James, *Apocryphal New Testament*, 183; J.-D. Kaestli and P. Cherix, *L'évangile de Barthélemy d'après deux écrits apocryphes* (Turnhout: Brepols, 1993) 195. For the date, James, *Apocryphal New Testament* 186, suggests fifth–seventh century; Kaestli and Cherix, *L'évangile*, suggest fifth–sixth century; cf., similarly, W. Schneemelcher in Schneemelcher, ed., *New Testament Apocrypha*, 1:557.

33. Cf. C. Trautmann, "Salomé l'incrédule, récits d'une conversion," in J.-E. Ménard, ed., *Écritures et Traditions dans la Littérature Copte: Journée d'Études Coptes Strasbourg 28 Mai 1982* (Cahiers de la Bibliothèque Copte 1; Louvain: Peeters, 1983) 67-68.

34. Robinson, *Coptic Apocryphal Gospels*, 196; Budge, *Miscellaneous Coptic Texts*, 673.

35. Note also the Coptic fragments published by E. Revillout, "Le Livre de Jacques: La sage-femme Salome et la princesse Salome," *JA* 5 (1905) 409-61; discussed by Trautmann, "Salomé," 61-72. These fragments, dependent on the *Protevangelium of James* but not recognizing Salome as a sister of Jesus, appear to tell a story of her life prior to her meeting with Joseph at the time of the birth of Jesus. She is a prostitute, daughter of Simeon the priest (Luke 2:25). She is converted and constructs a dwelling in the desert to receive travelers. It is here that Joseph encounters her. This story seems to be another attempt to explain who the Salome was who appears so inexplicably in the text of the *Protevangelium of James*. These fragments are also related in some way to the *Discourse by Demetrius*, as Trautmann, "Salomé," 70-72, shows.

36. Smith, *Clement*, 190-91.

of James the story of Salome's unbelief and healing was probably originally intended to be about Salome the sister of Jesus. (2) Because "Salome" was not widely known to be the name of a sister of Jesus, the Salome of the *Protevangelium of James* was identified either with the midwife or as a second midwife. (3) In Coptic tradition Salome the midwife was identified with Salome the disciple of Jesus. (4) In some versions of the Coptic tradition the story of Salome's unbelief and healing was dropped. That these versions preserve, as Smith seems to think,[37] an original, nonpolemical story of Salome the midwife and disciple of Jesus, antedating the extant texts of the *Protevangelium of James,* is highly improbable.

The Coptic tradition's identification of Salome the midwife with Salome the disciple of Jesus may be connected with the fact, to be established in the next section, that in earlier Egyptian Christianity Salome the disciple of Jesus was a better-known figure than she was in most other early Christian traditions. But the identification itself is an instance of the common Jewish and Christian exegetical practice of identifying people with the same names. The same practice led later writers (Theophylact, Euthymius Zigabenus, Nicephorus Callistus) who knew Salome the sister of Jesus from Epiphanius to identify her with the Salome of Mark 15:40, whom they also identified as the mother of the sons of Zebedee (Matt 27:56).[38] Occasionally such later writers also identify Salome's companion at the cross, Mary the mother of James and Joses (Matt 27:56; Mark 15:40), with Joseph's other daughter Mary.[39] But it is very unlikely that the tradition of these names for the sisters of Jesus *originated* as an interpretation of Mark 15:40, as H. B. Swete and J. Blinzler suppose.[40] There would be no reason to suppose that the women mentioned in Mark 15:40 were sisters of Jesus unless the sisters of Jesus were already known as Mary and Salome. The tradition of the names of the sisters of Jesus must antedate their identification with the women of Mark 15:40.

So is there any degree of probability that the tradition known to the *Protevangelium of James,* the *Gospel of Philip,* and the sources used by Epiphanius correctly preserved the actual names of two sisters of Jesus? Tal Ilan's study of the recorded names of Jewish women in Palestine in the period 330 BCE–200 CE finds that, although the 247 women whose names are known bore 68 different names in all, 61 of these 247 women were called Salome (including its longer version, Salomezion) and 58 were called Mary (Mariamme or

---

37. Smith, *Clement,* 190-91.
38. For references see Blinzler, *Brüder,* 36.
39. Blinzler, *Brüder,* 36.
40. H. B. Swete, *The Gospel according to Mark* (3d ed.; London: Macmillan, 1909) 113; Blinzler, *Brüder,* 36.

Maria).[41] In other words, these two names account for 47.7 percent of the women. Every second Palestinian Jewish woman must have been called either Salome or Mary. Individual sources for the names also show high percentages of these two names, making it likely that the sample is in this respect representative. The popularity of these names may derive from the fact that they were borne by members of the Hasmonean house, as were several of the most popular male names of the period.[42]

In the light of this statistical finding, it seems that the tradition which gives the names Mary and Salome to Jesus' sisters has a 50 percent chance of being correct, even if it was not based on historical memory! But the full significance of the statistic emerges only when we also consider the frequency of Jewish names *outside* Palestine. For this purpose, unfortunately, no such exhaustive collection of the surviving evidence is available. However, the list of 769 named Jewish women, from both Palestine and the diaspora, compiled by Günter Mayer, includes at least 21 women named Mary living in the diaspora,[43] but only two women named Salome living in the diaspora (Rome and Beirut).[44] Salome seems to have been a particularly Palestinian name.[45] Thus it is unlikely that a Gentile Christian living outside Palestine in the second century, wishing to invent names for the sisters of Jesus, would have hit on the two most common Palestinian Jewish women's names. He may well have called one sister Mary, but is unlikely to have called the other Salome. If the tradition is therefore to be traced back to Palestinian Jewish Christian circles, the chances of its being an accurate historical tradition are relatively high.

2. Salome the Disciple of Jesus

a. Salome in the Canonical Gospels

The name of Salome the disciple of Jesus occurs in the canonical Gospels only at Mark 15:40; 16:1. She is last of the group of three women whom Mark names

41. T. Ilan, "Notes on the Distribution of Women's Names in Palestine in the Second Temple and Mishnaic Periods," *JJS* 40 (1989) 186-200. The last figure could be increased to 59, since Ilan, 195, does not list Mary of Clopas (John 19:25), presumably — but probably incorrectly — considering her the same person as Mary the mother of James and Joses.

42. Ilan, "Notes," 191-92.

43. G. Mayer, *Die Jüdische Frau in der hellenistisch-römischen Antike* (Stuttgart: Kohlhammer, 1987) 104-6. The figure would be higher if the name Marion (and variant forms), used in Egypt, were included.

44. Mayer, *Jüdische Frau,* 106-7; cf. 109-10.

45. Cf. Mayer, *Jüdische Frau,* 42.

as among those women who had been disciples of Jesus in Galilee, had followed him to Jerusalem, and had watched his crucifixion from a distance (15:40-41). She is not named with the other two women as a witness of Jesus' burial (15:47), but is again the third of the group of three when they visit the tomb on Easter morning (16:1). But Matthew and Luke fail to mention Salome. The names given in the three Synoptic Gospels are as follows:

Mark 15:40 (cross):	Mary Magdalene Mary the mother of James the little and Joses Salome
Mark 15:47 (burial):	Mary Magdalene Mary of Joses
Mark 16:1 (empty tomb):	Mary Magdalene Mary of James Salome
Matt 27:56 (cross):	Mary Magdalene Mary the mother of James and Joseph The mother of the sons of Zebedee
Matt 27:61 (burial):	Mary Magdalene The other Mary
Matt 28:1 (empty tomb):	Mary Magdalene The other Mary
Luke 24:10 (empty tomb):	Mary Magdalene Joanna Mary of James

Since Matthew 27:56 refers to "the mother of the sons of Zebedee" where Mark 15:40 has "Salome," it has often been thought that these two women are the same.[46] But if Matthew is dependent on Mark[47] and thought that Salome was the mother of the sons of Zebedee, he would surely have mentioned her also at 28:1, where he simply drops Salome from Mark's list of women at the tomb, without replacing her by the mother of the sons of Zebedee. A better ex-

---

46. First by Origen, *In Matthaeum: Commentariorum Series* 141; and still asserted by Grassi, *Hidden Heroes,* 41. Witherington, *Women in the Ministry,* 120, leaves the possibility open.

47. The argument of this section assumes Markan priority, but could be adjusted to suit other views of Synoptic relationships.

planation is that Salome, though known by name to Mark's readers, was not known in Matthew's church. Just as Matthew drops Mark's reference to Alexander and Rufus, the sons of Simon of Cyrene (Matt 27:32 par. Mark 15:21), presumably because they were well known to Mark's readers but would mean nothing to Matthew's, so he drops the name Salome, of whom he judged his readers would not have heard. At 27:55 he includes instead the mother of the sons of Zebedee, who had already appeared in his Gospel (but nowhere else in the Gospel traditions) at 20:20 and was presumably known to him from the traditions of his own church. Since she was one of the women who traveled with Jesus to Jerusalem (20:20), he felt free to include her in the women at the cross, but not to add her, without any authority from tradition, to the witnesses at the empty tomb.

All three Synoptic Evangelists state explicitly that many women who had followed Jesus from Galilee were present at the cross (Matt 27:55-56; Mark 15:40-41; Luke 23:49). There is no reason why the three Matthew selects for mention by name should be the same as the three Mark selects. The two Marys were evidently well known as witnesses of the burial and the empty tomb and so both Matthew and Luke retain their names from Mark. But both Matthew and Luke drop the less well known Salome in favor of women who featured in their own traditions. Luke's women are anonymous at the cross (23:49), the burial (23:55), and the empty tomb (23:56–24:9); the representative three are named only retrospectively (24:10). This is because the reader of 23:55 will at once identify the women with those who have already appeared, in a passage peculiar to Luke, at 8:2-3. At 24:10 Luke selects the first two women (Mary Magdalene and Joanna) of the three named in 8:2-3 and adds, from Mark 16:1, Mary of James. He can the more easily drop Mark's Salome and substitute, from his own tradition, Joanna, because, unlike Matthew and Mark, Luke makes clear that more women than those he names went to the tomb on Easter morning (24:10). He is free to name those his readers will know — whether from oral tradition or from his own previous reference to them in 8:2-3. We may compare his preference for the list of the twelve that he draws from his own tradition (6:14-16) rather than Mark's list (Mark 3:16-19), as well as the fact that he drops the name Bartimaeus (Mark 10:46; cf. Luke 18:35), perhaps because Luke did not expect it to be known to his readers.[48]

48. The phenomenon of the presence and absence of personal names in the Gospel traditions needs much more discussion than is possible here. E. P. Sanders, *The Tendencies of the Synoptic Tradition* (SNTSMS 9; Cambridge: Cambridge University Press, 1969) 128-35, 145, 168-73, 184-86, 275, usefully collects some of the evidence, but his discussion and conclusions are unsatisfactory because he ignores necessary distinctions, e.g., between geographical and personal

That Salome is absent from John 19:25 is not surprising, since there is no reason to suppose that the Fourth Evangelist, whether or not he knew Mark's Gospel, was following Mark at this point. He follows a distinctive tradition, which refers to none of the women named in the Synoptic traditions apart from Mary Magdalene. Unlike the Synoptic picture of a large group of women distant from the cross, John has, close to the cross, a small group of those who were closest to Jesus.[49] They include two relatives of Jesus: his mother and an aunt.[50] The last of the group, Mary Magdalene, named here to anticipate her necessary appearance at John 20:1, was the one woman disciple of Jesus who was universally known in the early church and most tenaciously remembered in the traditions as a witness of the empty tomb.[51]

The canonical Gospels therefore seem to indicate that Salome, though a sufficiently prominent disciple of Jesus to be named in one Gospel, was not as widely known as Mary Magdalene or Mary the mother of James and Joses. This is sufficient explanation of the omission of her name by Matthew and Luke. Smith, however, makes the "presumption . . . that Salome was eliminated because persons of whom the canonical evangelists disapproved were appealing to her as an authority."[52] Whether this presumption has any plausibility we shall be able to judge only in the light of extracanonical material.

b. Salome as One of Four Women Disciples

According to two Gnostic works, Jesus had seven women disciples (*Soph. Jes. Chr.* 90:17-18; *1 Apoc. Jas.* 38:16-17),[53] but these seven are never named. Indeed, throughout the whole of Gnostic literature no more than six women disciples of Jesus are ever named (Mary [Magdalene], Martha, Salome, Arsinoe, Mary the mother of Jesus, Mary the sister of Jesus)[54] and no more than four in any

---

names, or between cases where a person who is anonymous in one text is named in another and cases where a name that can in any case be supplied from the context is present or absent at a particular point in the text.

49. Cf. J. McHugh, *The Mother of Jesus in the New Testament* (London: Darton, Longman & Todd, 1975) 243-244.

50. Cf. chap. 6 above.

51. *Gos. Pet.* 12:50, like John 20:1, names only Mary Magdalene at the empty tomb.

52. Smith, *Clement,* 190.

53. In *1 Apoc. Jas.* 38:15–39:8, the seven women disciples seem to be allegorized as the "seven spirits."

54. Mary Magdalene: Hippolytus, *Ref.* 5.7.1; 10.9.3; Origen, *C. Cels.* 5.62; Epiphanius, *Pan.* 26.8.1-3; *Gos. Phil.* 59:6-11; 63.33; *Soph. Jes. Chr.* 98:9; 114:8; *Gos. Thom.* 21, 114; *1 Apoc. Jas.* 40:25;

one work. So the number seven is probably merely conventional. However, a group of four women disciples are named in the *First Apocalypse of James* (40:25-26: Salome, Mary, Martha, and Arsinoe),[55] and this distinctive group of four names recurs twice in the Manichean *Psalms of Heracleides*.[56] In each case a list of the twelve apostles, each briefly characterized, is followed by a similar list of women disciples: Mary,[57] Martha her sister, Salome, Arsenoe. Furthermore, one of the Manichean fragments from Turfan (M-18) refers to Mary, Salome, and Arsinoe.[58] Though it appears to be dependent on the *Diatessaron*,[59] it refers to the women at the empty tomb, first as Mary, Salome, and Mary (cf. Mark 16:1), but then as Mary, Salome, and Arsinoe. Since these four lists of women disciples of Jesus are the only known references to a disciple named Arsinoe[60] and since all four lists name the same four women, with the exception of the omission of Martha in the Turfan fragment, it seems certain that they derive from the same distinctive Gospel tradition. Since the *First Apocalypse of James* refers to Addai (36:20-22), the apostle of Edessa, this tradition may belong originally to the Jewish Christianity of east Syria, which would explain also its availability to the Manicheans. There seems no reason why the name Arsinoe should not be regarded as an historical memory of a disciple of Jesus whose name has not survived in other traditions (just as Joanna and Susanna are known only from Luke). Though not otherwise attested as a Pales-

---

Dial. Sav. 126:17; 131:19; 134:25; 137:3; 139:8; 140:14, 19, 23; 141:12; 142:20; 143:6; 144:5, 22; *Gos. Mary,* passim; *Pistis Sophia,* passim.

Martha: *1 Apoc. Jas.* 40:26; *Pistis Sophia* 38-39, 57, 73, 80; Origen, *C. Cels.* 5.62.

Arsinoe: *1 Apoc. Jas.* 40:26.

Mary the mother of Jesus: *Gos. Phil.* 59:6-11; *Pistis Sophia* 59, 61-62.

Mary the sister of Jesus: *Gos. Phil.* 59:6-11.

55. The text is fragmentary and the possibility that there were originally more than four names cannot be ruled out; see the text and note by W. R. Schoedel in D. M. Parrott, ed., *Nag Hammadi Codices V.2-5 and VI with Papyrus Berolinensis 8502, 1 and 4* (Coptic Gnostic Library; NHS 11; Leiden: Brill, 1979) 98-99.

56. Allberry, *Manichaean Psalm-Book,* 192 lines 21-24; 194 lines 19-22.

57. Mary the sister of Martha and Mary Magdalene are considered identical: see 189 lines 13-23 with 192 lines 20-21.

58. Translation by Schneemelcher, "Gospel of Mani," in Schneemelcher, ed., *New Testament Apocrypha,* 1:402.

59. See W. L. Petersen, "An Important Unnoticed Diatessaronic Reading in Turfan Fragment M-18," in *Text and Testimony: Essays on New Testament and Apocryphal Literature in Honour of A. F. J. Klijn* (ed. T. Baarda, et al.; Kampen: Kok, 1988) 187-92.

60. She has nothing to do with the Arsinoe who appears in the shorter version of the *Acts of Thomas* 20-42 (text in M. R. James, *Apocrypha Anecdota II* [TextsS 5/1; Cambridge: Cambridge University Press, 1897] 32-37) and the Ethiopic *Preaching of St. Thomas in India* (E. A. W. Budge, *The Contendings of the Apostles* [Oxford: Oxford University Press, 1935] 269-74).

tinian Jewish woman's name,[61] it is not implausibly such,[62] since it was a royal name of the Ptolemaic dynasty and the other female royal name of that dynasty, Cleopatra, was used by Palestinian Jews.[63]

So it seems that Salome the disciple of Jesus was remembered in at least one strand of Gospel tradition independent of Mark.[64] It may be this particular east Syrian tradition, rather than Mark's Gospel, that accounts for Salome's appearance in *Gospel of Thomas* 61, which we shall consider in the next section. But the relationship to east Syrian tradition can be supported at this point by the evidence of the Manichean *Psalms of Thomas,* of which psalm 16 is devoted to Salome (see the appendix to this chapter for a translation of this text)[65] and adds to the evidence just noted from the *Psalms of Heracleides* and the Turfan fragments, pointing to the prominence of Salome as a disciple of Jesus in Manichean traditions. In the psalm she is depicted as building a tower, probably an allegorical figure of the church.[66] In a prayer to Jesus she claims: "I am not double-minded, one is my heart and one my intention, there is no thought in my heart that is split or divided." This prayer may well reflect Jesus' words to Salome in *Gospel of Thomas* 61: "I am he who is from him who is undivided . . . whenever one is undivided, he will be filled with light, but whenever one is divided, he will be filled with darkness."

c. Salome as Interlocutor of Jesus

The introduction of particular named disciples as interlocutors of Jesus is a stylistic convention of the tradition of the sayings of Jesus (e.g., Matt 18:21; Mark 13:3-4; Luke 12:41; John 13:36-37; 14:5, 8, 22; 2 *Clem* 5:3). It came into its own especially in Gnostic revelation dialogues in which the risen Christ is questioned by one or more of his disciples, but it was by no means confined to that genre.

61. For Egyptian Jews called Arsinoe, see W. Horbury and D. Noy, *Jewish Inscriptions of Graeco-Roman Egypt* (Cambridge: Cambridge University Press, 1992) nos. 33, 38.

62. It occurs on two Jewish amulets from Syria: R. Kotansky, "Two Inscribed Jewish Aramaic Amulets from Syria," *IEJ* 41 (1991) 267-81.

63. Ilan, "Notes," 194.

64. C. M. Tuckett, *Nag Hammadi and the Gospel Tradition* (ed. J. Riches; Edinburgh: T. & T. Clark, 1986) 97-100, finds no evidence of dependence on Mark by the *First Apocalypse of James.*

65. Allberry, *Manichaean Psalm-Book,* 222-23.

66. Trautmann, "Salomé," 69, connects this theme of building with the idea, found in one of the Coptic fragments published by Revillout, that Salome built a hostel in the desert, where Joseph found refuge at the time of the birth of Jesus. But this connection seems very uncertain.

Only in extracanonical literature do women disciples appear as interlocutors of Jesus. Most frequent in this role is Mary Magdalene,[67] who was not only the best-known woman disciple of Jesus but also the special favorite of Gnostics (cf., e.g., *Gos. Phil.* 63:33–64:5; *Gos. Mary* 18:10-15; *Pistis Sophia* 19, 97). Other women disciples who appear occasionally in the role of interlocutor of Jesus are Mary the mother of Jesus, Martha, and Salome.

Salome is an interlocutor of Jesus in four works: the *Gospel of the Egyptians*, the *Gospel of Thomas*, the *Pistis Sophia*, and the Syriac *Testament of Our Lord*. (The last of these will be discussed in §e below.) Of the content of the *Gospel of the Egyptians*, which may have been originally *the* Gospel of the Gentile Christians of Egypt,[68] we know only the conversation of Jesus with Salome that Clement of Alexandria quotes and refers to several times (*Strom.* 3.6.45; 3.9.63, 64, 66; 3.13.92; *Exc. Ex. Theod.* 67; see the appendix to this chapter for translations of these passages). The conversation reflects an Encratite view of salvation as the restoration of the original condition of humanity without sexual differentiation, a notion that was frequently taken up in Gnostic literature, but whether the *Gospel of the Egyptians* was merely Encratite or more precisely Gnostic we do not have sufficient information to tell. Its original status as *the* Egyptian Gospel, only gradually supplanted in orthodox usage by the canonical Gospels, would account for its rather widespread use: by the Encratite and Docetist Julius Cassianus, by the Valentinian Theodotus, by Clement of Alexandria, and by the Sabellians.[69] However, the *Gospel of the Egyptians* used by the Naassenes (Hippolytus, *Ref.* 5.7.9) was not, as Smith claims, this gospel, but the Nag Hammadi *Gospel of the Egyptians* (CG 3,2; 4,2).[70]

Three of the sayings of Jesus that occur in this conversation with Salome occur elsewhere without reference to Salome. "I have come to destroy the works of the female" is echoed in the *Dialogue of the Savior* 144:16–145:5, where Mary (Magdalene) is the questioner. "When you tread on the garment of shame" is found in *Gospel of Thomas* 37, where the disciples in general are the questioners

---

67. *Gos. Thom.* 21; *Soph. Jes. Chr.* 98:9; 114:8; *Dial. Sav.* 126:17; 131:19; 134:25; 137:3; 139:8; 140:14, 19, 23; 141:12; 142:20; 144:5, 22; *Gos. Mary* 10:10–17:7; Epiphanius, *Pan.* 26.8.2-3; *Pistis Sophia*, passim.

68. Cf. W. Schneemelcher, "Gospel of the Egyptians," in Schneemelcher, ed., *New Testament Apocrypha*, 1:215.

69. By the time of Origen's *First Homily on Luke* 1:1, it was evidently regarded as heretical by the orthodox.

70. Smith, *Clement*, 190; also Schneemelcher, "Gospel of the Egyptians," in Schneemelcher, ed., *New Testament Apocrypha*, 1:211-12. That the work used by the Naassenes was the Nag Hammadi *Gospel of the Egyptians* is shown by the prominence of the figure of Adamas, both in the latter and in Naassene teaching, according to Hippolytus, *Ref.* 5.7.1-9.

(cf. 21, where Mary is the questioner). "When the two become one . . ." is found in *Gospel of Thomas* 22, where again the disciples in general are the interlocutors, and in *2 Clement* 12:2, where the interlocutors are anonymous.[71] These last two sayings,[72] being in form answers to questions, require an interlocutor, but the identity of the interlocutor was evidently not a stable feature of the tradition of these sayings. There is no reason to suppose that the content of the conversation with Salome in the *Gospel of the Egyptians* was associated with Salome elsewhere than in the *Gospel of the Egyptians*.

The subject matter of the conversation makes a female interlocutor appropriate, and this is probably also the case in *Gospel of Thomas* 61 (see the appendix to this chapter for a translation of this text), where Salome makes her only appearance in that Gospel. The conversation is obscure,[73] but, like that in the *Gospel of the Egyptians*, it probably makes use of the idea of the transcendence of sexual differentiation by returning to an original unity. Gnostic literature rather characteristically introduces women disciples of Jesus when it represents Jesus as employing the image of the transcendence of sexuality (cf. *Gos. Thom.* 114; *Dial. Sav.* 144:16–145:5; *1 Apoc. Jas.* 40:25–41:18).

Salome features rather more prominently in the fourth-century Egyptian Gnostic work generally known as the *Pistis Sophia*.[74] That this work treats her as one of four women disciples, along with Mary Magdalene, Mary the mother of Jesus, and Martha, is probably due to her appearance in the *Gospel of the Egyptians* and in the *Gospel of Thomas*, which was certainly known to the author of the *Pistis Sophia* (cf. 42-43). In the *Pistis Sophia*, which is a lengthy postresurrection conversation between Jesus and his disciples, the number of interventions in the conversation by male disciples are as follows: John 9, Peter 6, Andrew 5, Philip 4, Thomas 4, James 3, Matthew 2, Bartholomew 1. These proportions reflect roughly the relative prominence of various disciples in both Gnostic and orthodox Gospel traditions (for the special prominence of John, see *Pistis Sophia* 97). The number of interventions by female disciples are: Mary Magdalene 72, Salome 4 (chaps. 54, 58, 132, 145), Martha 4, Mary the mother of Jesus 3. Mary Magdalene's immense prominence in this work (and cf. the state-

71. Cf. also *Gos. Phil.* 70:9-17.

72. On the tradition history of these sayings (or one two-part saying), see the full study in D. R. MacDonald, *There Is No Male and Female: The Fate of a Dominical Saying in Paul and Gnosticism* (HDR 20; Philadelphia: Fortress, 1987).

73. On the interpretation of the saying, see J. Ménard, *L'Évangile selon Thomas* (NHS 5; Leiden: Brill, 1975) 161-62; M. Lelyveld, *Les Logias de la Vie dans L'Évangile selon Thomas* (NHS 34; Leiden: Brill, 1987) 55-68; Buckley, *Female Fault*, 100-102.

74. For the date and place, see M. Tardieu and J.-D. Dubois, *Introduction à la Littérature Gnostique* (Paris: Cerf, 1986) 1:80.

ments about her in 19 and 97) reflects her status in some (though by no means all) other Gnostic works, where she is not only the woman disciple Jesus loved more than other women (*Gos. Mary* 10:2-3), but the disciple Jesus loved more than all the male disciples (*Gos. Mary* 18:14-15; *Gos. Phil.* 63:33–64:5). The passage involving both Mary Magdalene and Salome in *Pistis Sophia* 132, in which Mary is able to supply the answer to the question Salome asks Jesus, makes clear Mary's more advanced status as a disciple compared with Salome (cf. also the respective commendations of Mary and Salome in 19 and 54).

On the basis of the canonical Gospels alone, we should not expect Salome to be very prominent in later Christian tradition. She appears only in Mark and there only as a name given last in a list of three. We should expect her to be no more prominent than Joanna, who, despite her role as a witness of the empty tomb in Luke 24:10, seems never to be mentioned by name in Christian literature before the fourth century,[75] and less prominent than Martha, whose role in Gospel stories (Luke 10:38-42; John 11:1-22; 12:2) impressed her on the Christian memory and imagination and accounts for her quite frequently mentioned place among the women disciples of Jesus (*1 Apoc. Jas.* 40:26; *Pistis Sophia* 38-39, 57, 73, 80; Origen, *C. Cels.* 5.62; *Ep. Apos.* 9-10; Hippolytus, *On the Song of Songs* frg. 15; *Apostolic Church Order* 26; *Testament of Our Lord* 1:16; Ethiopic *Didascalia* 3:6). We should also remember that, among both orthodox and Gnostic Christians, Matthew's Gospel was much the most popular of the Synoptics, Luke the second most popular, and Mark, which alone refers to Salome, the least used, since it added so little to Matthew and Luke.[76] Thus it is not surprising that in Gospel traditions and specifically in Gnostic traditions Salome is much less prominent than Mary Magdalene. More surprising is that as an interlocutor of Jesus she is the second most prominent woman disciple, after Mary Magdalene.

This is probably to be attributed to extracanonical tradition. Salome's place in the *Gospel of Thomas*, as I have suggested, may well result from the independent east Syrian tradition that put her among four named women disciples (in *1 Apoc. Jas.* 40:25-26 the first named of the four). Whether the *Gospel of the Egyptians* was dependent on Mark we have no way of telling, just as we do not know which other disciples may have featured in it as interlocutors of Jesus, but it is quite possible that in this case too the name of Salome was taken from tradition independent of Mark. At the same time, we should remember that Mark's Gospel was probably from an early date more popular in Egypt than

---

75. Only Tertullian, *Adv. Marc.* 4.19.1 (alluding to Luke 8:2-3), refers to Joanna without naming her.

76. É. Massaux, *Influence de l'Évangile de saint Matthieu sur la littérature chrétienne avant saint Irénée* (Louvain: Publications Universitaires de Louvain; Gembloux: Duculot, 1950) 651-55; Tuckett, *Nag Hammadi*, 149-52. For Gnostic use of Mark, see also Irenaeus, *Adv. Haer.* 3.11.7.

elsewhere,[77] since it was in Egypt that two expanded forms of Mark's Gospel (the *Secret Gospel* as used by the orthodox and by the Carpocratians) were known, in both of which at least one other reference to Salome was added to canonical Mark's two (see §3 below). It is also important to remember that the *Gospel of Thomas* was known in Egypt from the late second century.[78] Thus it is not surprising that the work in which Salome gains most prominence as an interlocutor of Jesus is another Egyptian work, the *Pistis Sophia*.

Salome's prominence in Gnostic Gospel traditions should not be exaggerated. She appears only in the east Syrian tradition (from which the Manichean tradition about her probably also derives) and the Egyptian tradition (where we have also already noticed her appearance, identified with Salome the midwife, in orthodox Christian literature of a slightly later date). Most of Gnostic literature never mentions her, while Mary Magdalene is more important than Salome, not only in Gnostic traditions as a whole, but also in those two traditions in which Salome features.

d. Salome as a Source of Esoteric Tradition

Origen reports that in a list of Gnostic sects Celsus refers to "Simonians from Helen, Marcellians from Marcellina, Harpocratians from Salome, others from Mary [Mariamme], others from Martha" (*C. Cels.* 5.62). The Harpocratians here can be confidently identified with the Carpocratians.[79] The list seems designed to emphasize the derivation of various groups from women, but in the last three instances certainly gives examples of the common Gnostic claim to teaching transmitted from Jesus by esoteric tradition through named disciples of his. The reference to Mary might be to the Naassenes, who claimed teaching transmitted by James to Mary Magdalene (Hippolytus, *Ref.* 5.71; 10.9.3), but since there were also Gnostic writings that claimed to contain esoteric teaching communicated by Jesus directly to Mary Magdalene[80] (*Gospel of Mary*, and the *Great* and *Little Questions of Mary*, according to Epiphanius, *Pan.* 26.8.1-3), the reference is perhaps more probably to groups that used these writings. However, extant Gnostic literature does not contain the revelations to Salome and Martha that are referred to here. The roles of these disciples as interlocutors of

---

77. Cf. the tradition that Mark himself took his Gospel to Egypt: Eusebius, *Hist. Eccl.* 2.16.1; Clement of Alexandria, *Letter to Theodorus* 1.19-20.

78. P. Oxy. 654 dates from the end of the second or beginning of the third century.

79. Smith, *Clement*, 89-90; against Levin, "Early History of Christianity," 4287.

80. Cf. P. Perkins, *The Gnostic Dialogue: The Early Church and the Crisis of Gnosticism* (New York: Paulist, 1980) 136.

Jesus in the *Gospel of the Egyptians* (Salome), the *Gospel of Thomas* (Salome), and the *Pistis Sophia* (Salome and Martha, but in any case the work is later than Celsus) do not meet the requirement. What Jesus says to Salome in the extant section of the *Gospel of the Egyptians* and in *Gospel of Thomas* 61 could scarcely form the basis of the distinctive theology of the Carpocratians. The model of the *Gospel of Mary* (see especially 10:1–17:20) and the *Great Questions of Mary* (Epiphanius, *Pan.* 26.8.2-3) requires us to think rather of an esoteric revelation given exclusively and secretly to Salome. This reference to Salome by Celsus is the only extant reference that requires us to suppose that there must have been substantial material about Salome — in the form of teaching given to her — that is now lost. But this lost material was no doubt produced by the Carpocratians themselves and was peculiar to them. The particular prominence of Salome in Egyptian Gospel traditions, which I have already established, would explain why the Carpocratians selected her as the authority for their own claim to a tradition from Jesus.

e. Salome in Orthodox Writers

In one non-Gnostic work, the fourth-century Syriac *Testament of Our Lord,* Salome has the role, along with Martha and Mary, of interlocutor of Jesus in a postresurrection revelatory discourse. In 1:16 the group of women disciples, "Martha and Mary, and Salome," following the male disciples' request that the risen Christ instruct them about church order (1:15), ask Jesus to teach them their own role as women disciples. He does so briefly, but in a way that acknowledges that women have a place in the ministry of the church, something that is characteristic of this work. But the question of the women disciples should probably be regarded as preparing for the instructions about the roles of widows, presbyteresses, deaconesses, and female virgins in the church that are given later (1:19, 23, 35, 40-43, 46; 2:4, 19). In that sense, the women disciples of Jesus have a rather prominent place in the work. In a non-Gnostic work this is unusual, just as in its emphasis on the ministry of women in the church this work is unusual. For this author Martha, Mary, and Salome are presumably the most prominent female disciples of Jesus, just as Peter, John, Thomas, Matthew, Andrew, and Matthias are the most prominent of the twelve (1: intro. 2, 15).

The list of women is no doubt part of the tradition of works on church order. The Syriac *Didascalia* refers to the women disciples of Jesus (though not as interlocutors of Jesus) in the course of its own rather more carefully restricted instructions on the ministries of women (14-16 = 3:1-13). Its two lists are "Mary

Magdalene and Mary the daughter of James[81] and the other Mary" (15 = 3:6) and "Mary Magdalene and Mary the daughter of James and mother of Jose, and the mother of the sons of Zebedee" (16 = 3:12), but in the first the Greek fragment has Salome in place of "the other Mary,"[82] while the corresponding passage in the Ethiopic *Didascalia* has "Mary Magdalene and the sisters of Lazarus, Mary and Martha, and Salome." The *Apostolic Constitutions* at the same point (3:6) has the longest list of women: "the mother of our Lord and his sisters; also Mary Magdalene, and Mary the mother of James, and Martha and Mary the sisters of Lazarus, and Salome." Such lists may have a traditional character and a degree of independence of the canonical Gospels, though the writers' knowledge of the latter certainly also influenced them. It is striking that the peculiarly Lukan women disciples, Susanna[83] and Joanna, never appear in them, despite the latter's role in Luke's resurrection narrative. Even in accounts of the women's visit to the tomb that seem indebted, directly or indirectly, to Luke, Joanna is absent (*Ep. Apos.* 9-11: Martha, Mary her sister, Mary Magdalene; Hippolytus, *On the Song of Songs*, frg. 15: Martha and Mary; Turfan M-18: Mary, Salome, Mary; Mary, Salome, Arsinoe).[84] We might also compare Epiphanius's list of women at the cross: Mary of Clopas, Mary the mother of Rufus,[85] the other Mary, Salome (*Pan.* 78.13.2).[86] Only in some late Coptic accounts does Joanna appear with Mary the mother of Jesus, Salome, and other women.[87]

The case of Joanna shows that the relatively little reference to Salome in non-Gnostic literature cannot be construed as polemic against her role in Gnosticism. Joanna is ignored not only in orthodox but also in Gnostic literature. Moreover, if orthodox writers suppressed the women disciples of Jesus because of Gnostic appeals to their authority, Mary Magdalene, far more impor-

---

81. This is the way Μαρία ἡ τοῦ Ἰακώβου is rendered in the Old Syriac version of the Gospels.

82. R. H. Connolly, *Didascalia Apostolorum* (Oxford: Clarendon, 1929) 133n.; cf. p. xxi.

83. Origen, *C. Cels.* 1.65, refers to Susanna.

84. See also the quotation from Severianus of Gabala in W. Bauer, *Das Leben Jesu im Zeitalter der neutestamentlichen Apokryphen* (Tübingen: Mohr [Siebeck], 1904) 450n.3.

85. The best explanation of "Mary the mother of Rufus" that I can suggest is that she results from (1) identifying Mary Magdalene, present at the cross according all four Gospels, with Mary of Bethany (John 12:3); (2) supposing that Simon the leper (Mark 14:3), in whose house Mary of Bethany anointed Jesus, was Mary's husband; (3) identifying Simon the leper with Simon of Cyrene, the father of Alexander and Rufus (Mark 15:21; cf. Rom 16:13). Such a chain of identification of Gospel characters is not untypical of patristic exegesis.

86. Cf. also *Pan.* 79.7.3-4: Salome, the other Mary, the mother of Rufus, Martha.

87. *Book of the Resurrection by Bartholomew* 8:1, in James, *Apocryphal New Testament*, 183; Kaestli and Cherix, *L'évangile*, 195; Coptic *Dormition of the Virgin*, in Robinson, *Coptic Apocryphal Gospels*, 51, 59.

tant for Gnostics than Salome, should have been the disciple to disappear
entirely from orthodox tradition. Orthodox references to the women disciples of
Jesus simply do not correlate with the requirements of anti-Gnostic concerns. It
may well be true that, whereas the prominence of the women disciples of Jesus in
some Gnostic literature reflects the prominence of women leaders in some of the
Gnostic groups, the relatively few references to the women disciples of Jesus in
non-Gnostic literature reflects the increasing opposition to female leadership in
the church.[88] But this is not the same as saying that the treatment of the women
disciples in non-Gnostic literature is deliberate polemic against their treatment
in Gnostic traditions. Of deliberate polemic of this kind there seems to be no evidence. It follows that there is even less reason to suppose that Matthew's and
Luke's omissions of Mark's references to Salome had anything to do with appeals
to Salome's authority by persons of whom Matthew and Luke disapproved.

Morton Smith has two main pieces of evidence for deliberate polemic by
orthodox writers against the figure of Salome as a Gnostic authority.[89] One is
the story of Salome's disbelief in the virgin birth, which we have already seen in
§1 did not originate as a story about Salome the disciple of Jesus at all. The
other is a comment of Origen on Matthew's account of the women at the cross
and the burial (Matt 27:55-56, 61). Origen identifies the mother of the sons of
Zebedee in Matthew with Salome in Mark. Of the women who observed the
crucifixion, the three leading ones are named, he says, "as though watching
more intently, ministering more fully, and following better" (*In Matthaeum:
Commentariorum Series* 141). His concern is to use them as examples of discipleship. Following the crucifixion, "the affection *(charitas)* of the two Marys . . .
attached them to the new tomb because of the body of Jesus buried there." But
observing that Matthew (like Mark) mentions only the two Marys, not the
mother of the sons of Zebedee, at this point (Matt 27:61), he suggests that perhaps this was because the two Marys were "greater in affection" (*In Matthaeum*
144). It is by no means clear, as Smith claims,[90] that Origen excludes Salome
from witnessing the empty tomb. Since the extant Latin summary of the latter
part of his commentary on Matthew breaks off before Matthew 28:1, we do not
know how he resolved the difference between Matthew 28:1 and Mark 16:1 on
this point. The comment we have is solely concerned with explaining why, according to both Matthew and Mark, only two of the women named as present
at the cross were also present by the tomb at the time of the burial. It is clear

88. Cf. E. Pagels, *The Gnostic Gospels* (New York: Random House, 1979; London:
Weidenfeld & Nicolson, 1980) 59-69.
89. Smith, *Clement*, 190-92.
90. Smith, *Clement*, 191.

that his comment aims at explaining the text and has no intention of putting down Salome for reasons of anti-Gnostic polemic. After all, why should Origen have exalted Mary Magdalene at the expense of Salome if his purpose was anti-Gnostic? He must have known of Gnostic appeals to the authority of Mary Magdalene (cf. *C. Cels.* 5.62), generally more prominent in Gnostic literature than Salome, as well as of the Carpocratian appeal to Salome in particular.

Finally, I should mention that Clement of Alexandria, in his treatment of Salome's conversation with Jesus in the *Gospel of the Egyptians,* accepts the authenticity of the conversation and interprets it in a non-Encratite sense. He neither rejects the Gospel nor casts any aspersions on Salome. This failure of Clement to polemicize against Salome is of interest, since it is Clement, in his *Letter to Theodorus,* who rejects what he regards as the Carpocratian interpolations in the *Secret Gospel of Mark* that may have concerned Salome.

3. The *Secret Gospel of Mark*

Against Smith, I have shown that there is no evidence that Salome the disciple of Jesus was a "controversial figure," that orthodox writers denigrated her or diminished her importance in a deliberate polemic against her role in Gnosticism, or that "there must have been early traditions about Salome [now lost] to explain later developments."[91] Although it seems that Salome was remembered in extracanonical Gospel traditions independent of Mark, the only lost traditions about teaching of Jesus given to Salome that the evidence requires us to postulate are specifically Carpocratian traditions. With these conclusions we may approach the most puzzling reference to Salome: the sentence that, according to Clement of Alexandria (*Letter to Theodorus* 3.14-16), the *Secret Gospel of Mark,* as used in the church in Alexandria, added at Mark 10:46: "And the sister of the young man whom Jesus loved and his mother and Salome were there, and Jesus did not receive them." This is the second of the two passages Clement quotes from *Secret Mark.* It has naturally received a good deal less attention[92]

---

91. Smith, *Clement,* 191, 192.

92. Besides Smith, see R. E. Brown, "The Relation of 'The Secret Gospel of Mark' to the Fourth Gospel," *CBQ* 36 (1974) 480; J. D. Crossan, *Four Other Gospels: Shadows on the Contours of the Canon* (Minneapolis: Winston, 1985) 109; Levin, "Early History of Christianity," 4286-4387; W. Munro, "Women Disciples: Light from Secret Mark," *JFSR* 8 (1992) 46-64. M. W. Meyer, "The Youth in Secret Mark and the Beloved Disciple in John," in J. E. Goehring, et al., eds., *Gospel Origins and Christian Beginnings* (J. M. Robinson FS; Sonoma, Calif.: Polebridge, 1990) 94-105, focuses on the phrase "the youth whom Jesus loved" in the second quotation, but does not discuss the rest of the passage.

than the first and much longer quotation. But its significance is far more difficult to discern, and so it constitutes the greater challenge to the adequacy of theories about *Secret Mark*.

We recall that Clement, according to the *Letter to Theodorus*, knew three versions of Mark's Gospel: (1) our canonical Mark; (2) the *Secret Gospel of Mark* as used in the orthodox church in Alexandria: this was our canonical Mark with at least two additional passages, which Clement quotes; (3) the *Secret Gospel of Mark* as used by the Carpocratians: this included further passages additional to those in the orthodox version of *Secret Mark*, of which Clement quotes only two words. We cannot be quite sure whether the orthodox version of *Secret Mark* included any more additions to canonical Mark than the two that Clement quotes. Since his purpose in quoting these passages was to assure his correspondent, Theodore, that the unorthodox material that Theodore had quoted from the Carpocratian version of *Secret Mark* did not occur in the orthodox version, Clement may have quoted only those passages of the orthodox *Secret Mark* where the Carpocratian *Secret Mark* had further material in the same context. It is clear from what Clement says (3:11-13) that the Carpocratian *Secret Mark* expanded the first of Clement's quotations from the orthodox *Secret Mark*, the story of the young man Jesus raised from the dead and initiated into the mystery of the kingdom of God. It is less clear whether the further Carpocratian additions of which Clement speaks in very general terms after quoting the second passage from the orthodox *Secret Mark* ("the many other things about which you wrote both seem to be and are falsifications") occurred in connection with the second quotation from the orthodox *Secret Mark* or at other points in the Carpocratian version of the Gospel. The former, however, seems the more likely. In that case, it seems probable that the last words of the second quotation ("and Jesus did not receive them") were replaced in the Carpocratian version by a much longer account of what happened when the three women met Jesus in Jericho.

The second quotation as it stood in the orthodox *Secret Mark* is enigmatic in its brevity. There seem to be three possible explanations of its significance. The first two, it should be noticed, are compatible with either of the two possible views of the literary relationship between canonical Mark and the orthodox *Secret Mark* (that *Secret Mark* is a secondary expansion of canonical Mark,[93] or

---

93. F. Neirynck, "The Apocryphal Gospels and the Gospel of Mark," in J.-M. Sevrin, ed., *The New Testament in Early Christianity* (BETL 86; Leuven: Leuven University Press/Peeters, 1989) 168-70; J. P. Meier, *A Marginal Jew: Rethinking the Historical Jesus*, vol. 1: *The Root of the Problem and the Person* (New York: Doubleday, 1991) 120-22; J.-D. Kaestli, "L'*Evangile secret de Marc*: Une version longue de l'Evangile de Marc réservée aux chrétiens avancés dans l'Eglise d'Alexandrie?" in J.-D. Kaestli and D. Marguerat, eds., *Le Mystère Apocryphe: Introduction à une littérature méconnue* (Essais bibliques 26; Geneva: Labor et Fides, 1995) 85-106.

that canonical Mark is an abbreviation of *Secret Mark*),[94] but the third explanation is possible only on the supposition that *Secret Mark* is the product of a later redactor of canonical Mark. Thus, while it is not possible here to engage in a full discussion of the relationship of canonical Mark and *Secret Mark,* my demonstration that the third explanation of this passage of *Secret Mark* is preferable to the other two will contribute to establishing the priority of canonical Mark.

(1) One explanation for the curious brevity of the passage is that it is a tendentious abbreviation of an originally longer incident in Jericho: "The original text must have gone on to report some action or saying of Jesus." According to Smith, this omitted material was probably a conversation with Salome, whose content was unacceptable to the orthodox.[95] In this case, the words "and Jesus did not receive them" would have been substituted for the omitted material.

We should notice, first, that on this view the omitted material cannot have been specifically Carpocratian in origin. It is hardly likely that a version of Mark produced by the Carpocratians would have been taken over, even in edited form, by the orthodox. Therefore, if the omitted material was the same as the additional passage that the Carpocratian version of *Secret Mark* evidently had at this point, then the Carpocratians preserved in their version material that did not originate with them but that the orthodox found it necessary to edit out of their version. This is, of course, possible. But in this case the omitted material is unlikely to have focused on Salome more than on the other two women named before her. Any specifically Carpocratian addition at this point in the Gospel might well have singled out the figure of Salome, because of the special Carpocratian interest in her, but if the reference to the three women was originally written in order to introduce a longer passage than it does now, then there is no reason at all to suppose that Salome played a larger part in this passage than the other two women. Furthermore, when we remember that Clement himself accepted as authentic and interpreted in an orthodox way the conversation of Jesus and Salome in the *Gospel of the Egyptians,* it becomes necessary to suppose that the material allegedly omitted from the orthodox *Se-*

---

94. The latter view is taken by H. Koester, "History and Development of Mark's Gospel (From Mark to *Secret Mark* and 'Canonical' Mark)," in B. Corley, ed., *Colloquy on New Testament Studies: A Time for Reappraisal and Fresh Approaches* (Macon, Ga.: Mercer University Press, 1983) 35-57; Crossan, *Four Other Gospels,* 91-121; H.-M. Schenke, "The Mystery of the Gospel of Mark," *SecCent* 4 (1984) 65-82; Munro, "Women Disciples." M. Smith's view is basically that canonical Mark and the additional material in *Secret Mark* derive from the same source: cf. Smith, *Clement,* 192-94; idem, "Clement," 452-53. This view would be compatible with the third explanation, apart from Smith's conviction that canonical Mark 10:46 is an abbreviation; cf. Smith, *Clement,* 188-89, 194.

95. Smith, *Clement,* 122.

cret Mark was not just mildly unorthodox but radically incapable of an orthodox reading.

The problem with this theory of abbreviation is the difficulty of explaining why the abbreviation was not more radical. In other words, why was the text
not reduced to that of canonical Mark?[96] It becomes necessary to explain what
purpose the redactor saw in retaining the words that Clement gives as his second quotation from the orthodox *Secret Mark*. This quotation as it stands must
have had some significance of its own for the redactor of the orthodox *Secret
Mark;* it cannot be merely the residue of an abbreviation. Smith therefore offers
the second of our three explanations in combination with this first explanation.[97] The first explanation is admitted to be insufficient alone. But then its
plausibility is closely connected with that of the additional explanation with
which it has to be combined. If the latter (the second of our three explanations)
proves to be itself a sufficient explanation, then this first explanation becomes
redundant. If the second explanation proves implausible, then the first explanation falls with it. Only if the second explanation proves both plausible and insufficient alone will we need to take the first explanation seriously.

(2) Another possibility is that Clement's second quotation from *Secret
Mark* has a polemical intention. According to Smith, "the story, as it stands,
can have been invented and preserved only as polemic against these women or
their followers or persons who appealed to their authority (as the Carpocratians did to that of Salome)."[98] For this view to be at all plausible, we should
have to suppose that all three women have been deliberately chosen as targets
of the polemic. If the sister of the young man is identified (from the Johannine
parallel to *Secret Mark*'s story of his resurrection) as Mary of Bethany (indis-
tinguishable in Gnostic literature from Mary Magdalene), then the first
woman in the list of three is appropriately the woman disciple of Jesus who
was most popular as a Gnostic authority, though we may wonder why in this
case the polemic is obscured by her anonymity (especially since Mark names
Mary Magdalene at 15:40, 47; 16:1). The second woman, who could be, grammatically, either the mother of the young man Jesus loved or Jesus' own
mother, is more problematic. The mother of the young man is otherwise en-

---

96. It is not necessary to discuss here the view that Mark 10:46 in its canonical form must
represent an abbreviation of an originally longer text; see Smith, *Clement,* 122-23; Koester, "History," 42; Crossan, *Four Other Gospels,* 109-10; H. Koester, *Ancient Christian Gospels: Their History and Development* (London: SCM; Philadelphia: Trinity Press International, 1990) 301. Canonical Mark 10:46 is not at all as odd as these scholars claim. If Mark wished to say that Jesus
met Bartimaeus as he was leaving Jericho, then he had first to record Jesus' arrival in Jericho.

97. Smith, *Clement,* 121-22.

98. Smith, *Clement,* 121.

tirely unknown and could hardly be the object of polemic. In extant Gnostic literature Jesus' mother takes part in revelatory dialogues only in three passages of the *Pistis Sophia* (59, 61, 62), which is a century later than Clement. There is no other evidence that Gnostics appealed to her as an authority, though this is of course quite possible.

This explanation loses much of its plausibility when one realizes that there are no parallels elsewhere to this kind of denigration of the women disciples of Jesus for reasons of anti-Gnostic polemic. Smith's evidence for orthodox polemic against Salome I have found to be entirely inadequate. Perhaps it could be suggested, as a variation of this second explanation, that the polemic is not specifically against the role of the women disciples of Jesus in Gnosticism, but more generally against women's ministry in the church.[99] But again there are no parallels. Even the works of church order that refer to the women disciples of Jesus in the context of specifically prohibiting women from teaching (or baptizing) do not deny that Jesus and his male disciples were accompanied by women disciples. They simply point out that among the functions these women did perform, according to the Gospels, teaching (or baptism) was not included (Syriac *Didascalia* 3:6, 9, 12; *Apostolic Church Order* 26-28;[100] *Apost. Const.* 3:6, 9).

The lack of parallels does not entirely rule out this explanation, but it does lead us to ask whether a more probable explanation might not be available.

(3) The explanations of the significance of the passage that have been suggested hitherto have treated it separately from Clement's other quotation from *Secret Mark:* the story of the young man that *Secret Mark* inserted between verses 34 and 35 of Mark 10. Yet the opening words of the second quotation ("and the sister of the young man whom Jesus loved") link it closely with the first, while only one Markan pericope (10:35-45) intervenes between the two passages of *Secret Mark.* It seems likely that the function of the second passage is to be found not purely in itself, but in its reference back to the first passage. This will be the case especially if *Secret Mark* is an expansion of canonical Mark. A redactor who added to canonical Mark just these two passages (at least in this part of the Gospel) may well have intended the second to function as a means of integrating the first into the Gospel. This suggestion that the second passage has primarily a literary function in relation to the first meets the problem, raised by Smith, that the second passage is too brief to be in its original form: "The story, as Clement quotes it, is quite unlike any other NT story because it has no apparently significant content. There is no miracle, no saying, nothing

99. Cf. Levin, "Early History of Christianity," 4287.

100. J. P. Ardenzen, "An Entire Syriac Text of the 'Apostolic Church Order,'" *JTS* 3 (1901) 72-73.

but Jesus' refusal to receive, on occasion, three women."[101] According to this third possible explanation of the passage, the redactor was not intending to write a typical Gospel pericope, with a point of its own, but to integrate into the Gospel the material he had interpolated at Mark 10:34. The latter was his real interest: his brief insertion into Mark 10:46 (where the text of canonical Mark offered an opportunity for interpolation) has significance only in relation to the earlier interpolation.

Many readers and exegetes of the Gospels in the early church were interested in identifying the characters in the Gospels: they liked to identify a figure in one story with a figure in another, to identify two persons of the same name, and to identify named persons with anonymous persons. On the assumption that *Secret Mark* is an expansion of canonical Mark, the redactor clearly intended to identify the young man whom Jesus raised from the dead, in the story he interpolated at Mark 10:35, with the young man of Mark 14:51-52. Precisely the same phrase, "wearing a linen cloth over his naked body" (περιβεβλημένος σινδόνα ἐπὶ γυμνοῦ), is used of both. The author solves the enigma of Mark 14:51-52 by explaining who the young man was,[102] and does so not by tampering with the text of Mark 14:51-52 (so far as we know), but by alluding to it in a story parallel to John 11. Readers of John's Gospel would know that the young man Jesus raised from the dead — and therefore also the young man who fled in Gethsemane — was Lazarus. We need not here decide whether John 11 was actually the source of the story in *Secret Mark*, rewritten in Markan language,[103] or whether the redactor of *Secret Mark* drew the story from floating Markan tradition in which it existed independently of John 11. In either case, since John's Gospel was known in Egypt from an early date,[104] there is no difficulty in supposing that the redactor of *Secret Mark* knew it and could expect his readers to know it. But he does not give the young man the name Lazarus, because it would be incongruous for a character who had been named earlier in the Gospel to appear anonymously in Mark 14:51-52.

The redactor's second interpolation into Mark ties the first interpolation more fully into the narrative of the Gospel by suggesting further identifications between characters. Salome, the only one of the three women who is named, is the key to the redactor's intention. Readers familiar with Mark's Gospel would know that Salome appears elsewhere only in 15:40; 16:1, in both cases as the

101. Smith, *Clement*, 121.

102. Cf. W. L. Lane in Corley, ed., *Colloquy,* 84.

103. So, cautiously, Brown, "Relation," against Smith's view that John 11 and *Secret Mark* have a common source. For Smith's response, see "Clement," 454n.13. Crossan, *Four Other Gospels,* 104-6, 110, seems to think that John is dependent on *Secret Mark.*

104. Shown by P52.

third of a group of three women. It seems that the redactor of *Secret Mark* intended to refer to the same group of three women that appears later in Mark 15:40; 16:1. In that case, "the sister of the young man whom Jesus loved" is Mary Magdalene, and "his mother" is "Mary the mother of James the little and Joses." That these identifications are intended is entirely plausible.

Although the sister of the young man could be either Mary or Martha, the role she plays in *Secret Mark's* story of the raising of the young man is closer to that played by Mary than to that played by Martha in John 11.[105] In the early church Mary of Bethany was frequently identified with Mary Magdalene. The reason why she remains anonymous in the passages from *Secret Mark* will be similar to the reason why the young man is not given the name Lazarus. She has still to appear anonymously in the text of canonical Mark before being named as Mary Magdalene in 15:40 (the first time this name appears in Mark). Readers of John would know that the unnamed woman of Mark 14:3-9 was Mary of Bethany (John 12:1-8).

An identification of Mary the mother of James and Joses (Mark 15:40) with the mother of Jesus would have seemed plausible on the basis of Mark 6:3, and was made by others in the patristic period.[106] The reason why she is unnamed in *Secret Mark* will be that the redactor has in mind Mark 3:31-35, where Jesus' mother (unnamed) and his brothers come to see Jesus and he (implicitly) refuses to receive them. A repetition of this incident must have seemed to the redactor the simplest way of introducing a reference to Jesus' mother accompanied by two other women into the narrative of Mark. He need not have reflected on the significance of Jesus' refusal to receive the women. The incident is just a literary device intended to identify the sister of the young man Jesus raised from the dead with Mary Magdalene, to associate her with two other women who appear elsewhere in Mark, and so to integrate the story of the raising of the young man into the Markan narrative.

Seen in this way, Clement's second quotation from *Secret Mark* reveals itself as a secondary addition to canonical Mark. Mark himself cannot have identified Mary Magdalene, whom he knows came from Galilee (15:41), with a woman of Bethany. Nor is he likely to have followed up the incident of Mark 3:31-35, where Jesus rejects his physical relatives in favor of those women and men who do God's will, by an incident in which Jesus rejects two (would-be?)

---

105. See the parallels in Brown, "Relation," 471.

106. Blinzler, *Brüder*, 73-74n.2. Modern advocates of this identification are S. W. Trompf, "The First Resurrection Appearance and the Ending of Mark's Gospel," *NTS* 18 (1971-72) 308-30; and J. J. Gunther, "The Family of Jesus," *EvQ* 46 (1974) 30-35; but against them, see Oberlinner, *Historische Überlieferung*, 117-20; Bauckham, *Jude*, 13-15.

women disciples along with his mother. But such difficulties need not have impeded a second-century redactor of Mark.

Appendix: Some Extracanonical Texts about Salome the Disciple of Jesus

Gospel of the Egyptians

The following passages from Clement of Alexandria contain quotations from the conversation between Jesus and Salome in the *Gospel of the Egyptians*. The words of Jesus and Salome are here printed in bold type, to distinguish them from Clement's own comments.

> When Salome asked, **How long will death have power?** the Lord said, **As long as you women bear children,** not as if life were bad and creation evil, but as teaching the sequence of nature. For death always follows birth. (*Strom.* 3.6.45)

> Those who oppose God's creation by means of continence, which has an appealing name, also quote the words spoken to Salome which we mentioned earlier. They are contained, I think, in the Gospel according to the Egyptians. For they say: The Savior himself said, **I have come to destroy the works of the female,** by "female" meaning desire, and by "works" birth and decay. (*Strom.* 3.9.63)

> It is probably because the Word had spoken concerning the consummation that Salome said, **Until when will people die?** Scripture speaks of the human being in two ways, the visible appearance and the soul, and again, one who is being saved and one who is not. And sin is said to be the death of the soul. Therefore the Lord answered very carefully. As long as women bear children, that is, as long as the desires are active. (*Strom.* 3.9.64)

> For when she [Salome] said, **I have done well then in not having borne children,** as if it were improper to engage in procreation, then the Lord answered and said: **Eat every plant but do not eat the one which contains bitterness.** (*Strom.* 3.9.66)

> Therefore Cassianus says: When Salome asked when the things would be known that she had inquired about, the Lord said: **When you [plural] have trampled on the garment of shame and when the two become one and the male with the female is neither male nor female.** (*Strom.* 3.13.92)

And when the Savior says to Salome that **there will be death as long as women bear children,** he does not speak reproachfully of procreation, for that is necessary for the salvation of believers. (*Exc. ex Theod.* 67)[107]

Gospel of Thomas 61

Jesus said: Two will rest on a bed; one will die, one will live. Salome said: Who are you, man, and whose son? You have sat upon my couch and eaten from my table. Jesus said to her: I am he who is from him who is undivided; to me were given some of the things of my Father. [Salome said:] I am your disciple. [Jesus said to her:] Therefore, I say, whenever one is undivided, he will be filled with light, but whenever one is divided, he will be filled with darkness.[108]

Psalms of Thomas 16

Salome built a tower upon the rock of
truth and mercy. The builders that built it are the righteous,
the masons that hew stones for it are the angels.
The floor (?) of the house is Truth, the beams of the roof are alms,
faith is [the] . . . the Mind is the . . .
of its door. They that go into it rejoice, they
that come out of it, — their heart seeks after gladness. She
built it and gave it a roof, Salome gave a parapet
to the tower, she took (?) an *anēsh* of storax to purify (?) it,
she] took the . . . of incense into the palm of her hand
. . . forth, she set it upon her head, she went [into
it, she called my Lord Jesus, saying . . .
mayest thou] answer me, Jesus, mayest thou hear me, for
I] am not double-minded, one is my heart and one my
intention, there is no thought in my head that is split or divided.
Garland (?) me with the Brightnesses and take me up [to the] house of
peace. The governors and rulers, — their
eyes looked upon me, they wondered and marvelled that the
Righteous belonged to a single Lord.[109]

---

107. The translations of these passages are from W. D. Stroker, *Extracanonical Sayings of Jesus* (SBLRBS 18; Atlanta: Scholars Press, 1989) 10-12, 157 (where the Greek texts may also be found). In the third quotation I have made changes to eliminate sexist language.

108. Translation from Stroker, *Extracanonical Sayings,* 105, 35.

109. Translation from Allberry, *Manichean Psalm-Book,* 222-23.

Secret Gospel of Mark

[Added after Mark 10:34:] And they come into Bethany. And a certain woman whose brother had died was there. And, coming, she prostrated herself before Jesus and says to him, "Son of David, have mercy on me." But the disciples rebuked her. And Jesus, being angered, went off with her into the garden where the tomb was, and straightway a great cry was heard from the tomb. And going near Jesus rolled away the stone from the door of the tomb. And straightway, going in where the youth was, he stretched forth his hand and raised him, seizing his hand. But the youth, looking upon him, loved him and began to beseech him that he might be with him. And going out of the tomb they came into the house of the youth, for he was rich. And after six days Jesus told him what to do and in the evening the youth comes to him, wearing a linen cloth over his naked body. And he remained with him that night, for Jesus taught him the mystery of the kingdom of God. And thence, arising, he returned to the other side of the Jordan.

[Added at Mark 10:46 after "And they came to Jericho":] And the sister of the youth whom Jesus loved and his mother and Salome were there, and Jesus did not receive them.[110]

110. The translations of these passages are from Smith, *Clement,* 447.

CHAPTER 8

The Women and the Resurrection:
The Credibility of Their Stories

They were women that wept when he
was going to the Cross, and women
that followed him from the Cross,
and that sat by his sepulchre when he
was buried. They were women that
was first with him at his resurrection
morn, and women that brought
tidings first to his disciples that he
was risen from the dead.[1]

1. Introduction

In the Gospel narratives the women disciples of Jesus are the first people to find the tomb of Jesus empty. Moreover, they are the only witnesses to the empty tomb who had seen Jesus buried and therefore could vouch for the fact that the empty tomb really was the tomb in which Jesus' body had been laid two days before. According to two of the Gospels, the women were also the first to meet the risen Lord. In relation to this prominence of the women in the Gospel resurrection narratives many argue that, since women's testimony in the ancient world, including especially Jewish Palestine, was widely regarded as unreliable

---

1. John Bunyan, *The Pilgrim's Progress* (ed. R. Sharrock; Harmondsworth: Penguin, 1965) 316.

and untrustworthy, this role of the women in the Easter events is unlikely to have been invented.[2] As "an apologetic legend" (Bultmann's phrase) a story thus featuring women would be poor apologetic.[3] This view is also commonly

2. E.g., E. L. Bode, *The First Easter Morning: The Gospel Accounts of the Women's Visit to the Tomb of Jesus* (AnBib 45; Rome: Biblical Institute Press, 1970) 157-58 (citing earlier scholars), 160-61, 173; G. O'Collins, *The Resurrection of Jesus Christ* (Valley Forge, Pa.: Judson, 1973) = *The Easter Jesus* (London: Darton, Longman & Todd, 1973) 42-43; P. Perkins, *Resurrection: New Testament Witness and Contemporary Reflection* (Garden City, N.Y.: Doubleday; London: Chapman, 1984) 94; W. J. Lunny, *The Sociology of the Resurrection* (London: SCM, 1989) 112; B. Gerhardsson, "Mark and the Female Witnesses," in H. Behrens, D. Loding, and M. T. Roth, eds., *Dumu-E₂-Dub-Ba-A* (A. W. Sjöberg FS; Occasional Papers of the Samuel Noah Kramer Fund 11; Philadelphia: University Museum, 1989) 218; S. T. Davis, *Risen Indeed: Making Sense of the Resurrection* (Grand Rapids: Eerdmans; London: SPCK, 1993) 182; S. Coakley, "Is the Resurrection a 'Historical' Event? Some Muddles and Mysteries," in P. Avis, ed., *The Resurrection of Jesus Christ* (London: Darton, Longman & Todd, 1993) 100; B. Hebblethwaite, "The Resurrection and the Incarnation," in Avis, ed., *Resurrection,* 158; T. Lorenzen, *Resurrection and Discipleship* (Maryknoll, N.Y.: Orbis, 1995) 171; W. L. Craig, "John Dominic Crossan on the Resurrection of Jesus," in S. T. Davis, D. Kendall, and G. O'Collins, eds., *The Resurrection* (New York: Oxford University Press, 1997) 259; A. J. M. Wedderburn, *Beyond Resurrection* (Peabody, Mass.: Hendrickson; London: SCM, 1999) 57-60; S. Byrskog, *Story as History — History as Story: The Gospel Tradition in the Context of Ancient Oral History* (WUNT 123; Tübingen: Mohr [Siebeck], 2000) 193-94. Serious attempts to refute this argument are surprisingly rare. J. M. G. Barclay, "The Resurrection in Contemporary New Testament Scholarship," in G. D'Costa, ed., *Resurrection Reconsidered* (Rockport, Mass./Oxford: Oneworld, 1996) 23, comments: "The prominence of the women is . . . not as strong an argument [for the historicity of the empty tomb] as it seems, since it could arise simply from literary necessity: if Mark was working from a source which had only women as witnesses of the burial of Jesus, only they could be responsible for discovering the tomb empty." But one would have to ask: Why should any source used by Mark have been at all interested in witnesses to the burial of Jesus, unless this were treated as preliminary to the discovery of the tomb empty? Moreover, the variation between Mark's lists of women at the burial (15:47) and at the empty tomb (16:1) must be taken into account (see below). For an even less adequate response to the argument, see G. Lüdemann, *The Resurrection of Jesus* (Minneapolis: Fortress; London: SCM, 1994) 116-17. It is sometimes argued (e.g., Lorenzen, *Resurrection,* 173; T. Williams, "The Trouble with the Resurrection," in C. Rowland and C. H. T. Fletcher-Louis, eds., *Understanding, Studying and Reading: New Testament Essays in Honour of John Ashton* [JSNTSup 153; Sheffield: Sheffield Academic Press, 1998] 233) that women had to be represented as those who found the tomb empty, because it was common knowledge that the male disciples had all fled to Galilee; but Wedderburn, *Beyond Resurrection,* 58-60, rightly responds that there is no convincing evidence that the male disciples were ever thought to have returned to Galilee immediately after Jesus' death. They would, in any case, not have traveled on the Sabbath.

3. R. Bultmann, *The History of the Synoptic Tradition* (tr. J. Marsh; 2d ed.; Oxford: Blackwell, 1968) 290; similarly M. Dibelius, *From Tradition to Gospel* (tr. B. L. Woolf; London: Nicholson and Watson, 1934) 190. Lüdemann, *Resurrection,* 118, concurs in this description of Mark 16:1-8.

used to explain the absence of the women from Paul's account of the Easter events, the earliest we have, in 1 Corinthians 15.[4] Hence the subtitle of this chapter: the credibility of their stories. This is deliberately ambiguous, since it could mean the credibility of their stories for people at the time or the credibility of their stories to us in the twenty-first century. Rather paradoxically but entirely logically, the argument I have cited finds in precisely the stories' lack of credibility then a reason for their credibility now. Since these narratives do not seem well designed to carry conviction at the time, they are likely to be historical, that is, believable by people with a historically critical mind-set today. It seems to me important to add one qualification to that expression of the argument. As often put, it suggests that the women's stories would not be judged especially reliable by people in the first century, when of course what is meant is: by *men* in the first century. It is not at all obvious that the role of the women would handicap these stories for female tellers or hearers, a consideration that is relevant not only because at least as many women as men, perhaps more women than men, were attracted to early Christianity, but also because the first tellers of these tales may well have been the four women whose names appear in them.

This rather traditional argument about the women in the resurrection narratives has been given a further twist in recent feminist approaches, which argue that not only does patriarchal prejudice against women account for their absence from Paul's account in 1 Corinthians 15, but even the Gospel narratives have reduced and played down the role of the women in the origins of Easter faith.[5] Again, the effect is to make the historical role of the women all the more credible. If even the evangelists who record these stories were not entirely comfortable with them and sought to reduce their implications, then it is all the more striking that they record them at all. The role of the women must have already been so well established in the tradition that no Gospel writer could simply suppress it. Often an aspect of this feminist argument is the claim that issues of power and authority are involved. Easter witness conferred authority in the church, and the

---

4. E.g., Gerhardsson, "Mark," 225-26; B. Witherington III, *Conflict and Community in Corinth* (Grand Rapids: Eerdmans; Carlisle: Paternoster, 1995) 300.

5. E. Schüssler Fiorenza, *Discipleship of Equals* (New York: Crossroad; London: SCM, 1993) 78; T. K. Seim, *The Double Message: Patterns of Gender in Luke-Acts* (Nashville: Abingdon; Edinburgh: T. & T. Clark, 1994) 147-63; C. Setzer, "Excellent Women: Female Witness to the Resurrection," *JBL* 116 (1997) 259-72; J. Lieu, "The Women's Resurrection Testimony," in S. Barton and G. Stanton, eds., *Resurrection* (L. Houlden FS; London: SPCK, 1994) 34-44; A. Fehribach, *The Women in the Life of the Bridegroom: A Feminist Historical-Literary Analysis of the Female Characters in the Fourth Gospel* (Collegeville, Minn.: Liturgical, 1998) 163-64; T. Mattila, "Naming the Nameless: Gender and Discipleship in Matthew's Passion Narrative," in D. Rhoads and K. Syreeni, eds., *Characterization in the Gospels* (JSNTSup 184; Sheffield: Sheffield Academic Press, 1999) 167-68; Wedderburn, *Beyond Resurrection*, 58; Byrskog, *Story,* 197.

downplaying of the women's witness reflects the suppression of the authority women exercised in the earliest Christian communities but had lost in the contexts in which the Gospels were written. The issue therefore moves from one merely about the reliability of women's stories to one more explicitly about hierarchy and power. In its strongest form it belongs to a feminist reconstruction of Christian origins that, in my view, has rightly highlighted the neglected evidence of women's leadership roles in earliest Christianity, but has also sometimes pushed its thesis to an unverifiably speculative extreme. But we should certainly agree that denigration of women's credibility, if and where it existed, was an aspect of a patriarchal social structure in which men were publicly dominant and could decide to rule women's testimony out of court. It is also worth bearing in mind the contention that this may not have been the case in the early Christian communities in which these stories of women were first told and transmitted.

The argument that the women's stories are credible now precisely because they would not have been then (at least to men) has not, of course, convinced everyone. A strong tradition, especially in German scholarship[6] and represented recently by Gerd Lüdemann in his book on the resurrection,[7] sees the story of the empty tomb as a late legend. Here the guiding principle is the priority of Paul, sometimes involving not only the fact that both the empty tomb and the women go unmentioned in Paul's summary of the kerygma in 1 Corinthians 15, but also the allegedly nonphysical character of Paul's understanding of resurrection, in comparison with which the need for the dead body of Jesus to disappear from the tomb can be seen as a crude apologetic and materialistic development postdating Paul.

This chapter is not the place to take up the latter aspect of that issue, but it will be useful at this point to highlight the issue of the relationship between kerygmatic summaries, of which 1 Corinthians 15:3-7 is one, and Gospel narratives, of which the stories of the women at the tomb and the appearance of Jesus to women are examples. These are, of course, different genres (whether oral or literary). Paul's kerygmatic summary consists of a list of events, with some theologically interpretative comments, from "Christ died for our sins" through "he was raised on the third day" to a catalogue of the various postresurrection appearances of Jesus. We know such kerygmatic summaries also from other sources, especially the sermons in Acts, where the summaries include also the ministry of Jesus and look forward to his future coming in judgment.

---

6. For the origin of this approach in the form-critical work of Dibelius and its influence, see J. E. Alsup, *The Post-Resurrection Appearance Stories of the Gospel Tradition* (CTM 5; Stuttgart: Calwer, 1975) 23-24.

7. Lüdemann, *Resurrection*, 121

The argument for Pauline priority to the detriment of the Gospel narratives of the women at the tomb asserts that the stories developed out of the kerygma. In Mark's story, for example, the words of the mysterious young man in the tomb to the women, "You are looking for Jesus of Nazareth, who was crucified. He has been raised" (Mark 16:6), are said to be the church's original kerygmatic proclamation about Jesus (he was crucified and raised) around which the story has been constructed. At least two arguments against this approach seem convincing. First, it is unclear why this argument applies to the resurrection narratives and not to the stories of Jesus' ministry. Few, if any, believe that first there were only summary statements about Jesus' ministry such as we find in the Acts sermons, for example, Jesus "went about doing good and healing all who were oppressed by the devil, for God was with him" (10:38), and that the stories about Jesus' healings and exorcisms we find in the Gospels developed, in that sense, out of the kerygma. If such stories were told about Jesus from the beginning, why should not the women's and others' stories of the resurrection also have been told from the beginning, alongside such kerygmatic summaries as Paul quotes in 1 Corinthians 15? We are dealing with two genres — individual stories about Jesus and kerygmatic summaries of the Gospel story as a whole — that coexisted in the early church, serving different functions. There is no reason to believe that any of the former developed out of the latter.[8]

But, second, to the thesis that resurrection narratives developed out of the kerygma there is one massive obstacle: Paul's list of appearances in 1 Corinthians 15 and the resurrection narratives in the Gospels are remarkably — and puzzlingly — ill-matched.[9] It is not only that the two stories about the women — their discovery of the empty tomb and Jesus' appearance to them — find no place in Paul's summary (and the same could be said of the appearance to the disciples on the way to Emmaus), but also that there are no stories in the Gospels corresponding to three of the five appearances Paul lists (leaving aside the appearance to himself): the appearances to Peter, to more than five hundred people at once, and to James. Even the other two in Paul's lists — appearances to the twelve and to all the apostles — are not easy to correlate with the appearances to the apostolic group narrated in the Gospels. If the stories originated from the kerygma, why do we not have a story of the appearance to Peter (merely mentioned by Luke) or of the appearance to James (we have such a story only in a fragment of the Gospel of the Hebrews) or of the appearance to the five hundred, which seems quite unlike anything at all in the Gospels? This rather extraordinary lack of correspondence between the kerygmatic summary Paul quotes and the resurrection

---

8. This is argued by Alsup, *Post-Resurrection*.

9. See Alsup, *Post-Resurrection*, 55-61.

narratives in the Gospels surely confirms that we are dealing with two fundamentally independent (not necessarily unrelated) forms in which the Easter events were transmitted probably from the very beginning of the church.

2. The Formation of the Gospel Resurrection Narratives

In this section, as a preliminary to looking closely at the role of the women in the narratives, I shall briefly indicate the way I believe the evangelists composed their narratives on the basis of oral traditions. The many attempts to trace the development of these traditions, prior to their incorporation in the Gospels, I find largely unconvincing, at best unverifiable. As I shall argue later in this chapter, there are reasons for thinking that in many cases these units of tradition reflect rather directly the oral testimony of those who had been eyewitnesses of the events.

(1) It seems likely that what the evangelists knew in the oral tradition were a number of discrete narrative units, with no stable connections between them. Table 5 (on p. 263) lists the units that can be postulated and where they have been used in the Gospels. (I include extracanonical Gospel texts, which, even if dependent on the canonical Gospels and relatively late, have considerable comparative value in exercises of this kind. In some cases they may be dependent on oral tradition independently of the canonical Gospels even if they also knew one or more of the canonical Gospels. For the resurrection narratives the most interesting of these extracanonical texts are the Longer Ending of Mark [Mark 16:9-20], which I follow the overwhelming majority of modern scholars in regarding as a later addition to the text of Mark's Gospel; the *Gospel of Peter*, whose surviving text breaks off at the beginning of the first and perhaps only resurrection appearance narrative it included;[10] and the early-second-century *Epistle of the Apostles* [*Epistula Apostolorum*].)[11]

---

10. We know a little more about this appearance narrative from the Syriac *Didascalia* 21 (R. H. Connolly, *Didascalia Apostolorum* [Oxford: Clarendon, 1929] 183; cf. lxxv-lxxvi), where the reference to Levi makes it virtually certain that the source is the *Gospel of Peter*. It is remarkable that J. D. Crossan, *The Cross that Spoke: The Origins of the Passion Narrative* (San Francisco: Harper & Row, 1988), chap. 10, discusses the last three extant verses of the *Gospel of Peter* without any reference to *Didascalia* 21, while Alsup, *Post-Resurrection*, 130-31, discusses *Didascalia* 21 without referring to the *Gospel of Peter*.

11. In the latest study, C. E. Hill, "The Epistula Apostolorum: An Asian Tract from the Time of Polycarp," *Journal of Early Christian Studies* 7 (1999) 1-53, argues for its origin in Asia Minor within the period 117-148 CE; but cf. J.-N. Pérès, "L'*Épître des Apôtres* et l'*Anaphore des Apôtres*: Quelques Convergences," *Apocrypha* 8 (1997) 89-96, arguing for an origin in east Syria.

Table 5: Narrative Units in the Oral Tradition

	Mark	Matt	Luke	John	Gos. Pet.	Ep. Apos.	LEMk	Others
Guards at the tomb		●		●				Gos. Naz.?
Women find tomb empty	●	○	●	●	○	○		
Men find tomb empty			●	●				
Appearance to women	(●)[1]	●		●		○	○	
Appearance to travelers			●				○	
Appearance to James								Gos. Heb., 1 Ap. Jas.
*Appearance to disciples Easter evening			●	●[2]		○	○	
*Appearance to disciples mountain in Galilee		●						
*Appearance to disciples fishing in Galilee				●	●			
*Appearance to disciples on Mount of Olives?[3]								Acts, Ap. Pet., Gnostic Gospels
*Ascension			●			○	●	Acts, Ap. Pet., Ap. Jas.

● = Cases where I judge the text is not dependent on an extant literary source, and so where direct dependence on oral tradition is likely.

○ = Cases where dependence on an extant literary source is likely. *The Epistle of the Apostles* and the Longer Ending of Mark seem to be retellings of the traditions that are dependent on the canonical Gospels but without immediate literary use of the texts of the canonical Gospels. (In the column "Others" no judgment on this issue is made.)

*Narratives to which an apostolic commissioning is usually attached.

1. I think it likely that Mark derived the commission to the women to tell the disciples (16:7) from a story of Jesus' appearance to the women that he has not related.

2. John has two such episodes, on Easter evening and a week later.

3. It is hard to tell whether this existed as a narrative unit distinct from the ascension.

That the evangelists knew resurrection traditions as discrete narrative units can be concluded from the fact that in no case are two of these narrative units linked in the same way by more than one evangelist. Each evangelist has selected and combined units of tradition in his own way to compose his own distinctive narrative sequence. For example, both Luke and John relate the two stories in which the tomb is found to be empty: once by the women, once by Peter (and, in John, the beloved disciple). But whereas Luke links the two stories in a simple sequence, John breaks up the first story, inserting the second within it, and fuses the end of the first story closely with a third: the appearance of Jesus to Mary Magdalene at the tomb. It is also worth noticing that, whereas the canonical evangelists link the narrative units together in a variety of ways, the *Gospel of Peter* simply narrates the three narrative units it contains one after the other, as discrete units without narrative connections. In this respect it may be closer to oral tradition than the canonical Gospels, not in the sense that it is independent of any of the canonical Gospels,[12] but in the sense that whatever dependence on the canonical Gospels it has has been mediated by an oral process in which the influence of textual sources has been absorbed into a continuing oral tradition with distinctively oral features.[13]

(2) On the other hand, there is a broadly common structure to the overall narrative design of the Gospel resurrection narratives. It is sometimes said that the resurrection narratives differ from the Gospel passion narratives in that the latter follow a broadly common sequence of events, whereas the former have no such common structure.[14] That this is untrue can be seen from table 6 (on p. 265). With the exception of Mark's Gospel, which in its probable original form ends with the discovery of the empty tomb, the canonical Gospels all have a

12. The relationship of the Gospel of Peter to the canonical Gospels is debated, but even Crossan, *Cross,* chap. 9, thinks the pericope of the women at the empty tomb (12:50–13:57) is dependent on Mark and was not part of the early "Cross Gospel" to which he assigns most of the *Gospel of Peter* and which he claims antedates the canonical Gospels. However, H. Koester, *Ancient Christian Gospels* (London: SCM; Philadelphia: Trinity Press International, 1990) 238-39, does think even this pericope may be dependent on Mark's source rather than on Mark.

13. This is the view of R. E. Brown, "The *Gospel of Peter* and Canonical Gospel Priority," *NTS* 33 (1987) 321-43; whereas A. Kirk, "Examining Priorities: Another Look at the *Gospel of Peter*'s Relationship to the New Testament Gospels," *NTS* 40 (1994) 572-95, sees rather a process of textual redaction comparable to the classic view of Matthew's and Luke's relationship to Mark. In my view, the *Gospel of Peter* shows signs of "re-oralization," on which see Byrskog, *Story,* 16, 127, 138-44.

14. J. Jeremias, *New Testament Theology: Part 1: The Proclamation of Jesus* (tr. J. Bowden; New York: Scribner; London: SCM, 1971) 300; quoted with approval by Lüdemann, *Resurrection,* 21. Of course, the passion narratives have a much longer sequence of events in common.

Table 6: The Narrative Structure Common to
the Gospel Resurrection Sequences

	Empty tomb (double witness)	An appearance	An appearance with apostolic commissioning
Matthew	Opening: guards Empty: women	Women (2)	11 in Galilee (mountain)
Luke	Empty: women Empty: men	Travelers (2)	11+ on Easter evening
John	Empty: women Empty: men	Woman (1)	10+ on Easter evening (11+ a week later) 7 in Galilee (fishing)
Gospel of Peter	Exit: guards Empty: women		3 in Galilee (fishing) (commissioning?)
Epistle of Apostles	Empty: women	Women (3)	11 (immediately)
Mark with Longer Ending	Empty: women	Woman (1) Travelers (2)	11 on Easter evening

threefold structure,[15] beginning with a twofold witness to the empty tomb (either by female and male disciples, or by the guards and the women disciples), and ending with an appearance in which the apostolic group receives from the risen Christ their commission to witness and to evangelize. Between the empty tomb and the appearance to the apostolic group just one appearance is narrated (to the women in Matthew and John, to the two travelers to Emmaus in Luke). This appearance story has in all cases the essential function — not its only, but an essential, function — of making the literary transition from the tomb to the disciples gathered when the risen Christ appears to them. This transitional function takes different forms in each Gospel, but in each case the middle element of the three is given a transitional function. Probably the author of the Longer Ending of Mark intended to bring the end of Mark into conformity with this common structure that he observed in the Gospels of Luke and John, but did so by including both transitional narratives: the one he knew in John and the one he knew in Luke.[16] That this threefold structure occurs in Matthew, Luke, and John,

15. This is also recognized, rather less precisely, by G. Theissen and A. Merz, *The Historical Jesus* (tr. J. Bowden; Minneapolis: Fortress; London: SCM, 1998) 495.

16. I am inclined to think the Longer Ending of Mark dependent on both Luke and John (so, e.g., Lüdemann, *Resurrection*, 26-27), but some think the parallels with one or both of these Gospels are due to dependence on oral tradition: e.g., B. H. Streeter, *The Four Gospels* (London:

independently of one another (in my view), presumably means that it was deployed in oral preaching. What the evangelists achieve in writing is the integration of the three elements into a sequential narrative whole. One should also notice that this threefold structure entails a certain economy of narration, which the evangelists seem deliberately to have chosen. In other words, they likely knew other oral traditions of resurrection appearances, but chose in each case just one for the transitional position, which had to be a story that could be told in such a way as to effect the transition. Matthew and Luke chose just one story for the concluding element of the apostolic commissioning, a different one in each case. John exceptionally extends the concluding element, adding a second appearance to the apostolic group in Jerusalem in order to accommodate his story of Thomas, and, allowing himself the luxury of an epilogue, includes what is in effect a second commissioning story in chapter 21.

(3) What then accounts for the differences among the Gospel resurrection narratives, so often considered problematic?[17] I suggest the following five factors:

(a) Each evangelist *selected narrative units* from the tradition, both for narratological reasons, because he wished to create an integrated sequence of such units, and also as guided by his own theological interests and aims.

(b) The evangelists are dependent on *varying oral forms* of the same narrative unit. Thus, for example, in the case of the story of women visiting the empty tomb, while Matthew is dependent on Mark, Luke and John in my view are each dependent on the oral form of this story that each knew.[18]

Macmillan, 1924; New York: Macmillan, 1925) 348-50 (dependence on Luke, but not on John); R. H. Smith, *Easter Gospels* (Minneapolis: Augsburg, 1983) 208 (dependence on neither Luke nor John). I am also inclined to think it was composed in the form we have it to serve as an appendix to Mark's Gospel, though it may reflect an expanded kerygmatic summary of the resurrection appearances, whereas many scholars think it existed as a discrete text before being added to Mark (e.g., W. L. Lane, *The Gospel of Mark* [NICNT; Grand Rapids: Eerdmans; London: Marshall, Morgan & Scott, 1974] 604).

17. For the differences in the narratives of the women at the empty tomb as problematic for the credibility of the stories, see recently U. Ranke-Heinemann, *Putting Away Childish Things* (tr. P. Heinegg; San Francisco: HarperSanFrancisco, 1994) 135-40; Williams, "Trouble," 221-22.

18. The degree of verbal resemblance between Luke 24:1-9 and Mark 16:1-8 is remarkably small and quite insufficient to show literary dependence. Just because we know that Luke knew and used Mark, it does not follow that he modeled his version of this particular narrative on Mark. The enterprise, which many scholars have undertaken, of understanding Luke's alleged redaction of Mark in this passage rests on a premise that is highly questionable. The discussion of this issue by R. J. Dillon, *From Eye-Witnesses to Ministers of the Word: Tradition and Composition in Luke 24* (AnBib 82; Rome: Biblical Institute Press, 1978) 1-8, simply begs the question.

Unless we think Luke dependent on John or vice versa, we cannot ascribe the presence of two angels in their stories, contrasted with Mark's and Matthew's one, to the evangelist's redaction in either case. Two angels must already have featured in the oral forms of the story known to Luke and John.

(c) Each evangelist had to connect the narrative units they selected and to integrate them into an *overall narrative sequence*. Beyond the broad threefold structure that Matthew, Luke, and John all share, as I have noted, each had to integrate the units into a whole in their own way. Significant differences among the Gospels result. As already noted, Luke and John tell rather different stories because they have combined the story of the women's visit to the empty tomb with the story of the men's visit to the empty tomb in different ways.

(d) Other *narratological reasons* should not be neglected. The evangelists are skilled storytellers who exercised the freedom necessary to storytellers if they are to communicate a story in an appealing and effective way. Comparisons between the Gospels have focused too often on theological reasons for their differences to the detriment of narratological reasons. It is possible, for example, that considerations of storytelling partly account for the fact that John tells the story of the women's discovery of the empty tomb and of Jesus' appearance to the women as the story of Mary Magdalene alone, while at the same time indicating that she was not alone when she speaks in the plural: "we do not know where they have laid him" (20:2). Focalization on a single character gives readers a more vivid sense of that character's personality and reactions and enables readers to enter the scene by sharing that character's individual perspective. The one-to-one encounter between Mary and the risen Jesus is emotionally charged and involving in a way that Matthew's story of Jesus' appearance to the two Marys cannot equal. This is not to say that there is not also a theological dimension to John's focus on the one Mary; as we shall see, there is such a dimension but one served by and coherent with this narratological aspect.

(e) Finally, the *specific theological concerns* of each evangelist, of course, guide their retellings of the story. We shall notice some of these in due course.

(3) Table 7 (on p. 268) analyzes the various forms of the two narrative units involving the women: their discovery of the empty tomb and the appearance of the risen Jesus to them. It provides a conspectus of the correspondences and divergences between the accounts that it may be useful for readers to consult during the discussion of each canonical Gospels' presentation of the role of the women in §§4-7 below.

Table 7: The Two Narrative Units about the Women

A. The women find the tomb empty

	Mark	Matt	Luke	John	Gos. Pet.	Ep. Apos.
very early on first day	•	•	•	•	•Lord's	
women go to tomb	•3	•2	•3+	•1(+)	•1+	•3
bring spices	•		•		(?)	•
find stone rolled away	•		•	•	•	•
angel rolls stone away		•			[•]	
*woman weeping					•	
women see angel(s)	•1	(•1)	•2	•2	•1	
angel(s) tells of resurrection	•	•	•		•	
*angel tells to tell disciples	•	•				
women tell no one	•					
*women tell disciples		(•)	•	•		
*disciples do not believe			•			

B. Jesus appears to the women/woman

	Matt	Luke	John	Gos. Pet.	Ep. Apos.	LEMk
Jesus appears to women	•2		•1		•3	•1
*women weeping			•		•	
nonrecognition to recognition			•			
holding him mentioned	•		•			
they worship	•					
*he tells them to tell disciples	•		•		•twice	
brothers	•		•		•your	
*women tell disciples					•twice	•
*disciples do not believe					•twice	•

*Motifs listed in both A and B.

3. The Credibility of Women

According to Luke 24:10-11, when the women returning from the tomb report to the apostles (i.e., the eleven) the message of the angels to the effect that Jesus has risen from the dead, "these words seemed to them to be nonsense, and they did not believe them" (24:11). The Longer Ending of Mark says the same of

Mary Magdalene's report that she has seen the risen Christ: the disciples "would not believe it" (16:11). The *Epistle of the Apostles,* in a free retelling of the stories unconstrained by its knowledge of the canonical narratives,[19] has Jesus send two of the women in turn to tell the eleven disciples that he has risen from the dead. Each time they fail to believe. "What have we to do with you, O woman? He that is dead and buried, can he then live?" they scornfully respond (*Ep. Apos.* 10). Do these accounts imply simply that the content of the message the women bring is incredible, or does the gender of the messengers compound the incredibility of their message? Are the men disinclined to take such reports seriously because they are brought to them by women? The texts themselves are not conclusive on this, though the words of the men in the *Epistle of the Apostles* — "What have we to do with you, O woman?" — seem a fairly strong hint that gender is not irrelevant here.

However, the picture is not uniform. Matthew's narrative, while not reporting the reception the women's message got, presumes that it was believed, since this is the only narratively available explanation for the fact that the male disciples do in fact obey Jesus' instruction to go to Galilee (28:16). We must also notice that the accounts make use of the same motif of unbelief when the messengers are male. The Longer Ending of Mark — contrary to Luke's narrative of the travelers to Emmaus (see 24:34-35) — says that the two travelers were not believed by the rest of the disciples when they reported that they had seen the Lord. John, who omits mention of the reaction of the male disciples when Mary Magdalene reports her encounter with Jesus to them, portrays Thomas as refusing to believe the report of the other male disciples (20:24-25). The issue of belief — even when the disciples are in the presence of Jesus himself (Matt 28:17; Luke 24:37-41; EpApp 11) — is a major theme of the resurrection narratives and is not confined to the role of the women in them.

But if gender is not the only aspect of this issue and therefore not to be exaggerated in dealing with these texts, the question remains whether gender is not nevertheless *an* aspect. Is the presumed cultural context of these narratives such that the reports of the women would be especially liable to disbelief? Most often this question has been answered with reference to the fact that, at least as a general rule,[20] women were not eligible to be witnesses in Jewish courts.[21]

---

19. The *Epistle of the Apostles* is undoubtedly dependent on the Gospels of Matthew, Luke, and John. Its lively and original version of the story of the women at the tomb is probably to be explained as an example of "re-oralization," in which the storytelling freedom of the oral tradition continued in the period when Gospel texts were used in a still predominantly oral context.

20. The Mishnah allows women to testify in certain cases: see R. G. Maccini, *Her Testimony Is True: Women as Witnesses according to John* (JSNTSup 125; Sheffield: Sheffield Academic

Since our stories are not set in law courts, this piece of halakah may be less relevant than the reason Josephus purports to give for it: "because of the levity and impetuosity of their sex" (*Ant.* 2.219).[22] This is, of course, a version of the common ancient prejudice that women are less rational than men, more easily swayed by emotion, more readily influenced, all too prone to jump to conclusions without thoughtful consideration.[23] While this did not result in a consistent male policy of disbelieving women, it is hard to believe it would not affect judgments of credibility especially when what the women were reporting would take some believing anyhow.[24]

In the case of the women's reports about the resurrection, the most relevant comparative evidence is more specific. There is a good deal of evidence that in the Greco-Roman world in general women were thought by educated men to be gullible in religious matters and especially prone to superstitious fantasy and excessive in religious practices.[25] Strabo, for example, points out

---

Press, 1996) 68; T. Ilan, *Jewish Women in Greco-Roman Palestine* (Peabody, Mass.: Hendrickson, 1996) 163-66. Maccini, *Her Testimony*, 66-70, 95-96, 228, too easily assumes that the Mishnah informs us as to the law in operation in the late Second Temple period, as does R. J. Karris, "Women and Discipleship in Luke," *CBQ* 56 (1994) 18-19. Ilan claims: "The rabbis . . . disqualified women as witnesses but the judicial system in Palestine of that period [the Greco-Roman period] did not operate to any extent according to the Pharisees and in fact often needed testimony from women" (227). "Often" is vague enough to be plausible, as well as compatible with Josephus's general statement, but we should note that Josephus is a good witness, not for Pharisaic halakah, but for the actual practice of Jewish courts.

21. E.g., M. Hengel, "Maria Magdalena und die Frauen als Zeugen," in O. Betz, M. Hengel, and P. Schmidt, eds., *Abraham Unser Vater* (O. Michel FS; Leiden: Brill, 1963) 246; Jeremias, *New Testament Theology,* 306; Gerhardsson, "Mark," 217-18, 225; Seim, *Double Message,* 156; Byrskog, *Story,* 73-75.

22. He adds that slaves are also disqualified as witnesses: "because of the baseness of their soul, since whether from cupidity or fear it is like[ly] that they will not attest the truth."

23. Cf., e.g., Philo, *Quaest. Gen.* 4.15. But it is worth noting that Jewish literature by no means always endorses this view: see 2 Macc 7:21; Jdt 8:29; *Bib. Ant.* 33:1; 40:4.

24. Maccini, *Her Testimony,* 77-82, 96, 228-29, tends to discount gender as a factor in disbelief of women whenever it is not explicit in the texts. This is too stringent a principle, since it overlooks the prevalence of gender prejudice that can be assumed without needing to be explicitly mentioned.

25. Juvenal, *Sat.* 6.511-91; Plutarch, *De Pyth.* 25 (*Mor.* 407C); Fronto *apud* Minucius Felix, *Octavius* 8-9; Clement of Alexandria, *Paed.* 34.28; Celsus *apud* Origen, *C. Cels.* 3.55; 2 Tim 3:6-7. Cf. also R. MacMullen, *Christianizing the Roman Empire* (A.D. *100-400)* (New Haven: Yale University Press, 1984) 39, 137n.33; R. Shepard Kraemer, *Her Share of the Blessing: Women's Religions among Pagans, Jews, and Christians in the Greco-Roman World* (New York/Oxford: Oxford University Press, 1992) 3, 211n.1; M. Y. MacDonald, "Early Christian women married to unbelievers," *SR* 19(1990) 229-31; M. Y. MacDonald, *Early Christian Women and Pagan Opinion: The Power of the Hysterical Woman* (Cambridge: Cambridge University Press, 1996) 109, 123-24.

that "in dealing with a crowd of women . . . a philosopher cannot influence them by reason or exhort them to reverence, piety and faith; nay, there is need of religious fear also, and this cannot be aroused without myths and marvels" (*Geog.* 1.2.8).

We are fortunate to have an example of this prejudice directed specifically against Mary Magdalene as an alleged witness to the resurrection by the second-century pagan intellectual despiser of Christianity, Celsus: "after death he rose again and showed the marks of his punishment and how his hands had been pierced. But who saw this? A hysterical female, as you say, and perhaps some other one[26] of those who were deluded by the same sorcery" (*apud* Origen, *C. Cels.* 2.55).[27] Even allowing for Celsus's polemical intent in focusing on a female witness of the resurrection, it is notable that the appearance to Mary Magdalene was sufficiently prominent in what Celsus knew of the Christian claim about the resurrection of Jesus for him to be able to take it up in this way. There can hardly be any doubt that the gender of the "hysterical" or "crazed"[28] woman is important to Celsus's sneering polemic.

But what of the Jewish cultural-religious context in which the stories of the women at the tomb must first have been told? For this we can turn to some evidence that, so far as I know, has not been previously noticed in connection with the Gospel narratives.[29] It comes from Pseudo-Philo's *Biblical Antiquities*, which is still surprisingly neglected as evidence of Palestinian Judaism in the New Testament period. Pseudo-Philo's work gives remarkable prominence and significant roles in the history of Israel to women. On two occasions he (I use masculine pronouns for the author with caution, for this is a case where a female author certainly cannot be excluded)[30] portrays biblical women receiving

---

26. This term is masculine (τις ἄλλος).

27. Translation from H. Chadwick, *Origen: Contra Celsum* (2d ed.; Cambridge: Cambridge University Press, 1965) 109. Celsus attributes this passage to a Jew whom Origen considers an invented figure. For the view that Celsus himself, unlike his Jew, did not make anything of the gender of the first witness to the resurrection, see G. Stanton, "Early Objections to the Resurrection of Jesus," in Barton and Stanton, eds., *Resurrection*, 81. G. W. Bowersock, *Fiction as History: Nero to Julian* (Berkeley: University of California Press, 1994) chap. 5, describes the cultural background (such as apparent deaths and "resurrections" in the Greek novels) against which Celsus would have judged the report of Jesus' resurrection. He suggests that the popularity of the theme of resurrection at this period was due to the influence of the Christian message. But the issue of the credibility of women is not treated.

28. On the word πάροιστρος see MacDonald, *Early Christian Women*, 2-3 and n. 7.

29. C. S. Keener, *A Commentary on the Gospel of Matthew* (Grand Rapids: Eerdmans, 1999) 699, has a reference to *Bib. Ant.* 9:10, but does not consider its implications.

30. This is also the verdict of P. W. van der Horst, "Portraits of Biblical Women in Pseudo-Philo's *Liber Antiquitatum Biblicarum*," in van der Horst, *Essays on the Jewish World of*

and communicating revelation from God that is not believed by those for whom it is intended. In one case (*Bib. Ant.* 9:10), the woman is Moses' sister Miriam, whom the Bible calls a prophet (Exod 15:20) and to whom, as a young girl before the birth of her brother, Pseudo-Philo attributes a prophetic dream. It is one of his many elaborations on the biblical story:

> The spirit of God came upon Miriam one night, and she saw a dream and reported it to her parents in the morning, saying, "I had a vision this night, and behold a man was standing in a linen garment and he said to me, 'Go and say to your parents, "Behold the child who will be born of you will be cast forth into the water; likewise through him the water will be dried up. And I will work signs through him and save my people, and he will exercise leadership always."'" When Miriam reported her dream, her parents did not believe her.[31]

The parallel to the story of the women at the tomb is striking, though it is Mark and Matthew who have the command of the angel, "Go and tell," and Luke who reports that they were not believed. What is striking about Pseudo-Philo's account is that Miriam's parents are the righteous couple Amram and Jochebed. Amram has been portrayed as a man of great faith and faithfulness to God, approved by God. There does not seem to be any strong reason in the plot for their failure to believe their daughter's prophetic dream. It seems as though Pseudo-Philo sees their unbelief as the expected reaction, even by such admirable characters as Amram and Jochebed, to a claim by a woman to have received divine revelation. Yet there is no doubt that Pseudo-Philo portrays the revelation given to Miriam as authentic (at the end of the chapter he points out that it was fulfilled: 9:16) and readers are surely therefore entitled to think that Amram and Jochebed should have believed it.

Indirect confirmation of this understanding of the story is provided by the striking parallel and contrast in Josephus, who also records a dream predicting that Amram and Jochebed's child would deliver Israel. In this case, however, the dream is Amram's; it is Amram who then tells his wife about it; and they believe the promises of God (*Ant.* 2.210-18). Here the revelation is given by God to a man and there is no problem of belief. Whether Josephus knew the

---

Early Christianity (NTOA 14; Freiburg: Universitätsverlag; Göttingen: Vandenhoeck & Ruprecht, 1990) 122. The best case for female authorship of *Biblical Antiquities* is made by M. T. DesCamp, "Why Are These Women Here? An Examination of the Sociological Setting of Pseudo-Philo Through Comparative Reading," *JSP* 16 (1997) 53-80.

31. Translation from H. Jacobson, *A Commentary on Pseudo-Philo's Liber Antiquitatum Biblicarum*, vol. 1 (AGAJU 31; Leiden: Brill, 1996) 105.

tradition about Miriam's dream and corrected it,[32] or Pseudo-Philo knew the tradition Josephus records and transformed it, we cannot be sure. Josephus was certainly capable of correcting even a biblical text portraying revelation given directly to a woman. Whereas in Genesis Rebekah inquires of the Lord about her unborn children and receives a prophetic oracle about them (Gen 25:22-23), in Josephus it is her husband Isaac who prays and receives the prophecy from God (*Ant.* 1.257). Josephus does not consistently remove every case of God speaking directly to or through a woman that he found in his Scriptures, but he does seem to minimize them,[33] and largely restricts them to a few women whom the Bible calls prophets, such as Deborah (*Ant.* 5.200-209) and Huldah (*Ant.* 10.59-61), but not including Miriam, whom the Bible (Exod 15:20) but not Josephus calls a prophet.[34] It looks as though Josephus represents an opinion that was disinclined to believe that God communicates revelation directly to women and that Pseudo-Philo was concerned to counter this notion.

The second instance in Pseudo-Philo's work (*Bib. Ant.* 42:1-5) of this motif of revelation disbelieved when reported by a woman comes in his retelling of the biblical story of the birth of Samson. In Pseudo-Philo's version, Samson's parents Manoah and Eluma (as Pseudo-Philo calls Manoah's wife) quarrel over which of them is to blame for her childlessness. Eluma prays that this will be revealed to her. So God sends an angel to tell her that she is the sterile one, but that God will give her a son, Samson, who will be a Nazirite and deliver Israel from the Philistines. Thus, as in Judges, it is Samson's mother who is told about the coming birth by an angel, and she reports what the angel said to her husband Manoah:

32. This possibility is perhaps supported by the fact that *b. Soṭ.* 11b, 12b-13a, reports a prophecy (not a dream) by Miriam about Moses as the future savior of Israel.

33. In Josephus's retelling of the story of Manoah and his wife (*Ant.* 5.276-81) the theme of revelation is subordinated to the picture of Manoah as a jealously suspicious husband of a remarkably beautiful wife. Compare Pseudo-Philo's version discussed below.

34. B. Halpern Amaru, "Portraits of Biblical Women in Josephus' *Antiquities,*" *JJS* 39 (1988) 147, points out that Josephus omits the exchange between Sarah and God in Gen 18:15 (*Ant.* 1.213), which *Genesis Rabbah* considers the only occasion on which God "found it necessary to enter into a conversation with a woman" (20:6; 45:10; 48:20; 63:7). (*Genesis Rabbah* is distinguishing between God speaking to a woman and God holding a coversation with a woman, which happens in the Bible only in Gen 18:15.) But Josephus's motive here, if not simple abbreviation, may well have been to avoid putting Sarah in a negative light. For instances in Second Temple Jewish literature of biblical women portrayed as recipients of revelation, see R. D. Chesnutt, "Revelatory Experiences Attributed to Biblical Women in Early Jewish Literature," in A.-J. Levine, ed., *"Women Like This": New Perspectives on Jewish Women in the Greco-Roman World* (SBLEJIL 01; Atlanta: Scholars Press, 1991) 107-25; his main examples are Rebekah in Jubilees, Aseneth in Joseph and Aseneth, and Job's daughters in the Testament of Job.

She came to the house to her husband and said to him, "Behold, I put my hand over my mouth, and I will be silent before you always because I boasted in vain and did not believe your words. For the angel of the Lord came to me today and informed me, saying, 'Eluma, you are sterile, but you will conceive and bear a son.'" Manoah did not believe his wife, and being confused and sad he himself also went to the upper chamber and prayed and said, "Behold, am I not worthy to hear the signs and wonders that God has done among us or to see the face of his messenger?" (*Bib. Ant.* 42:4-5)[35]

Manoah's reaction to Eluma's report — he "did not believe his wife" — is neither explicit in nor a necessary deduction from the biblical text. It reveals again Pseudo-Philo's expectation that this is how a woman's claim to have received divine revelation is likely to be received. In Pseudo-Philo, as in the Bible, Manoah then prays, but Pseudo-Philo rewrites his prayer. What Manoah finds hard to believe is that the revelation should have been made to his wife rather than to him, the man. The way the story continues is a clear rebuke to this patriarchal prejudice: God does deem Manoah worthy to hear God's voice, but it is to his wife that the angel returns and it is she whom the angel sends to summon her husband (42:6-7). Pseudo-Philo is surely using the story to counter a prevalent belief that it is men with whom God communicates directly and revelation comes to women only through the mediation of men. He highlights a biblical case in which a revelation rather pointedly comes to a woman and only to her husband through her.

In the much later Jewish exegesis of the same story preserved in *Numbers Rabbah* we find a similar interpretation (which is therefore probably evidence of a common exegetical tradition). It is similar but not precisely the same as Pseudo-Philo's. The passage is a comment on Judges 13:12-13, where Manoah asks the angel, "Now when your words come true, what is to be the boy's rule of life; what is he to do?" and receives the response, "Let the woman give heed to all that I said to her":

And Manoah said: Now let thy word come. Manoah said to him: "Until now, what I have heard was from a woman, and women are not qualified to give directions nor are their words to be relied upon, *But now let thy word come;* I wish to hear from your own mouth, because I do not rely upon her words; she may have changed something while speaking, or omitted or added something. . . . *And the angel of the Lord said unto Manoah: Of all that I said*

35. Translation from Jacobson, *Commentary,* 163. Other translators do not read Manoah's prayer as a question, but I think he may well be right to do so.

unto the woman. This he said in order to show honour to the woman and to endear her to him. (*Num. Rab.* 10:5)[36]

Here Manoah is explicit about his reasons for not believing his wife: women's words are not to be relied on ("she may have changed something while speaking, or omitted or added something"). This is the usual prejudice against women's rational capacities. It may also be operative, though unstated, in Pseudo-Philo. It may explain why women are not thought suitable recipients and communicators of revelation. But the special value of the two examples from Pseudo-Philo is that they point to the importance of the issue of receiving revelation, which is exactly what is at stake in the resurrection narratives. That women should have been given the message of the resurrection runs up against an assumption of male priority in God's dealings with his people. It is an assumption Pseudo-Philo seems eager to counter throughout his work,[37] in part by portraying female counterparts to key male figures in the biblical history: Jephthah's daughter becomes a second Isaac,[38] Deborah a second Moses.

In this light we can see that, if there is a problem in their Jewish context about the role of the women in the resurrection narratives, it may be not so much their supposed unreliability as witnesses or their susceptibility to delusion in religious matters, but something even dearer to patriarchal religious assumptions: the priority of men in God's dealings with the world. In these stories women are given priority by God as recipients of revelation and thereby the role of mediators of that revelation to men. Is this not part of the eschatological reversal of status, in which God makes the last first and the first last, so that no one might boast before God?[39] In this light too we can well understand why Peter, in Luke's narrative, does not believe the women but nevertheless hurries at once to the tomb to see for himself, just as Manoah does not believe his wife's claimed revelation but very much wants to receive the same revelation himself.

36. Translation from J. J. Slotki, *Midrash Rabbah: Numbers*, vol. 1 (London: Soncino, 1939) 366.

37. Other instances in Pseudo-Philo of revelation to and through women are Melcha's prophecy about Abraham (*Bib. Ant.* 4:11) and Deborah's prophetic and teaching ministry (30; 32:14-15). C. A. Brown, *No Longer Be Silent: First Century Jewish Portraits of Biblical Women* (Louisville: Westminster/John Knox, 1992) 218, thinks Pseudo-Philo also portrays Jephthah's daughter and Hannah as recipients of divine revelation.

38. Cf. F. J. Murphy, *Pseudo-Philo: Rewriting the Bible* (New York/Oxford: Oxford University Press, 1993) 166-67.

39. B. Witherington III, *Women in the Earliest Churches* (SNTSMS 59; Cambridge: Cambridge University Press, 1988) 165, asks this question of Mark's narrative of the women at the tomb.

It seems not accidental that, among the canonical evangelists, it is Luke who parallels the motif we have observed in Pseudo-Philo.[40] Female recipients of revelation should not come as a surprise to readers of Luke's Gospel: all three women in his strongly gynocentric birth and infancy narratives are such.[41] Rather comparable to Pseudo-Philo's paralleling of women and men is Luke's oft-noted tendency to pair male and female characters or stories about them.[42] In Luke's resurrection narrative the reaction of the apostles to the women's report from the tomb functions similarly to the comparable motif in Pseudo-Philo: it counters the male prejudice about revelation to women. There is no doubt that the apostles ought to have believed the women.[43] When the travelers to Emmaus report what the women had said and imply that, though right about the empty tomb, they were evidently wrong about the risen Christ, since the men had not seen him (Luke 24:22-24), the incognito Jesus retorts: "O how foolish you are, and how slow of heart to believe all that the prophets have declared!" (24:25). Yet does not Luke's resurrection narrative in fact minimize the role of the women? They are the first to be told that Jesus is risen, but they are

40. A later occurrence of the motif is in the Gnostic *Gospel of Mary* 17:16-22, where Peter cannot believe that Jesus would have given revelation privately to a woman (Mary Magdalene) rather than to the male disciples.

41. See chaps. 3–4 above, and note the references to Pseudo-Philo in chap. 3.

42. The most recent discussion is Seim, *Double Message*, chap. 2.

43. It is remarkable that some feminist critics take the motif of the male disciples disbelieving the women, in Luke and the *Epistle of the Apostles*, as a denigration of the women's witness by these authors: Setzer, "Excellent Women," 265-66; B. E. Reid, *Choosing the Better Part: Women in the Gospel of Luke* (Collegeville, Minn.: Liturgical, 1996) 201-2. It is perfectly clear in both cases that the women's report is true and authorized by God and that the male disciples are at fault in not believing it. In relation to Luke, Seim, *Double Message*, 156-63, sees this clearly but in a quite contradictory way fails to follow it through. Against E. Schüssler Fiorenza's reading of Luke 24:11 as Luke's disqualification of the women as witnesses, see S. Barton, "The Hermeneutics of the Gospel Resurrection Narratives," in Barton and Stanton, eds., *Resurrection*, 45-48, concluding: "There are grounds for thinking . . . that an adequate understanding of the resurrection is not best served by the method Fiorenza has adopted, and that feminist interests themselves may not be best served by this approach either. . . . The weakness of her approach is that the interests her interpretation is trying to serve lead to a very partial and tendentious reading of the tradition. It is as if the search for largely hidden androcentric forces assumed to lie beneath the surface of Luke's narrative take the place of attending in an open and sympathetic way to what lies on the surface" (47-48). But this feminist interpretation of Luke 24:11 seems to build on prefeminist scholarship. For example, R. H. Fuller, *The Formation of the Resurrection Narratives* (New York: Macmillan, 1971; London: SPCK, 1972) 100-101, claims that the apostles' nonbelief "is intended to preserve the independence of the apostolic witness: apostles cannot come to faith as a result of the testimony of third parties. They must see and believe for themselves in order that they can provide first-hand witness." But there is no reason at all why they should not believe the women and then also see for themselves, as they do in Matthew.

not the first to see him. Does not their mediation of revelation to the men turn out to be of no permanent significance, since it is soon replaced by the risen Lord's appearances to the men and his commissioning of the men to be his witnesses in the world?[44] We must now turn to this broader question that can be put to all the Gospels in somewhat different ways: Is the role of the women not minimized by the way the evangelists incorporate it into their larger narrative of resurrection appearances?

4. The Women in Matthew

In looking more closely at the role of the women in each Gospel, we need to recall the threefold narrative structure that, as we have seen, is common to Matthew, Luke, and John. In this structure the first and third units are stable — the empty tomb and an appearance story featuring apostolic commissioning — while the second varies. In the first unit the role of the women is evidently essential. For Matthew and Luke, as also for Mark, the women have a unique qualification as witnesses to the empty tomb: they were also present at the cross when Jesus died and at the tomb when his body was laid in it. They know both that Jesus was dead when laid in the tomb and that the tomb in which he was buried was the same tomb they found empty on Easter Sunday morning. The guards in Matthew's story presumably also know this, but, since Matthew provides no indication that their story became known to anyone except the Jewish authorities, they do not function as witnesses in the way that the women do. The women's witness to the empty tomb and the angelic message was and therefore also remains uniquely theirs. No other visitor to the tomb, not even a male disciple, could reproduce it. Hence the Gospel stories of the empty tomb perpetuate the women's witness: all readers of them are confronted with *their* distinctive witness. And, while the empty tomb is of a different order from the appearances of the risen Christ himself, the place that all the Gospels give to it attributes considerable significance to it.

The second unit in the threefold structure is, I suggested, always transitional in the literary sense that it connects the empty tomb with the apostolic group to whom the risen Lord appears in order to commission them. In Matthew, the women, meeting Jesus on their way from the tomb, are instructed by him to tell the male disciples to go to Galilee, where they will see him. The as-

---

44. Cf. Seim, *Double Message,* 159 ("the tradition guaranteed by the women runs out into the sand"); P. Perkins, "'I Have Seen the Lord' (John 20:18): Women Witnesses to the Resurrection," *Int* 46 (1992) 33, 38.

sumption implicit in the narrative is that the women's message is delivered to the eleven, believed, and obeyed. This is how the eleven come to the mountain in Galilee where Jesus appears to them. The question we must consider is whether this transitional placing of the appearance to the women limits its significance to a mere preliminary to the appearance to the eleven men. I will make three comments.

First, the parallel provided by Pseudo-Philo's story of Eluma and Manoah is instructive. There the male assumption that revelation should come to men and be transmitted by them to women is overturned by a reverse process in which the woman is given the revelation to share with the man. The man himself does then meet the angel of the Lord, but only when the woman to whom the angel has appeared calls him. This ensures that, when he himself meets the angel, he cannot discount the woman's role and lapse into his normal assumption of male privilege. Similarly, in Matthew, both the two women and the eleven men see the Lord, but the experience of the women is not only chronologically prior but also indispensable for the men's experience. Only because the men believe and obey the revelation brought them by the women can they themselves see the Lord. The women's priority is really a kind of positive discrimination that, by reversing the normally expected priority of one gender over the other, has the effect of ruling gender privilege out of the new order the resurrection appearances constitute.

Second, the two women in Matthew, like Mary Magdalene in John, model the proper response of the disciple to the risen Lord. They acknowledge who he is by worshiping him, as the eleven then also do (Matt 28:9, 17). This is not an incidental detail, but in Matthew's rather spare narratives of the two appearances a prominent feature: it climaxes the Matthean theme of the worship of Jesus[45] that began with the magi in 2:11.[46]

But third, what is implied by Jesus' command to the women to go and tell the disciples (28:10), a command they have already received from the angel at the tomb (28:7)? Is this a command whose significance is exhausted when they have delivered the message to the eleven, leaving the women, and for that matter all other male disciples, out of the commission to make disciples of all nations with which Jesus charges the eleven (28:18-20)? Matthew surely does depict a special role for the eleven, but we need not conclude that the women's

45. Matthew uses προσκυνεῖν in a semitechnical way for the divine worship (rather than mere respect for a human superior) that is due Jesus and emphasizes that it expresses the proper response to Jesus. For the evidence, see R. Bauckham, "Jesus, Worship of," *ABD* 3:813.

46. It is therefore not correct to say that, in Matthew's resurrection narratives, "The identity of the risen one is not a concern" (E. M. Wainwright, *Shall We Look for Another? A Feminist Rereading of the Matthean Jesus* [Maryknoll, N.Y.: Orbis, 1998] 115).

resurrection witness is therefore merely a transitional, completed, and superseded role.[47] We have already noticed that the women's witness to the empty tomb undoubtedly continues, and the same must be said of their witness to the living Jesus himself. The command to "go and tell," given on both occasions, surely overreaches its immediate narrative applicability. It is inconceivable that the women would have stopped telling all who were subsequently willing to hear them. Thus their witness is not replaced by that of the eleven, but has its own continuing validity.

5. The Women in Luke

As far as Luke's account of the empty tomb goes, we have already noticed that, by means of his statement that the apostles did not believe the women, he makes explicit the rebuke to assumptions of male priority that the revelation given first to the women entails. The point is rubbed in when the two travelers to Emmaus repeat the story of the women (Luke 24:22-23) to the stranger who consequently rebukes them for their unbelief (24:25). We should note that Peter's visit to the empty tomb,[48] while it adds some confirmation to their report, cannot replace the women's witness, since only they knew which tomb was Jesus' (Peter must rely on them for this) and only they receive the angels' interpretation of the absence of Jesus from it (Peter's amazement [24:12] is not belief that Jesus has risen, as the words of the travelers [24:21-24] make clear).

The second unit of the threefold structure in Luke is the appearance to the two travelers. It performs the necessary transitional function in that Cleopas and his companion retell the story of the empty tomb and, having recognized the Lord, then travel back to Jerusalem to rejoin the group of disciples to whom the Lord then appears and whom he then commissions. Luke probably chose this story as his transitional one because it enabled him to develop the theme of the interpretation of prophetic Scriptures that is his own distinctive contribution to the themes of the resurrection narratives. But he therefore deprives the women of the privilege of being first to meet the risen Lord. On that subject, I must first dismiss a consideration that is frequently brought to bear on it but proves to be a scholarly red herring. This is the view that competition for authority in the early church took the form of rival claims to the first resur-

---

47. Contra Witherington, *Women in the Earliest Churches,* 174.

48. Most scholars now accept that 24:12 belongs to the original text of Luke, though R. Mahoney, *Two Disciples at the Tomb: The Background and Message of John 20.1-10* (Theologie und Wirklichkeit 6; Frankfurt: P. Lang; Bern: H. Lang, 1974) chap. 2, argues at length against its originality.

rection appearance.[49] All the evidence of the Gospels is decisively against this view. If it were the case, why does the strongly Petrine Gospel of Matthew, with its depiction of Peter as the rock on which the church will be built, attribute the first resurrection appearance to the women and make no mention of the appearance to Peter individually, of which we learn from Luke and Paul? If Luke were concerned to displace the women from their privileged position for this reason, why does he leave it entirely unclear whether the first resurrection appearance was to Peter or to the travelers to Emmaus?[50] Finally, why is it that John, who does indeed recount the Lord's commission to Peter to be the chief undershepherd of his flock, includes this in the story of the fourth resurrection appearance he narrates?[51] The suggestion that he downgrades Peter's commission by thus positioning it is quite implausible by comparison with the much more obvious conclusion that he gives it emphasis, along with the different role of the beloved disciple, by placing it in the epilogue to his Gospel, whose function is to preview the coming history of the church. I see no evidence that chronological priority in the resurrection appearances was thought, in itself, to confer special authority in the early church.[52]

49. G. W. Trompf, "The First Resurrection Appearance and the Ending of Mark's Gospel," *NTS* 18 (1971-72) 313, 325-27; E. Schüssler Fiorenza, *In Memory of Her* (New York: Crossroad; London: SCM, 1983) 51, 332; F. Bovon, "Le Privilège Pascal de Marie-Madeleine," *NTS* 30 (1984) 51-52; C. Osiek, "The Women at the Tomb: What Are They Doing There?" *Ex Auditu* 9 (1993) 105-6; J. D. Crossan, *Who Killed Jesus?* (San Francisco: HarperSanFrancisco, 1995) 207; Seim, *Double Message,* 159; S. Schneiders, "John 20.11-18: The Encounter of the Easter Jesus with Mary Magdalene — A Transformative Feminist Reading," in F. F. Segovia, ed., *"What Is John?": Readers and Readings of the Fourth Gospel* (Atlanta: Scholars Press, 1996) 160-61. The argument of G. O'Collins and D. Kendall, "Mary Magdalene as Major Witness to Jesus' Resurrection," *TS* 48 (1987) 631-46, is in part aimed against the view that Mary Magdalene's witness was seen as competitive with other resurrection appearance traditions.

50. Many commentators, probably influenced by 1 Cor 15:5, seem to think it obvious that the appearance to Peter was the first. Fuller, *Formation,* 112, even thinks Luke inserted the reference to Peter "because he does not agree with the impression created by his source that the Emmaus appearance was the primary one." If so, he made a poor job of correcting that impression. Why should not the appearance to Peter have occurred while the two travelers were on their way back from Emmaus to Jerusalem?

51. R. E. Brown, "John 21 and the First Appearance of the Risen Jesus to Peter," in E. Dhanis, ed., *Resurrexit* (Vatican City: Libreria Editrice Vaticana, 1974) 246-61, argues that John 21 incorporates a tradition of the first resurrection appearance to Peter, displaced because this chapter was added to the Gospel by a later redactor who wished to preserve Johannine fragments that had not been incorporated in the Gospel. I think John 21 is an epilogue that belongs integrally to the design of the Gospel.

52. The altercations between Peter and Mary Magdalene in *Gos. Thom.* 114 and *Gos. Mary* 17:7–18:21 make no reference to the issue of priority in resurrection appearances, nor do the references to Mary Magdalene in Gnostic writings, catalogued by Bovon, "Privilège," 53-56 (and

What then is the effect of Luke's omission of the appearance to the women (a question we can ask without presuming to know whether Luke knew that story)? His telling and retelling of the story of the women at the tomb has already sufficiently countered the assumption of male priority. This enables Luke (unlike Matthew) to include the women, without having to single them out for special mention, in the third element of the threefold structure of his narrative, that is, the group of disciples whom Jesus commissions as witnesses. That the women are present in this scene often goes unnoticed because too little attention is paid to Luke's generally inclusive picture of the large group of Jesus' disciples,[53] which is different from Mark's and Matthew's greater concentration on the twelve (with the addition of the women at a late stage). It is Luke who has Jesus send out the seventy as well as the twelve (with no indication that the seventy were all men). Both in Galilee and when he enters Jerusalem, Luke's Jesus is accompanied by a large number of disciples: "a great crowd of his disciples" (6:17: ὄχλος πολὺς μαθητῶν αὐτοῦ), "the whole multitude of the disciples" (19:37: ἅπαν τὸ πλῆθος τῶν μαθητῶν). When Luke, alone of the evangelists, in the context of the Galilean ministry refers to the women who accompanied Jesus during his Galilean ministry and names some of them (8:2-3), the effect of adding these to a mention of the twelve (8:1) is not, as some feminist exegetes complain, to make the women a group alongside the disciples, who are all male, or to subordinate them to the twelve, but to single out the twelve and the women as two notable groups within the larger body that Luke calls Jesus' disciples.[54] This is clear from the larger context in the Gospel. It is also confirmed by Luke 24:6, where the angels at the tomb tell the women to remember how Jesus told *them*, while he was still in Galilee, that he would die and rise again. Although the words of the passion prediction here are closest to 18:32-33, the fullest of the three passion predictions in Luke, which was spoken to the twelve (18:31), this prediction was not given in Galilee. The angels' reference must therefore be to 9:22 and/or 9:44, spoken to "the/his disciples" (9:18, 43). The women must be included in that term.

The large crowd of Jesus' disciples who hail him as the Messiah at the triumphal entry (19:37) had either traveled with him to Jerusalem (cf. 23:49) or ar-

---

see chap. 7 above). These references are interesting in the regard for this disciple and her symbolic value for Gnostic groups, but they do not demonstrate that this was linked to controversy about whether the resurrection appearance to her preceded that to Peter.

53. For the literature on this topic, see Karris, "Women," 10-12. I leave aside here the debated issue of whether the women are present at the last supper as Luke depicts it.

54. I differ from C. Ricci, *Mary Magdalene and Many Others* (tr. P. Burns; Minneapolis: Fortress, 1994) 50-61, who thinks that both the twelve and the women are distinguished from those Luke calls "his/the disciples," and that the twelve and the women are closer to Jesus than the disciples.

rived independently for the Passover. They must comprise most of those who, according to Acts, made up the body of about a hundred and twenty "brothers" prior to Pentecost (Acts 1:15). At the cross, although the twelve had fled, the spectators include the larger body of Jesus' disciples, called here "his acquaintances" for the sake of the echo of prophecy (Ps 38:11 [MT 12]; 88:8 [MT 9]): "all his acquaintances . . . *and* the women who had followed him from Galilee" (Luke 24:29: πάντες οἱ γνωστοὶ . . . καὶ γυναῖκες αἱ συνακολουθοῦσαι αὐτῷ ἀπὸ τῆς Γαλιλαίας). The "and" here means "including": the women are not mentioned as an afterthought, but singled out for special mention because they now become principal actors in the two narratives that follow: Jesus' burial and the discovery of the empty tomb.

Luke's resurrection narratives refer to the disciples in such a way as to make clear that not only the eleven but a larger group are in view, and also that the women belong to this larger group. When the women return from the tomb they report "to the eleven and all the rest" (24:9: τοῖς ἕνδεκα καὶ πᾶσιν τοῖς λοιποῖς).[55] The travelers to Emmaus, not members of the eleven, are called literally "two from them" (24:13: δύο ἐξ αὐτῶν), that is, "two of their company," and the travelers themselves refer to the women with an exactly parallel expression: literally "some women from us" (24:22: γυναῖκές τινες ἐξ ἡμῶν),[56] that is, "some women of our company." So when the travelers return to Jerusalem and find "the eleven and those with them gathered together" (24:33: τοὺς ἕνδεκα καὶ τοὺς σὺν αὐτοῖς), readers must surely assume that the women are included.[57] In

55. In v 10 the recipients of the women's message become "the apostles" (in Luke's terminology, the eleven), perhaps in order to heighten the effect of their refusal to believe the women (v 11). Not only as men but also as apostles, they assume that such a revelation should have been given to them, not to the women.

56. The omission of ἐξ ἡμῶν in D may be tendentious: the scribe wished to distance the women from the group of male disciples.

57. Scholars who recognize this include Dillon, *From Eye-Witnesses*, 8-9, 53-55, 291; Perkins, *Resurrection*, 167; Karris, "Women," 17; J. B. Green, *The Gospel of Luke* (NICNT; Grand Rapids: Eerdmans, 1997) 850. J. Plevnik, "'The Eleven and Those with Them' According to Luke," *CBQ* 40 (1978) 205-11, discusses the two phrases in 24:9 and 24:33 (he does not comment on 24:13, 22), and argues that Luke is preparing for the election of a replacement of Judas in Acts 1:15-26 and therefore making clear that there were others besides the eleven who fulfilled the condition of apostleship (Acts 1:21-22: "the men who have accompanied us during all the time that the Lord went in and out among us, beginning from the baptism of John until the day when he was taken up"). But despite Luke's emphasis on the special role of the twelve in the early church, his interest in "those who from the beginning were eyewitnesses" (Luke 1:2) is not limited to the twelve, as his references to the women (in Luke 8:2-3; Acts 1:14, as well as in the passion and resurrection narratives) show. The women fulfill the qualifications for apostleship, as Luke uses that term, confining it to the twelve, except that they are female. Moreover, I do not think we should read Luke 24 (or any part of the Gospel) only retrospectively with the narrative

this inclusive picture the women do not need their own commissioning; they belong fully to the whole group of disciples Jesus commissions. This is the natural conclusion from a sequential reading of Luke's Gospel, and it would be a methodological mistake to refuse it on the basis of the way Luke resumes the narrative at the beginning of Acts.[58]

6. The Women in John

There can be no doubt that John largely displaces the women from their role of witness to the empty tomb in favor of Peter and, especially, the beloved disciple. Since John does not record that any of the women observed the burial of Jesus, he is evidently not concerned with Mary Magdalene's ability to identify the right tomb. On the first of Mary Magdalene's two visits to the tomb, she sees, in the darkness, only that the stone has been removed and concludes that the body has been stolen.[59] It is Peter and the beloved disciple who first look inside. At this point, John's special concern to portray the beloved disciple as the perceptive witness[60] has displaced the role of the women, but, in a Gospel notable for its positive and vivid portraits of women as model disciples,[61] we can be sure that this is not a matter of gender bias. We must also notice that unlike Matthew, who explicitly excludes the women from the commissioning appearance to the apostolic group, and Luke, who includes them, John leaves it unclear whether women are present among the disciples on Easter Sunday evening (John 20:19-23). This means that the role of women in John's resurrection narratives is concentrated on the transitional episode: the appearance to Mary Magdalene. But this story — surely, with Luke's walk to Emmaus, one of the two most memorable of the

---

of Acts in view. The beginning of Acts refocuses Luke's understanding of the resurrection appearances with his particular concerns as he embarks on the narrative of the early church; it does not follow that Luke 24 must have precisely the same focus and concerns.

58. That there is a difference between the "general apostlic mandate given to the community at large" at the end of Luke 24 and the restriction to the eleven at the beginning of Acts is recognized also by Crossan, *Who*, 205-6.

59. This is hardly an "apostolic role" of witness to the empty tomb, pace M. Scott, *Sophia and the Johannine Jesus* (JSNTSup 71; Sheffield: Sheffield Academic Press, 1992) 225, 228.

60. See R. Bauckham, "The Beloved Disciple as Ideal Witness," *JSNT* 49 (1993) 21-44, reprinted in S. E. Porter and C. A. Evans, *The Johannine Writings* (Biblical Seminar 32; Sheffield: Sheffield Academic Press, 1995) 46-68.

61. T. K. Seim, "Roles of Women in the Gospel of John," in L. Hartman and B. Olsson, eds., *Aspects on the Johannine Literature* (ConBNT 18; Uppsala: Almqvist & Wiksell, 1987) 56-73; S. M. Schneiders, "Women in the Fourth Gospel," in M. W. G. Stibbe, ed., *The Gospel of John as Literature* (NTTS 17; Leiden: Brill, 1993) 129-30.

resurrection appearance narratives — amply compensates for John's neglect of the women in the first and third elements of the threefold structure.

For all three of the evangelists who employ the threefold structure, the second unit serves in part to model the proper response of believers to the risen Lord. In Mary Magdalene's case this is seen in her recognition of the Master who calls her by her own name and in her learning that she need not cling to the physical presence of Jesus for fear of losing him again.[62] The effect of the brief narrative owes much to the one-to-one intimacy of the encounter, distinctive among the canonical appearance stories (though John's subsequent narratives are notable for Jesus' attention to specific individuals within the larger groups present: Thomas [20:26-29] and Peter [21:15-22]). It coheres with what C. F. D. Moule called the "individualism" of this Gospel.[63] Mary Magdalene is represented as one of the sheep of the good shepherd's flock depicted in the parable of chapter 10. He knows his sheep and they know him. He calls each by name and they recognize his voice, as they will not recognize a stranger (10:3-5, 14, 27). Appearing to Mary, Jesus begins to fulfill his promise that he will show himself, not to the world, but to the disciples only,[64] and, moreover, individually to each one who loves and obeys Jesus: "The one who loves me will be loved by my Father, and I too will love that one and show myself to that individual (ἐμφανίσω αὐτῷ ἐμαυτόν)" (John 14:21).[65]

With regard to the relationship between this appearance story and the one that follows, in which Jesus commissions the group of disciples (20:21: "As the Father has sent me, so I send you"), two points are important. First (in view of John's highlighting of disciples other than the twelve: Nathaniel and the beloved disciple, as well as women),[66] the group is probably not limited to the twelve (or eleven) and, moreover, one of the twelve, Thomas, is not present at the commissioning. This shows that John intends the commissioning of the disciples to be representative, not exclusive. The exact composition of the

62. John 20:17 is, of course, an interpretive crux that has been extensively discussed and debated. We cannot enter that discussion here.

63. C. F. D. Moule, "The Individualism of the Fourth Gospel," in Moule, *Essays in New Testament Interpretation* (Cambridge: Cambridge University Press, 1982) 91-109.

64. Setzer, "Excellent Women," 268, claims that John does not consider Mary Magdalene a disciple because 21:14 counts only three appearances "to the disciples." It is surely obvious that only appearances to a group of disciples (plural) are being counted.

65. It is unfortunate that the NRSV, in order to avoid gendered pronouns, turns the singulars of vv 21, 23-24, into plurals, obscuring the striking and deliberate individualism of these verses.

66. On the relative unimportance of the twelve in John, see A. J. Kostenberger, *The Missions of the Jesus and the Disciples according to the Fourth Gospel* (Grand Rapids: Eerdmans, 1998) 147-48.

group present on the occasion narrated is left vague because it is unimportant: whichever disciples they were, they stand for all. It is the same in chapter 21, where the miraculous catch of fish, under Jesus' direction, is a symbol of the mission Jesus entrusts to the disciples. The disciples who go fishing are seven, because this is the symbolic number of completeness. For the sake of the realism of the narrative they cannot be more numerous, but as seven they are representative of all disciples. Moreover, when John names five but leaves two unnamed (21:2: ἄλλοι ἐκ τῶν μαθητῶν αὐτοῦ δύο), he is leaving one space for the always anonymous beloved disciple, but also another space representatively open for any other disciple to fill. Nothing prevents this other from being a woman. Again, in a realistic story of fishing the disciples have to be men, but in their representative role they can stand also for women.

Second, as in Matthew, it is clear that Mary's own commission to "go and tell" (20:17) is not exhausted in the delivering of her message to the disciples:[67] she is certainly more than an "apostle to the apostles."[68] But this is conveyed differently, and more emphatically, than in Matthew. In her report to the disciples, what stands out are the words in first-person direct speech: "I have seen the Lord" (20:18). This is exactly what the other disciples later say to Thomas: "We have seen the Lord" (20:25). In Paul this is the defining content and terminology of the apostolic witness: "Am I not an apostle? Have I not seen Jesus our Lord?" (1 Cor 9:1). John does not use the term "apostle,"[69] but the words of the witness given first by Mary belong to the theme of seeing and believing that runs through John's resurrection narratives, culminating in 20:29. John does not depreciate the seeing that is the privilege of the disciples to whom Jesus appeared. Others must believe without seeing (20:29), but in doing so are dependent on the witness of those who did see. In that sense, Mary's witness is in no sense superseded by or subordinated to that of the other disciples. Her confession, "I have seen the Lord," stands in John's Gospel because for every reader of that Gospel it goes on testifying to the reality of the risen Lord just as compellingly as the witness of the other disciples and Thomas does.

I conclude that there is no evidence to suggest that the role of the women in the resurrection stories has been depreciated or limited in the Gospel narratives of Matthew, Luke, and John. Where male prejudice against their credibility is explicitly evoked (Luke 24:11), this is so that it may be decisively overturned. Where readers may bring such prejudice to the texts, even though the texts give

---

67. Contra Lieu, "Women's," 39.

68. For this traditional title, see R. E. Brown, *The Community of the Beloved Disciple* (New York: Paulist, 1979) 190n.336.

69. ἀπόστολος occurs only in John 13:16, where the use is nontechnical.

no pretext for doing so, again the effect of the narratives will be to refute and to reverse assumptions of male priority and female unreliability. This is entirely coherent with the supposition that outsiders would find this aspect of the Christian narrative problematic, but it suggests that within the Christian communities themselves the role of the women as witnesses was highly respected. There seems to be no evidence that it became less so over time. It is one of a variety of striking aspects of early Christianity that belong to the countercultural nature of the Christian communities as societies in which God's eschatological overturning of social privilege was taken very seriously. This point will be supported in §8, which considers the place of these Gospel women themselves in the early Christian movement.

7. The Women in Mark

I have left Mark to last because it does not share the threefold structure of the other Gospel resurrection narratives, and because, in consequence, there are issues peculiar to the debate about the significance of the way Mark's Gospel ends (i.e., the way the original text ends at 16:8). These issues are important in our present context insofar as they entail judgments as to whether Mark's depiction of the women is finally positive or negative. In order to solve the puzzles of the end of Mark, it is important to recognize that there are several distinct, even if related, questions: (1) Why does Mark's Gospel end with the empty tomb rather than continue with narratives of appearances and apostolic commissioning? (2) Why do the women "say nothing to anyone" (16:8)? (3) Why does Mark choose this particular note on which to end his story of the empty tomb and his Gospel as a whole?

(1) That Mark is the only Gospel that ends as it does and that later readers and editors found this ending unsatisfactory and requiring the remedy of additional conclusions strongly suggest that Mark would have frustrated the expectations of his first readers by ending in this way. In explanation of this unexpected — premature, as it must have seemed — ending, there appear to be two plausible lines of thought, which are not mutually exclusive. One is that Mark's failure to narrate resurrection experiences expresses a kind of theological reticence that preserves the mystery of the risen one. In this sense Francis Watson links Mark's nonnarration of a resurrection appearance with his nonnarration of the event of resurrection itself.[70] A second form of explanation appeals to

---

70. F. Watson, "'He Is Not Here': Towards a Theology of the Empty Tomb," in Barton and Stanton, eds., *Resurrection*, 99-101.

Mark's understanding of discipleship as following Jesus on the way of the cross. The reader is prevented from coming to the end of the Gospel with a sense of having left behind the cross in order to be with the Lord in his now risen glory. Though the reader does, of course, now know that Jesus is risen, as he had predicted within the Gospel story, there is no postresurrection disclosure of the risen glory like the prefiguring of it at the transfiguration. The reader is therefore not tempted to Peter's misunderstanding when he wished to build dwellings for the glorified Jesus and his companions to remain (9:5). Instead, the young man's message (16:7), by referring back to Jesus' words at the last supper (14:28), thrusts the reader back into the Gospel story, where suffering and the possibility of failure in discipleship in the face of suffering are still a reality.

These lines of explanation *can* each be linked with a particular understanding of the women's silence in the last verse of the Gospel. If this silence is understood as the proper response to a theophany or supernatural disclosure, then it belongs to the narrative's means of inviting the reader to the same kind of awe-struck terror before the mystery of the resurrection. If, on the other hand, it represents the women's failure to carry out the command they have been given to tell the male disciples, then it joins the failure of the male disciples in Gethsemane, with its promised overcoming in Galilee, in portraying the way of discipleship of the crucified Christ as a way that holds out promise despite failure.[71] But these understandings of the women's silence are not necessary to the two lines of explanation of Mark's nonnarration of resurrection appearances.

(2) Why did the women say nothing to anyone (οὐδενὶ οὐδὲν εἶπαν, 16:8)? Mark says it was because they were afraid, but the meaning of this is very much a matter of dispute. One line of interpretation supposes that the women's silence means they do not deliver the message they have been given to Peter and the other disciples. In this way, just as the male disciples have failed, so in the end the women too, who have remained faithful up to this point, also fail: "ultimately women are no different from men — at least in terms of discipleship."[72] This is the interpretation that entails a finally negative view of the women in Mark, though no more negative than his view of the men among Jesus' followers. However, the proponents of this view seem to me to fail to explain why it is that the women do not deliver the message. What are they afraid of? Awe of the numinous figures in a vision usually leads to doing as they have instructed (e.g., in 2 Enoch 1, Enoch tells his sons what the angels have told him as they have told him to do). If, as these interpreters argue, the women's flight and fear are

---

71. A. T. Lincoln, "The Promise and the Failure: Mark 16:7, 8," *JBL* 283-300, especially 299.
72. Lincoln, "Promise," 289.

not the expected, proper reactions to a revelatory experience, but are to be evaluated negatively, what sort of fear is it that prevents the women giving the message to the disciples? Are they afraid the men will disbelieve and laugh at them? I can think of no better explanation, but the proponents of this view seem to offer none.[73]

At first sight it seems plausible that the women's flight parallels that of the men in Gethsemane (14:50, 52),[74] but only so long as we remain at the level of words instead of envisaging the realistic situations Mark depicts. The flight of the men in Gethsemane is a failure to stand by Jesus, a failure to follow him on the way of the cross, through fear of the danger to themselves. But there is no sense in which the women should have remained in the tomb in order to be faithful to Jesus. Their business in the tomb is in any case finished; the young man has told them to go. Their flight can hardly be a failure of discipleship, even if their failure to speak is.

The idea that the women's silence represents their failure is also not really helped by the fact that verse 7 refers indirectly to the failure of the male disciples. The reference back to 14:28 certainly means that the envisaged meeting of the risen Christ with Peter and the disciples in Galilee will entail restoration after their failure. (Peter is singled out for mention by name in 16:7 because of his role in 14:29-31.) But this promise of restoration is not given for the women,[75] whose failure has not even happened when the young man speaks to them. This might seem a pedantic point, but it is important to resist the assimilation of the female to the male disciples that the interpretation of the women's silence as failure promotes. Up to this point Mark has given the twelve and the women distinct roles, such that the women are still active in the narrative long after the male disciples have fled, effectively, out of the narrative. It must be problematic if the women finally have their own failure without their own promise of restoration.

---

73. H. Kinukawa, *Women and Jesus in Mark: A Japanese Feminist Perspective* (Maryknoll, N.Y.: Orbis, 1994) 110, suggests, following E. Moltmann-Wendel, that the women's flight might be because they fear the "danger of being blamed and arrested as followers of Jesus, since Jesus' corpse has now disappeared from the tomb, which could lead to rumors or riots." But it seems implausible that the women who were not afraid of arrest in 15:40 (as the male disciples had been) should become so now.

74. Lincoln, "Promise," 287; P. Danove, "The Characterization and Narrative Function of the Women at the Tomb (Mark 15,40-41.47; 16,1-8)," *Bib* 77 (1996) 390 (who refers also to 5:14; 13:14, claiming that these "frames evoked by ἔφυγον confirm the women's negative evaluation").

75. It seems unlikely to me, in view of the reference back to Mark 14:27-28 (where it is clear that only the male disciples are in view), that the women are included in the ὑμᾶς or the second-person plural verbs of Mark 16:7. This issue is discussed by Theissen and Merz, *Historical Jesus*, 497-98n.36, who think it cannot be decided with certainty, but incline to think the women are included.

The understanding of the women's silence as disobedience takes the silence in an absolute sense: they never say anything to anyone at all. As Andrew Lincoln points out, this would not prevent Jesus' promise that the male disciples will see him in Galilee being fulfilled, since the promise itself need not include the role of the women in bringing it to fulfillment.[76] (In the *Gospel of Peter,* for example, the women are given and deliver no message, but the disciples go to Galilee, just because going home seems the only thing to do.) But there is still a problem about taking the women's silence to be absolute: in that case, no one but the women would ever have known the story and Mark would not have been able to tell it. It is not plausible to read the end of Mark's story of the empty tomb as an ironic device that deconstructs the story's own truth claims.

There is no need to suppose that the women's silence is absolute or that it contradicts the young man's command to them to go and tell Peter and the others. Mark's Gospel itself provides a good analogy: in 1:44 Jesus tells the healed leper to "say nothing to anyone (μηδενὶ μηδὲν εἴπῃς); but go, show yourself to the priest" (cf. 16:8: οὐδενὶ οὐδὲν εἶπαν). The general prohibition is not contradicted by the specific command. What the women did not do was to make the news generally known. They did not stop everyone they met in the street to tell them. They did not tell anyone else, but they did deliver the message as instructed to the male disciples.[77]

In that case, if the women's silence is not disobedience, what explains it? What were they afraid of? On the view that Mark's depiction of the women remains positive to the end, their fear can be interpreted as part of the expected response to an epiphany, continuous with their "terror and amazement" (τρόμος καὶ ἔκστασις) earlier in verse 8. The whole of verse 8 then describes their reaction to the awe-inspiring disclosure they have witnessed and Mark's story ends by impressing on its readers this "destabilizing and disorienting"[78] effect of the message of the resurrection.[79] Lincoln objects that "fear" (ἐφοβοῦντο) is not elsewhere in Mark used in a positive sense of awe in the face of the numinous,[80] but this is not accurate. To take one clear example, it is true

---

76. Lincoln, "Promise," 292.

77. This is argued by D. Catchpole, "The Fearful Silence of the Women at the Tomb," *JTSA* 18 (1977) 3-10, which I have not been able to see; also by T. Dwyer, *The Motif of Wonder in the Gospel of Mark* (JSNTSup 128; Sheffield: Sheffield Academic Press, 1996) 191-92, who cites others who take this view (n. 174); and J. L. Magness, *Sense and Absence: Structure and Suspension in the Ending of Mark's Gospel* (Semeia Studies; Atlanta: Scholars Press, 1986) 100.

78. Watson, "He is not here," 101.

79. Dwyer, *Motif,* shows how this is the culminating instance of a theme to be found throughout Mark (and for a cautious approach to the effect on the reader, see 201).

80. Lincoln, "Promise," 286-87.

that, in the story of the stilling of the storm, Jesus connects the disciples' fear of perishing in the storm with their lack of faith (4:40), but the great fear they experience in the next verse (ἐφοβήθησαν φόβον μέγαν) is not that unbelieving terror but awe in view of the divine identity of Jesus disclosed in his command over the elements.[81] This verse alone is a sufficient parallel to a positive evaluation of the women's fear in 16:8. (Examples in which it is less clear that the fear is to be evaluated positively are 5:15, 33; 6:20, 50; 8:31; 9:6, 31; 10:33-34.)

But it is much less clear that silence is the expected response to a disclosure of the numinous.[82] Most alleged parallels are not really relevant,[83] but 2 Corinthians 12:4 may be genuinely so: Paul speaks there of hearing "things that are not to be told, that no human is permitted to repeat" (ἄρρητα ῥήματα ἃ οὐκ ἐξὸν ἀνθρώπῳ λαλῆσαι). It may well be that the women take the words of the young man to be an apocalyptic secret that they are to communicate to Jesus' disciples but that is strictly not to be revealed to anyone else. They could well be right in thinking this, in that the time for proclaiming the risen Christ to the world will not come until he appears to the disciples in Galilee. There is no suggestion in any of the Gospels that any of the disciples, women or men, communicate the news of the resurrection outside the circle of the disciples until the risen Lord explicitly commissions them to do so. I am inclined to think this the most convincing explanation of the women's silence in Mark 16:8. If it is correct, then the last six words of Mark actually depict the women *as obedient,* in not betraying the secret to the world. Not only do they remain faithful to the end of the Gospel; the Gospel ends by stressing their reverent obedience.

This comes close to suggesting that the so-called messianic secret continues to the end of the Gospel. In fact, the passages often grouped under the heading of "the messianic secret" are not homogeneous, but display a number of different motifs,[84] to which the secret of the resurrection in 16:8 could be

81. So, e.g., Dwyer, *Motif,* 109-11; J. Marcus, *Mark 1–8* (AB 27A; New York: Doubleday, 1999) 334.

82. There is some evidence for flight as a response to the numinous: Dan 10:7; 1 Enoch 106:4; cf. Mark 5:14.

83. Of the examples quoted from Pesch and Lightfoot in G. O'Collins, "The Fearful Silence of Three Women (Mark 16:8c)," *Greg* 69 (1988) 501, in 1 Sam 3:16 Samuel is afraid to tell Eli of the vision because it prophesied judgment on Eli's family; in Ezek 3:26; 24:27; Luke 1:20 the silence is miraculously imposed by God for special reasons; and Dan 7:15, 28; 8:17, 27; 10:7 do not state that Daniel kept quiet about what he might have revealed to others. There is a Hebrew Bible/OT motif that at a theophany all must "keep silence before the Lord" (Hab 2:20; Zeph 1:7; Zech 2:13 [MT 17]), but it can hardly be this that is evoked by the statement that the women said nothing to anyone.

84. J. D. G. Dunn, "The Messianic Secret in Mark," in C. Tuckett, ed., *The Messianic Secret* (IRT 1; London: SPCK; Philadelphia: Fortress, 1983) 116-31.

added as another. The messianic secret proper — that Jesus is the Messiah, the Son of God — is not in fact maintained in the Gospel narrative beyond the confession of Bartimaeus (10:46-52), that is, after the point at which the passion has come very close. The secret the women convey only to the male disciples is that Jesus has risen from the dead. Its proclamation to the world awaits its full disclosure through Jesus' own appearance to the disciples.

An alternative approach is suggested in a neglected contribution by Mary Cotes.[85] She points out that in the Markan examples of awe or fear in the face of the numinous, the latter produces not silence but speech. She argues that the women's silence is due to a fact generally neglected in the exegetical debate: their gender. Women were expected to be silent in public. Thus, although the women at the tomb will indeed communicate their message to the disciples, they are constrained by expected social roles from broadcasting it in public places. Their silence is "the typical reluctance of women to speak in the public arena."[86] Their fear is precisely of speaking in public:

> Quite simply, the women do not speak out because they are afraid of speaking out. And the reason for their fear of speaking is that, in the world in which they live, men are thought of as speakers in the public sphere; women, whose domain is deemed to be the interior, and whose position is deemed to be inferior, should be absent from, and silent in, the public arena.[87]

Cotes also points out that the Markan characters who have to be told by Jesus not to speak about what has happened to them or has been made known to them are all male. She has probably exaggerated the silence of women in public. We do not have the evidence to support such a strong social requirement, though it may well be true that respectable women would not normally have initiated conversations with men who were not relatives.[88] The Gospels (surprisingly, perhaps our best evidence of ordinary social mores in practice in first-century Palestine) do not often represent women as vocal in public places,

85. M. Cotes, "Women, Silence and Fear (Mark 16:8)," in G. J. Brooke, ed., *Women in the Biblical Tradition* (Studies in Women and Religion 31; Lewiston, N.Y.: Mellen, 1992) 150-66, especially 151-60.

86. Cotes, "Women," 166.

87. Cotes, "Women," 160.

88. For rabbinic advice against speaking with women in public, see Ilan, *Jewish Women*, 126-27. We cannot simply assume that it was followed by ordinary people. For evidence from Greco-Roman writers that women were expected not to speak to unrelated men in public, see J. H. Neyrey, "What's Wrong with This Picture? John 4, Cultural Stereotypes of Women, and Public and Private Space," *BTB* 24 (1994) 81.

though there are some exceptions (Matt 15:22; Luke 11:27; 13:13).[89] Cotes claims support from Mark 5:33, arguing that the hemorrhaging woman's fear and trembling are "a response to having to make a public declaration."[90] This would be quite a good parallel to Mark 16:8, but it is not at all clear that it is the correct interpretation. More likely the woman fears that Jesus will be angry with her for having touched him surreptitiously, though recent commentators seem to prefer the view that her fear, as in 4:41 and 5:15, is religious awe at the miracle done to her.[91] Moreover, Cotes surely neglects the fact that women did not need to speak to strangers in public in order to spread news. They would speak to their female friends and neighbors in their homes and at the wells and the market stalls; these women would tell their husbands, and the news would spread. Though the Samaritan woman in John 4 is not a model of respectable women's behavior, there is probably nothing improper about the way she spreads her news throughout her village (John 4:28-30, 39).

Nevertheless, there may be validity in the suggestion that, in first-century Jewish culture, there is a gendered aspect to silence. I do not think it is plausible that the women's fear in Mark 16:8 is simply reluctance to speak in public: this would be a rather banal end to the Gospel. But it may be that awe in the face of the numinous would more likely generate silence in women than in men because of women's cultural habit of reticence in male company. In this respect, the parallel between the women in Mark 16:8 and Peter in 9:6 is of interest. After reporting Peter's suggestion that they make three dwellings for Jesus, Moses, and Elijah, Mark explains: "He did not know what to say, for they were terrified" (ἔκφοβοι γὰρ ἐγένοντο). The last clause is a close parallel to the last words of the Gospel: ἐφοβοῦντο γάρ. The disciples' fear at the transfiguration is unexceptionable, but it should have left them dumbfounded. Not knowing what to say, Peter should have stayed silent, but instead he characteristically — both as the impetuous Peter of Mark's Gospel and as a man used to grasping a situation in

---

89. J. Dewey, "Women in the Synoptic Gospels: Seen but Not Heard?" *BTB* 27 (1997) 58, attributes the relative silence of women in the Synoptic Gospels to the androcentric bias of the writers. This may be an element, but in arguing that the Gospels' inconsistency shows they do not reflect social reality she does not allow sufficiently for distinctions of context (public or private) and interlocutors (relatives, family friends, strangers) or for whether it is the woman who initiates the conversation. There are very few cases in which a woman initiates conversation with a male stranger in a public place. Not even the unusually vocal women of the Fourth Gospel do this, while even John's Mary of Bethany, who speaks freely enough with Jesus in 11:32, just as her sister does, performs her anointing in silence, inhibited by the presence of a large number of men at the dinner table (12:1-8).

90. Cotes, "Women," 160.

91. R. A. Guelich, *Mark 1–8:26* (WBC 34A; Dallas: Word, 1989) 298; Dwyer, *Motif,* 118; Marcus, *Mark 1–8*, 359-60.

speech[92] — blunders into a serious misunderstanding. By contrast, the women remain silent. What has happened is mystery beyond their comprehension and they rightly do not attempt to explain it to others. This is perhaps another way in which the women could be understood to remain, at the end of the Gospel, a positive contrast to Mark's depiction of the failings of the male disciples.

In the universe of grace that is Mark's narrative world, it is not necessarily "better" not to have failed than to have failed. And Mark is certainly not engaged in a polemic against the twelve (a crass reduction of Mark's theology of discipleship to some kind of ecclesiastical power struggle).[93] But it is clear that Mark has deliberately used the two groups of followers of Jesus in which he is interested — the twelve and the women — to model the two possibilities of, on the one hand, failure and restoration, and, on the other hand, faithfulness that does not need restoration. Moreover, it is not accidental that the two groups are distinguished by gender. In the sociocultural context, false confidence in their own ability to follow Jesus even to death, exemplified by Peter (14:29-31), is more likely to have been a temptation for men than for women. For the women, faithfulness to loved ones through shame and death is a culturally expected role.[94] The men must become witnesses of the crucified and risen one through failure and restoration; the women, through the deeply disturbing encounter with the numinous that transforms their faithfulness into something more than their accepted cultural role: the vocation to be witnesses of a world-transforming event.

Finally, we should notice how Mark frames his passion narrative, in which the male disciples fail, with two stories including women: the anointing of Jesus at Bethany (14:3-9) and the visit of the women to the tomb. The woman who anoints Jesus is the first person in the narrative who accepts that Jesus has to die. The women at the tomb are the first to know that Jesus has risen.

(3) The point at which Mark stops telling his story is not the end of the story: "Absence from the text is not necessarily absence from the story."[95]

---

92. Presumably James and John remain silent, but Mark draws no attention to this.

93. J. Painter, *Mark's Gospel* (NT Readings; London/New York: Routledge, 1997) 212-13, extends this notion of Mark's polemic against the Jerusalem church leadership to the end of the Gospel, arguing that the women's silence implies that the disciples did not go to Galilee, in spite of Jesus' instruction, but were unfaithful in remaining in Jerusalem (cf. Acts 1:4!).

94. It may have been less dangerous for the women than for the male disciples to be present at the cross: the men would more likely risk arrest as suspected insurrectionists. But the fact that the women stand "at a distance" from the cross (Mark 15:40) should probably not be understood as cowardice (contra Mattila, "Naming," 169, 178). The Roman soldiers would not have allowed them to come closer. On the issue of the danger to the women, see Gerhardsson, "Mark," 220-21, who argues that they were probably not in much danger but were not in a position to judge this.

95. Magness, *Sense,* 121.

Readers know what is to follow, because Jesus in Mark's narrative has predicted it, and in this last passage of Mark's narrative they are reminded by the young man's words to the women (Mark 16:7) of Jesus' predictions. They know not only that the disciples will see Jesus in Galilee (14:28), but also that the gospel will be preached in the whole world (13:10; 14:9) amid suffering for disciples of Jesus (13:9-13), and that, after various other events, the Lord will come in glory (13:14-27).[96] Mark's ending thus employs the narrative device of "open closure"[97] or "suspended ending,"[98] whereby the readers are not left with a satisfying sense of a story brought to its conclusion but are left to imagine for themselves how the rest of the story will proceed. Those great literary models for the ancient world, the *Iliad* and the *Odyssey*,[99] as well as the influential *Histories* of Herodotus, also contain predictions of events that are to happen only after the narrated conclusions of these works.[100] For Mark's readers, the story after the end of Mark is one in which they themselves are involved, and so the device of open closure allows them both to project the end of the story from sufficient indications within the story and at the same time to imagine themselves within the story as it moves from the Gospel's ending to the story's ending and the world's.

Why does Mark make the women's silence the last thing he narrates? Perhaps because it accomplishes not absolute closure but an appropriate degree of closure. It means that no other events will be generated until the women deliver their message to the male disciples and the latter go to Galilee to meet Jesus. Although Mark 16:8 is not the end of the story, it does indicate that there will be no more story until what 16:7 requires takes place. There are not going to be new developments in the plot prior to those of which the readers know from Jesus' predictions: the appearance of Jesus to the disciples in Galilee and the preaching of the gospel in the world. The silence of the women tells readers that, although the women will pass on the news of Jesus' resurrection to the male disciples, the proclamation of the gospel to the world does not start at this point. It cannot start at this point, not because the women are women, but because the proclamation of the gospel, as all the Gospels indicate, must begin from a resurrection appearance in which Jesus commissions his witnesses. The

96. For these and more oblique "foreshadowings" of the way the story must continue beyond the narrated ending, see Magness, *Sense*, 108-13.

97. D. Marguerat, *La Première Histoire du Christianisme: Les Actes des Apôtres* (LD 180; Paris: Cerf; Geneva: Labor et Fides, 1999) 309.

98. Magness, *Sense*, 22 and passim.

99. Magness, *Sense*, 28-34.

100. Marguerat, *Première Histoire*, 313-15, uses the example of Herodotus to show that this device could be used in historiography.

women's witness to the empty tomb cannot in itself be the beginning of the preaching of the gospel, but it does become, as Mark's telling of the story shows, even ensures, part of the gospel that is proclaimed, just as the anointing of Jesus by a women does, according to Mark 14:9.

8. The Women as Authoritative Witnesses in the Early Church

In general, I would resist the tendency of many recent scholars to see the roles that women played in the early Christian communities reflected in the roles they play in the Gospel narratives. This is a form of allegorization that reads the Gospels as texts about the early church disguised as stories about Jesus.[101] It neglects the extent to which the Gospels make historical distinctions between the "then" of Jesus' ministry and the "now" of their readers.[102] Any argument from the Gospels to the role women played in the Christian communities must proceed with extreme caution. But, in the case of the resurrection narratives, I think we can discern not the roles of Christian women in general, but the role of the specific women who witnessed the empty tomb and the risen Lord. These women, I think we can say, acted as apostolic eyewitness guarantors of the traditions about Jesus, especially his resurrection but no doubt also in other respects. As we have seen, that their witness acquires textual form in the Gospels implies that it can never have been regarded as superseded or unimportant. For as long as these women were alive, their witness, "We have seen the Lord," carried the authority of those the Lord himself had commissioned to witness to his resurrection. We should beware of the well-established tendency in New Testament scholarship to envisage the oral traditions about Jesus as handed down anonymously in the early communities as though the disciples of Jesus, those who must first have told these stories and handed on these sayings, had all disappeared as soon as the Christian movement got going.[103] On the contrary, they were well-known figures and there were a large number of them. They surely continued to be active traditioners whose recognized eyewitness authority could act as a touchstone to guarantee the traditions as others relayed them and to protect the traditions from inauthentic developments. We should also

101. I agree with Karris, "Women," 4; see also R. Bauckham, ed., *The Gospels for All Christians: Rethinking the Gospel Audiences* (Grand Rapids: Eerdmans; Edinburgh: T. & T. Clark, 1998).

102. E. E. Lemcio, *The Past of Jesus in the Gospels* (SNTSMS 68; Cambridge: Cambridge University Press, 1991).

103. Cf. M. Hengel, *The Four Gospels and the One Gospel of Jesus Christ* (tr. J. Bowden; Harrisburg: Trinity Press International; London: SCM, 2000) 143-44.

remember that ancient historiography and historiographical theory set great store by the role of eyewitnesses. When the Gospels appear, as they sometimes do, to be naming individual eyewitnesses, indicating the presence in the stories of persons well known by reputation if not in person to their readers, we should expect them to be relatively close to the firsthand testimony of these figures. We can test this hypothesis in the peculiarly interesting case of the women at the tomb.

Samuel Byrskog has recently made an important contribution to Gospels studies that serves to correct the tendency just noted for scholars to distance the Gospels from the eyewitnesses of the events of Jesus' history.[104] He compares the practice of Greco-Roman historians with that of modern "oral history," and finds the role of eyewitness informants very similar in both. In accordance with the well-known saying of Heraclitus, which they sometimes cite, "Eyes are surer witnesses than ears,"[105] the historians valued as their sources direct experience of the events by involved participants in them. The eyewitness experience should be either their own or that of eyewitnesses whose living voices they could hear and whom they could question themselves: "Autopsy was the essential means to reach back into the past."[106] The ideal eyewitness was not the dispassionate observer, but the person who, as a participant, had been closest to the events and whose direct experience enabled him or her to understand and interpret the significance of what he or she had seen. The historians "preferred the eyewitness who was socially involved or, even better, had been actively participating in the events."[107] Eyewitnesses were "as much interpreters as observers."[108] Their accounts became essential parts of the historians' writings.[109]

Byrskog argues that a similar role must have been played in the formation of the Gospel traditions and the Gospels themselves by individuals who were qualified to be both eyewitnesses and informants about the history of Jesus. He is cautious, perhaps too cautious, about hypotheses that he judges unverifiable, such as Dibelius's conjecture that the naked young man (Mark 14:51) and Simon of Cyrene (Mark 15:21) are mentioned in Mark because they were the eyewitness informants behind the passion narrative. Other explanations can adequately account for their presence in the Markan story.[110] He looks for more

104. Byrskog, *Story.*
105. Byrskog, *Story,* 52-53.
106. Byrskog, *Story,* 64.
107. Byrskog, *Story,* 167.
108. Byrskog, *Story,* 149.
109. Byrskog, *Story,* 64.
110. Byrskog, *Story,* 36-37, 66.

definite clues to the oral history behind the texts,[111] and finds some such in several cases, among which the women at the cross and the tomb are a prominent example.[112] I suggest that they are an even better example than he realizes.

The way that all the Synoptic Gospels repeatedly make the women the subjects of verbs of seeing (Matt 27:55; Mark 15:40; Luke 23:49, 55) shows clearly that the Gospels are appealing to their role as eyewitnesses.[113] The primacy of sight (as in the saying of Heraclitus quoted above) was a feature of the ancient Greek theory of cognition[114] to which the historians' emphasis on autopsy corresponded: "they related to the past visually."[115] Of course, this does not mean that the other senses are excluded from the eyewitnesses' recollections and testimony, but the primacy of sight signifies the importance of having actually been there, as opposed to merely hearing a report of the events. Seeing is also prominent in the Gospel traditions, including in itself the act of hearing (e.g., Matt 11:4 par. Luke 7:22; Matt 13:16-17 par. Luke 10:23-24).[116] The women at the cross and the tomb are important mainly for what they see, but also for their hearing of the message of the angel/s.

They are not an anonymous group: all the Gospels name some of them, while also stating or implying that there were others (Matt 27:55; 28:1,[117] 6; Mark 15:41, 47; 16:6; Luke 24:10; John 20:2). The significance of this naming, and of the variations in the lists of names, seems never to have been properly appreciated. Byrskog supposes that specific names are given "perhaps because as female eyewitnesses they were already from the outset somewhat suspect."[118] But it is not really clear how suspicions of women's credibility could be much allayed by naming them. The naming is surely more likely to reflect how extraor-

111. Byrskog, *Story,* 46, 66-67.

112. Byrskog, *Story,* 75-82.

113. Cf. Gerhardsson, "Mark," 219-20, 222-23; Byrskog, *Story,* 75-78.

114. Byrskog, *Story,* 65.

115. Byrskog, *Story,* 64.

116. Byrskog, *Story,* 103-4.

117. W. Carter, "'To see the tomb': Matthew's Women at the Tomb," *ExpT* 107 (1996) 201-5, argues that Matt 28:1 indicates that the women are not mere witnesses, but "those who understand and trust Jesus' teaching enough to wait expectantly for his resurrection" (205). We might take this to mean that the women are *perceptive* witnesses, who understand the significance of what they witness, as the beloved disciple does in the Fourth Gospel. But I am not convinced the evidence supports this interpretation of Matt 28:1. Witherington, *Women in the Earliest Churches,* 171, following F. Neirynck, understands Matt 28:1 as a kind of title for the story that follows and not as describing the women's motive in going to the tomb: "The Evangelist is suggesting that, seen from the point of view of God's providential plan, the women come 'to witness' the empty tomb and go forth to witness about it, whatever their original intentions might have been."

118. Byrskog, *Story,* 77.

dinarily important, for the whole story of Jesus, were the events of which they are the sole witnesses.

The names are not the same in each Gospel, though Mary Magdalene appears in all, and Mary the mother of James and Joses appears in all three Synoptics. Comparison of the various lists of the named women is instructive. This is how they appear in the canonical and extracanonical sources:

Table 8: Named Women

	Cross	Burial	Empty tomb
Mark	Mary Magdalene	Mary Magdalene	Mary Magdalene
	Mary mother of James the little and Joses	Mary (mother) of Joses	Mary (mother) of James
	Salome		Salome
Matthew	Mary Magdalene	Mary Magdalene	Mary Magdalene
	Mary (mother) of James and Joseph	the other Mary	the other Mary
	Mother of sons of Zebedee		
Luke			Mary Magdalene
			Joanna
			Mary (mother) of James
John	Jesus' mother		Mary Magdalene
	His mother's sister Mary (wife) of Clopas		
	Mary Magdalene		
Gospel of Peter		Mary Magdalene	
Epistle of the Apostles			Sarah
			Martha
(Ethiopic text)			Mary Magdalene

We must resist the rather prevalent temptation to deduce from these lists that a woman named in one Gospel's list is the same person as a woman designated differently in another Gospel.[119] It is helpful to remember that Mary was an extraordinarily popular name: about a quarter of all Palestinian Jewish

119. Probably the most extensive recent example of this practice is J. Wenham, *Easter Enigma* (Grand Rapids: Zondervan; Exeter: Paternoster, 1984) chap. 3.

women were called Mary.[120] Any particular Mary had therefore to be distinguished in some way from others; so, among the Gospel women, we have one woman identified by reference to her sons (Mary the mother of James the little and Joses, a form of reference that is abbreviated in some of the texts), one by reference to her husband (Mary of Clopas), one by her hometown (Mary Magdalene), and the mother of Jesus (whose personal name John does not use at all). These designations function precisely to distinguish the women, and we entirely miss the point if we try to identify with one another the women they are designed to distinguish. That the Synoptic evangelists make clear that the women they name are no more than a few of the women there were makes the divergences between their lists quite intelligible. Each had his own reasons for naming the specific women he does.

We may conclude then that, in all, there are five named women (Mary Magdalene, Mary the mother of James and Joses, Salome, Joanna, and Mary of Clopas), together with two anonymous but specified women: the mother of the sons of Zebedee and the mother of Jesus.[121] The divergences between the lists are much more interesting and significant than is usually realized. No doubt the Torah's requirement of two or three witnesses (Deut 19:15) plays a role in the accounts. As Birger Gerhardsson rightly points out, the influence of this legal ruling extended far beyond the law courts to any situations in ordinary life where evidence needed to be assured.[122] It probably accounts for Jesus' sending out of the twelve in pairs (Mark 6:7). It is certainly notable that the Synoptics name two or three women on each occasion in the passion-resurrection narratives where they are cited as witnesses. (The naming of the three leading members of the twelve on several occasions in the Synoptics could be a comparable phenomenon: Mark 5:37; 9:2; 14:33.) But, of course, the requirement of two or three witnesses cannot explain the variations in the specific names given.

Gerhardsson suggests two possible reasons for the variations in the names. The first is that "the evangelists' need of naming two or three witnesses was stronger than their actual knowledge of the facts; they freely enumerated two or three familiar names." But this does not explain why, if Matthew and Luke knew Mark, they changed the names, nor why Mark himself varies the names on the three occasions (cross, burial, empty tomb). Gerhardsson's second possibility (which he thinks more probable) is that "several women visited the tomb and the single narrator wanted to mention two or three of them without any need of

120. T. Ilan, "Notes on the Distribution of Jewish Women's Names in Palestine in the Second Temple and Mishnaic Periods," *JJS* 40 (1989) 191-192.

121. Jesus' mother's sister (John 19:25) is probably not a fourth woman in John's group, but a description of Mary of Clopas; see chap. 6 above.

122. Gerhardsson, "Mark," 218.

being complete or of making the same selection as another narrator."[123] This is on the right lines, but fails to take sufficient notice of the detail of the variations in the lists and so misses the full significance of the point. In general, commentators show little interest in the names the evangelists have so carefully noted, and it is especially odd to find feminist critics acquiescing in the general neglect of the women other than Mary Magdalene by making the divergences among the Gospels grounds simply for dismissing these women from consideration without further attention.[124] It is usually only Mary Magdalene who is taken seriously as a witness, whereas the actual data of the texts points rather to the seriousness with which we should take all these named women as eyewitness informants whose accounts have informed the Gospel stories.

What is of considerable interest in the divergences among the lists is the scrupulous *care* they display in the naming of the women as witnesses. Mark names three women at the cross and the same three women as those who go to the tomb, but only two of the three are said to observe the burial of Jesus.[125] The explanation must be that in the known testimony of these three women, the two Marys were known to be witnesses of the burial but Salome was not. Similar care is perhaps even more impressive in Matthew. For Matthew Salome was evidently not a well-known witness and he omits her from the lists. At the cross he substitutes the mother of the sons of Zebedee, who has appeared earlier in his narrative (Matt 20:20) and is unique to his Gospel. He does not, however, add her to the two Marys at the burial or the empty tomb, surely because she was not known as an eyewitness to these events. Matthew could so easily have used her to make up the number at the tomb but instead he is scrupulously content with the only two women well known to him as witnesses. Luke, who names the women only at the end of his account of their visit to the tomb,[126] lists, besides the indis-

---

123. Gerhardsson, "Mark," 223.

124. Setzer, "Excellent Women," 260-61; cf. Lieu, "Women's," 42.

125. The persistent attempts (examples are cited in Bode, *First Easter*, 20-22) to explain the variations in Mark's lists of the women by postulating different sources are ludicrous. One theory thinks that Mark found two different women, "Mary of Joses" (Mark 15:40) and "Mary of James" (Mark 16:1), in two different sources, but identified them and harmonized the sources in 15:40, where he refers to "Mary the mother of James the little and Joses" (Bode, *First Easter*, 21). It is much easier to suppose that Mark first refers to this Mary by reference to both her sons, including the nickname of one, in order to facilitate readers'/hearers' identification of her, and then feels free to identify her more concisely, in two different ways, in 15:47 and 16:1, just as Matthew, having introduced her as "Mary the mother James and Joses" (Matt 27:56), can then call her "the other Mary" (Matt 27:61; 28:1).

126. This may be so that the naming of Mary Magdalene and Joanna can function as an *inclusio* with 8:2-3, reminding readers that the women have accompanied Jesus and his story from early in the Galilean ministry until the resurrection.

pensable Mary Magdalene, Joanna, who is peculiar to his Gospel and already introduced at 8:3, and Mary the mother of James. This third name may be Luke's only borrowing from Mark in his narrative of the empty tomb. His reference to Joanna surely indicates the distinctive source of his distinctive empty tomb story.[127] Like Matthew he omits Mark's Salome, but he does not simply reproduce the list of women followers of Jesus he had employed earlier in his Gospel (8:3: Mary Magdalene, Joanna, Susanna). Mary Magdalene and Joanna he knew to be witnesses of the empty tomb, Susanna he evidently did not.[128]

The prominence of Mary Magdalene among the women is clear: she appears in all the lists and she is named first in all the lists except John 19:25 (and the *Epistle of the Apostles*). We could compare the way Peter is always named first when the trio Peter, James, and John are named in the Synoptics (Mark 5:37; Luke 8:51; etc.). But we should also note that Mary the mother of James and Joses appears in all seven of the lists in the passion-resurrection narratives of the Synoptics. Obscure as she and her sons are to us, she was evidently a well-known figure for the evangelists and their first readers/hearers. She also receives, with Mary Magdalene, the resurrection appearance in Matthew 26:8-9, and should not be considered a secondary addition to a tradition in which, as in John 20:11-18, Mary Magdalene was originally the only person present with Jesus. In view of the care that all the evangelists, but especially Matthew, take in naming these women witnesses, it is much easier to understand the omission of names than the addition of names. John's exclusive focus on Mary Magdalene is readily explicable from his narrativizing tendency to focus on individuals, as well as his theological stress on individual relationship with Jesus, noted above in §6.

I must therefore take issue with Byrskog, who, having pointed out the prominence of Mary Magdalene in the traditions, writes: "Perhaps, therefore, the female witnesses and informants did not, at first, consist merely of a collective body of women. *The members of the early Jerusalem community might have realised that one woman in particular carried memories worthwhile telling and preserving.* They knew to whom to turn for information."[129] Byrskog is correct to claim, here as elsewhere, that not merely collectivities but specific individuals within them must have been the eyewitness informants behind the Gospel tra-

---

127. Similarly Luke's naming of Cleopas (Luke 24:18) may well indicate the eyewitness source of the Emmaus story.

128. It is tempting to conjecture that each evangelist's story or stories involving the women derives from a different woman, thus: Salome — Mark, Mary the mother of James — Matthew, Joanna — Luke, Mary Magdalene — John. But this is too speculative.

129. Byrskog, *Story*, 81; cf. Perkins, "I Have," 31-41, who in the course of a whole article about the women witnesses to the resurrection of Jesus names no woman except Mary Magdalene.

ditions: "groups and cultures do not remember and recall; individuals do."[130] His mistake in the case of the women is not to relate this principle to the conspicuous naming of several women in the resurrection narratives. The female eyewitnesses of the events were not a mere collective body, but nor are they reducible to the single, albeit prominent woman Mary Magdalene. The named women are all named precisely because they fulfilled this role. The women who acted as eyewitness informants in the early church with regard to the story of the empty tomb and the appearance of Jesus to some women were, specifically, Mary Magdalene, Mary the mother of James and Joses, Salome, and Joanna. Two of these, Mary Magdalene and Mary the mother of James and Joses, were known to have witnessed the burial. Three other specific women, Mary of Clopas, Mary the mother of Jesus, and the mother of the sons of Zebedee, were known to have been present at the cross, but did not act as witnesses to the burial or the empty tomb. These conclusions are not the result of methodologically dubious "harmonizing." They follow from the recognition that the variations in the lists of named women cannot be explained from inattention to the details or unfounded invention on the part of the evangelists, but make sense only as due to the particular care the evangelists took to list only such women as they knew to be witnesses of each event.

For the eyewitnesses behind the Gospel traditions, Byrskog writes, the history of Jesus "became their own oral history which they proclaimed to others. One needed their eyes as well as their ears."[131] It would be a mistake to envisage the women's role of eyewitnesses as a passive one. As participants in events that radically changed their own lives, the women, in telling and retelling the stories of the events of the passion and resurrection, were also interpreting the significance of these events. As I noted above in summarizing Byrskog's account of the practice of the Greco-Roman historians, autopsy was not "merely a matter of passive observation; it has to do with active understanding."[132] The women's participation in the events, as well as their commission by the risen Christ himself to be his witnesses, qualified them as the authoritative witnesses who shaped the way their own stories were told in the oral tradition and were available for checking the authenticity of the stories being told. They would not have told their stories only when male tradents of the Gospel traditions and male evangelists sought them out and asked them for their recollections, though this may well have happened. As prominent members of the early communities, probably traveling around the communities, they were doubtless ac-

130. Byrskog, *Story*, 255; cf. also 153n.44.
131. Byrskog, *Story*, 106.
132. Byrskog, *Story*, 147.

tive in telling the stories themselves. They may not usually, like the male apostles, have done so in public contexts, because of the social restrictions on women in public space. But this is no reason to deny them the role of authoritative apostolic witnesses and shapers of Gospel traditions, since there need not have been such restrictions in Christian meetings and since they could witness even to outsiders in women-only contexts such as the women's quarters of houses.[133]

There is no basis in the texts for Byrskog's adherence to the view that the women's witness has been significantly downplayed in the androcentric narratives of the Gospels, while at the same time the fact that the women are still present in the narratives evidences the influence they must have asserted against the androcentric grain of the early Christian traditions.[134] In view of my own studies (above) of the place of the women in the resurrection narratives, there is no reason to think that we have access to the women's own testimony through the distorting mirror of male tradents who decisively shaped their testimony into the stories we read. The presence of the individual women's names in the Gospel texts indicates, on the contrary, that they were the active tradents of their own oral history, and that what we have in the Gospel stories in which they appear is the textualized form of the stories they themselves told. The evangelists have, of course, exercised the freedom of all such storytellers to vary the particular performance of the oral tradition they themselves give, in this case a textualized form, and have also, as we have noticed, adapted the stories to fit an integrated narrative sequence and in the light of their own theological emphases. But we should not imagine a long process of male traditioning behind the evangelists' redaction, or rule out the real possibility that the evangelists themselves were in touch with these women. On the whole we can be confident that in reading these stories we do indeed see with the eyes of these named female eyewitnesses. To what extent this may be true of Gospel narratives outside the passion-resurrection stories is more difficult to ascertain, but remains to be adequately investigated.

If, as I have suggested and allowing for the evangelists' freedom as storytellers and redactors with their own interests, the stories of the women at the

---

133. Thus it is possible that Luke would have included the women among the eyewitnesses who were also "ministers of the word" (Luke 1:2), but it is hard to judge this. Loveday Alexander, *The Preface to Luke's Gospel* (SNTSMS 78; Cambridge: Cambridge University Press, 1993) 34-41, 80-81, 120-25, has shown that the *word* αὐτοψία and its cognates are not prominent in the writings of historians (she stresses instead their popularity with medical writers), but Byrskog, *Story*, chaps. 2–3, shows that this approach obscures the considerable importance of the *idea and practice* of autopsy in the Greco-Roman historians.

134. Byrskog, *Story*, 81-82.

empty tomb and at the appearance of the Lord to them are substantially as the women themselves told them, then we must regard the differences between the stories as irreducible. We cannot go behind them to a supposedly original version. Nor can we dispense with the angels and reconstruct a less mythologically laden event.[135] These are the stories as doubtless different women told them. They are different performances of the oral traditions, and their differences are such as would have been expected and unproblematic in performances of oral tradition, no greater and no more problematic than those between the three narratives of Paul's conversion that all occur in Acts. Did Paul's companions on the road to Damascus hear the voice that spoke to him or not (Acts 9:7; 22:9)? Did the women see one angel or two? We do not need to answer such questions in order to find their story credible.

9. The Women in the Kerygmatic Summaries

The previous section, suggesting that these women were themselves apostolic traditioners and eyewitness guarantors of their stories in the early Christian communities, makes all the more striking and puzzling the alleged absence of the women from the kerygmatic summaries. We shall need to consider the kerygmatic summaries in the sermons of Acts before turning finally to 1 Corinthians 15.

I have argued elsewhere that the kerygmatic summary, that is, a brief outline of the Gospel story from Jesus' baptism (or, later, his birth) to his future coming in glory, was a widespread oral form in the early church, fundamentally independent of the Gospel traditions (i.e., the stories about and sayings of Jesus).[136] This independence can be shown in part from the occurrence in the kerygmatic summaries of characteristic terminology that does not appear in Gospel traditions.[137] We have evidence of kerygmatic summaries not only in Acts and 1 Corinthians 15, but also in later Christian literature such as the *Ascension of Isaiah* and Ignatius, which can help to indicate the degree of stability and variation to be found in such summaries. I have argued that the kerygmatic

---

135. E.g., Bode, *First Easter,* 165-70. The claim that John 20:1-2 preserves the earliest form of the story of the visit of the women to the tomb (e.g., Jeremias, *New Testament Theology,* 304-5) is untenable, because analysis of the narrative units shows that John has adapted a single traditional unit in 20:1-2, 11-13, inserting another such unit (20:3-10) within it.

136. R. Bauckham, "Kerygmatic Summaries in the Speeches of Acts," in B. Witherington III, ed., *History, Literature, and Society in the Book of Acts* (Cambridge: Cambridge University Press, 1996) 185-217.

137. Bauckham, "Kerygmatic Summaries," 197-98, 214-15.

summary was a flexible form. On any one occasion, items from a stock of formulae could be selected as appropriate, though the key points of the story would no doubt normally appear. The form was open to improvisation and augmentation. One of its uses was no doubt as an outline for preachers, who could use it as a framework to be filled out by telling stories from the Gospel traditions. Even when used as a bare summary, no doubt influence from the Gospel traditions, either in phraseology or in the addition of items to the series of formulae, could occur. We can see this, for example, in the summaries in Acts, which are for the most part strikingly independent of Luke's Gospel, but sometimes show some influence from it (Acts 3:13b-14; 13:24-25, 28). The tradition of kerygmatic summaries and the tradition of Gospel stories and sayings were not unrelated, but they were basically independent, and the summaries seem to have retained their own integrity in oral use throughout the first century.

Luke has doubtless based his examples of preaching by Peter and Paul (Acts 2:14-36; 3:12-26; 10:34-43; 13:16-41) on the kind of kerygmatic summaries he knew. In what could only be a literary representation of a real (much longer) sermon, it was very appropriate to use the kind of kerygmatic summaries that Christian preachers used as outlines. Luke varies these summaries both in view of the audience each sermon has in his narrative and probably also simply so that readers should not find them tediously repetitive. But they also have much in common, so that we can observe both the relative stability and the flexibility of the form. This seems to imply that some common assumptions about Paul's kerygmatic summary in 1 Corinthians 15:3-7 are probably mistaken. Paul is citing the tradition for a particular purpose: for its relevance to the discussion of resurrection that follows in 1 Corinthians 15. Therefore it is intelligible that he begins the summary with Jesus' death. There is no need to suppose that the summary he knew did not include the ministry of Jesus, since this would not be relevant to his purpose in the context. What Paul does quote of the summary may well list resurrection appearances in more detail than was usual, again because these were so germane to Paul's purpose. Moreover, the inherent flexibility of kerygmatic summaries makes a certain amount of improvisation on Paul's part not untrue to the tradition. As has often been noticed, not only must verse 8 be Paul's addition to the traditional summary, but also at least part of verse 6 has to be his own contribution. He may, for his own purposes, have omitted appearances he knew in the tradition. Attempts to determine the precise parameters of the tradition Paul inherited, though they have been many,[138] are not appropriate to the nature of the form.

---

138. For a survey of views, see N. Taylor, *Paul, Antioch and Jerusalem* (JSNTSup 66; Sheffield: Sheffield Academic Press, 1992) 176-78.

None of the sermons in Acts cites a particular resurrection appearance. In 2:32; 3:15; (cf. 5:32), it is simply said that the apostles are witnesses of the fact that God raised Jesus. But in 10:40-41 Peter says: "God raised him on the third day and allowed him to appear, not to all the people, but to us who were chosen by God as witnesses and who ate and drank with him after he rose from the dead." In 13:30-31 (note the third-person form) Paul says: "But God raised him from the dead and for many days he appeared to those who came up with him from Galilee to Jerusalem and they are now his witnesses to the people." In neither case is it clear whether the reference is only to the twelve (to whom Luke, unlike Paul, restricts the term "apostle") or also to the many others we know from Luke's Gospel to have been with Jesus in Galilee as well as in Jerusalem and to have witnessed the risen Christ.[139] The parallels with Acts 1 (1:2 [chosen], 3 [forty days], 4 [eating?], 8 [witnesses], and 21-22) suggest the former, but this may be misleading. In Acts 1 Luke is overwhelmingly concerned with the twelve, who clearly have a special place as witnesses and who are to feature as the leaders of the earliest Christian community in the following chapters. From Acts 1:2-13 alone we could well conclude that only the eleven apostles met the risen Christ, but from verse 22 it is clear that this cannot have been the case, since there were others (of whom verse 23 names just two) who were qualified to replace Judas among the twelve, in the sense that they had been followers of Jesus from the baptism to the ascension and could witness, among other things, to his resurrection. One of these others must be selected to "become a witness with us [the eleven] of his resurrection" (1:22). Does this mean that only membership of the twelve made one a witness, and that all the others who were otherwise qualified for the role would not function as witnesses? It seems intrinsically unlikely that this could be Luke's view, and it is in direct conflict with the last chapter of his Gospel, where "the eleven and those with them" (24:33) are designated witnesses (24:48). Luke never makes clear exactly what the special role of the twelve is, but it surely cannot exclude a role for other witnesses.

If the references to witnesses in Acts 10:41 and 13:31 are not restricted to the twelve, then there is no reason why they should not include the women (whom Luke has taken pains to portray as among the most important founding

139. With reference to 10:41, for example, J. A. Fitzmyer, *The Acts of the Apostles* (AB 31; New York: Doubleday, 1998) 466, thinks more than the twelve are included (appealing to Luke 24:33); but C. K. Barrett, *A Critical and Exegetical Commentary on the Acts of the Apostles*, vol. 1 (ICC; Edinburgh: T. & T. Clark, 1994) 527, and B. Witherington, *The Acts of the Apostles: A Socio-Rhetorical Commentary* (Grand Rapids: Eerdmans; Carlisle: Paternoster, 1998) 358, think of the twelve only, whereas, with reference to 13:31, Barrett, *Acts*, 643, thinks more than the twelve are included, as Fitzmyer, *Acts*, 516, seems to assume (Witherington does not comment).

members of the earliest Christian community: 1:14).[140] This form of kerygmatic summary is quite open to being illustrated with stories of Jesus' appearances to the women alone or to women and men together (as I have argued Luke 24:36-53 should be understood). There is no reference to the empty tomb in any of the Acts summaries, a fact not often mentioned in discussion of whether 1 Corinthians 15:4 implies an empty tomb or proves Paul's ignorance of the story of the women's visit to the tomb. It is an important fact since there is no doubt that Luke knew such a story and gave it a significant place in his Gospel. He must have thought that the story of the women at the tomb was significant but not sufficiently essential to appear in a very briefly narrated kerygmatic summary. Since this is plausible enough to account for the lack of reference to that story in Acts, it is hard to tell whether, in these sermons preached, of course, to outsiders, Luke may have thought the women's story inappropriate because of its potential incredibility to male hearers (something Luke alone among the canonical evangelists has mentioned: Luke 24:11).

I need not discuss any further the absence from 1 Corinthians 15 of reference to the women at the tomb, but I must raise the question of the absence of an appearance to the women or to Mary Magdalene in particular in Paul's list of appearances. Of course, this has been taken as evidence that the tradition of such an appearance only originated later than 1 Corinthians.[141] If, however, the tradition was known, we could attribute its omission from the list either to the Jerusalem church leaders, from whom Paul presumably derived this kerygmatic summary, or to Paul himself. Some of the suggested explanations posit the former, some the latter:

(1) The omission could be due to the male prejudices against women's witness,[142] especially to the supernatural or to divine revelation, that I have discussed. It is important to note that the kerygmatic summaries were formulated to assist the preaching of the gospel to outsiders, and so it would be because of the prejudices of such outsiders that the appearance to the women was omitted from the summary Paul reports. This could have happened in the Jewish context of the Jerusalem church or (remembering Celsus's scorn for female witness to the resurrection) in the contexts in which Paul evangelized. Such an apolo-

---

140. Lieu, "Women's," 41, says that "Acts lists the Eleven and appends, almost apologetically, 'with [the] women and Mary the mother of Jesus and his brothers' (Acts 1:13-14)." But this is to miss how important the women are thus indicated to be. Of the 120 members of this community before Pentecost (1:15), Luke singles out the eleven, the women, and the brothers of Jesus as the three groups deserving special mention. If the three groups are being ranked, then it is remarkable that the women rank above the brothers of Jesus.

141. E.g., Fuller, *Formation*, 78.

142. E.g., Witherington, *Conflict*, 300; Perkins, "I Have," 40, 41.

getic omission is not necessarily in tension with the authority of the women's witness within Christian circles.

(2) Some kind of distinction between "official" and "unofficial witnesses" has often been suggested, with the appearance to the women belonging in the latter category and Paul's list being only of the former.[143] Unfortunately we do not know what the character of the appearances to Peter and James was, and cannot take for granted, as many scholars do, that they endowed Peter and James with leadership roles in the church. Moreover, whatever distinction between official and unofficial is offered, it is hard to see how the appearance to the five hundred (1 Cor 15:6) could qualify as official. But it is possible that the summary Paul knew listed (as might be appropriate in a summary designed to assist evangelistic preaching) those appearances in which the recipients were commissioned to proclaim the Gospel, and that the appearance to the five hundred was added by Paul because of its usefulness for his purpose in 1 Corinthians 15. (The comment "most of whom remain until now" must in any case be Paul's own contribution, and the appearance is valuable evidence for authenticating the resurrection, as Paul is evidently attempting to do here.) The focus of verse 9 on Paul's own status as "the least of the apostles," by virtue of the anomalously late resurrection appearance to him, could lend some support to this view of a list predominantly, at least, of apostolic commissioning appearances.

(3) A more specific variant of (2) is the contention that there was competition for first place among the resurrection appearances, since it implied special authority, and that Paul's kerygmatic summary has for this reason replaced the appearance to the women with that to Cephas (Peter).[144] This would be more plausible if attributed to the Jerusalem church than to Paul, though the matter is complicated by attempts to bring the appearance to James into the same field of postulated controversy. I have already argued that all the evidence of the Gospels is against the idea that this kind of significance was attached to priority in resurrection appearances (see §5 above). First Corinthians 15:5 is far too slender a basis on which to build such a theory against the evidence of the Gospels.

(4) In a novel argument Antoinette Clark Wire argues that part of Paul's polemic in 1 Corinthians 15 consists in opposing this closed list of resurrection appearances to the Corinthian women prophets' claims to present experience of the risen Christ and communication from him. Therefore he wishes "not to

---

143. E.g., Wedderburn, *Beyond Resurrection*, 58; and cf. the scholars reported in O'Collins and Kendall, "Mary Magdalene," 637-38.

144. Schüssler Fiorenza, *In Memory*, 332. For a quite complex view of factors alleged to be operative in the elimination of Mary Magdalene from the tradition in 1 Cor 15, see Bovon, "Privilège," 52.

provide support for women who prophesy in Corinth from the news that women's word was the genesis of the resurrection faith."[145] The plausibility of this view depends on much larger issues in the interpretation of 1 Corinthians. In my view, Paul is not opposing some kind of strongly realized eschatology, a claim that has been popular in exegesis of 1 Corinthians but is giving way to the view that what Paul opposed among the Corinthians was not some version of Christian theology different from his own, but the influence of their pagan background and context on their social values and beliefs. Furthermore, it seems to me that Paul affirms the women prophets in Corinth, criticizing not their message but their attire (11:2-16).

(5) Finally, Anthony Thiselton, following W. Künneth, argues that the priority of Peter in the pre-Pauline tradition behind 1 Corinthians 15:5 was because his public denial of Jesus made his experience of the risen Christ paradigmatic as an experience of transformation and restoration through the cross and resurrection. This was also congenial to Paul since for himself, as he explains in verses 8-10, his own late calling by the risen Lord to be an apostle was also overwhelmingly an experience of grace.[146] Paul's list of resurrection appearances thus begins and ends with the two apostles whose experience of the risen Christ was most obviously and strikingly one of grace. But this interpretation does not make it entirely clear why the appearance to Peter had to displace that to the women. It would be necessary to add that the list of appearances is chronological (as Paul's repetition of "then" in the list indicates) and that, since the appearance to the women was known to have preceded that to Peter, the women could not be assigned to second place in the list but only omitted altogether.

Explanations (1), (2) and (5) seem to me to have some plausibility. It is difficult to decide among them, but at least they illustrate that there are plausible reasons why Paul's kerygmatic summary should not refer to the appearance to the women. There is no need to conclude that the tradition of this appearance was a late development. Moreover, the fundamental independence of the tradition of kerygmatic summaries and that of Gospel narratives means that, whatever the reason for the absence of the women from the former, the stories about the women and the resurrection could still have been told among the latter. As observed in §1, the absence of the women is certainly not the only point at which the Gospel narratives and the kerygmatic summary in 1 Corinthians do not coincide. Indeed, noncorrelation between the two is much more obvious than cor-

---

145. A. C. Wire, *The Corinthian Women Prophets* (Minneapolis: Fortress, 1990) 162.

146. A. C. Thiselton, *The First Epistle to the Corinthians* (NIGTC; Grand Rapids: Eerdmans; Carlisle: Paternoster, 2000) 1204.

relation. The reasons may have to remain obscure, but the fact should not be considered a reason for treating the Gospel narratives as late legends.

Finally, we should notice that the women are not in fact, as so often assumed, absent from 1 Corinthians 15:3-7. Paul distinguishes between an appearance to the twelve and one to all the apostles, since, unlike Luke, he does not confine the term "apostle" to the twelve. At this appearance he would have assumed that other apostles he knew, such as Barnabas, Sylvanus, and James the Lord's brother, were present along with the twelve. Now that it is generally recognized that Paul knew and had great respect for at least one woman apostle, Junia (Rom 16:7), we must certainly also conclude that he would have taken for granted that women were included in an appearance to "all the apostles."[147]

147. This is recognized by Witherington, *Conflict*, 300.

Index of Names of Ancient People and Places

Index of Modern Authors

Index of Ancient Literature